American Civil War

American Civil War

THE ESSENTIAL REFERENCE GUIDE

James R. Arnold and Roberta Wiener, Editors

ABC-CLIO

Santa Barbara, California • Denver, Colorado • Oxford, England

Overview of the American Civil War

The American Civil War was a struggle to determine whether the United States would survive as a nation, and if so, what sort of nation it would be. In 1860, Republican candidate Abraham Lincoln won election to the presidency on a platform calling for the prohibition of slavery in the western territories. Recognizing that containment would mean the eventual end of the institution of slavery, white citizens in seven Deep South states— South Carolina, Georgia, Florida, Alabama, Mississippi, Louisiana, and Texas—did not wait for Lincoln's inauguration but hurried to declare themselves no longer part of the United States. The lame duck president James Buchanan did nothing to stop them, and the seceding states organized themselves into a new government they called the Confederate States of America. They selected Jefferson Davis of Mississippi as their president and inaugurated him before Lincoln took the oath of office as president of the United States on March 4, 1861.

Lincoln did not accept the validity of secession but recognized that he had no constitutional authority to end slavery under normal circumstances. He also believed it would eventually die out if contained. He therefore assured Southerners that he would not take the initiative in seeking to end slavery where it already existed but that he would do his best to maintain federal authority in the rebellious states by holding on to U.S. installations there. Only three remained that had not been seized by secessionists: Fort Pickens in Florida, Fort Jefferson in Florida's Dry Tortugas, and Fort Sumter in the harbor of Charleston, South Carolina. Sumter became the flash point. South Carolina was dominated by proslavery extremists who demanded that the Confederate government eject the small U.S. garrison from the fort. When Lincoln declined to remove the few dozen men and announced his intention of replenishing their nearly exhausted supply of food, Confederate forces around the harbor opened fire. After 36 hours of bombardment, the fort surrendered.

With war now a reality, both sides called for volunteers to form large armies. Four more states of the Upper South—Virginia, North Carolina, Tennessee, and Arkansas— faced with the necessity of fighting either for the Union or for the Confederacy, chose the latter. Three border slave states—Missouri, Kentucky, and Maryland—were sharply divided and provided recruits for both sides' armies. The newly expanded Confederacy established its capital at Richmond, Virginia.

An initial Union attempt to take Richmond resulted in an embarrassing failure at the First Battle of Bull Run, but Union offensives early in 1862 scored major successes,

A Currier & Ives illustration of the interior of Fort Sumter during the bombardment of April 12, 1861. (Library of Congress)

especially west of the Appalachians, where Union armies, cooperating with naval forces on the rivers and led by superior generals such as Ulysses S. Grant, advanced steadily into the heartland of the Confederacy.

Only in Virginia did Union forces seem incapable of making progress. Much was hoped from the dashing young Major General George B. McClellan, who trained and organized a large army and led it—very slowly—to the outskirts of Richmond in the spring of 1862. There he proved hesitant and irresolute, retreating in the face of attacks from Confederate general Robert E. Lee. Lincoln sacked McClellan, but his replacement fared no better. The president tried a succession of generals and even gave McClellan a second chance, but the results ranged from dismal to little short of disastrous.

At the outset of the war, Lincoln had hoped that the majority of white Southerners had merely been led astray by the strident proslavery leadership and would return to their allegiance under firm but restrained Union pressure. By mid-1862, it was clear this was not the case. In the face of Southern intransigence, Lincoln determined to raise the stakes and prepared to invoke his war powers as commander in chief to issue the Preliminary Emancipation Proclamation. Persuaded by his cabinet not to issue the document in the wake of Union defeats, Lincoln awaited a Union victory. The tactically drawn Battle of Antietam, which forced Lee to withdraw his army from Maryland, gave Lincoln the opportunity he wanted. He issued the proclamation, declaring that all slaves in areas still in rebellion against the United States as of January 1, 1863, would be forever free. On that date, Lincoln followed through with the actual Emancipation Proclamation, changing the war for Union and eventual emancipation into a war for Union and immediate emancipation.

Union frustration continued in the small but prestigious eastern theater of the war until July 1863, at Gettysburg in southern Pennsylvania. Lee's strategic overreach and a respectable performance by his opponent, Major General George G. Meade, combined to give the Union its first clear-cut—if largely hollow—victory in the East. Meanwhile, west of the Appalachians, Union forces continued to strike punishing body blows to the Confederacy. Simultaneous with the Union victory at Gettysburg, Grant won a far more significant triumph in the Siege of Vicksburg, Mississippi, sundering the Confederacy, reopening the Mississippi River to Union commerce, and capturing 30,000 soldiers the Confederacy could ill afford to lose. The Union army of Major General William S. Rosecrans maneuvered the Confederates out of the rest of Tennessee and weathered a concerted counterattack in the September 1863 Chickamauga Campaign. Union forces in the West then combined, under Grant's command, to finish the year's fighting in the Battle of Chattanooga, Tennessee.

For the 1864 offensive, Lincoln gave Grant overall command of all Union armies. Grant personally accompanied Meade's army in Virginia, virtually commanding it himself, while Major General William T. Sherman, acting under Grant's orders, led the western Union armies in a drive against Atlanta, Georgia. Grant and Sherman were relentless in their advances, and the Confederate defenders fought desperately. Both armies reached the outskirts of their target cities—Richmond and Atlanta—by midsummer, but casualty lists were long and Northern civilians began to despair of ever winning the war. Lincoln feared that he might lose that fall's presidential election to the Democratic candidate, none other than the failed General McClellan, running on a platform that called the war a failure.

Then, in early September, Sherman took Atlanta. That success, along with minor Union victories on other fronts, contradicted the Democratic platform's claim that the war could not be won. Lincoln swept into a second term with a resounding win in the November election.

In the months that followed, Lee's army continued its dogged defense of Richmond, but each day Grant pressed it further toward its breaking point. Elsewhere, Confederate power was already near collapse. The Confederacy's main army in the West suffered a crippling defeat in a desperate last-gasp offensive into Tennessee, while Sherman, with most of his forces, marched through Georgia and then the Carolinas, appropriating food and livestock and destroying railroads, depots, and sometimes more. When spring came, Sherman's western armies were moving northward through North Carolina on their way to join Grant in finishing off Lee. Before they could arrive, on April 2, 1865, Lee's lines broke, and Richmond fell. Lee's army fled westward toward the mountains, but never reached them. Lee surrendered on April 9, 1865, at Appomattox Court House, Virginia. The surviving remnants of Confederate forces surrendered over the next few weeks.

Steven E. Woodworth

Further Reading

Maury, Dabney H. *Recollections of a Virginian in the Mexican, Indian, and Civil Wars.* 2nd ed. New York: Charles Scribner's Sons, 1894.

Vinovskis, Mark A., ed. *Toward a Social History of the American Civil War: Exploratory Essays.* New York: Cambridge University Press, 1990.

Causes of the American Civil War

Immediate Causes

Lincoln's Election

The election of Abraham Lincoln as president of the United States brought the issue of slavery to a head for proslavery Southern extremists, known as "fire-eaters." The Republican Party was pledged to prevent the further spread of slavery into any U.S. territory where it did not already exist. On the other hand, Republican leaders had repeatedly stated that they lacked authority to interfere with slavery in the states where it already existed. The fire-eaters, however, refused to be assuaged by this. They professed to fear that enough additional free states would be admitted to the Union to provide the three-fourths majority necessary to pass a constitutional amendment banning slavery (although, with the 15 slave states then existing, that would have required a total of 60 states). They feared that Lincoln would use the federal government to undermine slavery in subtle ways, and they were alarmed by the fact that a president could be elected without a single Southern vote, an indication that the South might no longer wield the disproportionate influence it had held in the past. Finally, their pride was wounded by the realization that there would soon be an administration in Washington that believed that their cherished institution of slavery was immoral.

Failure of Compromise

Despite Lincoln's election and the fire-eaters' oft-repeated threats to secede in that case, some Americans in government believed that a compromise was possible. Sectional difficulties had been smoothed over by compromises in 1820 and 1850, and some thought it might be possible to create a "Compromise of 1861" as well. Various possible arrangements were discussed, especially one involving the possible extension of the Missouri Compromise Line (36°30′ north latitude) to the Pacific, with all territories south of that line being open to slavery.

Lincoln and his fellow Republicans were willing to concede much to achieve a compromise. They were even willing to go so far as to accept a constitutional amendment, supposedly unamendable, guaranteeing that the federal government would never interfere with slavery in any state where it presently existed. The one point on which they would not yield, however, was the central point of the Republican platform: no further spread of slavery into the territories. That was precisely the point that proslavery Southerners demanded the Republicans must surrender if there was to be a compromise. On that point neither side would give way, and the efforts at compromise failed. Viewed in retrospect, it is clear that, given the slaveholders' intransigence, no real compromise was possible—only another Northern surrender to Southern demands, as had occurred in 1820 and 1850.

Active Secessionists

The fire-eaters did not merely wait to see if the mass of their fellow Southerners would respond to Lincoln's election by clamoring for secession: they worked actively to bring about that result. Secessionists in the Deep South states were often influential men, and they used all of their political skill to maneuver their states into taking the fateful step. Their success in stampeding the first seven states into secession helped make compromise impractical.

Intermediate Causes

The Kansas-Nebraska Act

In 1854, congressman Stephen A. Douglas upset the precarious sectional truce with a piece of legislation aimed at securing federal support for a transcontinental railroad with its eastern terminus at Chicago. To achieve that purpose, Douglas's bill had to provide for the organization of the territory west of Iowa, through which the proposed tracks would run. Although the 1820 Missouri Compromise had promised that slavery would never exist in those lands, Douglas attempt to woo Southern support for his bill by proposing that the lands in question be divided into two territories—Kansas, lying directly west of the slave state of Missouri, and Nebraska, farther north—and that the status of slavery in these territories would be determined by "popular sovereignty," a vague doctrine that said the white settlers in the new territories should decide the status of slavery there. This gave proslavery forces a realistic chance of capturing the Kansas Territory for transformation into another slave state. Douglas successfully shepherded his

THE LITTLE GIANT_IN THE CHARACTER OF THE GLADIATOR.

Cartoon of Stephen Douglas as a gladiator. A gifted orator, Douglas was one of Lincoln's opponents in the 1860 election. (Bettmann/Corbis)

Kansas-Nebraska Act through Congress, and President Franklin Pierce signed it into law, but the backlash from outraged Northerners was enormous. As they saw it, the slave-power, by violating the sacred covenant of the Missouri Compromise, had shown that it would never be satisfied until the whole country adopted slavery. As a result, antislavery Northerners founded the Republican Party around the principle of banning the further spread of slavery.

Bleeding Kansas

In direct response to the Kansas-Nebraska Act, both proslavery and antislavery forces began encouraging their adherents to migrate to Kansas in order to secure it for their side. Violence soon broke out in the territory, and that civil conflict came to be known as Bleeding Kansas. Proslavery forces seized control of the territorial government through election fraud, and antislavery settlers responded by setting up an extralegal rival government. Newspapers throughout the country sensationalized the violence, each emphasizing the acts committed by the other side.

Bleeding Sumner

In May 1856, in the midst of the Kansas troubles, Massachusetts senator Charles Sumner made a speech in the Senate chamber. The speech, entitled "The Crime against Kansas," denounced Southern efforts to make Kansas into a slave state and also made personal slurs against certain proslavery senators. Two days later, Congressman Preston Brooks of South Carolina, the nephew of one of the senators thus insulted, entered the Senate chamber and caned Sumner, breaking his cane over the senator's head and leaving Sumner lying unconscious in a pool of blood. Northerners were outraged, and even more so when delighted Southerners expressed enthusiastic support for Brooks, even sending him several new canes. Tensions continued to rise.

The Dred Scott Case

In 1857, Supreme Court chief justice Roger B. Taney attempted to end the turmoil by legislating from the bench. The case before him was that of Dred Scott, the slave of an army doctor who had taken him as a personal servant to posts in the free state of Illinois and the free territory of Wisconsin. Scott sued for his freedom on the grounds that he could not have been a slave in those jurisdictions, but Taney, writing for the majority of the court, wrote that Scott, as an African American, had no standing to sue. Going farther, Taney

decreed that no one had the right to ban slavery in any territory and that no state had the right to prevent a slaveholding citizen of another state from entering and residing within its boundaries as long as he pleased. Instead of calming the sectional crisis, Taney's judicial power grab only raised the pitch of the debate, providing further evidence to Northerners that the slave powers were bent on control of the entire nation.

John Brown's Raid

One disturbed Northerner of strong antislavery convictions, but possessing an unstable mind, was John Brown. On October 16, 1859, Brown led a group of like-minded fanatics in taking over the U.S. arsenal at Harpers Ferry, Virginia (now West Virginia), in the hopes of sparking a mass slave revolt that would spread through the entire South. Instead, the result was the death of several locals as well as several of Brown's men, and the capture of the rest. Condemned on November 2, Brown was hanged a month later. Although many Northern leaders condemned the raid, expressions of support from many quarters in the North helped convince Southerners that those north of the Mason-Dixon Line were eager to instigate mass slaughter in the South.

Long-Term Causes
Slavery

There was only one fundamental cause of the American Civil War, and that cause was slavery. All other factors of dispute between the two sections—tariffs, state-rights, the governance of the territories—were merely footnotes to that one overriding issue.

Beginnings of the Slave South

The first slaves came to Virginia in 1619, although most labor in Virginia at that time

Consequences of the American Civil War

Immediate Consequences

Destruction of Life and Property

The most striking immediate consequence of the war was destruction and loss of life on a scale the country had never before imagined. Union war dead totaled 360,000; Confederate, 258,000. The combined total of 618,000 was significantly greater than the United States was to lose in World War II, its next bloodiest conflict, and World War II came at a time when the U.S. population was more than three times the size it had been in the 1860s. In terms of war dead per capita, no other U.S. conflict comes close to the Civil War, with its total of 181.7 war dead per every 10,000 people. By contrast, the comparable figure for the American Revolution was 117.9 and a distant 29.6 for World War II. In addition to those who died in the war, another 275,000 Union soldiers and 226,000 Confederates were wounded in the war, many of them maimed for life by the amputation of a leg or an arm.

The economic expense of the war, although of far less impact than the human cost, was nevertheless substantial. The Union spent some $2.3 billion on its war effort or about $98 per person in its population. The Confederacy, on the other hand, expended only $1 billion in its failed bid for independence, but that came to $111 per person for Southerners. The North continued to experience prosperity during the war, with its total wealth increasing by 50 percent during the decade of the 1860s. In stark contrast, the South was impoverished by the war. On top of its military spending, it suffered another $1.1 billion in war damage, or about 40 percent of its prewar wealth, including 40 percent of its livestock and 50 percent of its farm machinery. In addition to all of this, most of the South's invested capital—some $1.6 billion—was wiped out by the freeing of the slaves. Global cotton markets had found other sources during the war, and never again would Southern cotton command the consistently high prices it did in the antebellum years. All told, it took the South more than half a century to recover from the effects of the war.

Emancipation

The other most striking immediate consequence of the Civil War was the emancipation of 3.5 million slaves. Many of them were initially declared free by Abraham Lincoln in his January 1863 Emancipation Proclamation, which was aimed only at slaves in areas then still in rebellion against the United States. Subsequently, in 1865, the Thirteenth Amendment freed all slaves in the United States.

Fires during the Confederate evacuation of Richmond consumed parts of the city. (Library of Congress)

What to do with the newly freed millions was a difficult problem for the federal government in the waning days and immediate aftermath of the war. Plans were discussed for giving each freedman a farm—the much discussed "forty acres and a mule"—but nothing came of this. The government did establish a Freedmen's Bureau, headed by former Union general Oliver O. Howard, which helped to care for the needs of the recent slaves until they could establish themselves in their new lives. However, political realities made this difficult.

The Preservation of the Union

The United States remained united as a single nation, and for more than a century, secession remained discredited as a viable option.

Intermediate Consequences
Reconstruction

Although Union forces were victorious on the battlefield, the Union was preserved, and the slaves freed, white Southerners waged a long and ultimately successful struggle to achieve what was for many of them the chief purpose of the war: the maintenance of white supremacy in the South. The 12-year period after the end of the war is known as Reconstruction, during which federal authorities attempted to reestablish truly loyal governments in the Southern states and to secure the recognition of basic civil rights for the freedmen. Yet not all Northerners were united in desiring the accomplishment of these goals. Some believed preservation of the Union and perhaps freeing the slaves was all that the war should have accomplished.

Some believed it had already accomplished too much. This made it a constant struggle to achieve the degree of political support in the North necessary to continue to try to impose respect for black civil rights in the South. Southern whites closed ranks against anything of the sort, showing more unity in opposition to black civil rights than they ever did in defense of the Confederacy itself. Organizations such as the Ku Klux Klan waged a war of terror and intimidation aimed at persuading blacks and their white allies to refrain from voting or to leave the region entirely. These tactics finally prevailed. In 1877, the federal government terminated its efforts at Reconstruction, and over the next 20 years, the South developed a system of racial segregation and second-class citizenship for blacks known as "Jim Crow."

Reconciliation

The 1890s ushered in the era of sectional reconciliation. A desire for national unity at any price, concern for possible foreign threats, and the experience of the Spanish-American War all combined to encourage this informal movement. The era of reconciliation saw the dedication of the major battlefield parks and their commemoration with heroic statuary. It was also a time for the funerals of many great figures of the war, including generals such as Joseph E. Johnston and William T. Sherman, as well as political figures such as Jefferson Davis. Davis died in 1889, on the eve of the period of reconciliation, unrepentant to the last. His funeral was the occasion for outpourings of support in cities all across the South.

As part of the movement toward reconciliation, Southerners conceded that the preservation of the nation had been a good thing, while Northerners agreed that Confederates had been brave and heroic in fighting for "what they believed." Both sides were supposed to have been fighting for the principles of American freedom, and everyone was supposed to pretend that the war had had nothing to do with slavery. No one was supposed to mention the significance of black Americans or their present circumstances under Jim Crow, a system that was no longer completely relegated to the South. The full fruition of what had been won in the Civil War—what Lincoln called a "new birth of freedom"—had to wait for another era.

Long-Term Consequences
Civil Rights

The unfinished promise of the Civil War was eventually fulfilled by the civil rights movement of the 1950s and 1960s, culminating in the Voting Rights Act and the Civil Rights Act of 1964, securing the full privileges of citizenship and civil rights to the descendents of the slaves whom the war had freed.

A More Unified Country

Since the Civil War, most Americans have considered their primary governmental allegiance to be due not to their state governments but to the nation as a whole. Whereas before the war it was common to say, "The United States are," since the war, the country's name has been treated as a singular noun.

Increased Power of the Federal Government

In the short and intermediate term, the Civil War did not greatly increase the power of government. Once the conflict—including Reconstruction—was over, the government returned more or less to its accustomed course, not quite as small as it had been before the war but much smaller than it would later become. However, wars have a tendency to increase the power of the governments that fight them; the bigger the war, the greater the increase. The American tradition was so strongly opposed to powerful government that the effect was not immediately felt in the case of the Civil War. Nevertheless, the war had to some degree prepared the way for future increases in federal authority when external threat, internal crisis, or political agitation seemed to demand them. The Civil War, for example, had seen the imposition of the first U.S. income tax. The tax was discontinued after the war and even declared unconstitutional by the Supreme Court, but a half century later, another income tax was imposed, this time with the support of a constitutional amendment.

Another way in which the Civil War opened the way for increased government intervention in the life of average Americans was through the three Reconstruction amendments—passed by Congress and ratified by the states during the several years immediately following the war. Aimed at securing freedom, citizenship, and voting rights for the newly freed slaves, the three amendments—Thirteenth, Fourteenth, and Fifteenth—have come to be used in ways and for purposes their authors never dreamed of. The Fourteenth Amendment in particular has been the occasion for a vast increase in federal authority at the expense of a weakening of state governments. Its "equal protection" and "due process" clauses were used—beginning some 80 years after it was written—to take selected concepts from the federal Bill of Rights and apply them to the states. On this basis, federal judges have decided whether prayers can be said at a local public school and have made literal life and death decisions for citizens.

Steven E. Woodworth

A

Abolitionism

Abolitionists were divided over the means by which slavery should be eradicated in the United States, and the Civil War greatly exacerbated those divisions. Some abolitionists were pacifists and were opposed to armed conflict in general, while others perceived the war as an opportunity to finally destroy the institution, pressing President Abraham Lincoln to expand the war and make it an antislavery crusade. Abolitionists opposed slavery for a variety of reasons. A number were opposed to it on religious and moral grounds, while others saw it as an institution that would eventually destroy the United States. Still others opposed slavery because they believed that it stood as an impediment to economic growth and maturation.

Opposition to slavery during colonial times was manifested by religious groups such as the Society of Friends, or Quakers. Antislavery sentiments were also apparent in the natural rights ideology of the American Revolution, and slavery was abolished by most Northern states following independence in 1776. Slavery, however, grew in the South, especially with Eli Whitney's invention of the cotton gin in 1793 and the expansion of the cotton culture into the western territories. Concerned with the spread of slavery and also concerned that racial prejudice would prevent freed slaves from participating in American life, some antislavery advocates formed the American Colonization Society in 1817. This organization advocated transporting freed slaves back to Africa. Between 1817 and 1867, approximately 15,000 blacks

were sent to the Republic of Liberia, in West Africa, but the colonization approach foundered because of the high costs and the fact that many slaves were already generations removed from Africa.

A growing abolitionist movement was fueled in the 1830s by the religious ferment of the Second Great Awakening and evangelists such as Theodore Weld, who preached that slavery was a sin. Weld's antislavery endeavors were supported by wealthy New York merchants Arthur and Lewis Tappan, who paid the young abolitionist's way to Lane Theological Seminary in Cincinnati, Ohio. While attending the seminary, Weld led an 18-day debate on slavery, which led to his expulsion. Weld and his Lane followers then moved throughout the Midwest spreading the gospel of abolition. In 1839, Weld published *Slavery As It Is*, one of the most influential tracts describing the brutality of the slave system.

With the impetus of the British abolition of slavery in the West Indies in 1833 and the Second Great Awakening, the American Anti-Slavery Society was founded in 1833. Under the leadership of William Lloyd Garrison, editor of the antislavery newspaper *The Liberator*, abolitionists pushed for the immediate emancipation of slavery as opposed to the gradualist approach of the American Colonization Society. Among Garrison's most important early supporters was the eloquent Boston patrician Wendell Phillips, who refused to eat sugarcane or wear cotton shirts, as these items were produced by slave labor. Abandoning the idea of reform within the churches, Garrisonians also advocated

Stewart, James B. *Holy Warriors: The Abolitionists and American Slavery.* New York: Hill and Wang, 1996.

Walters, Ronald. *The Antislavery Appeal: American Abolitionism after 1830.* Baltimore: Johns Hopkins University Press, 1978.

African Americans, Confederate Army

The first military units of free African Americans for service in the Civil War were organized in the Confederate states at the very beginning of the war in 1861. However, these units did not remain in service. The *Charleston Mercury* recorded two weeks after the Union surrender of Fort Sumter in Charleston Harbor the presence of "one Negro company" from Nashville, Tennessee, in a military parade. In Memphis, Tennessee, in May 1861, a committee of three persons was established to organize a volunteer company of freemen for military service to the Southern cause.

New Orleans, which had a tradition of African American militia units dating to the French colonial era, boasted 1,400 African American men among the 28,000 troops reviewed by the state's governor in the New Orleans Grand Confederate Review of November 1861. The *New Orleans Picayune* remarked in February 1862 that "the companies of free colored men" were "all very well drilled and comfortably equipped." Louisiana has the distinction of providing more African American soldiers to the Confederate Army and to the U.S. Army during the Civil War than any other state of the Confederacy.

The 1st Regiment of Louisiana Native Guards had been organized by Jordan Noble, who had served as a drummer with a black regiment at the battle of New Orleans in the War of 1812. The Corps D'Afrique was a Native Guards unit of French-speaking soldiers. All were refused service in the Confederate Army. A few free African Americans from the state did serve in combat with Confederate units, and received Confederate pensions. Charles Lutz and Jean-Baptiste Pierre-Auguste are among those recorded in state archives. Leufroy Pierre-Auguste of St. Landry Parish is known to have fought with Confederate Army troops at the battles of Shiloh, Fredericksburg, and Vicksburg.

Until 1862, about 3,000 free African-descended residents of Louisiana served in Native Guards units within the state, including at least one company of cavalry. After Admiral David Farragut secured New Orleans for the federal government, the Corps D'Afrique was mustered into the U.S. Army by General Benjamin Butler.

Christian Fleetwood, a sergeant major in the 4th U.S. Colored Troops, wrote in 1895 that "the heart of the Negro was with the South but for slavery." In fact, many free African Americans in the South wished to keep their own status distinct from that of slaves or recently freed slaves. Fleetwood also believed that an early policy of enlisting free African Americans, while freeing all slaves who served in the Confederate Army, would have brought a rapid Confederate victory as well as early diplomatic recognition for the Confederacy from Great Britain.

But it was not until January 1864 that Patrick R. Cleburne, a Confederate general later killed in action, wrote to Confederate States of America President Jefferson Davis that it would be "madness not to look at our danger from every point of view" and recommended that the Confederacy "commence training a large reserve of the most courageous of our slaves."

Cleburne also proposed to guarantee freedom to every slave who remained loyal to the Confederacy. Confederate General Robert E. Lee, who had stated at the beginning of the war that if he owned all the slaves in the South, he would gladly free them to save the Union, promptly endorsed Cleburne's proposal. Not until March 13, 1865, however, did Davis reluctantly agree to the proposal, and the Confederate Congress authorized raising 300,000 additional troops "irrespective of color." Less than a month later, General Lee surrendered the Army of Northern Virginia at Appomattox, effectively ending the war and rendering the issue moot.

The philosophical foundations of the Confederacy made it difficult to accept General Cleburne's practical proposal. Confederate vice president Alexander Stephens wrote that "the cornerstone of the Confederate States of America" is that "the Negro is not equal to the white man." General Clement H. Stevens insisted that "I do not want independence if it is to be won by the help of the Negro . . . The justification of slavery in the South is the inferiority of the Negro. If we make him a soldier we concede the whole question."

Cleburne had foreseen and accepted this when he wrote Davis that "when we make soldiers of them we must make free men of them." While patriots dedicated to independence for the Southern states were willing to make these concessions, slave owners whose first priority was protecting their property in human beings were not. The latter predominated in positions of power in the Confederate government.

Charles Rosenberg

Further Reading

Buckley, Gail. *American Patriots: The Story of Blacks in the Military from the Revolution to Desert Storm.* New York: Random House, 2001.

Edgerton, Robert B. *Hidden Heroism: Black Soldiers in America's Wars.* Boulder, CO: Westview Press, 2001.

Gladstone, William A. *Men of Color: African Americans in the Civil War.* Gettysburg, PA: Thomas Publications, 1996.

McConnell, Roland C. *Negro Troops of Antebellum Louisiana: A History of the Battalion of Free Men of Color.* Baton Rouge: Louisiana State University Press, 1968.

Reidy, Joseph P., et al., eds. *Freedom's Soldiers: The Black Military Experience in the Civil War.* New York: Cambridge University Press, 1998.

African Americans, Union Army

African Americans made a major contribution to the Union war effort during the American Civil War. By the end of the war, the United States Colored Troops (USCT) constituted approximately 10 percent of the Union Army. Yet during the first two years of the war, President Abraham Lincoln was reluctant to allow African Americans to join the army. Indeed, he was concerned that African American recruitment might further alienate the South, anger Northern whites, and jeopardize the loyalty of the border states. Consequently, many free African Americans who tried to enlist for service early on were turned away.

African Americans made up less than 1 percent of the population of the North, but the need for manpower led Frederick Douglass and the abolitionists to press Lincoln to let African Americans serve. Douglass and others expected that military service would produce full citizenship rights. The first official black enlistment system, although the total was set low, began after the summer of 1862 under U.S. Congressional authorization.

Some of the approximately 180,000 black soldiers who served in the Union army. (Library of Congress)

By late 1862, Lincoln had determined that enlistment of African American troops would not only strengthen Union forces but, more importantly, would weaken the Confederate cause. Consequently, Lincoln threw his whole-hearted support behind African American enlistment as a war measure with the issuance of the Emancipation Proclamation, which took effect on January 1, 1863. The Proclamation stated that slaves in rebelling states as of that date were freed from slavery and that the Union would do everything in its power to ensure that they would remain free. Furthermore, the proclamation extended the first well-publicized invitation for African Americans to join Union military forces on land and sea and served to entice many Northern and Southern African Americans to join the Union Army.

African American soldiers encountered much discrimination. They served in strictly segregated units led by white officers, many of whom were reluctant to promote African Americans because they feared that white soldiers of lower rank would not take orders from black superiors. As a consequence, by the end of the war, only 100 or so African Americans were commissioned officers, and none rose higher than the rank of major. African Americans were also initially paid less than their white counterparts; they received $10 per month compared to $16 per month for white soldiers. Some USCT units refused to accept their pay in protest of the unequal treatment. Yielding to public pressure, Congress finally approved equal pay for the USCT in June 1864.

Duty assignments were also unequal. The USCT was often placed in labor rather than combat positions. Major General William T. Sherman, for example, refused to deploy African American troops to the front lines because he doubted their willingness and ability to fight. Instead, Sherman utilized African Americans in manual labor and support capacities. Furthermore, USCT troops often went into battle with inferior clothing, equipment, and weapons. African Americans also had to contend with the constant fear that Confederate forces might execute them on the spot or sell them into slavery if they were captured.

On July 18, 1863, the 54th Massachusetts Infantry Regiment led an assault on Confederate Fort Wagner guarding Charleston, South Carolina. The unit suffered heavy casualties, 281 of 600 men, during the fight. Among the dead was their commander, young white officer Colonel Robert Gould Shaw. The courage displayed by the 54th Regiment that day was a strong signal to Washington and the North that freed men and liberated slaves could indeed prove highly effective soldiers.

Some 200,000 African Americans served, mostly in labor units. In fact, more than 15 percent of the 1860 free African American population of the North served while more than 80 percent of the USCT hailed from the South. Total African American enlistment ultimately comprised as much as one-eighth of the Union Army in 166 regiments (145 infantry, 13 artillery, 7 cavalry, 1 engineer). African Americans also made up about 16 percent of Union naval strength. Although most African American soldiers were led by white officers, there were more than 100 African American lieutenants, captains, and surgeons, and this figure does not include some African Americans who passed as whites. It is estimated that more than 180,000 African Americans took part in more than 40 major battles and about 450 smaller engagements throughout the conflict. Twenty-three black soldiers and four black sailors were awarded the Medal of Honor.

The U.S. Colored Troops were disbanded at the end of the war, although Congress authorized four African American regiments thereafter; the 9th Cavalry and 10th Cavalry and the 24th Infantry and 25th Infantry regiments served with distinction in the American West and were the first for black volunteers in the peacetime U.S. Army. Not until 1877 did the first African American graduate from West Point, however.

Military service remained a source of much pride for African American families. For many years after the war, these families honored the fathers and grandfathers who had served in the war for the cause of freedom. Military service was also a source of respect in African American communities, and more than 130 African American veterans became political leaders during the Reconstruction era. However, with the end of Reconstruction in 1877, persistent racism and the emergence of Jim Crow laws blotted out the importance of African American military service during the Civil War. In fact, it was not until the 1950s that historians revived scholarly interest in the subject; in 1989 the motion picture *Glory* helped popularize the important role of and hardships experienced by African American soldiers.

Rolando Avila

Further Reading

Cornish, Dudley T. *The Sable Arm: Negro Troops in the Union Army, 1861–1865.* New York: W. W. Norton & Co., 1966.

Gladstone, William A. *Men of Color.* Gettysburg, PA: Thomas Publications, 1993.

Glatthaar, Joseph T. *Forged in Battle: The Civil War Alliance of Black Soldiers and White Officers.* New York: The Free Press, 1990.

Hollandsworth, James G. *The Louisiana Native Guards: The Black Military Experience during the Civil War*. Baton Rouge: Louisiana State University Press, 1995; 2004.

Miller, Edward A., Jr. *The Black Civil War Soldiers of Illinois: The Story of the Twenty-ninth U.S. Colored Infantry*. Columbia: University of South Carolina Press, 1998.

Antebellum Decade, 1850–1860

The decade preceding the outbreak of war featured a series of political crises. It began with the Compromise of 1850. By the terms of this compromise, people living in the new territories were to decide for themselves whether to form a free or a slave state. Thus, these territories became political battlegrounds between southern politicians and their supporters and their counterparts in the North and West. Southern leaders thought that they had to win these battles because as the nation's population increased, the southern people were becoming increasingly outnumbered. Southern leaders clung desperately to the equality of votes in the Senate because only here was the political balance level.

These facts set the stage for conflict when, in 1854, a Democratic senator from Illinois named Stephen A. Douglas proposed a bill to establish a new territorial government for the vast land between the Missouri River and the Rocky Mountains. Douglas's proposal became the Kansas-Nebraska Act. It proved to be one of the most important single events that pushed the nation into civil war. In order to secure southern votes to pass the Kansas-Nebraska Act, Douglas included a provision that gutted the Missouri Compromise, a national covenant that had bonded the nation for 34 years. Despite the fact that Kansas and Nebraska were north of the Missouri Compromise line, their settlers would now decide whether or not to allow slavery in the new states. Across the North, citizens met at hundreds of "anti-Nebraska" meetings to protest. Northern voters formed many new political parties, all of them based on opposition to slavery. The party that rose above the others was the Republican Party.

Meanwhile, after 1854, Kansas became not just a political battleground, but also a place where rival sides fought ruthlessly. An abolitionist zealot named John Brown wanted to "strike terror into the hearts of the pro-slavery people" in Kansas. Brown lived along the banks of Pottawatomie Creek, Kansas. During the night of May 24–25, 1856, Brown and a small group including four of his sons killed five proslavery men in cold blood. The killings at Pottawatomie Creek encouraged the proslavery forces in Kansas to respond. So continued a cycle of violence and revenge. "Bleeding Kansas" became a battleground featuring hit and run raids, arson, ambushes, and murder in the night.

The civil war in Kansas was the most important issue during the presidential election of 1856. The Republican Party managed to unite voters who opposed the repeal of the Missouri Compromise and the extension of slavery. A politician named Abraham Lincoln gradually emerged as the party's most articulate spokesman. Although a Democrat James Buchanan won the 1856 election, it was clear to all that the Republican Party was the power of the future. The strength of the new party became apparent during the Election of 1860.

National crisis came in 1860. Four decades of compromise between North and South had failed. Four honorable men representing four different ideas about the future of the nation competed to become president of the United States. Northern and western Democrats wanted Senator Stephen Douglas to be the Democratic candidate. Many southern Democrats bitterly disliked Douglas because they did not share his views on slavery. They preferred to lose the election rather than have Douglas be their candidate. They succeeded in splitting the party in two. About one-third of the delegates, almost all from the South, left the party and nominated John C. Breckinridge as their candidate. Breckinridge's platform was proslavery.

The Republican party selected Abraham Lincoln. A fourth candidate was John Bell of Tennessee. He represented a new party called the Constitutional Union party that tried to bridge the gap between North and South. Bell's party recognized no political principle other than "the Constitution . . . the Union . . . and the Enforcement of the Laws." It avoided taking a substantive stand on the issues of the day.

The election became two separate contests: Lincoln versus Douglas in the North; Breckinridge versus Bell in the South. Lincoln received only 40 percent of the nation's popular vote, but it comfortably gave him enough electoral votes to become president.

Few doubted the importance of Lincoln's election. Virginia had been a moderate southern state. A majority of its voters cast their ballots for Bell, the compromise candidate. Now, a Richmond newspaper gloomily wrote, "A party founded on the single sentiment . . . of hatred of African slavery, is now the controlling power." A New Orleans paper called the Republicans a "revolutionary party." Antislavery people agreed that the election did mark a revolution. "We live in revolutionary times," wrote an Illinois man, and "I say God bless the revolution." Given such attitudes, it is unsurprising that Lincoln's election precipitated secession conventions in the South.

James R. Arnold

Further Reading

Abrahamson, James L. *The Men of Secession and Civil War, 1859–1861*. Wilmington, DE: SR Books, 2000.

Bowman, Shearer D. *At the Precipice: Americans North and South during the Secession Crisis*. Chapel Hill: University of North Carolina Press, 2010.

Catton, Bruce. *The Coming Fury*. Garden City, NY: Doubleday and Company, 1961.

Potter, David M. *Lincoln and his Party in the Secession Crisis*. New Haven, CT: Yale University Press, 1942.

Walther, Eric W. *The Shattering of the Union: America in the 1850s*. Wilmington, DE: Scholarly Resources, 2004.

Antietam, Battle of (September 17, 1862)

The Battle of Antietam Creek, or Sharpsburg, September 17, 1862, was one of the most important military engagements of the American Civil War. It is known by these two names because the North usually named its battles after the nearest body of water, in this case, Antietam Creek, while the South usually chose the nearest town, which was Sharpsburg, Maryland.

Following the March 1862 duel between USS *Monitor* and CSS *Virginia*, Union Army major general George B. McClellan's Army of the Potomac began a glacial advance up the peninsula formed by the York and James rivers toward the Confederate capital of Richmond. In the resultant fighting, Confederate commander General Joseph E. Johnston was badly wounded, and General Robert E. Lee took command of the Army of Northern Virginia and forced the overcautious McClellan's withdrawal. Lee was determined to strike at Union forces before they could reunite and drive south against Richmond. On August 29–30, 1862, Confederate major generals Thomas J. Jackson and James Longstreet surprised and defeated Union major general John Pope's new Army of Virginia in the Second Battle of Bull Run/Manassas.

Pope now withdrew to the defenses of Washington, and Lincoln reluctantly replaced

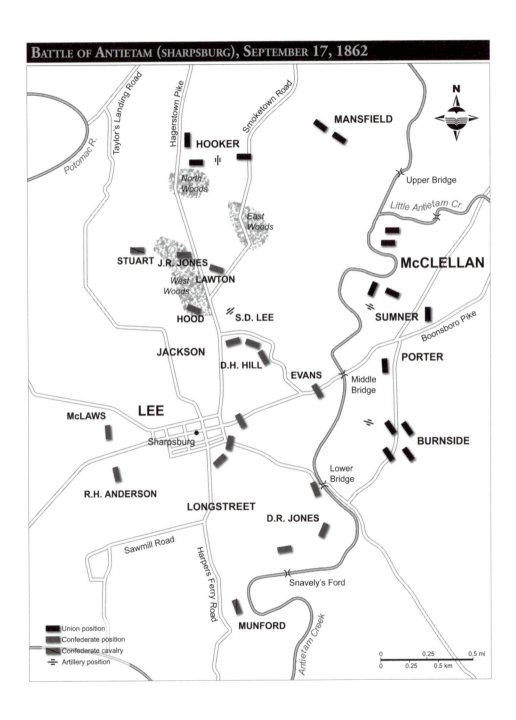

BATTLE OF ANTIETAM (SHARPSBURG), SEPTEMBER 17, 1862

Taylor's Landing Road

Hagerstown Pike

Smoketown Road

Potomac R.

MANSFIELD

HOOKER

North Woods

Upper Bridge

Little Antietam Cr.

East Woods

STUART J.R. JONES

West Woods LAWTON

McCLELLAN

HOOD   S.D. LEE

JACKSON

SUMNER

Boonsboro Pike

D.H. HILL

EVANS

Middle Bridge

PORTER

McLAWS   LEE

Sharpsburg

BURNSIDE

Lower Bridge

R.H. ANDERSON

LONGSTREET

D.R. JONES

Sawmill Road

Harpers Ferry Road

Snavely's Ford

Union position
Confederate position
Confederate cavalry
Artillery position

MUNFORD

Antietam Creek

0   0.25   0.5 mi
0   0.25   0.5 km

him with McClellan, for on September 4, Lee and his Army of Northern Virginia had begun an invasion of the North. Lee hoped to cut key rail lines west and isolate Washington, with Harrisburg as his probable objective. Southern leaders believed that a significant land victory might bring British and French diplomatic recognition of the Confederacy.

Lee's army crossed the Potomac River east of the Blue Ridge Mountains. Arriving at Frederick, Maryland, on September 7, Lee gambled, dividing his army into five separate parts, three of which were to converge on and take the major Union arsenal at Harpers Ferry. Outnumbering Lee's force two-to-one but overestimating Lee's strength, McClellan proceeded with his customary caution.

McClellan fumbled away an incredible intelligence advantage. Near Frederick, Maryland, some of his soldiers discovered a copy of Lee's orders, wrapped around three cigars and verified by a Union officer who identified the handwriting of Lee's adjutant. McClellan now knew the entire disposition of Lee's forces. Despite this information, McClellan moved with the same glacial speed that had earned him the nickname of the "Virginia Creeper" during the Peninsula Campaign. He delayed a full 18 hours before putting his army in motion and pushing through the Blue Ridge Mountain passes. On September 14, in small, intense engagements in the battles of South Mountain and Crampton's Gap, Confederate forces delayed the Union advance.

Lee's army was then split into three main bodies across 20 miles. Although initially inclined to retreat on learning of McClellan's

Confederate soldiers marching through Frederick, Maryland, during the Antietam Campaign. This image is the only known photo of Confederate soldiers on campaign in enemy territory. (Courtesy of the Historical Society of Frederick County, Maryland)

moves, Lee decided to stand and fight, ordering his remaining forces to join him as soon as possible and positioning his three available divisions along a low ridge extending about four miles north to south, just east of Sharpsburg and west of Antietam Creek. Hilly terrain here enabled Lee to mask his inferior resources. The resultant battle was very much a fragmented fight, in large part because of the terrain.

On the afternoon of September 15, the major part of the Army of the Potomac was within easy striking distance of Lee's then 18,000 men. Had McClellan attacked, Lee would have been routed. However, Lee predicted McClellan would not move that day or the next. Indeed, McClellan wanted first to rest his troops, then spent the entire day of September 16 placing his artillery and infantry and inspecting the line.

While McClellan dallied, Jackson's corps arrived from Harpers Ferry, giving Lee 30,000 men and leaving absent only three of his nine divisions. Even with Jackson's corps, Lee would be outnumbered 41,000 to 87,000. McClellan said after the battle that he thought Lee had 120,000 men. This is hard to believe, for he planned a double envelopment to hit Lee's flank and then smash the Confederate center.

During the battle, Lee was in position to observe and command throughout. In sharp contrast to McClellan, Lee also gave great latitude to his subordinate commanders. McClellan remained more than a mile to the rear, unable to observe the battle in progress and with little idea of what was going on. McClellan also failed to take advantage of his superior numbers. He withheld an entire corps (20,000 men failed to see battle) and he employed a piecemeal rather than simultaneous form of attack. Each Union corps was committed by successive oral orders from headquarters, without informing the other corps commanders and without instructions for mutual support. This process was compounded, as corps commanders sent their own divisions to the attack in piecemeal fashion. McClellan also failed to employ his cavalry to cut Confederate lines of communication and prevent Confederate reinforcements from moving to the battlefield from the south. Even a delay of an hour or two would have changed the battle.

The Battle of Antietam opened early on the morning of September 17 with an attack by Major General Joseph Hooker's 12,000-man I Corps against the Confederate left held by Jackson's corps. Hooker's men drove the Confederates back into the West Woods. Lee called up Brigadier General John Bell Hood's Texas Brigade, which repulsed the Union attack.

Amid the smoke and ground fog, the battle lines were only 50 or even 30 yards apart. Units were shattered soon after they began to fight. In the intense fighting for the cornfield, the 1st Texas Regiment of Hood's Brigade lost more than 82 percent of its men killed or wounded in 20 minutes, the highest percentage losses North or South of any regiment in the war. Successive Union attacks on the Confederate left by Major General Joseph Mansfield's XII Corps and Brigadier General Edwin Sumner's II Corps were poorly managed and also failed.

At the Confederate center, meanwhile, a crisis developed as some 3,000 Confederates under Major General Daniel H. Hill fought to hold the Sunken Road, which came to be known as "Bloody Lane." Here, Major General William B. Franklin's VI Corps mounted three separate assaults, all of which failed. Then two Union regiments were able to enfilade the Confederate position on the Sunken Road, forcing the Confederates there to fall back and opening a gap between

Confederate dead at Antietam, photographed two days after the battle by Alexander Gardner. Mathew Brady displayed this graphic image at an exhibition, one of the first times the shocked public witnessed the reality of war. (Library of Congress)

the Confederate center and left. Confederate troops under Hill managed to plug the hole in time. Lee then ordered Jackson to counterattack the Union right, a move that was not successful. McClellan on his part failed to take advantage of the situation and did not commit his reserve, which remained inactive during the entire battle.

On the Union left, Major General Ambrose Burnside's IX Corps spent the morning trying to carry a bridge over Antietam Creek. Finally, Union forces crossed the creek via fords, but the Confederates withdrew to higher ground. By the time Burnside was ready to renew the attack, the last division of Lee's army, commanded by Major General Ambrose P. Hill, had arrived. Despite being exhausted from their forced

march, they defeated the Union assault. The Battle of Antietam was over.

In the battle, Union casualties amounted to 2,108 dead, 9,540 wounded, and 753 missing (15%). Confederate losses were 1,546 dead, 7,752 wounded, and 1,018 missing (26%). It was the bloodiest single day of fighting of the entire war.

Lee waited a day and then pulled back into Virginia. McClellan failed to pursue. Lincoln was furious and soon removed McClellan from command. McClellan might have destroyed Lee on the 17th or the day after, but in the words of one historian of the battle, he was "so fearful of losing that he would not risk winning" (Sears 1983).

Nevertheless, this inconclusive battle had important results. Lee's defeat weakened

Confederate hopes of securing recognition from Britain and France. Never again was the Confederacy this close to winning recognition abroad. It also helped ensure that the Democrats did not win control of the House of Representatives in the November elections. A one percent shift in the vote would have brought Democratic control and trouble for Lincoln. The Union victory also allowed Lincoln the opportunity on September 22 to issue the Preliminary Emancipation Proclamation, which freed, as of January 1, 1863, all slaves in areas still in rebellion against the United States. This document transformed a war to preserve the Union into a struggle for human freedom.

Lee W. Eysturlid and Spencer C. Tucker

Further Reading

Gallagher, Gary W., ed. *Antietam: Essays on the 1862 Maryland Campaign.* Chapel Hill: University of North Carolina Press, 1999.

McPherson, James M. *Crossroads of Freedom: Antietam.* New York: Oxford University Press, 2002.

Murfin, James V. *The Gleam of Bayonets: The Battle of Antietam and Robert E. Lee's Maryland Campaign, September 1862.* Baton Rouge: Louisiana State University Press, 2004.

Priest, John M. *Antietam: The Soldier's Battle.* New York: Oxford University Press, 1994.

Sears, Stephen. *Landscape Turned Red: The Battle of Antietam.* New York: Ticknor and Fields, 1983.

Appomattox Court House and Surrender

Located 25 miles east of Lynchburg, Virginia, and three miles east of the town of Appomattox, Appomattox Court House is the small village in which Confederate General Robert E. Lee surrendered to Union Lieutenant General Ulysses S. Grant on April 9,

1865. Lee's surrender, which occurred in the home of Wilmer McLean, essentially ended the Civil War. In 1940, the U.S. Congress created the Appomattox Court House National Historical Monument to commemorate the event.

In Virginia, it was common practice to establish county seats in towns and then rename the towns after the county. Residents added the term *Court House* after the county's name to distinguish the new town from the county. In addition to containing the county court house, the county seat was also home to the county's post office. By 1839, residents in the area of Clover Hill, where Appomattox Court House now stands, increased pressure on the state legislature to create a new county. They cited the considerable distance they had to travel to their respective county courthouses every time they had to vote, serve as jurors, or attend militia muster. On February 6, 1845, the Virginia state legislature voted to establish Appomattox County, and local voters chose the village of Clover Hill to be the new county seat. The residents of Clover Hill immediately changed the name of the village to Appomattox Court House. By 1860, about 150 people, many of whom earned their living from growing tobacco, lived in Appomattox Court House. The small hamlet included the courthouse, a tavern, the county jail, law offices, three stores, two blacksmiths, and several farms and homes.

On April 8, 1865, Union cavalry under by Major General George Armstrong Custer captured the supply trains waiting for Lee at Appomattox Station, a few miles away from Appomattox Court House. The failure of the Confederate forces to dislodge the Union troops in the Battle of Appomattox Court House on the morning of April 9, 1865, convinced Lee to surrender to Grant. When he made the decision to surrender,

Lee reportedly said, "Then there is nothing left for me but to go and see General Grant, and I had rather die a thousands deaths."

Lee subsequently sent his aide, Colonel Charles Marshall, to find a suitable place in Appomattox Court House for the surrender. Because it was a Sunday, the courthouse was closed. Marshall then chose the three-story brick home of Wilmer McLean, a retired major in the Virginia Militia who had not participated in the war. McLean willingly agreed.

For the surrender ceremony, Lee and Grant met in the parlor of McLean's home. Lee, dressed in an immaculate uniform, arrived at the McLean home at 1:00 p.m. Grant arrived 30 minutes later dressed in what was described as a dirty uniform. Lee rose from his chair and greeted Grant with a handshake in the middle of the room. After briefly reminiscing about their previous encounter in the Mexican-American War (1846–1848), Grant offered Lee generous terms of surrender. Lee's officers and soldiers were to be paroled and all weapons, with the exception of officer's swords and private horses, were to be confiscated by the Union Army. Lee and his men would not be charged with treason. At 4:00 p.m., Lee and Grant shook hands and Lee departed the McLean house.

When Lee met his troops, he told them: "Men, we have fought the war together, and I have done the best I could for you. You will all be paroled and go to your homes until exchanged. My heart is too full to say more." On April 10, Lee and Grant met for a second time at the McLean home. Lee requested that his men be issued parole passes to protect them from arrest or annoyance. Grant ordered that 30,000 parole passes be issued to the former Confederate soldiers.

After the Civil War ended, the town fell on hard times, although the railroad station prospered. Many of the residents in Appomattox Court House moved to Appomattox Station. Even the McLean family left town in 1867. When McLean defaulted on a bank loan, his brick home in Appomattox Court House was sold at public auction on November 29, 1869. In 1891, Myron Dunlop purchased the McLean home. He had planned to exhibit the home at the Chicago World's Fair in 1893. Although the McLean home was dismantled and packed for shipping to Chicago, Dunlop experienced financial difficulties and the home remained dismantled for half a century. The fate of Appomattox Court House was equally bleak. In 1892, the courthouse in Appomattox Court House burned and the county seat was transferred to Appomattox Station. The residents of Appomattox Station then shortened the name of their town to Appomattox. By 1900, Appomattox Court House was entirely abandoned.

In 1930, the federal government purchased the land around the abandoned village. Five years later, the federal government initiated discussions to establish a national monument at Appomattox Court House, and the U.S. Congress created the Appomattox Court House National Historical Monument on April 10, 1940. In February 1941, archeologists began the reconstruction of the historical site. On April 9, 1949, the National Park Service finally opened the reconstructed McLean house to the public. Robert E. Lee IV and Ulysses S. Grant III cut the ribbon at the dedication ceremony on April 16, 1950. Thousands of tourists visit the Appomattox Court House National Historical Monument annually.

Michael R. Hall

Further Reading

Altsheler, Joseph. *The Tree of Appomattox.* Kila, MT: Kessinger, 2007.

Davis, Burke. *To Appomattox: Nine April Days, 1865.* Springfield, NJ: Burford Books, 2002.

Marvel, William. *A Place Called Appomattox*. Chapel Hill: University of North Carolina Press, 1999.

Wiley, Bell I. *The Road to Appomattox*. Baton Rouge: Louisiana State University Press, 1994.

Artillery

Civil War field artillery was organized into four- and six-gun batteries. According to regulations, Union batteries numbered between 80 and 156 men, while regulation Confederate batteries numbered 70 to 150 men. A total of 19 Regular Army and 1,647 volunteer batteries served in the Federal Army. The South mustered between 227 and 261 field batteries. At the beginning, batteries on both sides used whatever equipment was available. There were some 163 field guns and howitzers available in the Federal inventory, while the Confederates secured 35 field pieces when they took over federal arsenals. However, few weapons on either side were modern rifled pieces. There were only seven four-gun batteries in the entire U.S. Army when the war began and all the weapons were smoothbore (with maximum effective ranges of 1,500 yards). Consequently, early war batteries utilized a mix of cannon with individual units often having three different types.

As time passed, the North's superior industrial might took effect. Union gunners exchanged older weapons for newly manufactured, modern rifled cannon with effective ranges out to 2,400 yards. In the East, both the Army of Northern Virginia and particularly the Army of the Potomac standardized the weapons assigned to the artillery. Both armies discarded the obsolete 6-pound cannon. Three types came to dominate: the 12-pound Napoleon smoothbore; the 3-inch Ordnance Rifle; and the 10-pound Parrott rifle. The South equipped its batteries via some internal manufacture, some delivery of guns through the blockade, and most importantly, battlefield capture. At Chancellorsville (May 1863) the Federal artillery employed seven long-range rifles to three smoothbores (all Napoleons). Because of their canister-firing capacity, Napoleons probably inflicted more casualties than all other types combined. At Chancellorsville, the rebel artillery had a ratio of about two rifled cannon to three smoothbore. By the time of Gettysburg, two months later, both sides had a roughly 50–50 split of rifles to smooth bores. Lee's gunners took a handful of 12-pound howitzers to Gettysburg and found them near useless. Afterward, they exchanged them for better weapons.

In contrast, the Western armies received second call on equipment of all sorts. At the Battle of Shiloh (April, 6–7 1862) Confederate artillery consisted of 23 batteries. Eighty-five percent of the tubes were smoothbore 6-pound cannon and 12-pound howitzers. These inferior weapons were at a disadvantage in long-range artillery duels. Seventeen months later, the Army of Tennessee's artillery arsenal, which fought at Chickamauga (September 20–21, 1863), still included everything from the obsolete 6-pound smoothbore to the modern 3-inch rifled gun. Likewise the 192 field pieces supporting the Union infantry at Chickamauga comprised 9 different types of weapons including 10 6-pound smooth bores, 16 12-pound howitzers, and 4 mountain howitzers.

Throughout the war southern gunners suffered from materiel inferiority including poor artillery ammunition, unreliable fuses, and poor friction primers. As time passed, the shortage of draft animals reduced the mobility of the Confederate artillery.

Siege artillery types included 8-inch and 10-inch howitzers, which were smoothbore,

Heavy artillery such as this 15-inch Rodman Gun was used in fixed fortifications. (Library of Congress)

muzzle-loaders with ranges of more than 2,000 yards. Likewise, there were 8-inch and 10-inch siege mortars. The siege weapons' lack of mobility greatly limited their usefulness, although on the Union side they did participate effectively at Malvern Hill and Shiloh.

Confederate gunners extensively utilized seacoast cannon for coastal defense and to guard inland waterways. This class included 32- and 42-pound seacoast guns; 8- and 10-inch seacoast howitzers mounted on barbette carriages; 8-, 10-, and 12-inch Columbiads; as well as a variety of heavy cannon such as the Blakely, Parrott, Rodman, Dahlgren, and Whitworth types. Some of the most effective seacoast types were English manufactures brought through the blockade. However, events proved that Confederate gunners using even the most modern types

had trouble hitting moving ships. Union ships routinely steamed past rebel batteries guarding inland waters. On the other hand, ship mounted cannon seldom could silence heavy artillery protected by well-designed earthworks. Thus, the Union navy received heavy punishment at Fort Donelson, Drewry's Bluff, and Charleston Harbor.

James R. Arnold

Further Reading

Boatner, Mark M., III. *The Civil War Dictionary*. New York: David McKay Co., 1959.

Daniel, Larry J. *Cannoneers in Gray: The Field Artillery of the Army of Tennessee 1861–1865*. Tuscaloosa: University of Alabama Press, 1984.

Hazlett, James C., Edwin Olmstead, and M. Hume Parks. *Field Artillery Weapons of the*

Civil War. Urbana: University of Illinois Press, 2004.

Naisawald, Louis V. *Grape and Canister: The Story of the Field Artillery of the Army of the Potomac, 1861–1865*. New York: Oxford University Press, 1960.

Olmstead, Edwin, Wayne E. Stark, and Spencer Tucker. *The Big Guns: Civil War Siege, Seacoast, and Naval Cannon*. Bloomfield, ON: Museum Restoration Service, 1997.

Wise, Jennings C. *The Long Arm of Lee*. Lynchburg, VA: J.P. Bell and Company, 1915.

Atlanta Campaign

Between May 6 and September 1, 1864, Major General William T. Sherman led more than 98,000 Union troops on the most successful campaign of the Civil War, capturing the important Confederate manufacturing and rail center of Atlanta, Georgia. At a cost of only 20,000 casualties, as compared to at least 27,000 men for the much smaller Southern army, Sherman was able to drive the Confederates some 140 miles into Georgia and capture a city as important to the Southern cause as Richmond. The capture of Atlanta, just three months before the 1864 presidential election in the North, has often been credited with ensuring President Abraham Lincoln's reelection and the continuation of the war.

In March 1864, Ulysses S. Grant had been promoted to lieutenant general and given command of all Union forces. His strategic plan called for all Union forces to go on the offensive on the same date, roughly May 5, 1864. Earlier in the war, the Confederates had been able to move their resources to different theaters depending on which Union army was active, thus partially neutralizing the North's numerical superiority. Grant's strategy, which had the strong support of President Lincoln, would prevent this. The two main thrusts would be aimed at the two major Confederate armies, the Army of Northern Virginia under General Robert E. Lee and the Army of Tennessee under General Joseph E. Johnston.

The Armies of the Potomac and the James, under Grant's direction, would move into Virginia in the so-called Overland Campaign with the goals of destroying Lee's Army of Northern Virginia and taking Richmond. The commander of the Department of the Mississippi, Major General Sherman, was to take the Armies of the Ohio, the Tennessee, and the Cumberland and defeat Johnston's army in Georgia, seizing Atlanta.

Johnston's 45,000-man Army of Tennessee was in a strong defensive position in the mountains of north Georgia, north and west of Atlanta. Nevertheless, it had two major weaknesses: it was supplied by just a single railroad from Atlanta, and it faced a force of 98,000 Union troops, more than twice its own size.

On May 6, 1864, the Union army began the drive toward Atlanta. The forward-most Union position was 23 miles south of Chattanooga, about 120 miles from Atlanta, while Johnston's Confederate army was in and around Dalton, Georgia. Sherman's plan was simple. Major General James B. McPherson's Army of the Tennessee would move through the mountain passes to the west of Dalton, placing itself behind Johnston along the railroad. This move would either trap the Confederate army at Dalton, or force it to retreat. While this flanking movement was under way, Major General George Thomas's Army of the Cumberland would press Johnston's front to distract the Confederates from McPherson's movements.

General Johnston, realizing that his position was untenable, soon abandoned Dalton and moved his army south, some 18 miles

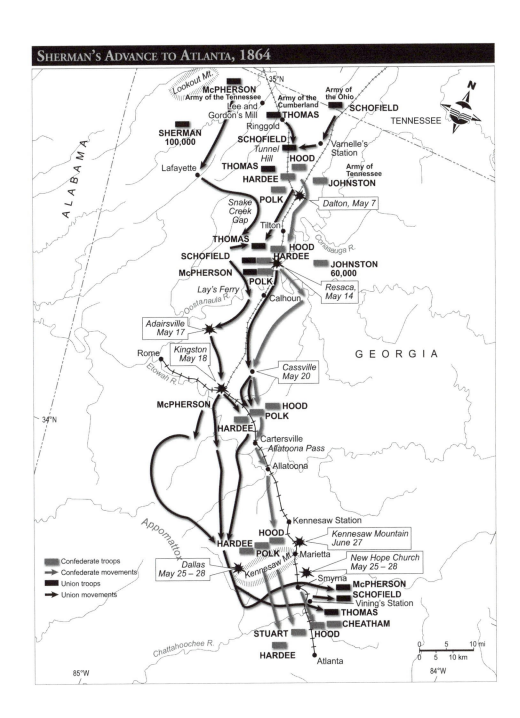

SHERMAN'S ADVANCE TO ATLANTA, 1864

to Resaca. Union soldiers were overjoyed at having driven the Confederates from such a well-fortified position, and many in the Confederate government in Richmond now doubted that Johnston would be able to defend Atlanta.

In Resaca, the Confederates dug in behind earthworks surrounding the city. Major General William Hardee commanded Johnston's right wing, Lieutenant General John Bell Hood held the center, and Major General Leonidas Polk commanded the left wing of the Southern army.

On May 14, Sherman ordered his forces to press Resaca on all fronts. The Battle of Resaca lasted two days. Johnston made a determined effort to hold Resaca, but in the end, Sherman again threatened his line of retreat, and he was forced to fall back closer to Atlanta. The Confederate Army abandoned the town during the night of May 15, crossing the Oostenaula River on pontoon bridges. In the battle Johnston had sustained some 5,000 casualties, while Sherman suffered 6,000. A tactical Confederate victory, it was a strategic gain for the Union side.

Johnston continued to move his army south, crossing the Etowah River and burning the bridge behind his army. The Confederate army fortified Allatoona Pass in the Etowah Mountains, which blocked any direct advance toward Atlanta. Sherman decided to repeat his flanking strategy that had proven successful against Dalton and Resaca. On May 23, he sent his army west toward Marietta, Georgia. He believed that by threatening this important city he could force Johnston to abandon Allatoona Pass.

Johnston detected the Union move toward Marietta and was able to place part of Hood's and Hardee's corps at New Hope Church directly in the path of the Union army. On May 25, Brigadier General Joseph Hooker's

command was surprised by this Confederate force behind earthworks. In the ensuing battle of May 25–27, Hooker lost some 1,600 killed or wounded, the Confederates far less.

Sherman now ordered New Hope bypassed, forcing Johnston to abandon that position. Standing between Sherman's position and Marietta were three mountains. The closest to the Union line was Kennesaw Mountain, some 1,200 feet high. Kennesaw Mountain was the center of the Confederate line. Instead of his usual flanking movement, Sherman ordered a direct assault on the entrenched Confederates on Kennesaw Mountain on June 27. Major General George Thomas's Army of the Cumberland carried out the main assault. The battle was a one-sided Confederate victory. The Union army sustained more than 3,000 casualties, compared to perhaps 750 for the Confederates. Sherman has been criticized for the terrible loss of life incurred, in consequence of his impatience with the flanking strategy.

Following the battle, Sherman once again sent the Army of the Tennessee on a wide flanking movement, forcing Johnston to abandon Kennesaw Mountain and Allatoona Pass. By July 3, Johnston retreated across the Chattahoochee River. The Union army followed closely, bridged the river in two places, and began moving forces across. Johnston withdrew again, moving the majority of his army and guns into Atlanta.

As Johnston moved south, he moved closer to his supplies while Sherman was more removed from his own. Also, the farther south Sherman moved, the smaller his army became as he was forced to leave men behind to guard the railroad. Johnston's plan was to preserve the strength of his army while drawing Sherman into a weaker position. Then he would wait for his foe to make a mistake.

Considering the numerical disadvantage faced by the Confederates, Johnston's strategy was the wisest course to follow. Confederate President Jefferson Davis disagreed, however. Fearing that Johnston would not defend Atlanta, he replaced him with his subordinate, John B. Hood on July 17. Much has been made of the personal animosity between Davis and Johnston that made Davis quick to believe any negative report about his field commander.

Sherman and his senior officers were relieved to learn that Hood was the new commander, as they had much less respect for him than they did for Johnston. Despite having lost the use of his arm at Gettysburg and losing his leg at Chickamauga, Hood retained his belief in aggressive military tactics.

On July 20, Hood ordered his men to attack the Union army, which formed a semicircle just north of the city. This engagement, known both as the Battle of Peach Tree Creek, and Hood's second attack, the Battle of Atlanta on July 22, were disasters for the Confederates, who lost more than 8,000 men to only 3,000 for the Union. Nevertheless, General McPherson was killed during the fighting on July 22, the only Union commanding general killed in battle during the war.

Hood retreated into the Atlanta defenses, while Sherman's men fortified outside the city and fired artillery into the city. After nearly a month, on August 27, Sherman changed his approach. Leaving a small force to guard the railroad bridge over the Chattahoochee River, Sherman sent the rest of his force to the west of Atlanta again to attempt to cut the Confederate supply line.

Thinking that the Union army was withdrawing, Hood was slow to respond. On August 30, the Army of the Tennessee under its new commander Major General Oliver Otis Howard had reached the city of Jonesboro, cutting the Macon and Western Railroad, Hood's only line of retreat and supply. Hood then ordered General Hardee and Lieutenant General Stephen Lee to Jonesboro to drive Howard out and reopen the rail line. In the two-day Battle of Jonesboro (August 31-September 1), the Confederates sustained heavy casualties and were unable to retake Jonesboro.

On the night of September 1, General Hood and the Confederates destroyed their supply stocks and munitions inside Atlanta and evacuated south to Lovejoy Station. The next day the Union forces entered Atlanta.

The objective of the campaign, the destruction of the Confederate army, was not achieved, as Hood had escaped with what remained of his army. However, Sherman had accomplished a great deal. Although Hood's army was still active in the field, Sherman was free to move largely unchallenged to Savannah. The news of the fall of Atlanta was received with joy in the North and gloom in the South. Most believed that once Atlanta fell, the Confederacy no longer had a chance to win the war.

Wesley Moody

Further Reading

Castel, Albert. *Decision in the West, The Atlanta Campaign of 1864*. Lawrence: University Press of Kansas, 1992.

Johnston, Joseph E. *Narrative of Military Operations, Directed, During the Late War Between the States*. New York: D. Appleton, 1874.

Key, William. *The Battle of Atlanta and the Georgia Campaign*. Atlanta, GA: Peachtree, 1981.

Sherman, William T. *Memoirs of General W. T. Sherman*. New York: Library of America, 1990.

B

Beauregard, Pierre Gustave Toutant (1818–1893)

Born into a powerful Louisiana family in Saint-Pierre Parish on May 28, 1818, Pierre Gustave Toutant Beauregard prepared for a life of public prominence. His fascination with Napoleon Bonaparte led him to select a military career, over the objections of his parents. Beauregard entered the U.S. Military Academy, West Point, in 1834, graduating second in a class that included future Civil War generals Richard Ewell, Jubal Early, and Irvin McDowell. He excelled at artillery tactics to the point that the Academy invited Beauregard to stay on as lecturer in the subject for an additional year. He then served for two years with the Army Corps of Engineers, involved in the placement of gun batteries in various fortifications around the country.

The outbreak of the Mexican-American War in 1846 found Captain Beauregard supervising the construction of fortifications near Tampa, Florida. Eager for combat experience to enhance his chances of promotion, Beauregard received permission to go to Mexico in 1847 as part of Major General Winfield Scott's campaign against Mexico City. Reporting to Scott's command, Beauregard (along with captains Robert E. Lee and George B. McClellan) served as a staff officer to Scott, learning the intricacies of staff work, logistics, and personnel matters. With his knowledge of artillery and engineering, Beauregard played several important roles in the war. He supervised the use of siege artillery at Veracruz, demonstrated initiative

against the Mexicans at the Battle of Contreras by revealing an opportunity to flank the enemy, and was one of the few staff officers to agree with Scott that a direct assault on the heights at the Battle of Chapultepec was the best option to capture Mexico City. However, whereas Scott singled out a number of officers for specific praise in his official reports, Beauregard received none, creating a paranoia about recognition that haunted him for the remainder of his military career.

Following the war, Beauregard returned to New Orleans as an engineering officer. He dabbled in Democratic local politics (including an unsuccessful campaign for mayor of New Orleans). He also worked to ensure the election of Mexican-American War veteran Franklin Pierce as president in 1852. Pierce, however, selected another veteran, Jefferson Davis, as his secretary of war. Beauregard hoped that these fellow officers would assist him in gaining promotion. Beauregard also courted and married Catherine Deslonde, the sister-in-law of John Slidell, the powerful Democratic senator from Louisiana, a marriage that improved Beauregard's chances of advancing his military career.

Through Slidell's influence, Beauregard became the superintendent of West Point in January 1861. Only five days later, however, he resigned the post when his native Louisiana seceded from the Union to protest the election of the Republican Abraham Lincoln. A month later, Beauregard received a commission as brigadier general in the Confederate Army from Jefferson Davis, now Confederate president. Utilizing Beauregard's experience as an artilleryman, Davis sent him to Charleston, South Carolina, to assume command of local forces confronting the Union enclave at Fort Sumter. On April 12, 1861, Beauregard received orders from Davis to remove the Union garrison by force, and Beauregard's subsequent bombardment forced a Union evacuation two days later.

Arriving in the Confederate capital of Richmond to a hero's welcome in May 1861, Beauregard seemed destined for the accolades he believed to be long overdue. Instead, he found himself embroiled in personality clashes with his commander-in-chief. Jefferson Davis was perhaps somewhat envious of Beauregard's position as hero of the hour. He certainly did not appreciate Beauregard's advice on military matters. Beauregard believed he was in Richmond to supervise Confederate military efforts as senior commander, while Davis, the former secretary of war, believed himself quite competent to do that himself. Davis simply wanted Beauregard to supervise the defense of Richmond as commander of the local army, under command of General Joseph Johnston, who held the post of department commander. Beauregard favored a direct offensive action against Washington, D.C., with himself in command. At the First Battle of Bull Run, Beauregard commanded the victorious Confederate Army. Thereafter, he expected the accolades of the victor, but instead he felt snubbed when other heroes, such as Thomas J. Jackson, captured the public's attention. Continually irritating Davis over strategic policy and chafing under Johnston's command, in January 1862 Beauregard found himself sent to Tennessee.

Assigned to the western theater, Beauregard served as a corps commander under General Albert Johnston, but similar irritations soon emerged. Beauregard continually offered unsolicited advice on operational

matters and constantly planned, without Johnston's knowledge, for autonomous attacks by his corps into Tennessee and Missouri. These plans went on hold when Union forces under Brigadier General Ulysses S. Grant and Flag Officer Andrew Foote captured Fort Henry and Fort Donelson, forcing a Confederate retreat back to their railhead at Corinth, Mississippi. Beauregard joined his corps with Johnston's army in preparation for a counterstroke against the Union advance at Pittsburgh Landing, Tennessee. The resulting Battle of Shiloh (April 6–7, 1862) proved a professional disaster to Beauregard. Johnston's initial attack went well, routing the Union troops out of their unprepared camps. Johnston, however, was mortally wounded and it took some time to locate Beauregard to inform him that he was now in command. By that time, the daylight had faded, and Beauregard, anticipating the final destruction of Grant's army the next day, called off the attack for the night and sent off a triumphant telegram to Jefferson Davis and the Confederate War Department informing them of his great victory. Beauregard soon had to eat those words. The next day, Grant, reinforced by troops from Major General Don Carlos Buell's army, launched a counterattack that drove Beauregard's army from the field in disarray. Falling back to Corinth, Beauregard eventually evacuated this important position a month later. In retrospect, Beauregard did not deserve to take the brunt of the blame for the Confederate defeat. Although initially successful, Johnston's attack was already bogging down when he was killed. Had he been alive, it is doubtful that Johnston could have done any better than Beauregard on the second day of Shiloh or during the time preceding the evacuation of Corinth. Unfortunately for Beauregard, he was in command and had to take the blame. Davis removed Beauregard from command, replacing him with his own personal friend, Major General Braxton Bragg.

Beauregard found himself in the backwater of the war, once again commanding Confederate forces around Charleston. For the remainder of 1862 and throughout 1863, Beauregard ably defended the city, repulsing several serious Union attempts against Charleston from the sea. While successful in protecting the city, the failure of Union efforts resulted more from the daunting city defenses than from any tactical brilliance on Beauregard's part. In early 1864, Beauregard assumed command of the Department of North Carolina, embracing North Carolina and regions of Virginia south of the James River. Beauregard again ably defended the right flank of Richmond as Grant's Overland Campaign ground its way toward the Confederate capital in the summer of 1864. The primary task was containing Union Major General Benjamin Butler's assault at Bermuda Hundred. Once again gaining prominence, Beauregard soon ruined his credibility. When Confederate General Robert E. Lee's Army of Northern Virginia became locked in a siege in defense of Petersburg, Beauregard assumed (since Petersburg was within his department) that he would at least be the equal of Lee in coordinating the battle.

Instead, Davis dissolved his department and placed Beauregard and his men under Lee's command. Instead of accepting the demotion, Beauregard complained, and Davis shipped him off again. The last months of the war found Beauregard in a series of unredeemable situations. He served briefly under Major General John Hood in his disastrous campaign into Tennessee in late 1864, and tried unsuccessfully, as part of Joseph Johnston's army, to stop Major General William Sherman's campaign through the Carolinas in early 1865. Released from the army when Johnston surrendered in 1865, Beauregard returned to New Orleans.

In the postwar years, Beauregard prospered in a variety of business ventures, wrote his memoirs, and served in several public offices before his death in New Orleans on February 20, 1893. Perhaps the best summary of Beauregard's career is that he did specific important military tasks well, but could not translate that success onto a larger stage. But, in his defense, he was also never given the opportunity to try.

Steven J. Ramold

Further Reading

Basso, Hamilton. *Beauregard: The Great Creole*. New York: Scribner's, 1933.

Williams, T. Harry. *P.G.T. Beauregard: Napoleon in Gray*. Baton Rouge: Louisiana State University Press, 1954.

Blockade of the Confederacy

On April 19, 1861, President Abraham Lincoln announced a naval blockade of the Southern coast from South Carolina to Texas. On April 27 he issued a second proclamation extending the blockade to Virginia and North Carolina. To help man the ships required, on May 3 the president called for the enlistment of an additional 18,000 seamen.

In implementing the blockade, the Union grappled with a fundamental contradiction. The North maintained throughout the war that the Confederate States of America did not exist and that the Federal government faced merely a domestic insurrection. If that was indeed the case, foreign governments had no justification for recognizing or aiding the Confederacy. But at the same time, if the Confederate States did not exist, could the Union legally blockade its own southern coastline? U.S. Secretary of the Navy Gideon

Welles, taking such legal complications seriously, personally opposed a "blockade," favoring instead a policy of "closing" Southern ports, a traditional technique in times of domestic insurrection. Yet for practical military, political, and diplomatic reasons, President Lincoln and Secretary of State William H. Seward chose to ignore the legal technicalities of the issue and continued to maintain both positions—that the Confederate States did not in fact exist but that the Union could blockade the coastline.

Lincoln's proclamation created practical problems for both the Union and Confederate governments. With only a handful of ships available to blockade some 3,000 miles of Southern coastline, the Union faced the challenge of turning a paper blockade into a real one. Secretary Welles disbanded overseas squadrons and called home their ships. He also proceeded to buy or commandeer virtually every steamer available. These were soon armed with a few guns and converted into blockaders. At the same time, he instituted a massive shipbuilding program that bore fruit later.

Welles organized the ships into three squadrons: the Home Squadron, based at Fortress Monroe; the Coast Blockading Squadron (soon redesignated the Atlantic Blockading Squadron), with the Potomac Flotilla (centered on the Potomac and Rappahannock rivers and charged with the defense of Washington); and the Gulf Coast Blockading Squadron. The Atlantic Blockading Squadron had responsibility for enforcing the blockade all the way from Alexandria, Virginia to Key West, Florida, a distance of some 1,000 miles. The Gulf Coast Squadron covered the even greater distance from Key West to Brownsville, Texas. Given the vast distances involved, in October 1861 Welles further divided the squadrons. He separated the Atlantic blockaders into two: a North

Atlantic Blockading Squadron, responsible for the Virginia and North Carolina Coasts, and a South Atlantic Blockading Squadron for the Southern coastline from South Carolina to Key West, Florida. In February 1862 Welles also divided the Gulf Coast Blockading Squadron, making four Federal blockading squadrons in all. The East Gulf Coast Blockading Squadron patrolled from Cape Canaveral on the Atlantic coast of Florida to St. Andrews Bay on the Florida Gulf Coast. The West Gulf Coast Blockading Squadron had responsibility for the Southern coast from St. Andrews Bay to Brownsville.

Few vessels were available at first. Ships returning from foreign station required repairs, and it was many months before the navy was able legally to blockade many Southern ports. At first, single warships took up station off key Confederate ports. On May 10, the screw sloop *Niagara,* just returned from Japan, initiated the blockade of Charleston, while on May 26 the *Brooklyn* arrived off the Mississippi River, and on June 8 the *Mississippi* set the blockade of Key West.

Confederate President Jefferson Davis embraced a plan, although it was never officially announced as policy, to suspend cotton exports in the mistaken belief that this "Cotton Diplomacy" would bring about British intervention. Southern leaders assumed that this would impose such economic pressure as to force the British government to dispatch warships to assist in breaking the Union blockade. It did not happen. Not only were cotton markets accessible to Britain in Egypt and India, but Northern "corn" (grain) was immensely important to Britain.

The South thus missed a great opportunity. Before the Union blockade could become effective, the Confederacy should have rushed all available cotton to European markets in order to purchase arms and manufactured goods. Instead, when its gold

THE BLOCKADE ON THE "CONNECTICUT PLAN".

A Currier & Ives cartoon poking fun at the early, and ineffective, Union blockade. As the war progressed, the blockade became much more effective. (Library of Congress)

reserves soon became exhausted, the Confederacy reversed its policy. By then it was too late, for the Union blockade had become much more effective.

Blockade running was triangular, with its three main corners at the South, the West Indies, and Europe (or sometimes even the North itself). Because of its proximity to the Confederacy, Nassau, Bahamas, was the headquarters of blockade-running operations. Other common destinations included Bermuda, St. Thomas, Havana, Jamaica, and Nova Scotia. Large ships, mostly British, would travel there, where their cargoes would be offloaded into smaller, faster ships for travel to the South. Major Confederate ports for blockade runners included Wilmington, North Carolina; Charleston, South Carolina; Savannah, Georgia; Mobile, Alabama; and, especially in the last year of the war when other ports had been closed, Galveston, Texas.

Blockade duties were tedious and routine-centered. Union ships had to remain on station in tropical summer heat and the gales and cold of winter, and they had to contend with operations in unfamiliar coastal shoal waters. Crews also had to be on constant guard against the possibility of a sudden Confederate attack. Each side sought to thwart the other. Signal rockets on the Union side might be countered by false Confederate signals to lure off the blockaders in another direction.

Despite the best Union efforts, most blockade runners made it through. Runs out were safer than runs in, simply because captains had the benefit of knowing the location of the Union ships and could plan accordingly. The most dangerous time to attempt to pass through the blockade was in daylight. If a blockade runner arrived off the coast in daytime and was sighted by Union warships, whether the blockade runner would escape rested solely on speed.

Although few blockade runners returned substantial profits, the financial rewards could be considerable, even if a ship were ultimately lost. The *Ella and Annie*, capable of carrying up to 1,300 bales of cotton, made eight trips through the blockade. Combined with profit on inbound cargo, it returned a profit of about $200,000 per round trip. Financial reward remained the chief motivation for blockade running, and high returns explain why so many people participated in the activity. Sailors on blockade duty could hope for prize money from any captures, but the sums realized were generally far less than supposed.

Slowly but surely, the number of blockaders increased. By January 1865, the Union Navy had 471 ships with 2,245 guns in the effort. During the course of the war these took a total of 1,149 ships of all types and destroyed another 351. The totals include 210 steamers captured and 85 destroyed, along with 569 schooners taken and 114 destroyed. In 1861, 2,465 steamers and sailing ships made it past the blockade. In 1864, the last full year of war, the total was 619.

With Confederate domestic production never reaching 50 percent of military needs, goods brought in by blockade runners were essential to the Southern war effort. Historian Stephen Wise has estimated that the South brought in through blockade running at least 400,000 rifles (more than 60 percent of the Confederacy's modern arms), 2,250,000 pounds of saltpeter (two-thirds of that needed) and 3 million pounds of lead (one third of army requirements). The runners also carried clothing, chemicals, and medicine. Without these supplies, the Confederacy could not have survived as long as it did.

The effectiveness of the blockade remains a hot topic of debate. Its critics note that the vast majority of blockade runners were successful. They point out that the economic collapse of the Confederacy was not because of the blockade but the deterioration of the Southern railroad system. Critics of the blockade argue that even a more effective blockade would not have prevented the South from continuing the war. Confederate defeat did not result from lack of war materials; rather, the South simply ran out of manpower.

Defenders of the blockade acknowledge its shortcomings. They admit to its incomplete nature and the fact that the South never lacked the essential weapons with which to fight and win battles; and they note that the Confederacy was hard pressed in such essential items as artillery, clothing, shoes, harnesses, medicines, and even blankets. The blockade also affected the entire Southern economy. The loss of rolled iron rail was particularly harmful, leading to the collapse of the Confederate transportation system, bringing with it serious distribution problems, even of food, that affected soldier and civilian alike. The blockade also disrupted patterns of intra-regional trade by water, sharply increasing the burden on the already inadequate Southern railroad net.

The blockade was certainly the chief cause, directly or indirectly, of Southern economic distress. The figures given of successful passages through the blockade are also misleading, as they include vessels exiting, as well as entering, Southern ports. Each stop by an individual coastal packet at a different port is counted a "successful attempt." Two coastal steamers making up to 10 stops per trip made almost 800 of the runs in 1861.

Historian David G. Surdam notes the role played by cotton, by far the most important prewar Southern export, in the blockade equation. He believes that the effectiveness of the blockade should be measured not in goods smuggled through it or the success rate of the ships. Rather, the total volume of trade was sharply reduced and the cost of shipment dramatically increased.

The under-industrialized Confederacy had to import manufactured goods to win the war, yet the higher shipping costs consumed much of its purchasing power and sharply eroded its ability to make purchases overseas. The increased cost in transporting cotton to Europe accounted for almost all of the increase in its price in Europe and the North. Although European goods could always reach the South, this increasingly occurred through less convenient ports, such as via the Mexican port of Matamoros to Brownsville, Texas. Also, increasing shortages of consumer goods impacted civilian morale.

The Federal government spent $567 million on the navy during the war (1879 calculation). This was roughly one-twelfth of the expenses of the entire war ($6.8 billion). Yet the entire cost of the navy was equal to or exceeded by the loss in revenue to the South from the export of raw cotton. Given the fact that the North was far richer than the South, it was far easier for it to bear the expense of the blockade than it was for the South to sustain the loss in export revenue.

Critical in the success of the blockade was the decision taken by Washington early in the war to secure bases from which the blockading squadrons could operate. The Union side demonstrated great ability in setting up and maintaining repair and supply facilities as well as the logistics network that went with this. The effort here was a vast one, and it is largely unsung in histories of the war. It certainly appears to have been an effective use of Northern resources.

Kenneth J. Blume and Spencer C. Tucker

Further Reading

Bradlee, Francis B. C. *Blockade Running during the Civil War and the Effect of Land and Water Transportation on the Confederacy.* Salem, MA: Essex Institute, 1925.

Browning, Robert M., Jr. *From Cape Charles to Cape Fear: The North Atlantic Blockading Squadron during the Civil War.* Tuscaloosa: University of Alabama Press, 1993.

Browning, Robert M., Jr. *Success Is All That Was Expected: The South Atlantic Blockading Squadron during the Civil War.* Dulles, VA: Brassey's, 2002.

Dalzell, George W. *The Flight from the Flag: The Continuing Effect of the Civil War upon the American Carrying Trade.* Chapel Hill: University of North Carolina Press, 1940.

Soley, James R. *The Blockade and the Cruisers.* New York: Charles Scribner's Sons, 1983.

Surdam, David G. *Northern Naval Superiority and the Economics of the American Civil War.* Colombia: University of South Carolina Press, 2001.

Taylor, Thomas E. *Running the Blockade: A Personal Narrative of Adventures, Risks, and Escapes During the American Civil War.* Annapolis, MD: Naval Institute Press, 1994.

Wise, Stephen R. *Lifeline of the Confederacy: Blockade Running during the Civil War.* Columbia: University of South Carolina Press, 1988.

Border States

The border states during the American Civil War were Maryland, Delaware, Kentucky, and Missouri and were identified by the Abraham Lincoln administration as such. West Virginia, admitted to the Union in 1863 after it seceded from Virginia, is sometimes considered a border state. These states were considered border states because of their geographical location, divided political loyalties, and strong ties to both the North and the South. These ties were economic as well as cultural and familial. When the Civil War began in 1861, slavery existed in Maryland, Delaware, Kentucky, and Missouri, albeit on a scale much diminished from the states in the Deep South. Because they occupied strategic locations, President Lincoln strove mightily to keep the border states loyal to the Union.

Maryland was a state of deep divides, with a distinctively Southern cultural bias and many families with Southern blood-lines. Many pro-Confederate Marylanders pushed for recognition of the Confederacy and abhorred radical abolitionists. By the same token, however, most did not support secession. In March 1861, rioting occurred in Baltimore when pro-Southern sympa-thizers attempted to stop Union troops from passing through the city on their way to Washington, D.C. Much property was de-stroyed, and dozens of people were killed or wounded.

In response, the federal government arrested and imprisoned the city's mayor, po-lice chief, and a number of Maryland legisla-tors who were deemed to be pro-Confederate. Martial law was imposed on Maryland, and Baltimore was treated as an occupied city until the end of the war in 1865. Federal troops continuously garrisoned the state as well. On April 27, 1861, the Maryland legis-lature voted to reject secession, but Lincoln was constantly wary of Maryland's sharply divided loyalties.

In Delaware, loyalties were not nearly as divided. In the winter of 1861, when the Con-federacy asked the state to join it, the state's legislature overwhelmingly rejected the pro-posal. Thereafter, Delaware remained loyal to the Union, and its many industries con-tributed to the Union war effort. Although there were small pockets of Southern sym-pathizers in the state, Delaware never posed a serious threat to the Union, and Lincoln worried least about Delaware of all of the border states.

Kentucky, like Maryland, was a state sharply bifurcated by conflicting cultures and political loyalties. Lincoln was most concerned about keeping Kentucky out of the Confederates' grasp, once remarking that "to lose Kentucky is nearly the same as to lose the whole game. Kentucky gone, we cannot hold Missouri, nor Maryland." Kentucky never officially seceded from the Union, but a group of pro-Southern sym-pathizers did form their own government, which the Confederacy officially recog-nized. When the war began in April 1861, pro-Southern governor Beriah Magoffin refused to heed Lincoln's call for troops, which outraged the state's pro-Union fac-tions. In May 1861, the state declared its neutrality, which proved to be short-lived. By the early fall of 1861, Confederate troops had moved into western Kentucky, and in response, Union troops occupied Paducah. As a result of the incursions, the Kentucky legislature ordered Confederate, but not Union, troops to withdraw from the state immediately. Magoffin tried to block the resolution but to no avail.

Pro-Southern factions in Kentucky were dismayed by the legislature's actions, and in November 1861 a delegation gathered at Russellville, Kentucky, to form a shadow government, based in Bowling Green. The Russellville Convention witnessed the elec-tion of an alternate governor and the ratifi-cation of the Confederate Constitution. In December 1862, the Confederacy admitted Kentucky as a state. The Confederate gov-ernment in Bowling Green never seriously threatened Kentucky's overall loyalty to the Union, but the war that saw Kentuckians fighting on both sides tore the society apart and resulted in much fratricide.

In Missouri, there were also sharply di-vided loyalties. In February 1861, a state convention defeated a measure to secede from the Union and declared the state's neutrality. But when Union troops moved into the state, first moving against a pro-Southern militia encamped at St. Louis, the state was neutral in name only. Indeed, the Union incursion pushed a good number of Missourians into supporting the Confederate cause.

In June 1861, the pro-Southern governor of Missouri, Claiborne F. Jackson, fled the state capital at Jefferson City as Union forces marched toward it. That autumn Jackson set up a pro-Southern government, which passed a secession ordinance and was admitted into the Confederacy in November. Meanwhile, the federal government installed a provisional governor at Jefferson City in the person of Hamilton Gamble. Missourians served in the armies of both North and South, which resulted in sons fighting fathers and brothers fighting brothers. Guerrilla warfare paralyzed parts of the state and wrecked its economy.

President Lincoln had to tread delicately in regard to the border states lest he push one or all into the Confederate camp. He did not, for example, include any of the states in his 1863 Emancipation Proclamation, which angered many abolitionists and radical Republicans. Slavery would not be officially abolished in the border states until the Thirteenth Amendment was passed in 1865. Federal troops in the border states were circumscribed in their activities for fear of creating an anti-Union backlash.

Paul G. Pierpaoli, Jr.

Further Reading

Hansen, Harry. *The Civil War: A History*. New York: Signet Classics, 2001

McPherson, James M. *The Battle Cry of Freedom: The Civil War Era*. Westminster, MD: Ballantine, 1989

McPherson, James M. *For Cause and Comrades: Why Men Fought in the Civil War*. New York: Oxford University Press, 1997

Bragg, Braxton (1817–1876)

Braxton Bragg was one of the most controversial of Confederate generals. He was the fifth-ranking general and commanded the most important Confederate forces in the west for much of the war. Although an able administrator, his mediocre performance as a field commander and his harsh methods of discipline lost Bragg the confidence of his superiors and his soldiers. Personality traits also prevented Bragg from succeeding. The conflicting mix of ability and faults was displayed as early as Bragg's military service during the Mexican-American War.

Bragg was born on March 22, 1817, in Warrenton, North Carolina. After attending local schools, he enrolled at the U.S. Military Academy at West Point in 1833. Bragg's intellect and discipline distinguished him, and he graduated fifth in a class of 50 in 1837. He was appointed a second lieutenant in the Third Artillery and sent to Florida to participate in the removal of the Seminoles. Bragg's health failed as a result of heat, humidity, and stress and he spent most of 1838 recovering from fever, dyspepsia, and boils. He also gained a reputation as a rigid commander, quarrelsome and critical of faults among superiors and subordinates. He also lacked tact in delicate situations and made his dissatisfaction known publicly.

In 1845, Bragg was assigned to the Army of Occupation under General Zachary Taylor in Texas. During the Mexican-American War, Bragg distinguished himself through

C

Cavalry Organization and Tactics

During the war, cavalry on both sides followed a tactical system known as the "Poinsett tactics," named after the U.S. Secretary of War who ordered its publication. Published in 1841, it was essentially a translation of a French cavalry tactical system. The U.S. Cavalry Tactics had three volumes covering dismounted drill, mounted drill, and the evolution of a regiment. Numerous subsequent manuals simplified the tactics manual. All emphasized the mounted charge in line with the saber as the arbiter of battle, an emphasis that proved woefully misplaced on the Civil War battlefield.

Both the Union and Confederates organized their cavalry regiments into ten companies with each regulation company numbering between 56 and 72 privates in the Union army and 64 and 100 privates in the Confederate service. The Union army mustered 258 regiments and 170 independent companies; the Confederate army between 127 and 137 regiments and 47 to 143 assorted cavalry battalions. By regulation, Union troopers carried a saber, revolver, and carbine. Confederate cavalry typically made do with less, often substituting shotguns and muskets for the carbine and doing without the saber. By mid-war, Union troopers in the East enjoyed the benefit of repeating carbines, most notably the seven-shot, breech-loading Spencer. Western Union cavalry, like their infantry and artillery comrades, had to use leftover equipment. One innovative western cavalry leader, Colonel John Wilder, took out a bank loan to purchase Spencers for his troopers.

Confederate manufacturing could not mass-produce repeating carbines.

Basic equipment for the trooper included a haversack, canteen, cap box secured to the waist belt, holster on the right side, and revolver cartridge box on the back. Carbines were slung from the left shoulder to the right-hand side with the cartridge box attached to the strap and carried in back. A complete set of horse equipment included bridles and saddles, halter, surcingle, pair of spurs, currycomb, horse brush, picket pin, saddle blanket, lariat, and pair of saddlebags.

Fundamental to a trooper's efficiency was the possession of a trained, fit horse. The Federal government provided horses for its troopers. Dismounted troopers were sent back to the cavalry depot to obtain a new mount. In contrast, rebel cavalrymen had to provide their own horses. When the war began, this meant that the typical Confederate trooper possessed a superior animal. The drawback of the Confederate approach became apparent as the war lasted longer than anyone had supposed and horses died from combat, disease, malnutrition, and exposure. The Confederate war department issued General Order No. 67, dated May 25, 1863, which decreed that a dismounted Confederate trooper who could not replace his horse could be ordered into the infantry or artillery. At this time, a horse cost much more than a Confederate private's monthly wage. The only alternative for most men was to secure permission to depart the ranks and join horse-stealing raids behind Union lines. Once a trooper was away from regimental discipline, he faced strong temptations not to return. The lack of a centralized

Chattanooga, Battle of

The great Confederate victory at Chickamauga, September 19–20, 1863, drove William S. Rosecrans's Army of the Cumberland behind its fortifications at Chattanooga. Outside the city, Braxton Bragg's victorious Army of Tennessee occupied the heights overlooking Chattanooga. With its back to the Tennessee River, and only a single mountain road linking Rosecrans's army with the rear, the Army of the Cumberland began slowly to starve. Forage was so scarce that the army's horses sickened and died, rendering the field army almost immobile.

Recognizing the crisis at Chattanooga, General Henry Halleck directed a splendid logistical exercise that moved 12,000 men by rail from Virginia to Tennessee. The former commander of the Army of the Potomac, Joseph Hooker, commanded this force. These reinforcements helped ensure the survival of the Union army at Chattanooga. Also at this time of crisis, the Lincoln Administration

summoned Ulysses S. Grant. Henceforth, Chattanooga became the Union's focus of strategic operations with some 37,000 reinforcements eventually reaching the Chattanooga area. Grant relieved Rosecrans and replaced him with the hero of Chickamauga, George S. Thomas. On the evening of October 23, 1863, Grant arrived in Chattanooga. Within 24 hours, he had adopted a campaign scheme and set it in motion to relieve the city.

After Chickamauga, Bragg had expected Rosecrans to evacuate Chattanooga. Surprised by the Union stand, he limited himself to ordering cavalry raids against the vulnerable Union supply line. Meanwhile, he fell to quarreling with many of his senior subordinates including generals Leonidas Polk, D. H. Hill, and Thomas Hindman. The morale of the Army of Tennessee plummeted. Over the period October 26–30, Grant implemented a plan to open a decent line of supply for the malnourished Union troops in Chattanooga. The complex, well-executed plan succeeded. On the morning

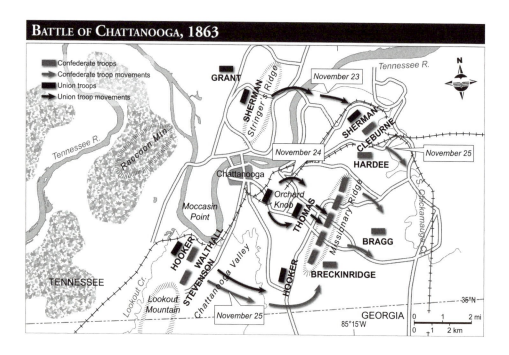

of October 30, 1863 a steamer delivered 40,000 rations and tons of forage for the starving horses. The opening of the so-called Cracker Line raised the morale of the Army of the Cumberland.

For the next three weeks, Union strength grew. Bragg, in contrast, weakened his army by getting rid of another unwanted subordinate, James B. Longstreet. On November 17, Bragg foolishly detached him and sent his command to Knoxville, Tennessee to confront a Union force commanded by Ambrose Burnside. Bragg was left with a mere 34,000 men. On November 23, 1863, Grant's 60,000 Union troops began an offensive to break the siege. Thomas's Army of the Cumberland advanced out from Chattanooga to occupy Orchard Knob, about half way to the Confederate lines on Missionary Ridge. Thomas's preliminary advance supported a two-pronged envelopment by other Federal contingents. Hooker's mission was to storm Lookout Mountain on the Confederate left while elements of Grant's Army of the Tennessee, under the command of William T. Sherman, tried to turn the Confederate right. On November 24, Hooker easily carried Lookout Mountain, although without threatening Bragg's main army. Sherman's corps meanwhile encountered greater resistance among the broken hills at the northeastern tip of Missionary Ridge and his advance bogged down.

On November 25, while Hooker worked to envelop the Confederate left, Sherman renewed his effort to turn the Confederate right. A combination of Union bungling and skillful Confederate resistance from a division commanded by the Irish-born general, Patrick Cleburne, defeated Sherman's thrust. To assist Sherman, Grant ordered Thomas to capture the Confederate trench line at the base of Missionary Ridge. In one of the most improbable charges of the war, Thomas's 18,000 men occupied the first trench line and then ignored orders and began scaling the 500-foot heights of Missionary Ridge. The attackers advanced like an irresistible tide led by a division commanded by 32-year-old major general Philip Sheridan. Their determined attack up Missionary Ridge routed Bragg's demoralized army. Bragg's army retreated in disorder, having suffered 8,700 killed, wounded, or captured. Grant lost about 6,000 men.

Chattanooga was an important strategic victory for the North. It opened the way for Sherman to advance on Atlanta the following spring. Sheridan's leadership during the fighting made a favorable impression on Grant. Grant would employ Sheridan in an important role the next year. For Grant himself, his performance at Chattanooga came on the heels of his brilliant victory at Vicksburg. These victories convinced Lincoln to offer him the top military command in the entire U.S. Army. From a Confederate viewpoint, the loss of Chattanooga severed a vital line of lateral communications. It also led to the relief of Braxton Bragg and his replacement as commander of the Army of Tennessee with Joseph E. Johnston.

James R. Arnold

Further Reading

Arnold, James R. *The Armies of U.S. Grant.* London: Arms and Armour Press, 1995.

Boatner, Mark M., III. *The Civil War Dictionary.* New York: David McKay Co., 1991.

McDonough, James L. *Chattanooga: A Death Grip on the Confederacy.* Knoxville: The University of Tennessee Press, 1984.

U.S. Military Academy. *The West Point Atlas of American Wars, Volume I, 1689–1900.* New York: Frederick A. Praeger Publishers, 1959.

Chickamauga, Battle of

Following a seven-month lull after the Battle of Stones River, Union General William Rosecrans launched an offensive in Tennessee. His cleverly conceived attack began on June 26, 1863.

Opposing Rosecrans was the Army of Tennessee commanded by Braxton Bragg. In nine days of skillful maneuver, Rosecrans's Army of the Cumberland drove Bragg's army out of central Tennessee. The Union army stood poised to advance on Chattanooga, the gateway to the Confederate heartland.

Confederate President Jefferson Davis looked at the strategic chessboard and everywhere he saw trouble. In Virginia, Lee's defeated army was trying to recover from its mauling at Gettysburg. In the west, Grant's victorious army had captured Vicksburg. And now, with Rosecrans's advance, the Confederate center appeared vulnerable. At this moment of crisis, Davis made the strategic decision to strip forces from all the other major Confederate armies in order to reinforce Bragg. Thus strengthened, Bragg would try to destroy Rosecrans's army and regain Tennessee.

When the reinforcements arrived, Bragg commanded over 50,000 men to oppose Rosecrans's 53,000 men. Bragg had the advantage of surprise. Rosecrans mistakenly thought that Bragg's army was demoralized and in retreat. Thus, on the night of September 17, when Bragg issued orders that initiated the Battle of Chickamauga, Rosecrans had little notion that he was about to face a major Confederate offensive. The Army of the Cumberland stood dispersed and vulnerable on the west bank of Chickamauga Creek.

Bragg's plan called for a crossing of Chickamauga Creek and a turn left to sweep south toward the Union center. A mixed wood forest covered most of the ground where the battle took place. With typical sight lines extending no farther than 100 yards, command and control of the fighting formations was exceedingly difficult.

On September 18, Bragg's army began to cross the creek. By day's end, Bragg thought that his forces were in position to assault Rosecrans's left flank. Alarmed at last, Rosecrans began concentrating his army. George Thomas's corps made a hard, fast march to take up a position on the Union left flank. On the morning of September 19, Thomas ordered one of his divisions to move forward to attack what he thought was an isolated Confederate brigade. Both sides fed in reinforcements and a general battle began. During the afternoon, three separate Confederate assaults almost shattered the Union position. But Confederate inability to coordinate the assaults limited their success.

During the night Thomas's men felled trees and built log breastworks. Meanwhile, the balance of Rosecrans's army shifted north to connect with Thomas's line. Bragg, in turn, resolved to continue his attack the next day. That attack would feature an effort to turn Thomas's left flank, followed by a series of assaults moving from the Confederate right to the Confederate left. Personality conflicts between Bragg and his subordinates delayed the start of the Confederate attack. When it did begin, the attacks were disjointed. Still, as the pressure against Thomas increased, that general asked Rosecrans for help. Rosecrans, in turn, decided to reinforce Thomas at the expense of all else. Command confusion delayed the movement of reinforcements to Thomas. Meanwhile, the Confederate right wing hurled itself against Thomas's line.

Around 11 a.m., a Union division mistakenly moved out of line to reinforce Thomas. This movement took place just as

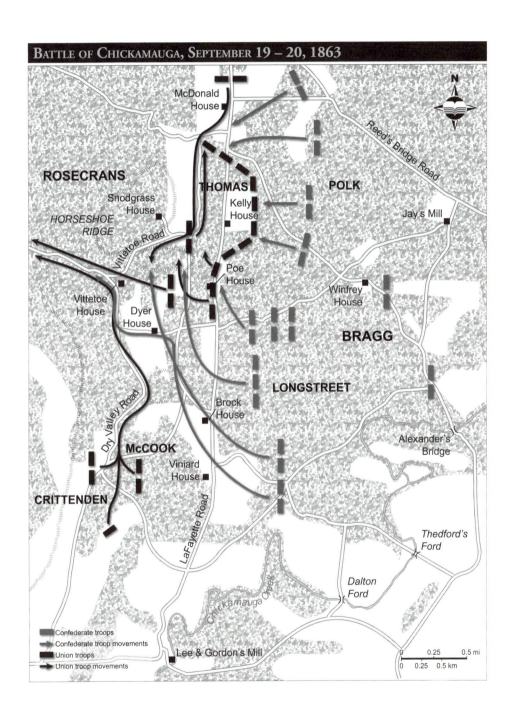

BATTLE OF CHICKAMAUGA, SEPTEMBER 19 – 20, 1863

McDonald House

Reed's Bridge Road

N

ROSECRANS

THOMAS

POLK

Snodgrass House

Kelly House

Jay's Mill

HORSESHOE RIDGE

Vittetoe Road

Poe House

Winfrey House

Vittetoe House

Dyer House

BRAGG

Dry Valley Road

LONGSTREET

Brock House

Alexander's Bridge

McCOOK

Viniard House

CRITTENDEN

LaFayette Road

Thedford's Ford

Dalton Ford

Chickamauga Creek

Confederate troops
Confederate troop movements
Union troops
Union troop movements

Lee & Gordon's Mill

0   0.25   0.5 mi
0   0.25   0.5 km

enforced around Richmond, where War Department clerk J. B. Jones reported signing an average of 1,350 passes a day. Stephens denounced the measure as utterly wrong and without legal authority. But such measures kept desertion in the Confederate Army to a lower rate than in the United States Army, at least until 1864. Conscription and military discipline were also matters of dispute between the states and Confederate government throughout the war. The governors of Georgia and North Carolina flatly opposed conscription.

Governor Brown engaged in lengthy correspondence with then Confederate secretary of war James A. Seddon, beginning in May 1863, demanding that Georgia volunteer regiments serving in the Confederate army be allowed to elect their own replacement officers. The entire series of correspondence was published in pamphlet form by the state printer. Seddon upheld the authority of the general in the field to make such promotions by appointment, which the governor denounced as a violation of the rights of the regiment as well as the state. The Georgia government was such a fierce advocate of states' rights that when Jefferson Davis proclaimed a national day of Thanksgiving, the state nullified the proclamation, and then proclaimed another day of Thanksgiving a few weeks later.

There was little suppression of newspapers by the Confederate government or Confederate states. Since the 1830s, criticism of slavery in the press had been a criminal offense in most slave states, and no editors remained in business in the South motivated to attack the peculiar institution. When William W. Holden, editor of the *North Carolina Standard*, advocated peace and rejoining the Union in 1863, Georgia troops passing through Raleigh, North Carolina wrecked his office and printing plant. A persistent editorial critic of the Davis administration, Nathan B. Morse of the *Augusta* (GA) *Chronicle and Sentinel*, was challenged to a duel by a rival editor, John Forsyth of the *Mobile Register and Advocate*, for advocating peace with the federal government. No official Confederate act was invoked against either editor.

Special precautions were taken to control slaves when Federal troops were close by. Vigilante organizations often met to keep a wary watch for untoward moves by slaves. Patrols on waterways and on land with bloodhounds sealed off escape routes. When units of the United States Army arrived in a local community, slaves would briefly be freed under the Emancipation Proclamation. As the soldiers moved on, local Confederates joined to whip and shoot those slaves who had been most cooperative with Union troops and send the rest back to work. At times, the Confederate Army removed all able-bodied male slaves ages 18–45 from the path of advancing Union troops. Rebel cavalry, scouts, and guerrillas all intercepted runaways, who were put to work on fortifications. Lists were published of those slaves seized to enable their owners to reclaim them from the military.

Charles Rosenberg

Further Reading

Ash, Stephen V. "A Wall Around Slavery: Safeguarding the Peculiar Institution on the Confederate Periphery, 1861–1865." In *Nineteenth Century America: Essays in Honor of Paul H. Bergeron*. Edited by W. Todd Grace and Stephen V. Ash. Knoxville: University of Tennessee Press, 2005.

Neely, Mark E., Jr. *Confederate Bastille: Jefferson Davis and Civil Liberties*. Milwaukee, WI: Marquette University Press, 1993.

Risley, Ford. *The Civil War: Primary Documents on Events from 1860 to 1865*. Westport, CT: Greenwood Press, 2004.

Civil Liberties, Union

Civil liberties in the United States during the Civil War turned principally on the application or suspension of the Writ of Habeas Corpus, freedom of the press, and the arrest of civilians by military authorities. Battlefields and army posts frequently overlay civilian population areas, which set up specific problems when dealing with civil liberties. At least 4,271 civilians were tried by military commission during the war, a practice later criticized by the United States Supreme Court in the 1866 case *Ex parte Milligan*. Arrests of civilians by Confederate military authorities were, proportional to the Southern population, similar in magnitude.

John Merryman, a Confederate sympathizer in Maryland, presented the best-known habeas corpus case during the first year of the war. In March and April 1861, control of Washington, D.C., and the movement of troops through Maryland to defend the capital were threatened. Baltimore was a flashpoint for secessionists, and the Federal government made wholesale arrests, suspending the writ of habeas corpus there. In May, shortly after Brigadier General Benjamin Butler led 1,000 Union troops into Baltimore to enforce the law there, Merryman was arrested by soldiers from Fort McHenry. He was suspected of being a lieutenant in a pro-Confederate military outfit and of possessing arms stolen from Federal depots. U.S. Supreme Court Chief Justice Roger B. Taney, who ruled on the famous *Dred Scott* decision, promptly issued a writ of habeas corpus. Major General George Cadwalader sent a staff member to respond that President Abraham Lincoln had authorized him to suspend the writ for reasons of public safety.

Taney then sent Lincoln a legal opinion on the history of the writ, warning that the nation's chief executive should not violate the law. Many asserted that Congress, not the president, should make the decision that a state of rebellion existed, which would constitutionally justify suspending the writ. But Lincoln noted that the Constitution is silent as to who should exercise that power. As most civilians in Maryland rallied to support the Federal government, the state was never placed under military occupation. Lincoln reassured a commission of the Maryland legislature in May 1861 that because Maryland had not taken hostile actions toward the Federal government, the U.S. military would not occupy communications in the state, nor seize the property of its citizens.

Major General Charles C. Frémont, briefly commanding the Department of the West, declared martial law in Missouri on August 10, 1861, authorizing military officers to shoot any rebels found armed inside Union lines, and to confiscate all property of anyone who fought in a Confederate military unit. He also ordered that any slaves of such persons were to be summarily declared free. Lincoln asked Frémont to rescind the orders, then overrode them, reserving political matters to the civilian government rather than military law. Frémont was soon relieved of command because he was losing control of the military situation in Missouri, despite the fact that a majority of the people and legislature remained loyal to the United States.

The May 1863 arrest for treason of former Ohio congressman Clement Vallandigham provoked another high-profile controversy over civil liberties. Vallandigham had deliberately violated General Order No. 38, issued by Major General Ambrose Burnside, then commanding the Department of the Ohio. The broadly-worded military order banned "the habit of declaring sympathy for the enemy." Vallandigham had made a passionate speech calling on Union soldiers to desert en masse, and the people to "hurl King Lincoln from his throne" (Goodwin 2005, 522). A military tribunal then sentenced Vallandigham to imprisonment for the duration of the war. Republicans and prowar Democrats, as well as copperheads (Northern Democrats who opposed the war), criticized Burnside's violation of free speech. Lincoln publicly supported Burnside but nevertheless commuted Vallandigham's sentence to deportation behind Confederate lines.

Freedom of the press also became an issue in the Vallandigham case when Burnside shut down the *Chicago Times* after it had denounced the tribunal. Secretary of War Edwin M. Stanton subsequently instructed military authorities not to suppress newspapers. The president was repeatedly urged to take action against the *Times* and other northern papers favorable to secession, but responded that only the very sternest necessity could justify abridging the liberties of the people, even in time of war.

Ownership of slaves was, at the time, a civil liberty protected by law, which the Federal government had no power to infringe. In the midst of war against a rebellion bent on preserving and expanding slavery, military necessity often prevailed. Major General Butler established the expedient that slaves owned by rebels should be treated as contraband of war. Soon enough, slaves were fleeing in droves to Union lines. Until ratification of the Thirteenth Amendment to the U.S. Constitution in 1865, however, the Federal government lacked constitutional authority to free slaves whose owners remained loyal to the Union.

Lincoln asserted that the whole issue of the war was whether government by the people

Engraving depicting the arrest of Clement Vallandigham in Dayton, Ohio, May 5, 1863. (Library of Congress)

could sustain itself, or whether every time a minority disagreed, they could break apart the nation. Lincoln exercised many powers without prior authorization from Congress, spending millions of dollars for military measures without appropriations. U.S. marshals seized copies of telegrams from every major telegraph office in the northern states. Calling up militias from all states that would respond and imposing a naval blockade of all Confederate ports were undertaken without prior legislative approval. The House of Representatives and the Senate did pass resolutions on August 5, 1861 approving all acts, proclamations, and orders of the president that related to calling up the militia and recruiting volunteers. However, broader resolutions giving formal legality to many other acts were never brought to a vote.

Charles Rosenberg

Further Reading

Catton, Bruce. *This Hallowed Ground.* New York: Doubleday & Company, Inc., 1956.

Goodwin, Doris K. *Team of Rivals: The Political Genius of Abraham Lincoln.* New York: Simon and Schuster, 2005.

Linfield, Michael, ed. *Freedom under Fire: U.S. Civil Liberties in Times of War.* Cambridge, MA: South End Press, 1990.

Congress, Confederate

The Congress of the Confederate States of America was modeled directly after the U.S. Congress, with a House of Representatives and Senate. Representatives were elected by district by popular vote; senators were elected by state legislative bodies.

Following the election of Abraham Lincoln as president of the United States in November 1860, South Carolina called for a state convention in which delegates voted to secede from the Union. By February 1, 1861, South Carolina, Mississippi, Florida, Alabama, Georgia, Louisiana, and Texas had all seceded. Representatives from these states met on February 4, 1861, as the Provisional Congress in Montgomery, Alabama. There they named Jefferson Davis as provisional president of the CSA until official elections could be held in November. The congress also drafted a constitution, which was largely copied from the United States Constitution. There were subtle differences, however, such as the president serving a single six-year term and the explicit mention of slavery. The document also gave more power to individual states, which were initially more responsible for raising troops.

Elections for the First Confederate Congress were not held until November 6, 1861, following the secession of four additional states: North Carolina, Arkansas, Tennessee, and Virginia. The First Congress met in the Confederate capital of Richmond, Virginia, from 1862 to 1864. One of the more pressing issues facing it was figuring out a way to adequately defend the Confederacy while not upsetting the sovereignty of the states. Also, the CSA was home to just 9 million people, of whom more than 33 percent were slaves. The United States, by comparison, had a population of more than 22 million people, all of whom were free. Faced with this manpower dilemma, the Congress passed several laws, including the Partisan Ranger Act (April 1862), which called for the creation of "irregular" troops who would carry out raids on Union troops. The Congress also passed the Bounty Law (May 1861), which enabled the president to hire privateers, or state-sponsored pirates, to attack Union ships and carry supplies to and from Europe. Among the most controversial acts passed by the Confederate Congress were the three Conscription Acts, passed in April 1862, October 1862, and February 1864. Many state governments were outraged by the laws because they claimed that the central government was overstepping its power, which ironically was one of the South's chief complaints about the Union government prior to secession.

Another controversial piece of legislation stated that any African American soldiers captured wearing a Union uniform would be executed alongside their white officers. This action led to an explosion of outrage in the North, with the United States Congress calling for an equal number of Confederate prisoners to be executed if this was to be carried out. The Confederate Congress and the president agreed to rescind the law.

The Second Congress, elected in November 1863, served only one year of its term and adjourned on March 18, 1865, two weeks before Richmond fell. In desperate circumstances it passed General Order 14 (March 13, 1865), which called for the creation of African American regiments comprised of freed slaves. Although two companies were raised, none saw action before the end of the war.

Throughout the war the Confederate Congress desperately tried to manage a major war while keeping the nation unified. This was made especially difficult because many citizens, as well as members of the government itself, believed that the states should have more power than the central government. Individual members of the Confederate Congress also tried to stymie President Davis's war agenda when they believed it was encroaching on congressional prerogative.

Seth A. Weitz

Further Reading

Davis, William C. *Government of Our Own: The Making of the Confederacy*. New York: The Free Press, 1994.

Davis, William C. *Look Away: A History of the Confederate States of America*. New York: The Free Press, 2002.

McPherson, James M. *Battle Cry of Freedom: The Civil War Era*. New York: Oxford University Press, 1988.

Thomas, Emory M. *The Confederate Nation: 1861–1865*. New York: Harper and Row Publishers, 1979.

Congress, Union

During the Civil War, the U.S. Congress was in session three times. These sessions, the 37th, 38th, and 39th, are some of the most important in American history because they dealt with both the management of the war and the plans for Reconstruction once the fighting concluded. Congress strove to accomplish these goals while some members of Congress were either sympathetic to the Southern cause or not supportive of President Abraham Lincoln.

The 37th Congress opened when Lincoln took the oath of office on March 4, 1861. It concluded on March 3, 1863. In a special session convened by Lincoln on July 4, the Congress passed numerous emergency war measures, which established a pattern whereby legislators generally acceded to executive demands in the name of prosecuting the war. That summer, Congress officially declared the existence of a state of rebellion and called for 500,000 volunteers, who would be asked to serve three-year tours of duty.

One of the most important actions of this Congress was the various laws that paved the way for the Emancipation Proclamation. This edict would declare all slaves living in states not under Union control free unless those states returned to the Union by January 1, 1863. Congress had been moving gradually toward emancipation since August 6, 1861, when it passed the First Confiscation Act. This law called for the seizure of Confederate "property," including slaves, by Union soldiers. Congress would later declare that the federal government would compensate any slave owners who voluntarily freed their slaves. This led to the abolition of slavery in the District of Columbia on April 16, 1862. In June 1862, Congress forbade slavery in U.S. territories. This solved one of the major issues that had divided the nation in the decades before the Civil War. Furthermore, on July 16, 1862 Congress passed the Second Confiscation Act, which liberated all slaves held by those in rebellion against the United States.

Perhaps the most controversial legislation passed by the 38th Congress (from March 4, 1863, to March 3, 1865) dealt with conscription. The first draft call-up occurred in July 1863 and was highly contentious, sparking the infamous New York City Draft Riots, which killed as many as 75 people. Some states also balked at the draft laws, arguing that they were illegal.

Another major issue for the 38th and 39th Congress (March 4, 1865 to March 3, 1867) was postwar Reconstruction. Lincoln wanted the Southern states returned to the Union as soon as possible and proposed the 10 Percent Plan, which would have allowed states to re-enter the Union after 10 percent of their voters from 1860 rolls had sworn an allegiance to the United States. He was opposed in this by members of his own party, the so-called Radical Republicans, who favored harsher reconstruction measures to punish the South. Indeed, they proposed and passed the controversial Wade-Davis Bill in July 1864, which would have admitted seceded states only after they had passed numerous tests, and only after a majority of the population had sworn the oath. Lincoln exercised a pocket-veto of the bill. In the end, following Lincoln's assassination in April 1865, his lenient approach to Reconstruction gave way to the more punitive approach favored by the Radical Republicans.

Among the more important nonwar legislation passed by Congress were the Morrill Land Grant, Homestead, and Pacific Railroad Acts, and the Legal Tender Acts. Also Congress agreed to increase the power of the federal government by allowing it to directly tax U.S. citizens to pay for the war, provide aid to industries, and sizably augment internal infrastructure improvements. During the war, Congress also created the Department of Agriculture, a cabinet-level federal agency that helped American farmers and by doing so stabilized the U.S. economy.

Although Democrats were decidedly in the minority in Congress after 1861, they nevertheless made their presence felt, especially those who demanded reunion with no preconditions (War Democrats). Congress remained in Republican control for the duration of the war, but a split soon developed between the moderate Republicans (who most often supported Lincoln) and the Radical Republicans. The moderates supported the Emancipation Proclamation and Lincoln's gentler vision for Reconstruction. By early 1864, so-called Peace Democrats in Congress clamored for immediate negotiations with the Confederacy to end the war, even if it meant permanent disunion. In general, however, most Democrats allied themselves with moderate Republicans, which temporarily checked the power of the Radical Republicans. Despite these many factions, however, Congress passed appropriations for both military and civilian purposes with surprising unanimity.

Seth A. Weitz

Further Reading

Ambrosious, Lloyd E. *A Crisis of Republicanism: American Politics during the Civil War Era*. Lincoln: University of Nebraska Press, 1990.

and military defeats, forced the Confederacy to enlist slaves in its ranks. The conscription laws never garnered enough popular support for the Confederate war effort.

Charles F. Howlett

Further Reading

Moore, Albert B., ed. *Conscription and Conflict in the Confederacy, Southern Classics Series*. Columbia: University of South Carolina Press, 1996.

Conscription, Union

The U.S. government enacted six draft laws during the Civil War. Throughout the conflict, the draft was a source of irritation to many, but its existence nevertheless induced the necessary number of voluntary enlistments to successfully prosecute the war.

On March 3, 1863, President Abraham Lincoln signed into law the Enrollment Act. Prior to passage of this legislation, the Federal Militia Act of 1862 had authorized the president to draft 300,000 men. Widespread opposition to this measure, including the Pennsylvania Supreme Court decision *Kneedler v. Lane*, which first held the federal Draft Act unconstitutional but reversed itself on re-argument, led to its suspension. The act was replaced by volunteer enlistments with generous bounties for signing up for armed service.

Similar to the Confederate experience, the toll of war and personal sacrifice on the home front saw the number of volunteers decline. That was coupled with increasing agitation on the part of the Copperheads (Peace Democrats) opposed to the war. The Copperheads actively discouraged men from volunteering for Union service.

In an effort to increase Union Army troop strength, Congress passed the Enrollment Act or "An Act for Enrolling and Calling Out the National Forces, and For Other Purposes" on March 3, 1863. The act contained 38 parts. Its most important provisions were the following: (1) males between the ages of 20 and 45 would be subjected to the draft first, followed by married men between the ages of 36 and 46; (2) eligible males between the ages of 17 and 20 could serve based upon parental or guardian permission; (3) each congressional district was responsible for drafting men based upon a house-to-house enrollment conducted by government agents; and (4) a lottery was to be conducted in each congressional district to secure the necessary numbers. If each district obtained the necessary number of volunteers, then the draft would not be implemented. The result of this law led to recruiting drives throughout the North in an effort to avoid activating the draft.

Throughout the duration of the war, there were six drafts, beginning in June 1863 and ending in December 1864. The first called for drafting 100,000 men for six months of service; the second, 500,000 men for three years; the third, 200,000 men for three years; the fourth, 85,000 men for 100 days; the fifth, 500,000 men for one, two, and three years; and the sixth, 300,000 men for one, two, and three years.

Administration of the federal draft was handled by the Provost Marshal General's Office in the War Department. The office established 185 congressional districts headed by a local provost marshal who was responsible for registering and mustering in those who had been drafted. Persons resisting the draft or encouraging opposition to enlistments were subject to arrest or detention. The first Enrollment Act also established military commissions with the power to try and convict civilians disloyal to the Union cause. In some instances, the death penalty was imposed.

Exemptions to the draft were permitted, especially for physical and mental disabilities. The law also permitted exemptions to any son responsible for the care of his parents and to fathers of motherless children. Other forms of exemption, similar to the Confederate draft laws, included substitution and commutation. A draftee could avoid military service by paying a $300 fee or securing a substitute. This provision, designed to offset the law's unpopularity, did lead to criticisms that the rich could buy their way out of service, thus leaving it to the poor men to fight the war.

Conscientious objectors fared better in the North than in the South. Initially, that was not the case after the Enrollment Act was first passed. Pacifists who refused to serve were tried and sentenced to death, although that penalty was never carried out. Many who refused to serve or pay for an exemption suffered physical abuse and were placed in a military stockade. In 1864, Congress, after hearing pleas from senators Charles Sumner and Thaddeus Stevens, established provisions for conscientious objectors to perform hospital work or care for freedmen in place of military service.

The Enrollment Act remained in effect until the end of the war. Despite the repeal of the commutation provision in March of 1864, opposition to the draft was widespread. The most notable event occurred in New York City in July 1863, when for more three days Irish immigrants burned and ransacked buildings in protest of the draft. Many were angry at the prospects of freeing blacks who would then be in competition with them for jobs. In various parts of Pennsylvania, numerous deaths were reported in draft riots as federal troops fired upon protestors in Luzerne and Columbia Counties. A notable riot occurred in the town of Port Washington, Wisconsin. In southern Indiana, a Copperhead stronghold, martial law was imposed and became the basis for the noted U.S. Supreme Court decision, *Ex Parte Milligan* (1866), which declared it unconstitutional to try civilians in military courts. Despite the many protests, only 6 percent of Union forces over the entirety of the war were draftees. The draft laws were not very effective in the Northern states, but they did give an additional boost to volunteerism for the war's duration.

Charles F. Howlett

Further Reading

Geary, James W. *We Need Men: The Union Draft and the Civil War*. Dekalb: Northern Illinois University Press, 1991.

Leach, Jack F. *Conscription in the United States: Historical Background*. Rutland, VT: Charles E. Tuttle Publishing Company, 1960.

Murdock, Eugene C. *One Million Men: The Civil War Draft in the North*. Westport, CT: Greenwood Press, 1980.

Paludan, Phillip S. *"A People's Contest": The Union and the Civil War, 1861–1865*. Lawrence: University Press of Kansas, 1988.

and northwestern Illinois. In 1831 he suffered a severe case of pneumonia, which left him permanently susceptible to respiratory ailments. The following year he served in the Black Hawk War and was assigned the duty of escorting the captured chief to Jefferson Barracks near St. Louis. In 1833 Davis won promotion to first lieutenant and assignment to the newly organized First Dragoon Regiment and was transferred to Fort Gibson, Oklahoma. Meanwhile, however, he had become romantically involved with Sarah Knox Taylor, daughter of Colonel Zachary Taylor. The colonel disapproved the match, and so Davis resigned his commission and married Knox, as she was called, at the home of her aunt and uncle near Louisville, Kentucky, in June 1835. Davis's older brother Joseph, 23 years his senior and a virtual father to him after the death of his parents, was a wealthy lawyer and planter and gave Jefferson a plantation adjoining his own on the banks of the Mississippi River north of Natchez, Mississippi. Arriving there with his new wife, Davis named the plantation Brierfield. A few weeks later, however, both newlyweds contracted malaria. After a brief but severe illness at the nearby home of Davis's sister, he recovered, but Knox succumbed, a bride of only three months.

For the next few years Davis directed his slaves in working and developing Brierfield and gained a reputation as a relatively humane slaveholder. In 1843 he began his political career, running unsuccessfully for legislature. The following year he campaigned for James K. Polk's successful presidential bid and also ran successfully in his own right for a seat in the U.S. Congress. In 1845 the 36-year-old widower married 18-year-old Varina Howell, daughter of a prominent Natchez family. With the outbreak of the Mexican-American War in 1846, Davis resigned his seat in Congress to accept the colonelcy of the First Mississippi

Rifle Regiment, in command of which he served under his first father-in-law, Zachary Taylor, and won accolades for gallantry at the battles at Monterey and at Buena Vista, at the latter of which he suffered a wound in the foot. Now a national military hero, he turned down President Polk's offer of a commission as brigadier general and left the military with the expiration of his regiment's term of service.

He did accept an appointment from the governor of Mississippi to fill the U.S. Senate seat of the recently deceased Jesse Speight, and the state legislature subsequently reelected him to a full term. In the Senate he quickly became chairman of the Committee on Military Affairs, but in 1851 he resigned his Senate seat, at the behest of the Mississippi Democratic party, in order to enter the race for governor against Whig candidate Henry S. Foote, with whom Davis had recently fought a brawl in a Washington, D.C., boarding house. Davis campaigned on a platform of opposition to the Compromise of 1850 and lost. The defeat returned him to his plantation but only to semiprivate life, as he remained active in Democratic politics and campaigned vigorously for 1852 Democratic presidential candidate Franklin Pierce. Having won the election, Pierce appointed Davis secretary of war. In that office Davis gave his approval to the War Department's ongoing modernization, and especially agitated for the building of a transcontinental railroad along a southern route. As one of the most influential members of Pierce's cabinet, he took a leading role in securing the president's approval for the 1854 Kansas-Nebraska Act, which repealed the antislavery portion of the venerable Missouri Compromise and reopened the sectional turmoil that led to civil war seven years later. At the expiration of Pierce's term, Davis left the war office, and the Mississippi legislature returned him to the U.S. Senate, where he naturally returned to his place in the Committee on Military Affairs. In 1858 he made several speeches during a tour of New England, in which he deprecated secession.

As 1860 began and the presidential election approached, Davis introduced a series of six strongly proslavery resolutions in the Senate. Their chances of passage were nil, but Davis meant them to become a rallying point for the Southern Democrats, a position that would rule out the preferred platform of likely Democratic nominee Stephen A. Douglas of Illinois. When the party convention met in Charleston that summer, it split. Several weeks later a rump Southern convention nominated Vice President John C. Breckinridge of Kentucky on a platform similar to the position Davis had staked out, while what was left of the national Democratic Party nominated Douglas on a platform calling for popular sovereignty. When the general election took place that fall, victory went neither to Breckinridge nor to Douglas but to Republican candidate Abraham Lincoln. In response, seven Deep South states, including Mississippi, declared themselves out of the Union. Davis strongly approved, despite his earlier statements against secession, and resigned his Senate seat.

In February 1861, a convention of the seceding states organized themselves as the CSA and chose Davis as their president. From his first capital in Montgomery, Alabama, Davis energetically began preparing the Confederate government for the war that he believed would immediately follow. When in April Lincoln declined to pull U.S. troops out of Fort Sumter in the harbor of Charleston, South Carolina, Davis ordered his forces to open fire. Thirty-three hours later the fort surrendered. The North mobilized for war, and four Upper South states, including Virginia, chose to join the Confederacy rather than fight against slavery. The Confederacy

promptly moved its capital to Richmond, Virginia, which became the scene of most of Davis's service as Confederate president.

On the whole, Davis performed ably as president. He ran the machinery of government that raised armies totaling about one million men and kept them at least minimally supplied. Until the final few months of the war, he invariably got the legislation he wanted from the Confederate congress. In the Virginia theater of the war, he chose and then sustained Robert E. Lee as commander of the Confederacy's largest army. In the decisive western theater of the war, however, Davis proved less successful, despite three extended western inspection tours. He cycled through a series of ineffective western commanders whom he did not sufficiently support and sometimes inadvertently undermined.

With the fall of his capital impending, Davis fled Richmond in hopes of carrying on the war from somewhere in the western portion of the Confederacy, perhaps west of the Mississippi, but Union cavalry apprehended him near Washington, Georgia. He was imprisoned for two years in Fort Monroe, Virginia, during which time he was kept in irons for a total of three days—a short, unpleasant interlude that won him great sympathy among Southern whites. Although he had obviously committed treason, the government ultimately dropped the case against him since the crime had been committed chiefly in Richmond, Virginia, and it was clear that no Richmond jury would convict him.

After his release, Davis served as president of the Carolina Life Insurance Company of Memphis, Tennessee, until its financial collapse. In 1877, he moved to the Beauvoir estate near Biloxi, Mississippi, as a guest of its owner, Miss Sarah Dorsey, who willed the estate to him on her death in 1879. There he wrote his two-volume memoir, *The Rise*

E

Early, Jubal (1816–1894)

Jubal Early was born in Franklin County, Virginia, on November 3, 1816, the son of a tobacco farmer and 1 of 10 children. His father had been a county sheriff, a colonel of militia, and a state legislator. Early attended local schools before going on to the United States Military Academy, West Point. He graduated in 1837 and was commissioned in the artillery. Early served in the Second Seminole War in Florida in 1838. He then resigned from the army and took up a legal career, which he pursued in both Franklin and Floyd counties in Virginia from 1840 to 1846. He also served one term in the state legislature during 1841–1842.

During the Mexican-American War (1846–1848), Early was a major in the 1st Virginia Regiment; however, his unit was assigned mainly to garrison duty and he saw little action. Following the war, he returned to his legal career and became a delegate to the Virginia General Assembly; he also served as Commonwealth attorney until 1852.

Early opposed secession and voted against it in the Virginia Convention of 1861. When his state, seceded, however, Early offered his services. Appointed as a colonel in Virginia's forces, Early was sent to Lynchburg, Virginia, to help to raise three regiments. He then entered Confederate service as commander of the 24th Virginia Infantry Regiment. He distinguished himself at Blackburn's Ford (July 18, 1861) and also fought well at the First Battle of Bull Run (July 21, 1861), where he commanded the 6th brigade.

In the spring of 1862, Early, now promoted to the rank of brigadier-general, was assigned to General Joseph E. Johnston's forces to stop the advance of Federal forces under Major General George B. McClellan up the peninsula between the York and James rivers. Early's brigade fought at Williamsburg on May 5, 1862, and he himself was wounded while leading an attack. He had recovered sufficiently to command a brigade under Major General Thomas J. "Stonewall" Jackson at Malvern Hill on July 1. Here his command became lost in woods on the battlefield and took little part in the battle.

During the second Manassas campaign, Early fought well at both Cedar Mountain on August 9, 1862, and the Battle of Second Bull Run on August 28–30. During the Battle of Antietam on September 17, Early commanded a division when Major General Alexander Lawton was wounded. He performed well enough here to retain divisional command. At Fredericksburg on December 13, 1862, Early played an important role in counterattacking the Federal units under Major General George Meade when it seemed as if the Union troops were about to break the Confederate line.

Promoted to major general rank from January 1863, Early commanded a division both at Chancellorsville (May 1–3, 1863) and at Gettysburg (June 1–3). During the winter of 1863–1864, Early was based in the Shenandoah Valley. In 1864, he fought in the Battle of the Wilderness (May 5–7), taking command of Lieutenant General A. P. Hill's III Corps. He also fought at Spotsylvania Court

Mahan, Alfred T. *Admiral Farragut: First Admiral of the United States Navy*. New York: D. Appleton & Company, 1879.

Foreign Involvement

In 1860 the United States was growing into a power that threatened the economic dominance of western Europe. Consequently, many European statesmen and their governments greeted with satisfaction the apparent implosion of a disliked rival. Great Britain had the additional pleasure of seeing a rebellious, former colony fall apart due to internal rebellion. European attitudes toward the civil war in America presented foreign policy challenges for the United States and for the Confederate States.

A particular flash point was the Union naval blockade. European powers (but not the United States) had signed a legal agreement stating that to be binding, blockades had to be maintained by forces strong enough to prevent access into the blockaded ports. This condition manifestly did not prevail in 1861 when the war began and the United States announced that it had begun a blockade of Southern ports. Blockade runners easily passed through the U.S. Navy's loose cordon. Confederate diplomats sought to persuade Great Britain that the blockade was therefore illegal. Thus, they argued, the Royal Navy should intervene to protect British trade with the South. Indeed, throughout the war, everyone knew that foreign intervention had to include Great Britain. Other European countries might join the effort, but Great Britain had to lead.

British prime minister Palmerston's government was too cagey to become embroiled in a war on mere legal pretext. Then, on November 8, 1861, a U.S. warship stopped the British mail steamer *Trent*, removed two Confederate diplomats, James Mason and John Slidell, and sent them to prison in Boston. This outrage, called the *Trent Affair*, provoked war fever in England. The Lincoln Administration wisely released the Confederate diplomats and so averted hostilities.

Thereafter, British merchants enjoyed the benefits of neutrality. They maintained a very lucrative blockade-running trade with the South. When Confederate raiding ships drove American merchantmen from the seas, British merchantmen happily picked up the trade. Crop failures in western Europe in 1860–1862 compelled the import of American grain and flour. Union states doubled their grain export, supplying nearly half of British imports. Notably, much of this grain was shipped aboard British merchantmen. So, the British economy benefitted from war in America.

In spite of the economic advantages of neutrality, the Palmerston regime again came close to intervention in the late summer of 1862. It was the time of greatest British labor unrest caused by unemployed textile workers suffering from the absence of Southern cotton. Robert E. Lee had just driven Union armies out of Virginia and stood poised to invade Maryland. In the western theater, Braxton Bragg and Kirby Smith were launching their invasion of Kentucky. British Foreign Minister Lord Russell predicted to Palmerston that in the next month "the hour will be ripe for the Cabinet" to discuss intervention. Lee's subsequent defeat at Antietam and Bragg's retreat from Kentucky ended all serious talk of British intervention for the remainder of the war.

Just as British merchants took advantage of American difficulties, so Louis Napoleon of France sought to benefit from America's internal preoccupations by sending French soldiers to Mexico. Napoleon wanted to overthrow Mexico's government and establish the Hapsburg Archduke Ferdinand Maximilian as Emperor of Mexico. Napoleon's motive related to the shifting alliances and balance of power in Europe. In the event, 35,000 French soldiers captured Mexico City in June 1863. This attracted Lincoln's attention. He was determined to assert the Monroe Doctrine and accordingly, after Grant captured Vicksburg in July 1863, ordered forces to move into Texas as a counterpoise to the French presence in Mexico. Again, when the 1864 campaign season began, Lincoln ordered resources diverted to Texas to check the French. The ill-fated Red River Campaign ensued, a campaign that proved an unnecessary diversion of U.S. military resources because Napoleon had lost interest in his Mexican adventure.

The rest of the world, excepting Canada, watched the American Civil War unfold with either indifference or, like Russia, supported the North diplomatically because of the slavery issue. Lincoln's Emancipation Proclamation in the fall of 1862 helped solidify European support for the United States. Canada was a unique case. Some 50,000 Canadians walked south over the border to enlist in the Union army. Some sought adventure, most were attracted by the lure of the recruiter's bounty payment.

James R. Arnold

Further Reading

Adams, Charles. *Slavery, Secession, and Civil War: Views from the United Kingdom and Europe, 1856–1865*. Lanham, MD: Scarecrow Press, 2007.

Donaldson, Jordon, and Pratt, Edwin J. *Europe and the American Civil War*. New York: Houghton Mifflin, 1931.

Ferris, Norman B. *The Trent Affair: A Diplomatic Crisis*. Knoxville: University of Tennessee Press, 1977.

Lonn, Ella. *Foreigners in the Union Army and Navy*. Baton Rouge: Louisiana State University Press, 1951.

Forrest, Nathan Bedford (1821–1877)

Nathan Bedford Forrest was born on July 13, 1821, in Bedford County, Tennessee, 1 of 11 children of an impoverished backwoods family. In 1834 Forrest's father, William Forrest, moved the family to Chickasaw Territory in northeastern Mississippi. Three years later, William Forrest died, with responsibility for the family falling on Nathan, the eldest son.

By sheer hard work and his own abilities, by 1840, Forrest had turned the ramshackle family homestead into a flourishing farm that finally enabled his family to live with a degree of financial security. In 1841, he joined a group of volunteers eager to join the fight to gain independence for Texas. However, upon arriving there he discovered that the Texans did not need his help. He returned to the family farm, where he expanded his business dealings from agricultural production to speculation in cattle and horses. As his interests broadened, his income increased.

In 1851, confident in his business ability and hoping to become involved in the cotton industry and slave trade, Forrest moved his family to Memphis, Tennessee, where he ventured into real estate. By 1859, he had built up such substantial wealth that he retired from his business dealings to look after his numerous landholdings.

With the beginning of the Civil War, Forrest joined the 7th Tennessee Cavalry he sent Smith and two of his brigades along the west bank of the river to prevent reinforcement from that direction and cut off a Confederate escape. Brigadier General John A. McClernand's division with a brigade from Smith mounted the main Union land effort on the east bank.

On the night of February 5, meanwhile, Tilghman called together his officers. None believed they could withstand a Union attack, and at 10:00 a.m. the next morning Tilghman ordered all the men save the artillery company manning the batteries to withdraw to Donelson. Tilghman hoped to delay the attackers long enough for the rest of his command to escape.

At 10:50 a.m. on February 6, the Union flotilla got under way, the ironclads formed in line abreast and lashed together because of the narrowness of the river. The timberclads trailed a half-mile behind. With no sign of the Union troops, Foote decided to begin the battle alone. At 11:45 a.m., from about 1,700 yards' range, the gunboats opened fire. At about a mile the water battery responded, and firing then became general.

The Confederate fire was both lively and accurate; indeed, all the gunboats were hit, but most damage was slight. A total of 43 men were killed or wounded. The Union fire was also accurate, and several Confederate guns were soon out of commission. With only four guns operable and Union fire sweeping the fort, at 2:00 p.m. Tilghman surrendered. Confederate losses were 5 dead, 11 wounded, 5 missing, and 110 surrendered.

Battle of Fort Donelson and the capture of Gen. Simon Buckner and his army on February 16, 1862. Forts Donelson and Henry comprised the strategic center of Confederate operations in the West during the Civil War. Gen. Ulysses S. Grant set out to capture the forts in early 1862 and by February 16, 1862, Buckner conceded to Grant's demand for an unconditional surrender. (Library of Congress)

Fort Donelson was the next Union objective. Located on the west bank of the Cumberland River 2 miles north of Dover, Tennessee, Donelson was situated on a bluff overlooking several miles of river. The fort itself was only about 15 acres, but its outer works extended over 100 acres with 400 log cabins as barracks. Donelson had two river batteries cut into the ridge facing downriver; the lower contained 10 guns and the upper contained 3. The fort itself had eight additional guns. On February 7, Fort Donelson's garrison numbered only about 6,000 men, including the troops from Fort Henry.

Confederate western theater commander General Albert Sidney Johnston reinforced Fort Donelson with 12,000 men. Johnston's intention was to hold Grant until he could complete the retreat of his main body to Nashville. Brigadier General John B. Floyd assumed command of Donelson. He and his second-in-command, Brigadier General Gideon J. Pillow, were incompetent. Brigadier General Simon Bolivar Buckner was the only effective senior Confederate officer present.

On February 12, 1862, Grant moved from Fort Henry to Fort Donelson by land. Simultaneously, Foote moved his gunboats and the troop transports, arriving near Fort Donelson on the night of February 13. That day, 15,000 unentrenched Union troops confronted 21,000 entrenched Confederates; but fortunately for Grant, Floyd made no effort to attack.

Shortly after noon on February 13, despite Grant's order not to bring on a general engagement, Brigadier General John A. McClernand ordered his men to capture a battery in the center of the Confederate line, but repeated Union assaults failed. Grant was displeased, but the action served to mask Union inferiority in numbers. That afternoon the weather changed dramatically from near-summer to winter conditions, bringing suffering to both sides.

By February 14, the Confederates were completely invested, save along the Cumberland above Dover, where the river had flooded. As Grant strengthened his lines, the Confederate commanders decided to attempt to break out, but Floyd countermanded an effort that day.

Grant's plan was to hold the Confederates within the fort from the land while the Union flotilla destroyed the water batteries. Shortly before 3:00 p.m. on February 14, the Union flotilla attacked with four ironclads; again the vulnerable timberclads formed a second division far to the rear.

The Union ships closed to within 400 yards. This time, plunging fire hit the sloping Union armor at right angles, disabling three of the four ironclads, which then drifted downstream. The other ships then withdrew. In the 90-minute engagement, the flotilla had 11 men killed and 43 wounded (the latter including Foote). Although none of the gunboats were fatally damaged, from this point on the navy contributed little to the battle. The fort was little damaged in the attack.

Meanwhile, Union troop reinforcements continued to arrive. Before dawn on February 15, Grant departed for a meeting with Foote, instructing his commanders not to initiate an engagement. Knowing that their position was untenable, on the night of February 14 the Confederate generals agreed that they would attempt to break out along the west bank of the Cumberland River. Pillow was to open an escape route by rolling up the Union right while Buckner sortied against the Union center. When the Union right flank had been pushed back, Pillow would lead the retreat and Buckner would serve as the rear guard.

Pillow's attack at 6:00 a.m. on February 15 caught the Union troops by surprise and

Northern states quickly enrolled the required number of militia and more. Lincoln asked Indiana for 6 regiments, the governor offered 12. Ohio's governor telegraphed Lincoln to plead for permission to enlist additional units because so many men were volunteering. More than 100,000 volunteers responded to Lincoln's initial call.

However, Lincoln's request backfired in the South. It caused a bitter outcry from the four Southern states that had yet to secede. The governor of Virginia replied that Lincoln had chosen to begin civil war; he would send no troops. The governor of Arkansas answered that his people "will defend to the last extremity their honor, lives, and property" against the North. In response to Lincoln's call, Virginia (April 17, 1861), Arkansas (May 6, 1861), North Carolina (May 20, 1861), and Tennessee (June 8, 1861) joined the Confederacy.

The vice president of the Confederacy, Alexander Stephens, cried "Lincoln may bring his 75,000 troops against us. We fight for our homes, our fathers and mothers, our wives, brothers, sisters, sons, and daughters! We can call out a million of peoples if need be, and when they are cut down we can call another, and still another, until the last man of the South finds a bloody grave." President Davis was more restrained. He announced, "All we ask is to be let alone."

James R. Arnold

Further Reading

Boatner, Mark M., III. *The Civil War Dictionary*. New York: David McKay Co., 1959.

Bostick, Douglas W. *The Union is Dissolved!: Charleston and Fort Sumter in the Civil War*. Charleston, SC: History Press, 2009.

Bowman, Shearer D. *At the Precipice: Americans North and South during the Secession Crisis*. Chapel Hill: University of North Carolina Press, 2010.

Burton, E. Milby. *The Siege of Charleston 1861–1865*. Columbia: University of South Carolina Press, 1970.

Catton, Bruce. *The Coming Fury*. Garden City, NY: Doubleday & Company, 1961.

G

Gettysburg Campaign (June–July 1863)

The Gettysburg campaign began in the early days of June 1863 and culminated in the epic Battle of Gettysburg on July 1–3. In the spring of 1863, Confederate forces had been buoyed by a recent series of successful battles, particularly at Chancellorsville on May 1–4. But the scenario for the South was far from rosy. Chancellorsville had been costly in that Robert E. Lee's brilliant subordinate, Lieutenant General Thomas "Stonewall" Jackson, was severely wounded and subsequently died of pneumonia. Lee himself was ill with laryngitis and with chest pains determined to be a heart condition called pericarditis. Furthermore, by the spring of 1863, the Confederacy was reeling from escalating inflation, the Union blockade, and critical shortages of both men and materiel. Nevertheless, Lee's considerable army of some 76,000 was in good spirits, which encouraged him to carry the war into the North.

A number of factors affected Lee's thinking, some of which countered concerns about the pressures the Confederate armies in Tennessee and western Georgia were then facing. Lee considered that a movement into the North might cause the Union to respond to the threat and thus ease their western campaign. Further, there was the prospect that a large Confederate presence might weaken support in the North for the war, boost the Union peace movement, bring about European recognition, and perhaps even result in the capture of Harrisburg, the Pennsylvania capital, and other Northern cities. Important too would be his army's ability to forage from the Maryland and Pennsylvania countryside. Naturally, the prospect of sweeping Union forces out of the upper South and at the same time probing military access to Washington, D.C., were also potential bonuses of a successful invasion of the Northern.

On June 3, 1863, Lee took his army on a march that was to shape the future of the Civil War and generate much controversy about his military judgment. Lieutenant General Richard Ewell had replaced Stonewall Jackson and spearheaded the movement west of the Shenandoah Valley, which screened the Confederate advance. Lee had counted on Major General J.E.B. Stuart's cavalry to provide reconnaissance for the march, but during this crucial campaign Stuart failed Lee. Stuart's first error was to allow his cavalry to be surprised by Union cavalry at Brandy Station on June 9. The Battle of Brandy Station, although inconclusive, displayed the mettle of Union cavalry and ended the first stage of the Gettysburg campaign.

Lee's army stretched across almost 100 miles by June 25. On that day Lee made the critical mistake of giving Stuart permission to cross the Potomac River east of the Blue Ridge Mountains and launch a raid against the Army of the Potomac. Stuart subsequently suffered numerous delays and was not seen again by Lee until July 2.

In the absence of an effective cavalry screen, Ewell led his corps into Pennsylvania, capturing York and Carlisle before turning to move on to Harrisburg. The foraging exercises of the Confederate invasion had proven successful beyond expectation, as foodstuffs of all kinds, livestock, horses, clothing, shoes, and even free blacks, were confiscated by the army. Trailing in Ewell's wake came Lieutenant General James Longstreet and Lieutenant General A. P. Hill's corps, which moved on Chambersburg on June 28. Here Lee learned from a Confederate spy that Major General George Meade had replaced Major General Joseph Hooker, and that the Army of the Potomac, which slightly outnumbered the Confederate army, was at Frederick, Maryland. Lee immediately saw the peril: Meade's army was in position to defeat the Confederates in detail.

Lee decided to concentrate his forces east of the mountains and prepare for battle. On June 30, 1863, both armies began focusing on Gettysburg because the small town was an important road hub.

The first day of battle at Gettysburg, July 1, took place along high ground west and north of the town. It was a meeting engagement with the ebb and flow of battle depending on which side received timely reinforcements and where those reinforcements appeared. Fortuitously for the Confederates, Ewell's Corps arrived on the Union flank and helped drive the Federal forces through the streets of Gettysburg. However, as dusk approached, there was a lull as Ewell vacillated about continuing the attack. This gave the Union forces the opportunity to rally on the high ground south of town.

The first day's battle had been especially costly for the Union side. However, during the night additional Union reinforcements allowed Meade to occupy a strong defensive position along the so-called Fishhook. The Fishhook ran from Culp's Hill southeast of the town east to Cemetery Hill, then curved sharply south along Cemetery Ridge to Little Round Top and Round Top. This terrain was Meade's greatest advantage during the battle. It enabled Meade, on interior lines,

to shift resources much more quickly than Lee, who occupied far longer exterior lines outside the Union arc.

For July 2, Lee conceived a sequential attack beginning against the Union left and extending toward the Union center. He intended Ewell's Corps to contribute by attacking the Union right. During the event, however, Longstreet's flanking movement to the Round Tops developed slowly, hampered by a lack of knowledge of the area and the desire to avoid Federal detection. As a result, Longstreet's attack did not commence until 4:00 p.m. But the Confederates were given a magnificent opportunity, thanks to an impetuous decision of Union III Corps commander Major General Daniel Sickles. On his own initiative, Sickles moved his 11,000 men forward in advance of the Fishhook to a small rise around the Peach Orchard. Sickles had almost completed his deployment when Longstreet's corps slammed into his position and inflicted heavy casualties on the Union defenders. Sickles's decision had both isolated his corps and exposed the entire Union left flank.

As fighting for the Peach Orchard raged, the remainder of Longstreet's corps headed for the Round Tops. The seizure of this high ground would allow the Confederates to dominate the entire Union line. Longstreet's men easily drove off the few Federals on Round Top and then prepared to assault Little Round Top. Meade's Chief Engineer, Brigadier General Gouverneur K. Warren, discovered Little Round Top unoccupied and sent an appeal for immediate assistance. Union reinforcements in the form of Colonel Strong Vincent's brigade arrived just in time. Colonel Joshua Chamberlain's 20th Maine Regiment took the brunt of the Confederate attack. His men repulsed several Confederate charges. Then, almost entirely out of ammunition, Chamberlain ordered his men to fix bayonets and charge. The Union troops

One of the war's iconic photos showing a dead Confederate at Devil's Den on the Gettysburg battlefield. The photographer arranged the scene for dramatic effect. (Library of Congress)

drove the surprised Alabamians facing them down the hill. It was one of the most memorable actions of the entire war and may have saved the battle for the Union.

Meanwhile, desperate fighting raged back and forth in both the Wheat Field and Peach Orchard. Finally, the Confederates broke through Sickles's position, but Hancock, who had collected reserves, drove them back. Meade shifted most of his XII Corps to assist his left flank. This left only one Union brigade to hold Culp's Hill. Fortunately for the Union side, the Confederates could not coordinate their flanking attacks. Ewell's attack on Culp's Hill did not begin until dusk at 7:00 p.m. The attacks narrowly failed when confronting Union troops behind prepared positions.

Although his plan had failed, Lee sensed that he had struck the Army of the Potomac a severe blow and that one more attack would collapse it. Lee had tested both Union flanks; now he would try the center. Stuart's cavalry had finally arrived about noon and Major General George E. Pickett's division from Longstreet's Corps had also come up and was now available. On the Union side, VI Corps also appeared on the field. The entire Army of the Potomac was thus in place. Meade informed his commanders that the next day Lee would test the Union center.

Lee's attack of July 3 was indeed against the center of the Union line. Hancock's II Corps held this section of the Union line. The more than one mile separating the two armies was open and rolling terrain, offering no cover or concealment for the attackers. Lee planned to utilize three divisions: Pickett's fresh men and two others from Hill's III Corps, under temporary commanders Brigadier General Pettigrew and Major General Isaac Trimble. Both of the latter divisions had suffered heavily in the first day's fighting. As part of the Confederate plan, Lee ordered Ewell to launch a simultaneous attack on Culp's Hill, while Stuart's cavalry would swing wide from the north and threaten the Union rear.

The third day's fighting began at about 4:30 a.m., when the Union XII Corps began an artillery bombardment of Confederate positions at Culp's Hill. Ewell then commenced his attack. There were heavy casualties on both sides, but the Confederates here accomplished nothing to support Lee's plan.

At about 1:00 p.m., 160 Confederate guns massed in the center of the line opened what would be the largest artillery duel in the history of North America. Fewer than a hundred Union guns replied in a two-hour-long cannonade. The Confederate fire failed to soften up the Union center. At about 2:00 p.m., the Union guns fell silent to preserve ammunition. The Confederate assault then began, with the three divisions in line a mile wide, flags flying, as if on parade. Under furious Union artillery fire, the Confederates pressed the attack. The attackers managed to cross the stone wall at the center of the Union position, an achievement referred to as "the High tide of the Confederacy," but were driven back by Union reserves. Of some 12,000 Confederates who began the attack that day, some 6,500 (55%) were casualties in what would forever be known as Pickett's Charge. That afternoon, Union cavalry defeated the Confederate cavalry about five miles east of the battlefield. For all practical purposes, the Battle of Gettysburg was over.

Regrouping the still considerable remnants of his army, Lee now prepared for a possible Union counterattack that he hoped would take place but never materialized. Meade was wary of a still dangerous enemy force. Under the cover of darkness and heavy rain, Lee disengaged on July 4. Lee's main task was to get his army across the rain-swollen Potomac and into friendly Virginia territory. A tense 10 days followed as Meade gained reinforcements and cautiously pursued the southern army. By July 14, the Potomac's flooding had subsided, and Lee took his army across hastily constructed pontoon bridges to the relative safety of Virginia.

In the Battle of Gettysburg, Meade lost perhaps 23,000 men. Lee's losses were at least as great and possibly as high as 28,000 men. Lee's Gettysburg campaign would confound survivors and historians alike, as they questioned Lee's overconfidence, poor decisions, and indecisiveness. The Confederate defeat at Gettysburg, combined with the Union victory at Vicksburg, marked a great turning point in the war.

Jack J. Cardoso, Keith D. Dickson, and
Spencer C. Tucker

Further Reading

Coddington, Edwin D. *The Gettysburg Campaign: A Study in Command*. New York: Charles Scribner's Sons, 1968.

Gallagher, Gary. *Lee and his Generals in War and Memory*. Baton Rouge: Louisiana State University Press, 1998.

Gallagher, Gary, ed. *The Third Day at Gettysburg and Beyond*. Chapel Hill: University of North Carolina Press, 1994.

Jones, Archer. *Civil War Command and Strategy: The Process of Victory and Defeat*. New York: The Free Press, 1992.

Thomas, Emory M. *Robert E. Lee: A Biography*. New York: W. W. Norton & Company, 1995.

Grant, Ulysses S. (1822–1885)

Ulysses S. Grant was one of the greatest of U.S. generals but is regarded as a failure among U.S. presidents. Born into a middle-class family in Point Pleasant, Ohio, on April 27, 1822, Ulysses Hiram Grant (his name changed with an error when he was appointed to West Point) secured an appointment to the U.S. Military Academy, West Point, in 1839. Grant performed well in certain courses, such as horsemanship, but struggled with mathematics and engineering, finishing 21st among 39 graduates in 1843. Posted to the 4th Infantry Regiment upon graduation, Second Lieutenant Grant accompanied his unit to Louisiana in 1844. A few months later, the United States Army placed the 4th under Major General Zachary Taylor near Corpus Christi for operations in the disputed border region between Texas and Mexico.

When Taylor's presence helped to trigger the Mexican-American War in 1846, Grant was in the thick of the fighting. He fought with distinction with his regiment at the battle of Palo Alto and the battle of Resaca de la Palma. He aided in planning Taylor's set-piece assault on fortified Mexican positions at Monterrey, and took part in some of the most brutal house-to-house fighting there before a ceasefire gave Taylor control of the city. The violent clash at Monterrey temporarily brought the fighting in northern Mexico to an end, and most of Taylor's Regular Army units were then shifted to Major General Winfield Scott for his 1847 invasion of central Mexico. Grant spent most of his time organizing logistics for Scott's army, a vitally important part of Scott's operations. Grant earned further attention in the subsequent campaign, taking part in fighting at the battle of Veracruz, the battle of Molino de Rey (where he was brevet promoted to first lieutenant), and the battle of Chapultepec (where he was brevet promoted to captain). In recognition of his wartime service, Grant received the substantive rank of first lieutenant two days after the capture of Mexico City. Immediately after the war, he married Julia Dent in St. Louis in 1848.

Grant's luck seemed to run out in peacetime, however. With the 4th Regiment constantly relocating, Grant had to move his family around the country, from Mississippi, to Michigan, and to New York. In 1853, Grant received a promotion to captain and orders to accompany the 4th to Fort Humboldt, California. Separated from his wife and unsatisfied with his dimming chances for higher rank, Grant began to drink. Historians differ widely on the relationship between Grant and the whiskey bottle. Post–Civil War

Lt. Gen. Ulysses S. Grant at Cold Harbor, June 1864. (National Archives)

revisionists considered Grant an abject alcoholic, but contemporary accounts seemed to indicate that Grant, while not an alcoholic, did not handle alcohol well. Whatever his dependence upon whiskey, Grant became melancholy and depressed when drinking, a noticeable change from his normal demeanor. Rumors, truthful or not, circulated that Grant's drinking made him unreliable and unsuitable for command. Disillusioned with army life, Grant resigned his commission in 1854, and returned to St. Louis.

Failure continued to dog Grant, however. His father-in-law gave him a small farm near St. Louis, but Grant could not turn a profit and he lost the farm. He ran for county political office, but lost badly. Grant worked in a variety of increasingly unsuitable jobs to care for his family until, finally, he was reduced to working as a clerk in his father's leather goods store in Galena, Illinois.

War has a way of changing fortunes, and no one's fortunes changed more in the Civil War than Grant's. Offering his services as a recruiter to Illinois Governor Richard Yates, Grant helped in the formation of a number of regiments in central Illinois. Initially hesitant to assume command, Grant finally agreed to be colonel of the 21st Illinois. He led the regiment in a raid against pro-secession forces on the Salt River in July 1861, giving Grant his first, albeit small, victory of the war. Buoyed by that success, Grant received a promotion to brigadier general of volunteers in July 1861, where he aided in keeping Kentucky in the Union by seizing Paducah in September 1861 and raiding Confederate camps along the Mississippi River. Operating under the command of Major General Henry Halleck, commander of the Department of Missouri, Grant took a more aggressive step in the assault and seizure of Fort Henry and Fort Donelson, guarding the entrances to the Tennessee and Cumberland, respectively, with the assistance of river gunboats under the command of Flag Officer Andrew Foote.

The capture of the two forts had two long-lasting effects upon Grant's career. First, it demonstrated to Grant the value of combined operations with naval forces. Second, it made Grant a celebrity. When Grant imposed unconditional surrender terms upon Fort Donelson, the press had a field day and Grant became the hero of the day.

Grant pursued the retreating Confederate forces under General Albert Johnston toward their railhead at Corinth, Mississippi. He nearly made a fatal mistake. Not expecting Johnston to attack him first, Grant failed in adequately fortifying his assembly camp near Pittsburgh Landing, Tennessee. Johnston caught Grant unaware in the ensuing Battle of Shiloh and nearly defeated him. Reinforced by units of Major General Don Carlos Buell's Army of the Ohio, Grant counterattacked on the second day and drove the Confederates back into Corinth. Corinth itself fell a few weeks later, but Grant nearly lost his command to Halleck's jealousy of his successful subordinate. Only his previous celebrity and the recognition that he was a fighting general saved him from an ignominious end. Grant assumed full command of Halleck's department when the latter went to Washington as Lincoln's military advisor.

Grant immediately began plans to reduce the Confederate stronghold of Vicksburg, the last bastion defending the Mississippi River Valley. Thwarted by poor terrain options and relentless attacks on his supply lines, Grant failed in numerous attempts to take the city in early 1863. In May, however, Grant opted to move his army across the Mississippi River to better ground south of Vicksburg, and, emulating Scott's Mexican campaign, live off the land instead of relying on fixed logistics. Gambling boldly and moving rapidly to keep two separate Confederate forces off balance, Grant managed to defeat the Confederates first at Jackson and then at Champion Hill. He then laid siege to Vicksburg, and forced its surrender in July 1863. For his efforts, Lincoln elevated Grant to command all Union forces in the western theater. In his new capacity, Grant oversaw the relief of Chattanooga, besieged by Confederate forces after the debacle at Chickamauga. Again rewarded for his success, Grant assumed command of all Union forces in March 1864 in the revived rank of lieutenant general, and went east to supervise Union offensives against Richmond and the Confederate Army of Northern Virginia.

In the spring of 1864, Grant began a massive coordinated offensive toward Richmond, with the aim of destroying the Army of Northern Virginia, commanded by General Robert E. Lee. At the same time, Union armies in the west, now commanded by Major General William Sherman, would press toward Atlanta. Grant's offensive led to a series of horrendous battles marked by ghastly casualties on both sides. Grant first clashed with Lee at the Battle of the Wilderness (May 5–6, 1864). However, in the grim mathematics of warfare, Grant understood that while he lost more men than Lee, Lee had actually lost a larger percentage of his smaller army. Moreover, Grant could replace his losses; Lee could not. Instead of retreating to rebuild his army like the previous commander of the Army of the Potomac, Grant moved forward in a series of flanking movements, trying to get between Lee and Richmond. Major clashes occurred over the following weeks at Spotsylvania Court House, the North Anna River, and Cold Harbor. Union casualties in these battles amounted to more than 50,000 men, but Grant had eroded both the reserves and the

morale of Lee's army. Moreover, when the campaign ended in the summer of 1864 with Grant and Lee locked in a siege at Petersburg, Virginia, Lee had lost all strategic initiative. Lee's greatest asset was his ability to move rapidly and strike from an unexpected direction, but now unable to leave Petersburg without risking the fall of Richmond, Grant forced Lee into a grinding war of attrition that Lee could not win.

The siege of Petersburg ground on from the fall of 1864 into the spring of 1865, but the result was never in serious doubt. Finally, stretched to the breaking point, Lee's lines around Petersburg collapsed on March 29, 1865, and Lee's army fled to the west in a desperate attempt to escape. Grant's forces pursued Lee, and finally contained him near Appomattox Court House, Virginia, on April 8. Unable to escape, Lee accepted the inevitable and met with Grant to negotiate surrender terms. Instead of "Unconditional Surrender Grant," Lee found that Grant offered generous surrender terms in the spirit of national conciliation promoted by Abraham Lincoln.

After the war, Grant remained in the Army as commanding general, promoted to the rank of full general, the first U.S. officer to wear four stars. He continued in this post until 1869, managing to avoid the political controversy that led to the impeachment of President Andrew Johnson. He supervised a dwindling army that continually failed in adequately enforcing Reconstruction in the defeated South. In 1868, Republicans convinced Grant to run for president, and he won handily and won another term four years later. Grant's presidency, however, was a disappointment. His campaign slogan, "Let Us Have Peace," indicated a president unwilling to enforce Reconstruction policies, and southern traditionalists soon undid most of the Reconstruction efforts. His administration suffered the embarrassment of scandal after scandal (although Grant himself was not involved), and a major economic panic in 1873 ended his administration on a negative note. After leaving the White House, Grant's old economic woes returned, and he was soon broke. Even worse, doctors diagnosed terminal throat cancer. Working against the clock, Grant wrote and published his memoirs. The well-written volume was an instant best-seller, and Grant died at Mount McGregor, New York on July 23, 1885 knowing that he had provided for his family. Grant's life was one of continual success and failure, but a dogged persistence that ultimately triumphed over failure came to symbolize the man, the general, and the president.

Steven J. Ramold

Further Reading

Goldhurst, Richard. *Many Are the Hearts: The Agony and the Triumph of Ulysses S. Grant.* New York: Crowell, 1975.

Perret, Geoffrey. *Ulysses S. Grant: Soldier and President.* New York: Random House, 1997.

Simpson, Brooks D. *Ulysses S. Grant: Triumph Over Adversity.* Boston: Houghton, 2000.

Guerrilla Warfare

Guerrilla, or irregular, warfare during the Civil War was unconventional warfare involving small groups of irregular combatants employing highly mobile tactics to fight larger conventional armies. Guerrilla fighters usually originated from within the local population, from which they drew support and shelter. Irregular warfare in the Civil War was especially common in the hinterlands of the border states (Arkansas, Kansas, Missouri, Kentucky) and in Tennessee, and Northwestern Virginia/West Virginia. Savage, no-holds-barred, neighbor-against-neighbor fighting was often the hallmark of guerrilla warfare.

Guerrilla warfare in the border areas frequently sprang from local conflicts. These conflicts featured Union versus anti-Union sentiment. The conflicts often arose from class differences or stemmed from the great social divide regarding slavery. These issues predated the war's outbreak. Such clashes spawned local self-defense groups that evolved into loosely organized partisan bands that sought to protect their own communities while terrorizing those of their opponents. The most infamous of the pro-Confederate guerrilla bands (known as bushwhackers) operated along the Kansas-Missouri border and were led by William Clarke Quantrill and William "Bloody Bill" Anderson. Other notorious partisan bands, led by Thomas Steele and Champ Ferguson, operated in Arkansas and the Kentucky-Tennessee-Western Virginia areas, respectively. Federal militias, often composed of local Unionists, were also organized for the same purposes and often exceeded their Confederate counterparts in the atrocities they committed. Most notable among these were the Redlegs, raised by the abolitionist U.S. senator from Kansas, James K. Lane, and the Jayhawkers, raised by Lane's ally, Charles Jennison. Dozens of these local bands terrorized the border regions, bringing total war that lasted until the end of the Civil War and often beyond.

The activities of the Confederate guerrillas put the Confederate leadership, both at Richmond and on the state level, in a quandary. On the one hand, they were effective in disrupting Union communication and supply lines and in tying down thousands of Union troops. On the other hand, the individualistic nature of the Confederate guerrilla bands, the difficulty in controlling them, and their capacity for uncontrolled violence against civilians proved a constant source of embarrassment to the Confederate government. Confederate partisans often resorted to mere outlawry that indiscriminately victimized any civilians they encountered. Atrocities against Unionists threatened to create a backlash that could hurt the Confederacy politically. As the war went on, guerrilla bands became refuges for deserters and individuals wishing to avoid conscription. In 1864, criminal activity among supposedly pro-Confederate guerrillas in Arkansas, for example, became so widespread that the Confederate authorities ordered a brigade of regular cavalry under Colonel Joseph Shelby to hunt them down.

In early 1862, the Confederate Congress sought to resolve the problem by passing the Partisan Ranger Act, which sought to limit and control the guerrillas by giving President Jefferson Davis sole authority to authorize guerrilla units and commission their commanders. Unfortunately, the legislation was vaguely worded and caused more problems than it solved. The Partisan Ranger Act displayed the Confederate government's preference to raise and use partisan units as part of the Confederate Army. They could thus directly support the Confederate armies in the field, and equally importantly, be controlled by the Confederate government. However, numerous Confederate guerrilla organizations showed no interest in having a close association with the distant government in Richmond.

Perhaps the best example of guerrilla violence occurred on August 21, 1863, when Quantrill's band attacked the Unionist town of Lawrence, Kansas. Quantrill's raiders, who were essentially a band of outlaws, indiscriminately killed 148 military-age males, both black and white, and burned most of the town to the ground. Then and thereafter,

Quantrill's supporters claimed that the raid was a reprisal for atrocities committed against pro-Confederate civilians in Missouri. Nevertheless, the raid was a great embarrassment to the Confederate leadership in Richmond. It also led to major reprisals against the pro-Southern communities in western Missouri.

The Union's response to guerrilla activities was uniformly harsh. Anti-guerrilla operations were brutal and aimed at punishing communities for the actions of guerrillas who may or may not have been members of those communities. The cycle usually began with an upsurge of guerrilla activity in a given area followed by a punitive operation by Federal units resulting in the burning of homes, farms, and even small towns. The best example of such a Union response was General Order Number 11, issued by the United States Army District of the Border in Kansas City on August 25, 1863, in response to the Lawrence Raid. It forced all residents in Clay, Bates, and Jackson Counties in Western Missouri out of their homes and resulted in massive destruction of homes and crops in those areas.

Throughout history, guerrillas have traditionally targeted an invader's line of supply. The Civil War was no exception. Union armies advancing south relied upon railroads for their supplies. The rail lines were vulnerable to guerrilla attack. Both the Federal offensives down the Mississippi through Tennessee were greatly impaired by Confederate guerrillas as well as the operations of more formally organized cavalry raiders. In the east, John Singleton Mosby's guerrillas were so effective at interrupting Federal control that a wide swath of territory to the south and west of Washington, D.C., became known as "Mosby's Confederacy." In contrast, Union guerrillas in east Tennessee and in northern Alabama seldom had the same was frequently intoxicated, a report Halleck knew to be false. Halleck had proceeded to remove Grant from command before Grant's congressman, Elihu B. Washburne, prompted Lincoln to support the victor of Forts Henry and Donelson and force Halleck to restore him. When newspapers criticized Grant after the narrow victory at Shiloh, Halleck seized the opportunity to sideline his subordinate again.

Taking the field for the only time in his Civil War career, Halleck pulled together all three field armies within his department, placed Grant in a meaningless second-in-command slot, and with his massed forces advanced with glacial slowness against the Confederate rail hub at Corinth, Mississippi, covering 20 miles in a month. He took the town but let the Confederate army guarding it escape.

Despite such a lackluster result, Lincoln, who was desperately seeking a general to mastermind and coordinate the movement of all the Union armies, selected Halleck for that task. Halleck went to Washington in the summer of 1862, but his efforts to direct the movements of such inadequate commanders such as Major Generals John Pope and George B. McClellan during the campaign in Virginia that summer proved a dismal failure. By its close, Halleck, who had never been comfortable actually directing operations in the field, all but refused to give further orders to his subordinate generals. Thereafter he made it an article of military faith that the general on the spot should always be left to make the decisions with nothing more than advice—albeit sometimes persistent, almost nagging advice—from Halleck in Washington. A frustrated Lincoln complained that Halleck amounted to little more than "a first-rate clerk."

In his capacity as a virtual clerk, however, Halleck performed useful service not only as an advisor to the field commanders but also as a mediator between them and the administration. When political Major General John A. McClernand wangled vague authorization from Lincoln to lead an independent expedition within Grant's department, Halleck quietly saw to it that the order was worded in such a way as to allow Grant to assume command and keep McClernand in his deservedly subordinate role.

When Grant was appointed to supersede Halleck as general in chief, he retained Halleck in the de facto role he had already been filling, that of chief of staff. In that capacity Halleck continued to advise generals in the field, including Grant, to transmit Grant's wishes into orders to the various armies, and to convey the impressions of the president and secretary of war to Grant and other field commanders. In the final analysis, despite his early shortcomings, Halleck made an important contribution to Union victory.

After General Robert E. Lee's April 1865 surrender, Halleck commanded the Military District of the James. That August, he took command of the Division of the Pacific; in 1869, he took control of the Division of the South. Halleck died in Louisville, Kentucky on January 9, 1872.

Steven E. Woodworth

Further Reading

Ambrose, Stephen. *Halleck: Lincoln's Chief of Staff.* Baton Rouge: Louisiana State University Press, 1962.

Marszalek, John F. *Commander of All Lincoln's Armies: A Life of General Henry W. Halleck.* Cambridge, MA: Belknap Press of Harvard University Press, 2004.

Woodworth, Steven E., ed. *Grant's Lieutenants: From Chattanooga to Appomattox.* Lawrence: University Press of Kansas, 2008.

Hardee, William J. (1815–1873)

William Hardee was born in Savannah, Georgia, on November 10, 1815. He graduated from the U.S. Military Academy, West Point, in 1838 and was commissioned a second lieutenant and sent to Europe to study cavalry tactics. During the Mexican-American War (1846–1848), he served under both Major Generals Zachary Taylor and Winfield Scott. After the war, he served in the 2nd Cavalry Regiment in Texas under Colonel Albert S. Johnston and Lieutenant Colonel Robert E. Lee.

In 1855, Hardee authored the *Rifle and Light Infantry Tactics for the Exercise and Maneuvers of Troops When Acting as Light Infantry or Riflemen*, a manual of infantry tactics that became the standard reference guide for infantrymen in both the Union and Confederate armies during the Civil War. Hardee was commandant of cadets at West Point from 1856 to 1861. He resigned his army commission as a lieutenant colonel after his home state of Georgia seceded from the Union. Although entering the Confederate army as a colonel, he was promoted to brigadier general by June 1861. In October 1861, he was advanced to major general, and in October 1862 he became a lieutenant general.

Hardee spent most of the war fighting with the Confederate Army of Tennessee. A thorough trainer, he was much admired by his men, who called him "Old Reliable." Hardee's first assignment was to organize an Arkansas brigade. He commanded a corps at Shiloh (April 6–7, 1862) and was there wounded in the arm. His command was then merged into General Braxton Bragg's Army of Tennessee. Not impressed with Bragg as a military leader, Hardee commanded the left wing of Bragg's army in the Battle of Perryville

(October 8, 1862). In his most successful battle, Stones River (December 31, 1861–January 2, 1863), Hardee's II Corps carried out a major surprise attack that almost defeated Union forces under Major General William S. Rosecrans. He briefly commanded the Confederate Department of Mississippi and East Louisiana, then returned to Bragg's command to take over command of Lieutenant General Leonidas Polk's corps besieging Chattanooga, Tennessee. Hardee's corps was forced to withdraw when Union troops under Major General George H. Thomas assaulted Missionary Ridge (November 25, 1863). One of Hardee's divisions then served as the Confederate rear guard. Hardee was one of a group of Confederate officers who finally convinced Confederate President Jefferson Davis to remove Bragg from command.

After General Joseph E. Johnston took command, Hardee continued in command of his corps for the Atlanta Campaign. Hardee had no confidence at all in Johnston's replacement, Lieutenant General John Bell Hood, however, and requested a transfer. From October 1864 to February 1865, Hardee commanded the Department of South Carolina, Georgia, and Florida. Although unable to stop Union Major General William T. Sherman's March to the Sea, Hardee was able to evacuate Confederate troops from Savannah before the Union occupation of the city. Hardee's troops then withdrew into North Carolina. Hardee's last battle with Union troops was at Bentonville, North Carolina, on March 19–21, 1865, where his only son was killed in battle. Hardee surrendered to Union forces at Greensboro on April 26, 1865.

After the war, Hardee retired to his wife's Alabama plantation. He then moved his family to Selma, where he was in the warehousing and insurance business. He was

Hood, John Bell. *Advance and Retreat; Personal Experiences in the United States and Confederate States Armies*. Bloomington: Indiana University Press, 1959.

McMurray, Richard M. *John Bell Hood and the War for Southern Independence*. Lexington: University of Kentucky Press, 1982.

O'Connor, Richard. *Hood: Cavalier General*. New York: Prentice-Hall, 1949.

Hooker, Joseph (1814–1879)

Joseph Hooker was born in Hadley, Massachusetts, on November 13, 1814. In 1837, he graduated from the U.S. Military Academy at West Point as a second lieutenant of artillery. That year, he shipped south for duty in Florida's Second Seminole War and rose to first lieutenant by November 1838. Hooker subsequently returned to West Point as its adjutant, and during the Mexican-American War, he served on the staffs of generals Zachary Taylor and Winfield Scott. He apparently enjoyed fighting and won three consecutive brevet promotions to lieutenant colonel for bravery in the Battle of Monterrey, the National Bridge, and the Battle of Chapultepec.

After the war, Hooker was assigned to the Division of the Pacific, where he remained until 1851. He performed well, but his sharp tongue and knack for insubordination cost him the friendship of Henry W. Halleck, the future chief of staff. Dissatisfied with slow promotion, Hooker went on furlough before resigning from the army in 1853 to pursue farming in Sonoma, California. He served as superintendent of military roads in Oregon in 1858 and the following year, became a colonel of the California militia.

When the Civil War began in April 1861, Hooker ventured to Washington, D.C. to secure a Union commission and became a brigadier general of volunteers. He spent the year commanding troops in the capital district before Major General George B. McClellan assigned him to the Army of the Potomac in May 1862. Hooker quickly established himself as one of the Union Army's most talented combat commanders. At a time when the Army of the Potomac was desperate for competent leadership in its highest echelons, he fit easily into the role of a brigade, division, or corps commander. Hooker performed well during McClellan's ill-fated Peninsula Campaign. A misinterpretation of an Associated Press tag line caused the press to dub Hooker "Fighting Joe" (a name he was never fond of). He was also one of the few senior officers to distinguish himself at the Second Battle of Manassas under John Pope. His aggressive leadership prevailed again on September 14, 1862 at the Battle of Turner's Gap. At the September 17, 1862, Battle of Antietam, Hooker exposed himself recklessly and sustained a bad foot wound. After the Battle of Fredericksburg in December 1862, Hooker adroitly played his political chips and received command of the Army of the Potomac from President Abraham Lincoln in January 1863. Hooker also raised political eyebrows by publicly stating that a military dictatorship, with him at the head, might be necessary to win the war.

Once in charge, Hooker initiated a much-needed reorganization of Union forces. He proved a surprisingly skilled administrator, improving the army's nutrition and health and modernizing its intelligence and medical services. In April 1863, the opening moves of his Chancellorsville Campaign brought 132,000 men to bear against Lee's 62,000 through a brilliant march around Lee's left flank and a rapid crossing of the Rappahannock and Rapidan rivers. On May 1, Hooker's force emerged from the

Wilderness, a tangle of second growth forest, into a position to attack Lee's exposed flank. However, when Lee unexpectedly advanced against Hooker instead of retreating as Hooker had expected, the general suddenly lost his nerve. Against much protest, he ordered the army back into the Wilderness and assumed a defensive posture. In a bold gamble, Lee seized the initiative on May 2, detaching Lieutenant General Thomas J. "Stonewall" Jackson's corps on a dangerous march across Hooker's front to a position to attack Hooker's unsecured right flank. Unnerved by Jackson's surprise attack, Hooker refused to commit his entire strength to the battle. Hopelessly confused, he first withdrew his army into a tight defensive shell and subsequently retreated. Hooker's debacle at Chancellorsville cost his army 17,000 casualties. Lee's domination of Hooker, cited by subsequent historians as "Lee's Masterpiece," cost the Army of Northern Virginia 12,000 casualties. Hooker maneuvered capably during the initial phases of the Gettysburg Campaign, but the Lincoln Administration had lost confidence in him. Major General George G. Meade replaced Hooker on June 28, 1863.

Transferred to the West, in the fall of 1863 Hooker partially regained his reputation as a corps commander. He fought well during the November 1863 Chattanooga Campaign, contributing to the victory at Lookout Mountain, Tennessee on November 24, 1863. He then served with Major General William T. Sherman's army during the Atlanta Campaign. However, when Major General James B. McPherson was killed in July 1864, Sherman passed over Hooker and appointed a less senior officer, Oliver O. Howard, to replace him. Hooker resigned in protest. He spent the rest of the war commanding the Northern Department, the Department of the East, and the Department of the Lakes, before tendering his resignation on October 15, 1868. Hooker then lived in quiet seclusion until his death in Garden City, New York, on October 31, 1879.

James R. Arnold

Further Reading

Boritt, Gabor, ed. *Lincoln's Generals*. New York: Oxford University Press, 1994.

Gallagher, Gary W., ed. *Chancellorsville: The Battle and Its Aftermath*. Chapel Hill: University of North Carolina Press, 1996.

Sword, Wiley. *Mountains Touched with Fire: Chattanooga Besieged, 1863*. New York: St. Martin's, 1995.

Woodworth, Steven E., ed. *Civil War Generals in Defeat*. Lawrence, KS: Univ. of Kansas Press, 1999.

Industry

The Civil War occurred as the United States was in the process of moving from the water-powered to the steam-powered phase of its own Industrial Revolution. Since the nation's first textile mill had opened in Pawtucket, Rhode Island, in 1793, moving water had provided the vast bulk of the energy that had driven America's steadily increasing number of manufacturing establishments. It was in part because of this dependence on relatively fast-moving rivers that the great majority of America's factories during the antebellum era were located in New England and other northeastern states, where such streams abounded.

While textile and other industries had flourished in the North and especially the Northeast, the South had lagged far behind the other regions of the country in manufacturing. This was largely a result of slavery. The South's Peculiar Institution drew off capital investment, and the abundance of cheap (slave) labor reduced the need for mechanical innovation. Slaves could be used to run manufacturing establishments, such as an iron forge in Virginia's Shenandoah Valley, but even there, the enforced stability of the slave labor force contributed to stagnation and use of outmoded equipment. Overall, slave-based agriculture dominated the southern economy.

Thus, when the war began the Northern and Southern states differed markedly in industrial development. Of the 128,300 industrial establishments in the United States,

only 18,026 were in the states that became part of the Confederacy. In 1860, Massachusetts alone produced more than 160 percent of the amount of manufactured goods produced in all of the Confederate states combined, Pennsylvania nearly 200 percent, and New York more than that. While 110,000 industrial workers labored in the South, the North's total of such employees was 1.3 million. In 1860, the nation's total annual value of industrial product came to $1.9 billion, but of that total, the future Confederate states contributed only $145.3 million, or 7.5 percent.

The North's economy was many times larger than that of the South, in terms not only of industrial output but also wealth that could fuel future growth. In addition to its far greater population, the North also had a more educated and more urbanized citizenry. Some 26 percent of the northern population lived in large towns or cities, as compared to only 10 percent in the South. The North's large middle class and far greater wealth, coupled with a well-developed banking system, facilitated economic development.

The Confederacy had very few large banks, scant industrial assets, a proportionally much smaller middle class, and not much in the way of financial prowess, making it difficult to raise money and ramp up production for the war. Much of the South's economic assets were tied up in land, which was not liquid and could not contribute in the short term to productive capacity, and slaves, which were vulnerable to escape and seizure by Union forces. On the eve of the

Civil War, the South boasted 30 percent of total U.S. assets, but it possessed just 12 percent of the circulating currency and only 21 percent of the nation's banking assets.

The entire South had less manufacturing capacity than New York City. The South lacked facilities for forging steel and was unable to construct machine tools—major liabilities in the age of machine war. In 1860, Northern states produced 93 percent of the nation's pig iron and manufactured 97 percent of its firearms. While very little of the North's industrial might in 1860 was devoted to arms and related manufacturing and it would take time to mobilize its great industrial assets for military production, at least the resources and means of expansion were readily available.

The South possessed abundant natural resources, including substantial iron and coal deposits and vast amounts of timber, but facilities to transport the raw materials to manufacturing sites were inadequate. In 1861, the North had 21,827 miles of railroad; the South only 8,947 miles; and, with the South unable to manufacture or secure rails or steam locomotives in any number, its railroads deteriorated throughout the conflict. The inability of the South to transport men, supplies, and foodstuffs easily by rail would prove costly.

The Southern economy was overwhelmingly agricultural. Cotton was the chief staple. As the world's leading producer of raw cotton, the South sold to the North and exported cotton abroad to Britain, France, and other nations, then purchased the manufactured goods it needed. The attempt by Southerners at the beginning of the war to withhold cotton from the market in order to use it as a bargaining tool to secure European recognition of the Confederacy failed. It had unfortunate consequences for the South in that the decision to withhold the cotton crop

from export denied the South access to such important European manufactured goods as machine tools, steam locomotives, and arms at the beginning of the war, when the Union naval blockade was yet porous.

Even in agriculture, Northern production exceeded that of the South. The North grew many more bushels of wheat, corn, and oats, and it sent to market more animals than did farmers in the South. However, the Southern states nevertheless raised two times more foodstuffs per capita than the Northern states. Just prior to the war, the South possessed half the horses and milk cows in the country, along with two-thirds of the mules, oxen, meat cattle, and swine. These animals not only provided foodstuffs for the South, but also provided hides for tanning and making leather.

The South had 1,246 tanning and leather shops capable of manufacturing four million pairs of shoes and boots annually. Yet even in this area, the North far surpassed the South. Massachusetts alone manufactured 40 million pairs of shoes and boots annually for internal consumption and export.

In 1861, the North had five facilities capable of producing heavy guns, the South but one. Prewar shipbuilding was centered in the North, and the South lacked modern shipbuilding facilities. During the war the North was able to build large numbers of technologically advanced ships, while Southern facilities to construct and repair ironclad vessels were limited and skilled labor was in short supply.

During the course of the war, the Confederacy of necessity began to develop an industrial base of its own. Many of the new factories were located in northern and central Alabama, but others included the enormous Augusta Powder Works in Augusta, Georgia. The Tredegar Iron Works, the South's only major prewar facility of its

The North's industrial capacity greatly surpassed that of the South. A New York City ship shipyard, ca. 1863. (Getty Images)

kind, continued to be a vital industrial asset to the Confederacy.

Despite the relative success of its efforts at industrialization, the Confederacy faced severe limitations in that area. Some scholars believe the Confederacy over-mobilized its white population, placing too many men under arms and leaving too few to support its industry. Efforts to use slaves in place of the departed soldiers were hampered by the tendency of slaves to seek their freedom by means of escape.

In the North the situation was much different. After an initial period of adjustment at the beginning of the war, northern industry rose to the challenge of wartime production, turning out vast quantities of weapons and war supplies. Although the Union had to import rifles during the early stages of the war, after 1863 importation of weapons became unnecessary as northern factories produced not only an abundance of weapons but also innovative new types of firearms, such as the repeating rifles. The northern labor force remained ample throughout the war, despite the enlistment of some 2 million northerners as soldiers. This was in part due to the region's larger population and in part thanks to the continued influx of foreign immigrants, 800,000 of whom arrived during the war.

The American Civil War demonstrated the strategic importance of industrial capacity. By every measure, the North enjoyed a dominant industrial advantage over the South.

Gerald D. Holland Jr. and
Steven E. Woodworth

Further Reading

Gordon, John S. *An Empire of Wealth: The Epic History of American Economic Power.* New York: Harper Perennial, 2005.

Nevins, Allan. *War for the Union, 1861–1865.* New York: Konecky and Konecky, 1971.

Roberts, William H. *Civil War Ironclads: The U.S. Navy and Industrial Mobilization*. Baltimore, MD: Johns Hopkins University Press, 2002.

Weigley, Russell F. *A Great Civil War: A Military and Political History, 1861–1865*. Bloomington: Indiana University Press, 2000.

Wilson, Harold S. *Confederate Industry: Manufacturers and Quartermasters in the Civil War*. Jackson: University Press of Mississippi, 2002.

Infantry Combat in the Civil War

Most Civil War battles took place in closed, wooded terrain with combat at extremely close range. Infantry was the queen of battle. Cavalry contributed little on the battlefield, artillery was decidedly a supporting arm. Combat centered around the infantry firefight. This involved two opposing lines—both sides deployed in loose, two-deep formation— blazing away at one another until one or both wavered and withdrew. It was a time, recalled one officer, "when all consideration for tactics is lost." In a Civil War firefight, there was no substitute for raw courage.

In past wars, infantry wielding smoothbore muskets had little chance of hitting an enemy soldier standing 200 yards away. Civil War soldiers carried improved weapons. A French captain named Minié developed a conical bullet (called a Minie ball by Civil War soldiers) with a tapered hollow, the base of which was fitted with a small iron cap. When a soldier squeezed the trigger, the force of the explosion drove the cap into the hollow, thereby expanding the bullet so that it engaged the rifling tightly. This reduced the windage, the difference between the bullet's and the gun-bore's diameter. Minié's bullet appeared in 1849. A trained rifleman firing a Minie ball on a proving ground could hit a man-sized target at 500 yards at least half the time. A decade of additional technological improvement gave Civil War marksmen a deadly weapon capable of killing at a heretofore unsurpassed distance.

However, three factors prevented soldiers from killing every enemy encountered. First, the accuracy a tester achieved on the firing range was very different from that achieved when the shooter was himself under fire. Second, the Civil War–era weapons had low muzzle velocity compared to modern weapons. This meant a soldier had to fire high to reach a distant target, in effect lobbing his shot at his foe. This required precise assessment of range. Last, regardless of theoretical ranges, most battles occurred in wooded, uneven terrain. Sighting ranges were often less than 100 yards. This greatly reduced the tactical impact of Captain Minié's invention. Still, shoulder arms, whether smoothbore or rifled, were by far the war's biggest combat killers. Medical statistics for the whole war showed that bullets caused 94 percent of all wounds, with artillery fire responsible for most of the rest.

In theory, the bayonet was an even more lethal killer. Experienced Mexican-American War officers believed that a spirited bayonet charge could win the day every time. They did not understand that a bayonet charge was formidable because of the psychological stress it placed upon the defender. In the Mexican-American War, the Mexican defenders were generally low morale troops. Many U.S. officers had seen the Mexican infantry run from their trenches when the American infantry pressed home a bayonet charge. They expected the same to occur in the Civil War. Consequently, at the beginning of the war, they became obsessed with the physical aspects of bayonet drill without realizing that the usefulness of the drill was to teach the recruit confidence and discipline.

Dead Confederate soldiers in the trenches of Fort Mahone at Petersburg, Virginia, April 1865. (Library of Congress)

In the Civil War, if defenders held firm, they typically repulsed a bayonet charge with their own firepower before the attackers came close enough to wield their bayonets. During the war, edged weapons of all sorts, including sabers, produced only 0.4 percent of all casualties. When hand to hand fighting did occur—such as on Little Round Top during the second day of Gettysburg (July 2, 1863) and at the Bloody Angle (Spotsylvania, May 12, 1864)—the actions became famous largely because of their rarity.

The standard tactical manuals used by both sides were inappropriate to the emerging conditions of the Civil War battlefield. The manuals carefully prescribed three different movement paces: common time at 70 yards per minute; quick time at 86 yards per minute; double quick time at 109 yards per minute. Conscientious officers drilled their men to use these three paces, only to find that in combat they were irrelevant. Likewise, drill manuals specified with great detail unit frontages, intervals, and the like, but on the battlefield, formal shoulder-to-shoulder maneuvering was as irrelevant as parade ground pacing. Instead, veteran units quickly learned how to disperse to take advantage of all available cover while retaining sufficient cohesion to react to their officers' orders.

The drill manuals never reflected such tactical realities. Consequently, close order bayonet assaults against waiting lines of equally determined defenders produced the staggering casualties characteristic of offensive action during the early part of the Civil War. Brave attackers broke a defending line, but at terrible cost. John Bell Hood's charge at Gaines's Mill on June 27, 1862, set the offensive tone for Lee's Army of Northern Virginia. One in four participants in the two assault brigades fell. In the 4th Texas, Hood's old regiment, all the field officers were killed or wounded. This battle, the first major engagement of the Seven Days' Battles, foreshadowed the future. Lee's relentless assaults cost the South over 20,000 casualties during the Seven Days.

Over time, individual officers and units acquired valuable combat experience and devised tactical innovations. Yet it remains striking how neither the North nor the South had a system to circulate tactical lessons. Instead, officers continued to train the soldiers with the same tactics used when the war began and to employ the same formations. From the beginning to the end of the open battle phase of the war—in other words, before the comprehensive use of fieldworks—there was little tactical evolution despite the fact that the tactical challenge remained unchanged. No one figured out how to maintain command and control in the wooded terrain that typified Civil War battlefields. Generals continued to try to maneuver long battle lines through thick woods without using tactical reconnaissance. The situation reached a terrible climax in Virginia in 1864 when two utterly determined, bloody-minded commanders—Lee and Grant—opposed each other. Given the paucity of tactical thinking, all the advantages went to the defender. The advent of trench warfare in 1864 accelerated this trend.

By the end of 1863, there was sufficient evidence to show that the era of open battle was giving way to a new kind of warfare in which the defenders fought exclusively from behind fieldworks and fortifications. In the West, the Army of the Cumberland did not entrench before the Confederate attack at Stones River in December 1862. It preferred fighting in the traditional 'stand up' style. After the first day of its next battle, along Chickamauga Creek in September 1863, it spent the night felling trees and preparing a long line of breastworks. In the east, neither side prepared extensive fieldworks during the Battle of Gettysburg. Less than five months later, Lee's army responded to a Federal advance by immediately building an imposing line of works along Mine Run. By the spring of 1864, western and eastern armies alike immediately constructed works whenever they were in the enemy's presence.

A handful of forward-thinking officers tried to develop assault tactics appropriate to the new conditions. The simplest and most effective was to order the men to charge with uncapped weapons so they could not stop to shoot during the advance. This compelled the soldiers to charge through the lethal zone before the buildup of losses stopped them. Another alternative, used most famously by the brilliant Union officer, Emory Upton, at Spotsylvania in May 1864, was to form a deep, but narrow, assault column. Only the leading rank carried rifles ready to fire. Upton's first assault on May 10 featured 12 regiments formed in four lines of three regiments each. The charge overran the Confederate works, but eventually failed due to lack of support from adjacent units. Two days later, an entire corps employed Upton's formation, with the leading division advancing in a solid rectangle some forty ranks deep. The subsequent breakthrough led to the bitter fighting at the Bloody Angle.

Such breakthroughs were the exception during the late war. Veteran soldiers, if not their generals, understood the futility of charging enemy works. They would obey orders to charge by rising from their trenches and advancing. Upon receiving first fire, they halted and lay down. Even as late as the Siege of Petersburg, green troops did not understand the wisdom of such behavior. In June 1864, the 1st Maine Heavy Artillery, with 950 men serving as infantry, charged the rebel works and lost 115 killed, 489 wounded, and 23 missing within 10 minutes. A notable late-war exception to the veterans' pronounced reluctance to charge fortifications occurred at the Battle of Franklin (November 30, 1864). Hood had recently impugned the courage of his army. They responded with suicidal courage in their attack against the Union works. Of 26,897 rebels engaged, 6,252 were lost including five generals killed.

The Civil War witnessed a transition from open field battle involving troops maneuvering in shoulder-to-shoulder formation to trench warfare where the defender enjoyed an enormous advantage over the attacker. This transition led to the stalemated trench warfare of World War I.

James R. Arnold

Further Reading

Abernethy, Byron R., ed. *Private Elisha Stockwell, Jr. Sees the Civil War*. Norman: University of Oklahoma Press, 1958.

Coggins, Jack. *Arms and Equipment of the Civil War*. New York: Doubleday, 1962.

Dawes, Rufus R. *Service With the Sixth Wisconsin Volunteers*. Madison: State Historical Society of Wisconsin, 1962.

Fox, William F. *Regimental Losses in the American Civil War*. New York: Brandow, 1898. (Reprinted by Morningside Bookshop, 1974.)

Frank, Joseph A., and George A. Reaves. *"Seeing the Elephant": Raw Recruits at the Battle of Shiloh*. Westport, CT: Greenwood Press, 1989.

Howard, McHenry. *Recollections of a Confederate Soldier, 1861–1866*. Dayton, 1975.

Nevins, Allan, ed. *A Diary of Battle: The Personal Journals of Colonel Charles S. Wainwright, 1861–1865*. New York: Harcourt, Brace & World, 1962.

Robertson, James I., ed. *The Civil War Letters of General Robert McAllister*. New Brunswick, NJ: Rutgers University Press, 1965.

Watkins, Sam R. *"Co. Aytch"*. New York: Macmillan Publishing Company, 1962.

Infantry Organization and Equipment

Both the Union and Confederate armies organized volunteer infantry regiments into ten-company units. U.S. Regular battalions had only eight companies. Both U.S. Regular and U.S. volunteer companies officially numbered between 64 and 82 privates. Confederate volunteer regiments had companies with between 64 and 125 privates. During the war the North raised 1,696 infantry regiments. Because of poor record keeping and confusing consolidation, the exact number of Confederate infantry units is difficult to assess. There were between 259 and 642 infantry regiments, 85 to 163 battalions, and some 62 independent companies that served on active duty.

According to regulations followed by both sides, a regiment's frontage equaled the number of files (front and rear men in double rank) multiplied by the 20 inches occupied by each man. Thus, a 100-man company had a frontage of 27.7 yards while a regiment had a frontage of about 277 yards. When accounting for regimental intervals, a five-regiment brigade deployed in two-deep line extended across a 1,460 yard front. This long frontage made command and control extremely difficult, particularly when, as was often the case, the battle took place in wooded terrain. During the war's opening battles, the regiment was the largest tactical unit. As armies expanded, the need for higher levels of organization became apparent. This led to the formation of brigades and divisions. Neither organization was ever

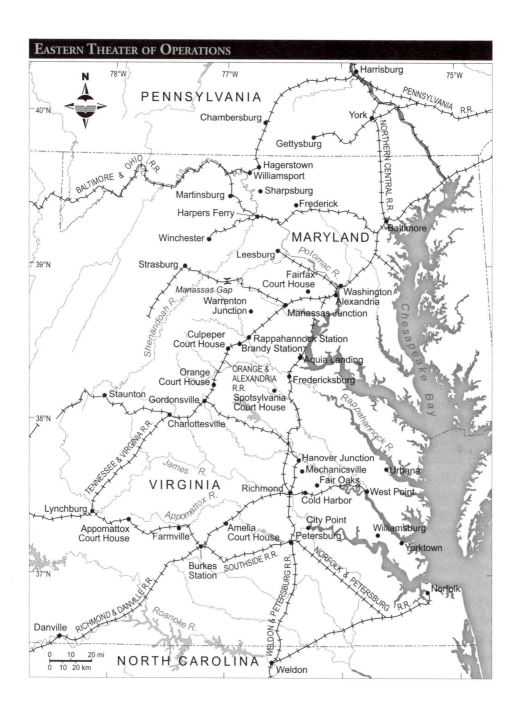

EASTERN THEATER OF OPERATIONS

carrying out Lee's plan to destroy McClellan. Jackson's command then moved northwest and played a key role in the subsequent Confederate victory over Union forces under Major General John Pope in the Second Battle of Bull Run/Manassas (August 29–30). Jackson accompanied Lee in his subsequent invasion of Maryland. His troops forced the surrender of the Union garrison at Harpers Ferry on September 15, rejoining Lee in time to participate in the bloody Battle of Antietam on September 17.

Advanced to lieutenant general and given command of II Corps in Lee's Army of Northern Virginia in October 1862, Jackson commanded the Confederate right flank in the Battle of Fredericksburg, Virginia (December 13, 1862), where he helped prevent a Union breakthrough. In the Battle of Chancellorsville (May 1–4, 1863), Lee, outnumbered two to one by Union forces under Major General Joseph Hooker, ordered Jackson to carry out a flanking attack against the Union right. Jackson's brilliant execution of the plan on May 2 caught Union forces off guard and rolled up the Union right. Only darkness prevented Jackson from inflicting greater damage. That night Jackson and his staff rode past the Confederate line on a reconnaissance. During their return, they were mistaken for Union troops and fired upon by Confederate soldiers. Jackson was badly wounded, necessitating amputation of his left arm. He subsequently contracted pneumonia and died at Guiney Station, Virginia, on May 10, 1863. He was buried in Lexington, Virginia. Jackson's death was perhaps the greatest single military personnel loss to befall the Confederacy. Lee never found an adequate replacement for Jackson. Personally brave, self-confident, and resolute, Jackson was also extremely religious, hard, and absolutely uncompromising. It was said of him that he lived in the New Testament but fought in the Old.

Spencer C. Tucker

Further Reading

Cook, Roy B. *The Family and Early Life of Stonewall Jackson*. Richmond, VA: Old Dominion Press, 1925.

Robertson, James I., Jr. *Stonewall Jackson: The Man, the Soldier, the Legend*. New York: Macmillan, 1997.

Tanner, Robert G. *Stonewall in the Valley. Thomas J. "Stonewall" Jackson's Shenandoah Valley Campaign, Spring 1862*. Mechanicsburg, PA: Stackpole Books, 1996.

Vandiver, Frank E. *Mighty Stonewall*. New York: McGraw-Hill, 1957.

Johnston, Albert Sidney (1803–1862)

Albert Sidney Johnston was born in Washington, Kentucky, on February 2, 1803. In 1822, he received an appointment to the U.S. Military Academy at West Point. He graduated eighth in his class in 1826 and while at the academy struck up a lifelong relationship with fellow cadet Jefferson Davis. Johnston joined the 2nd U.S. Infantry as a second lieutenant and served six years at Sacket's Harbor, New York, and Jefferson Barracks, Missouri, before fighting as the regimental adjutant during the Black Hawk War of 1832. Johnston resigned his commission in April 1834 to attend to his ailing wife, and after her death in 1835, he relocated to Texas.

When the Texas Revolution erupted in 1836, Johnston enlisted as a private in the small Texas Army and rose rapidly to brigadier general within a year. This meteoric ascent offended many individuals, and in 1837, Johnston was severely wounded in a duel with his predecessor. Nevertheless, he gained appointment as the Texas secretary of war. In 1840, when Johnston had a disagreement with President Sam Houston, he resigned his commission to take up farming.

During the Mexican-American War, Johnston served as colonel of the First Texas

Run on July 21, 1861, and gained promotion to full general. However, his quarrelsome nature and insistence on greater rank alienated Confederate president Jefferson Davis.

The president's antipathy for the general manifested itself during initial phases of the 1862 Peninsula Campaign when Johnston slowly gave ground before the superior numbers of Union General George B. McClellan. Regarding Richmond as threatened, Davis and others clamored for him to stand fast. When McClellan awkwardly divided his army into two wings separated by the Chickahominy River, Johnston pounced. At the ensuing Battle of Seven Pines, May 31 1862, Johnston was severely wounded. As fate would have it, his replacement, General Robert E. Lee, would command the Army of Northern Virginia for the rest of the war.

Returning to duty in November 1862, Davis assigned Johnston to head up the Department of the West. It was a tremendous responsibility involving two major Confederate armies; Braxton Bragg's Army of Tennessee and John C. Pemberton's army centered around Vicksburg, Mississippi. Johnston, who craved another combat command, failed to rise to the challenge of coordinating western operations. General Ulysses S. Grant commenced operations against Vicksburg in December 1862. By May 1863, Grant had isolated Vicksburg from outside help. Unable to reinforce the city in time, Johnston directed Pemberton to withdraw before he was trapped. However, Johnston exhibited little energy in trying to assist Pemberton. On May 14, 1863, General William T. Sherman drove Johnston away from the key rail hub at Jackson, Mississippi. Pemberton surrendered his army in Vicksburg after a two-month siege. During this time Johnston again failed to apply himself energetically to breaking the siege.

Davis personally blamed Johnston for the debacle at Vicksburg and restricted him to minor duties until the next crisis arrived. In December 1863, Grant and Sherman smashed Bragg's Army of Tennessee at Chattanooga, which resulted in Bragg's resignation. With some reluctance, Davis appointed Johnston to succeed him.

Throughout the spring of 1864, Johnston entrenched himself at Dalton, Georgia, with 62,000 men. In May, Sherman advanced on him with 100,000 soldiers and expertly maneuvered the defenders out of their positions. The Confederate general nevertheless fell back slowly and in good order toward Atlanta. His defensive skills exasperated Sherman, who was goaded into attacking at Kennesaw Mountain in June 1864 and badly repulsed. Unfortunately, Johnston's strategy angered Davis, who accused him of failing to halt the enemy. Johnston was partially to blame for Davis's anger because he declined to keep the president informed about his plans. On July 17, 1864, Davis relieved him. John Bell Hood, who succeeded him and may have played a role in his dismissal, promptly launched a series of attacks against Sherman, all of which failed and eventually caused the loss of Atlanta.

Johnston, marooned again without a command, remained idle until February 1865, when Lee reinstated him as commander of the greatly reduced Army of Tennessee now operating in the Carolinas. His mission was to prevent Sherman from attacking the Army of Northern Virginia from the rear and Johnston, outnumbered four to one, resorted to his usual defensive tactics. He fought and lost a final engagement to Sherman at Bentonville, North Carolina, on March 19, 1865, finally surrendering to him at Durham Station on April 26.

After the war, Johnston sold insurance before winning election to the U.S. House of Representatives in 1879. Six years later, he was appointed railroad commissioner by President Grover Cleveland and, while living in Washington, D.C., befriended his former antagonist, Sherman. Johnston also found time to pen his memoirs and excoriated Davis and others for losing the war. He died in Washington, D.C., on March 21, 1891, from pneumonia contracted while attending Sherman's funeral.

John C. Fredriksen

Further Reading

Davis, William C. "Jefferson Davis and His Generals." In *The Cause Lost: Myths and Realities of the Confederacy*. Lawrence, KS: University Press of Kansas. 1996.

Newton, Steven H. *Joseph E. Johnston and the Defense of Richmond*. Lawrence: University Press of Kansas, 1998.

Symonds, Craig L. *Joseph E. Johnston: A Civil War Biography*. New York: Norton, 1992.

at Lexington before proceeding on to the Kentucky capital of Frankfort to make arrangements for the inauguration of Richard Hawes as the short-lived Confederate governor on October 4.

Buell reacted slowly to the Confederate threat, but once the direction of their movements was clear, he moved swiftly to save Louisville. Collecting three additional divisions supplied by Major General Ulysses S. Grant and bringing his total strength to some 50,000 men, Buell's army arrived at Louisville on September 29. Buell's men advanced in four columns with the main Union effort against Bardstown. Bragg had expected the principal Union thrust to be against Frankfort and had sent some of his men there to reinforce Smith. On October 7, Union troops encountered Bragg's remaining 16,000 men at Perryville. On the morning of October 8, competition for the region's only water source, Doctor's Creek, which served as the middle ground separating the rival armies, escalated into a general engagement. A series of hard-hitting Confederate attacks achieved considerable success. Even though his nearly 37,000 soldiers substantially outnumbered Bragg, Buell failed to take advantage of his superior numbers. Because of an acoustic shadow, neither Buell nor two of his corps commanders even realized that a battle was under way. Thus, only nine of his twenty-four brigades participated in the fighting. Still, the nine fighting brigades were enough to mount a counter-attack that regained the Union position. Buell planned an all-out attack for the morning of October 9, but the Confederates decamped during the night. The Battle of Perryville claimed 4,200 Union and 3,400 Confederate casualties.

Smith and Bragg rejoined at London, Kentucky, and there concluded that Kentuckians were not going to flock to the Confederate cause in any great numbers. In any case, the Southerners were experiencing difficulty feeding and supplying their men, many of whom were sick and wounded. By October 26, the last Confederate forces were back in Tennessee. The Kentucky Campaign featured a series of Confederate botches, with Bragg and Smith failing to take advantage of several tantalizing opportunities. The campaign did nothing to boost Confederate morale and served only to showcase lackluster generalship on the part of both Confederate leaders. Buell, who despite superior numbers, had failed to bring the Confederates to decisive battle, was relieved of command of the Army of the Ohio.

Leah D. Parker and Spencer C. Tucker

Further Reading

McDonough, James L. *War in Kentucky: From Shiloh to Perryville*. Knoxville: University of Tennessee Press, 1994.

McWhiney, Grady. *Braxton Bragg and Confederate Defeat*, Vol. 1, *Field Command*. New York: Columbia University Press, 1969.

Noe, Kenneth W. *Perryville: This Grand Havoc of Battle*. Lexington: University Press of Kentucky, 2001.

L

Lee, Robert E. (1807–1870)

Robert Edward Lee was born on January 19, 1807, in Stratford, Virginia. He was the third son of American Revolution hero Henry Lee. He gained appointment to the U.S. Military Academy at West Point in 1825 and graduated second in his class four years later without a single demerit. Lee subsequently joined the elite Corps of Engineers as a second lieutenant, rose to captain in 1838, and distinguished himself in a variety of engineering tasks along the Mississippi River. During the opening phases of the Mexican-American War, he accompanied General John E. Wool's campaign to Saltillo and in 1847, joined the army of General Winfield Scott during the advance on Mexico City. Lee fought with distinction at Veracruz and Cerro Gordo, where his daring reconnaissance determined Scott's flanking movements. After additional fighting at Churubusco and at Chapultepec, where he was wounded, Lee gained a brevet promotion to colonel and returned home.

In 1852, Lee was appointed superintendent of cadets at West Point, a post he felt unqualified for, but he revitalized and tightened the school's curricula. Furthermore, he was a strict disciplinarian and nearly expelled his own nephew, Fitzhugh Lee, on account of poor grades and behavior. In 1855, Lee left the academy to become lieutenant colonel of the Second U.S. Cavalry under Albert S. Johnston, a unit renowned for training large numbers of future Confederate officers. In 1859, while on a furlough home, Lee was called on to suppress abolitionist John Brown's uprising at Harpers Ferry, which he did bloodlessly with a company of marines. Lee advanced to colonel of the First U.S. Cavalry and was commanding the Department of Texas in 1860 when the specter of civil war awakened a crisis of loyalties.

As a soldier, Lee supported neither secession nor slavery, but he felt deeply obliged to support his native state of Virginia. When President Abraham Lincoln offered him command of all federal armies, he respectfully declined and tendered his resignation in April 1861. By May, he was made a lieutenant general of Confederate forces by President Jefferson Davis. Lee, however, bungled his initial assignment to subdue the western counties of Virginia, due mostly to uncooperative subordinates. Criticized by politicians, newspapers, and the public, he briefly became known as "Granny Lee." Davis, however, recognized his potential and assigned him to shore up the defenses of the southern Atlantic coast. Lee returned to Richmond to serve as Davis's military adviser. In this capacity, Lee relieved Union pressure on the Confederate capital of Richmond by enabling General Thomas "Stonewall" Jackson's famed Shenandoah Valley Campaign of 1862.

Lee's fortunes, and the Confederacy's, changed dramatically on June 1, 1862, when he assumed command of the Army of Northern Virginia after General Joseph E. Johnston had been wounded at the Battle of Seven Pines on May 31, 1862. He had never commanded in battle before. Although outnumbered substantially, Lee soon respected in the North and revered throughout the South. His citizenship was officially restored by an act of the U.S. Congress in 1975.

James R. Arnold

Further Reading

Freeman, Douglas S. *Lee's Lieutenants: A Study in Command.* 3 vols. New York: C. Scribner's Sons, 1942–1944.

Long, Armistead L. *Memoirs of Robert E. Lee: His Military and Personal History.* New York: Books Sales, 1991.

Thomas, Emory M. *Robert E. Lee: A Biography.* New York: W. W. Norton & Company, 1997.

Lincoln, Abraham (1809–1865)

Abraham Lincoln is perhaps the most loved of all the U.S. presidents. A photograph of Lincoln taken toward the end of the Civil War shows a gaunt, exhausted leader whose visible anguish moves nearly every American. His words, always simple and eloquent, exhorting preservation of the Union, then asking forgiveness and peace for all who fought and suffered in the war, are equally familiar and moving. For most people, Lincoln personifies the American spirit of freedom and equality.

Lincoln was born on February 12, 1809, and grew up on frontier farms in Kentucky and Indiana. From an early age, despite his father's discouragement, he was obsessed with obtaining an education. The goal had to be innate, for, as he observed later, Indiana offered "absolutely nothing to excite ambition for education." Lincoln always attributed his love of books to his mother. "I owe everything I am to her," he said. She died when he was nine, but his stepmother encouraged him to continue his studying.

The year after the family moved to Illinois in 1830, Lincoln decided to live on his own. A job as a store clerk in New Salem gave him access to books and plenty of time to read. During the Black Hawk War, a conflict between the Sauk and Fox Indians and the United States in 1832, Lincoln served a short stint in the militia but did not see combat. When he returned to New Salem, he ran unsuccessfully for the state assembly in a predominantly Democratic district as an anti-Jackson Whig. After his defeat, he purchased a general store with a partner. Their venture failed because of the partner's alcoholism. Although it took Lincoln 15 years, he paid off all their debts in full, earning the nickname "Honest Abe."

In 1834, Lincoln won the first of his four two-year terms to the Illinois state assembly. As a state legislator, he generally supported internal improvements and the development of the nation's resources and was soon the leader of the Whig minority. In addition to his work in the assembly, Lincoln began to study law. After moving to the new state capital in Springfield, he was admitted to the bar in 1836. In 1842, Lincoln married Mary Todd, and in 1846, he was elected to the U.S. House of Representatives. In his single term in the House, Lincoln opposed the Mexican-American War and the extension of slavery into the territories and supported the right of voters in the District of Columbia to be able to abolish slavery.

In 1848, Lincoln vigorously campaigned across New England for Zachary Taylor. He was so disappointed when he did not obtain an expected appointment as commissioner of the general land office that he withdrew from politics and concentrated on his law practice for five years.

Lincoln returned to the political arena when reaction to the Kansas-Nebraska Act helped forge the new Republican Party.

President Abraham Lincoln, little more than a week before he gave the Gettysburg Address, November 8, 1863. Photo by Alexander Gardner. (Library of Congress)

In 1856, he campaigned throughout Illinois, delivering speeches in favor of antislavery Republican presidential candidate John C. Frémont. In 1858, the Illinois Republican Party nominated him to run for the Senate against Democrat Stephen A. Douglas.

In his subsequent speech accepting the nomination, Lincoln succinctly summed up his view of the situation the nation was in due to slavery: "A house divided against itself cannot stand. I believe this government cannot endure, permanently half slave and half free." Slavery, he warned, was a threat to free labor, and there was no way to reconcile it with a free society. By preventing its expansion, its ultimate extinction could be gradually obtained. Lincoln's preferred solution to this vexing social problem was to recolonize African Americans outside the country. Though he opposed slavery, he was not free of his era's pervasive racism.

From town to town during the 1858 campaign, in a series of debates, Lincoln and Douglas appeared on the same stage. What they said was reported across the nation because Douglas was widely regarded as the front-runner for the Democratic Party's presidential nomination in 1860. In his speeches, Lincoln repeated that slavery was morally wrong and attacked his opponent's "declared indifference" to it:

> I hate it because of the monstrous injustice of slavery itself. I hate it because it deprives our republican example of its just influence in the world—enables the enemies of free institutions, with plausibility, to taunt us as hypocrites—causes the real friends of freedom to doubt our sincerity, and especially because it forces so many really good men amongst ourselves into an open war with the very fundamental principles of civil liberty—criticizing the Declaration of Independence, and insisting that there is no right principle of action but self-interest.

The Republicans won 4,000 more popular votes than the Douglas Democrats (125,000 to 121,000), but the Democrats still managed to win more seats in the state legislature, and Douglas was returned to the Senate. Friends consoled the disappointed Lincoln with the advice that, although he had lost the Senate race, he was now a strong candidate for the Republican nomination for president. Lincoln replied, "I . . . admit that I am ambitious, and would like to be President . . . but there is no such good luck in store for me." A prominent figure after the debates, Lincoln toured the nation giving speeches to increasingly enthusiastic crowds prior to the 1860 Republican convention. At the convention, he was nominated on the third ballot over front-runner William H. Seward.

Louisiana and in Missouri. He then served with the 8th Infantry Regiment in Florida.

During the Mexican-American War (1846–1848), Longstreet first served under Major General Zachary Taylor in northern Mexico and took part in the Battle of Monterrey in September 1846. He then served under Major General Winfield Scott in the Veracruz to Mexico City Campaign. Longstreet was brevetted a captain following the Battle of Churubusco in August 1847 and a major after the Battle of Molino del Rey that September. He was badly wounded in the Battle of Chapultepec the same month.

With the beginning of the Civil War, Major Longstreet resigned from the U.S. Army on June 1, 1861, and accepted a commission as a brigadier general in the newly formed Confederate Army on June 17. He commanded troops in fighting at Centreville, Virginia, on July 18 and earned recognition in the First Battle of Bull Run/Manassas (July 21, 1861). Promoted to major general on October 7, he commanded a division in the Peninsula Campaign at Yorktown and then fought a skillful delaying action at Williamsburg (May 5, 1862). During the Battle of Seven Pines/Fair Oaks (May 31), however, his failure to move swiftly threw off Confederate commander General Joseph E. Johnston's plans, but Longstreet performed well under General Robert E. Lee during the Seven Days' Battles (June 25–July 1, 1862).

Lee dispatched Longstreet, in command of five divisions representing more than half of Lee's infantry, to join with forces under Major General Thomas J. Jackson. Under Lee's command, the combined forces defeated Major General John Pope's Army of Virginia in the Second Battle of Bull Run/Manassas (August 29–30, 1862). Although he opposed Lee's invasion of Maryland, Longstreet fought well at South Mountain (September 14) and in the Battle of Antietam (September 17). He was promoted to lieutenant general in October 1862. In the Battle of Fredericksburg (December 13), his I Corps held Marye's Heights, defending it against numerous costly Federal assaults.

In early 1863, Lee sent Longstreet on foraging operations (the Suffolk Campaign), and he thus missed the Battle of Chancellorsville. Following the death of Jackson from wounds sustained in that battle, Longstreet became Lee's chief subordinate, known as Lee's "Old War Horse." Longstreet opposed Lee's decision to fight at Gettysburg (July 1–3) and especially Lee's failed frontal assault (Pickett's Charge) on July 3.

Sent west with his men to reinforce General Braxton Bragg, Longstreet arrived there in time to fight in the Battle of Chickamauga (September 19–20, 1863), where he was able to take advantage of Major General William Rosecrans's critical error that shifted a Union division out of the line. Longstreet's men exploited the hole in the Union line and helped rout Rosecrans's army. Then while Bragg besieged Chattanooga, Longstreet moved against Union major general Ambrose E. Burnside at Knoxville, but Longstreet failed to dislodge him and had to begin a siege, which denied Bragg support at Chattanooga.

In April 1864, Longstreet rejoined Lee in Virginia. Longstreet and his men fought effectively against the Union forces in Grant's Overland Campaign of 1864. Wounded in the Battle of the Wilderness (May 5–6), Longstreet relinquished command to recuperate. Returning to duty that November, he fought in the remaining actions of the war near Petersburg and Richmond, serving with Lee's Army of Northern Virginia to the final surrender at Appomattox Court House on April 9, 1865.

After the war, Longstreet alienated Southerners when he became a Republican, renewed his friendship with Grant, and served in a variety of U.S. government posts, including minister to the Ottoman Empire (1880). Many proponents of the Lost Cause found it easy to make Longstreet a scapegoat, blaming him, for example, for his delay in attacking on the second day of the Battle of Gettysburg as well as for mistakes made by Lee there. Longstreet wrote extensively to defend his role in that battle, publishing his memoirs in 1896. He initially settled in New Orleans, Louisiana, but he later moved to Gainesville, Georgia, where he died on January 2, 1904. Greatly respected by his men, who called him "Old Pete," Longstreet, while careful and judicious in his planning, was an able commander and tactician with a talent for defensive warfare. A fine corps commander, he lacked the aptitude for independent command.

Spencer C. Tucker

Further Reading

Eckenrode, Hamilton J., and Bryan Conrad. *James Longstreet: Lee's War Horse*. Chapel Hill: University of North Carolina, 1986.

Freeman, Douglas S. *Lee's Lieutenants: A Study in Command*. 3 vols. New York: Scribner, 1970.

Longstreet, James. *From Manassas to Appomattox: Memoirs of the Civil War in America*. New York: Da Capo, 1992.

Wert, Jeffery D. *General James Longstreet*. New York: Simon and Schuster, 1993.

M

McClellan, George Brinton (1826–1885)

Born in Philadelphia on December 3, 1826, George Brinton McClellan graduated from the United States Military Academy at West Point in 1846. He served in the Mexican War and received two brevets. After the war, McClellan served mainly on the western frontier, performing various surveys and explorations. He also was one of the U.S. observers of the Crimean War (1853–1856) and wrote a much studied report of his observations. In 1857, McClellan resigned his commission to become a railroad executive.

When the Civil War began, McClellan became commander of Union troops in Ohio at the rank of major general of volunteers. His first assignment was to secure the western counties of Virginia. Thanks to able subordinates, Confederate miscues, and the support of the local populace, the area was largely secured for the Union by mid-summer 1861, with McClellan hailed in northern newspapers as "the Napoleon of the present war."

The fame came at an opportune moment for, in the wake of the July 21 Union debacle at the First Battle of Bull Run, Lincoln was looking for a suitable general to replace the discredited Brigadier General Irvin McDowell. Given the job, McClellan showed skill in organizing and training the army and restoring morale. Yet throughout the fall months, much to the dismay of the president, McClellan did not advance. In November, general-in-chief Winfield Scott, with whom McClellan had frequently quarreled, went into retirement. McClellan received Scott's duties in addition to his previous ones, but the added authority did not make him any more inclined to move forward. McClellan was also an open Democrat who approved of slavery and made no secret of his contempt for abolitionists and Republicans.

In January 1862, Lincoln ordered McClellan to advance toward Richmond. In response, McClellan finally revealed that he had a scheme for taking the army down Chesapeake Bay by water, landing on the Virginia peninsula between the York and James rivers, and advancing toward Richmond from the east. Lincoln had misgivings about the plan, and some in Lincoln's cabinet thought it looked suspiciously like leaving Washington open to a Confederate counterstroke. Nevertheless, the president reluctantly gave his approval, although he relieved McClellan of his duties as general-in-chief, leaving him to command only the Army of the Potomac.

McClellan's Peninsula Campaign (March–August 1862) grew out of his desire to restore the Union with a minimum of damage to Southern society and especially to the institution of slavery. Ironically, his timid implementation of the plan helped prolong the war and accomplish exactly the results he wished to avoid. After advancing slowly to the outskirts of Richmond, McClellan lost his nerve and retreated after heavy attacks by Confederate forces under General Robert E. Lee.

The president now decided to withdraw McClellan's troops from the peninsula and from McClellan's command, transferring them to the army of Major General John

Seven Days' Battles, June 25 – July 1, 1862

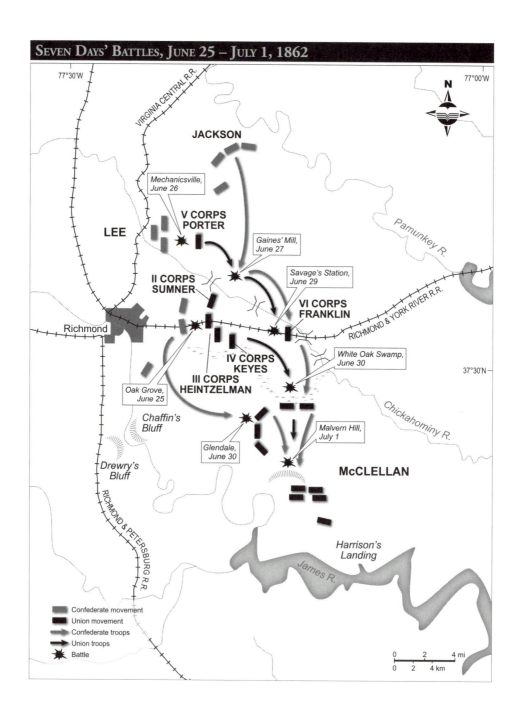

77°30'W

77°00'W

N

VIRGINIA CENTRAL R.R.

JACKSON

Pamunkey R.

Mechanicsville,
June 26

V CORPS
PORTER

LEE

Gaines' Mill,
June 27

II CORPS
SUMNER

Savage's Station,
June 29

VI CORPS
FRANKLIN

RICHMOND & YORK RIVER R.R.

Richmond

White Oak Swamp,
June 30

37°30'N

IV CORPS
KEYES

III CORPS
HEINTZELMAN

Oak Grove,
June 25

Chaffin's
Bluff

Chickahominy R.

Malvern Hill,
July 1

Glendale,
June 30

McCLELLAN

Drewry's
Bluff

RICHMOND & PETERSBURG R.R.

Harrison's
Landing

James R.

Confederate movement
Union movement
Confederate troops
Union troops
Battle

0   2   4 mi
0   2   4 km

Maj. Gen. George B. McClellan commanded Union forces early in the Civil War but his excessive caution may have cost the Union the chance to end the Civil War quickly and led to his removal from command. He ran against Abraham Lincoln for the presidency in 1864. (National Archives)

Pope in northern Virginia. McClellan moved so slowly in transferring them that Lee was able to defeat Pope at the Second Battle of Bull Run (August 29–30, 1862) before most of them arrived. Many leading Republicans suspected that McClellan and several of his loyal subordinates had hoped for just such an outcome. Still, with Pope's army demoralized and the victorious Lee advancing into Maryland, Lincoln believed he had little choice but to restore McClellan to command of the Union forces opposing Lee, hoping that McClellan's popularity with the soldiers would help restore morale.

McClellan's reinstatement did restore morale. Then a stroke of luck gave McClellan a complete copy of Lee's orders for the operation, showing that the Confederate army was spread out and vulnerable. Yet McClellan moved so slowly that Lee was able to regroup his forces and face him behind Antietam Creek in western Maryland. Although McClellan outnumbered Lee by about two to one at Antietam, he overestimated Lee's numbers by a factor of four, as he had done in all his previous operations. Holding almost half his force in reserve, on September 17, 1862, McClellan launched a series of piecemeal attacks that nearly succeeded in driving Lee into the Potomac River. In the end, McClellan allowed Lee to escape. Several weeks later, fed up with McClellan's slowness and lack of drive, Lincoln relieved him of command.

McClellan now plunged into Democratic Party politics and challenged Lincoln unsuccessfully in the 1864 presidential election. McClellan then traveled widely, worked as a civil engineer, wrote a patently self-adulatory memoir, and was governor of New Jersey during 1878–1881. He died in Orange, New Jersey, on October 29, 1885.

Steven E. Woodworth

Further Reading

Rafuse, Ethan S. *McClellan's War: The Failure of Moderation in the Struggle for the Union.* Bloomington: Indiana University Press, 2005.

Sears, Stephen W. *George B. McClellan: The Young Napoleon.* New York: Ticknor and Fields, 1988.

Meade, George (1815–1872)

George Gordon Meade was born in Cádiz, Spain, on December 31, 1815. His father was a U.S. naval agent, whose early death after finishing with one patient and beginning on another.

Nearly three out of four wounds were to arms or legs. The heavy, large-caliber bullets of the era shattered bones and opened hideous wounds in whatever part of a body they hit. Surgeons had little choice but to amputate mangled limbs. They worked without stopping for long hours after every battle. The surgeon, his helpers, and their tools became covered in blood, so that they looked more like butchers than like medical workers. The amputated limbs were tossed aside, and piled up outside the shelters where the surgeons labored. Federal surgeons could control a patient's pain during surgery by giving anesthetics, such as chloroform,

ether, or opium. The South had fewer supplies of all sorts. Confederate surgeons often operated on their patients without anesthetics. They tied the patients down, giving them gags or bullets to bite on to endure the pain; hence the expression, "bite the bullet."

If a wounded soldier survived surgery, he had about a one in five chance of getting an infection, which often proved fatal. The lightly wounded returned to their units to fight again. The badly wounded returned home, often living the rest of their lives maimed, crippled, and in severe pain.

Union and Confederate army medical officers—surgeons, assistant surgeons, stretcher-bearers, and hospital stewards—were assigned initially at the regimental

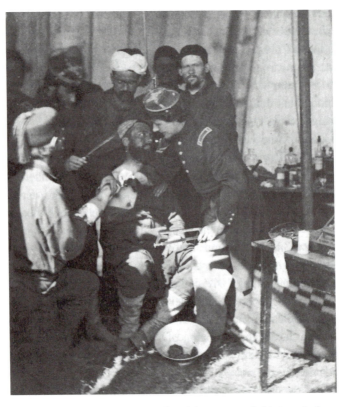

Zouaves tending a wounded soldier at a field hospital as the surgeon prepares to amputate his arm, 1861. (Library of Congress)

level, later at the divisional level. Some ten thousand medical officers served with the Union army during the war. Initially, medical officers were subject to capture, but by mid-1862, the opposing generals had agreed to treat all medical personnel as neutral.

At first, regimental band members, even the youngest drummer boys, removed the wounded from the field. Later, specialized ambulance corpsmen performed casualty clearance. They were the only military men, marked by white or yellow armbands, who were permitted to leave the field during combat. Leaving and returning repeatedly to the field of fire took enormous willpower.

The wounded were supposed to receive first aid where they fell, and then be transported to a field hospital, which could be a house or barn, or a hastily-erected tent. After treatment, patients went by train, boat, or wagon to a general hospital.

The Union army operated more than 200 general hospitals by war's end. Many were established in existing buildings, such as schools, hotels, or houses. The Confederates built Chimborazo Hospital in Richmond to accommodate the increasing overflow from its existing hospitals. Chimborazo had 250 buildings, making it the largest military hospital in the world, capable of housing 10,000 patients at a time.

Civilian surgeons staffed the hospitals, and volunteer nurses took up most of the slack in patient care. Dorothea Dix organized female nurses under the U.S. War Department. More than 3,000 women worked as nurses in Union hospitals, and an equal number of women worked in Confederate hospitals. They also tended the sick and wounded at field hospitals, and women living near battlefields took wounded soldiers into their homes and helped care for them. On both sides, after the bloody work of surgery was done, soldiers depended on dedicated nursing care to save their lives. The North had a central organization for volunteer hospital nurses under the U.S. War Department, while the South did not have such an organization.

Clara Barton, known to soldiers as "the angel of the battlefield," organized a medical supply service for the Union army collecting donations to buy the supplies and arranging their delivery to the battlefields. Dr. Mary Edwards Walker, only 20 years old when the Civil War began, spent three years as a nurse.

Having received her MD degree in 1855, Mary Walker sought a formal commission as a military surgeon when the Civil War broke out. When the Federal government agreed to hire her as a nurse, not a doctor, Walker volunteered her services instead. She tended to the sick and wounded first at the so-called Indiana Hospital, housed in the U.S. Patent Office, and later in the field at Warrenton, Virginia. (National Archives)

ironclad *Monitor*. Designed by John Erics-son, like the *Virginia* the *Monitor* was only just commissioned. The *Monitor* had but two guns—11-inch Dahlgren smoothbores in a single large turret protected by eight inches of iron plate. With only 18 inches of freeboard, the ship resembled a hat floating on the water. Lieutenant John L. Worden commanded a crew of 10 officers and 48 seamen. The men were exhausted from their two-day trip south from New York, during which the ironclad had nearly foundered on several occasions.

At about 9:00 p.m., the *Monitor* pulled alongside the frigate *Roanoke*, where Worden conferred with Captain John Marston, senior Union officer in the roads. Marston ordered Worden to defend the *Minnesota*, the Union fleet's flagship that had grounded while try-ing to evade the *Virginia* and seemed likely to be the Confederate ironclad's next target.

At about 6:00 a.m. on March 9, the *Vir-ginia* got under way. The sea was again calm and the day clear. Jones ordered the *Virginia* to make for the Union flagship. At 8:00 a.m., Worden saw the *Virginia* and its consorts steam out into the main channel and head for the *Minnesota*, and he immediately or-dered battle preparations. The *Monitor* was far more maneuverable than the *Virginia*, but it also was only a fraction of the Confederate ship's size and mounted but two guns to the ten on the *Virginia*.

Jones intended to ignore the Union iron-clad until he had finished off the *Minnesota* with hot shot. At about one mile from the grounded Union ship, Jones commenced fire. Almost immediately a round struck the *Minnesota* and started a fire. Shot from the *Minnesota*'s stern guns simply ricocheted off the *Virginia*'s armor. Worden now set the *Monitor* straight for the Virginia.

The *Minnesota* and *Virginia* exchanged fire until the *Monitor* had closed the range.

Its small pilot house forward prevented the Union ironclad's guns from firing directly forward, so Worden conned the *Monitor* par-allel to the *Virginia*. At 8:45 a.m., the *Moni-tor* fired the first shot of the battle.

The battle was fought at very close range, from a few yards to more than 100. The crew of the *Virginia* was surprised that the Union guns did not inflict greater damage. Not a single shot struck the *Virginia* at its vulnerable waterline. The Confederates be-lieved that the *Monitor*'s crew simply fired their guns as rapidly as possible (every five or six minutes) without aiming. The *Virginia* was also extremely vulnerable when it ran hard aground and the *Monitor*, with half the draft, could circle its antagonist and fire at will. With the *Virginia*'s very survival now at stake and its boiler safety valves tied shut to provide maximum steam, the *Virginia* at length pulled free.

Following two hours of battle, Worden disengaged to re-supply with ammunition, which had to be hoisted up from a storage bin below deck through a scuttle that re-quired the ship to be stationary. Jones took advantage of the respite to try to sink the *Minnesota*, but shoal water halted the *Vir-ginia* almost a mile away from its target. Nonetheless, shot from its guns did dam-age the Union flagship. The *Monitor* then returned, and the struggle between the two ironclads resumed.

With his fire having no apparent effect and unaware of the loss of his own ship's ram, Jones decided to ram and then board the Union ship. Seeing a chance, Jones ordered his ship forward at full steam, but Worden was able to turn the more nimble *Monitor* aside and it received only a glancing blow. The attempt actually hurt the *Virginia* more, opening up another hull leak. *Virginia* also sustained shell damage inflicted by the *Monitor* when the wooden backing behind the armor plate on the Confederate vessel cracked and splintered. Although the more numerous Confederate guns fired many more shot and shells than did the Monitor, only 24 struck and the only results were dents in the *Monitor*'s armor.

A few minutes after noon, Worden's attempt to ram the stern of the *Virginia* ended in a near miss. Just as the Union ship passed the stern of the *Virginia*, a 7-inch shell exploded in a direct hit on the *Monitor*'s pilot house, stunning and temporarily blinding Worden. He ordered the *Monitor* to sheer off to assess damage, and the ironclad drifted away toward Fort Monroe. Twenty-two-year-old executive officer Samuel Greene took command. Jones, meanwhile, decided to return to Norfolk for repairs. Greene declined to pursue, on account of his orders to protect the *Minnesota*. Each side subsequently claimed the actions of the other meant that its opponent was beaten.

The battle in fact was a draw. Aboard the *Monitor*, Worden was the only serious casualty, while the *Virginia* sustained two dead and 19 wounded. The fight might have gone differently had the *Virginia* concentrated its fire on the *Monitor*'s pilot house, a difficult target in the best of conditions, or if solid shot or bolts had been available for the rifled guns. On the other hand the *Monitor*'s fire should have been directed at its opponent's waterline. Its guns should also have employed 30-pound powder charges instead of the 15 pounds decreed. Following gun explosion in 1844, the Navy Department had decreed that no gun could be fired with a powder charge more than half that for which it had been designed. This order was revoked only after the *Monitor-Virginia* engagement. Ericsson was furious. He claimed that had the *Monitor* taken up position at 200 yards range with its guns exactly level and fired with the 30-pound charges he had sought,

that the shot would have gone clear through the *Virginia*.

Tactically, the engagement between the two ironclads was a Northern victory. The *Monitor* had saved the flagship *Minnesota*, assured the safety of the Union transports and supply ships, and hence the continuation of the Peninsula campaign. However, the South could claim a strategic victory, for as long as the *Virginia* remained in being, Norfolk and Richmond were safe from Union warships; and the *Virginia*'s mere presence acted as a brake on McClellan's drive toward Richmond.

The battle between the two ironclads was not renewed, but it did signal a new era in naval warfare. The first time that ironclad vessels had fought one another, it gave new impetus to the revolution in naval warfare then in progress. Both ships also became models for ironclad construction on their respective sides.

Spencer C. Tucker

Further Reading

Davis, William C. *Duel Between the First Ironclads*. Garden City, NY: Doubleday, 1975.

deKay, James T. *Monitor*. New York: Walker and Co., 1997.

Holtzer, Harold, and Tim Mulligan, eds. *The Battle of Hampton Roads: New Perspectives on the USS* Monitor *and CSS* Virginia. New York: Fordham University Press, 2006.

Johnson, Robert U., and Clarence C. Buel, eds. *Battles and Leaders of the Civil War*. Vol. 1. *From Sumter to Shiloh*. Secaucus, NJ: Castle, 1887.

Quarstein, John V. *C.S.S. Virginia: Mistress of Hampton Roads*. Appomattox, VA: H. E. Howard, 2000.

Smith, Gene A. *Iron and Heavy Guns; Duel Between the Monitor and Merrimac*. Abilene, TX: McWhiney Foundation Press, 1998.

N

Native Americans

On the eve of the Civil War, the small Union Army consisted mainly of a few western constabulary outposts used primarily for mapmaking, building roads, and the pacification of Native American tribes. As the war continued, the growing armies of the Union and, to a lesser extent, those of the Confederacy, continued to enforce Indian policies. For example, U.S. forces and volunteers saw action against the Sioux in Minnesota in 1862 and the Apache and the Cheyenne at Sand Creek on November 29, 1864 (the Sand Creek Massacre). Native Americans also actively supported both sides of the conflict in significant numbers. They participated in both conventional battles and guerrilla actions, often in an attempt to further their own tribal goals.

As many as 20,000 Native Americans took an active role in the Civil War. Even when they chose different sides, the reasons for their support were much the same. The poverty of many tribes and their dependence on the U.S. government for protection and survival encouraged their entry into the conflict. Tribes that had been effectively assimilated into the surrounding white populations usually supported the cause espoused by nearby settlers. Others were geographically located so as to be vulnerable to one side or the other. This latter was primarily the case for the Creek, Osage, and Seminoles in Indian Territory (around present-day Oklahoma); the Catawba of South Carolina; and the eastern band of the Cherokee in North Carolina, who became Confederate allies.

Many Native groups, such as the Cherokee who followed Stand Watie, one of their leaders and a Confederate Army brigadier general, hoped to avenge old grievances by joining the Rebel cause. Indeed, they hoped to settle a score with the tribal faction that had signed the 1835 Treaty of New Echota that removed them from their ancestral lands as well as with the U.S. government that had carried out the forced removal from their traditional homeland. A number supported the Confederacy simply because they themselves were slaveholders.

Native Americans participated in a number of conventional and unconventional military operations. In the March 7–8, 1862, Battle of Pea Ridge, Arkansas, then-colonel Stand Watie led the Cherokee Mounted Rifles in an assault to capture Union artillery batteries. When members of the 31st U.S. Colored Infantry of the Army of the Potomac fought at the July 30, 1864, Battle of the Crater at Petersburg, Virginia, they were met by Catawba warriors of the 17th South Carolina. Two Seneca brothers served the Union cause faithfully: Isaac Newton Parker was a noncommissioned officer in the 132nd New York State Volunteer Infantry, while his brother, Ely Samuel Parker, was a colonel on Lieutenant General Ulysses S. Grant's staff.

Throughout the war, Confederates formed four mounted infantry regiments from among the Cherokee, Chickasaw, Choctaw, Creek, and Seminole nations. The loyalties of the Cherokee Nation were particularly divided, as many of the original Confederate Cherokees eventually deserted to join the Union cause. Many Native Americans also

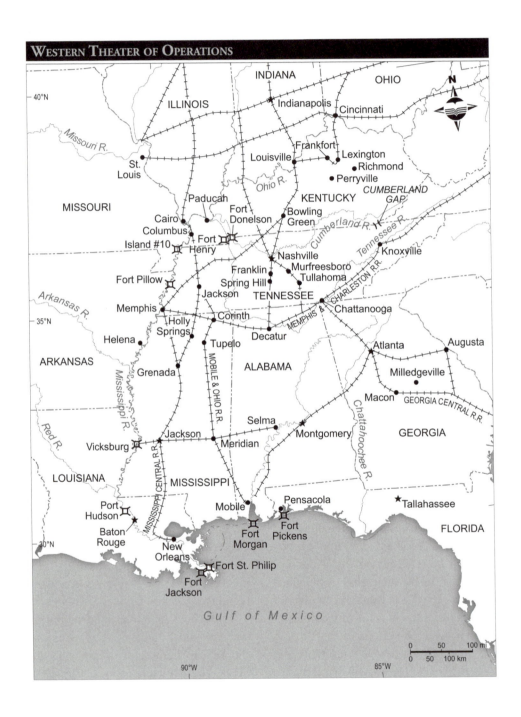

WESTERN THEATER OF OPERATIONS

provided valuable transportation services, as river pilots and individuals guarding vital lines of communications and the rail links critical to military operations.

A particularly sad chapter in U.S.–Native American relations during the war unfolded in the far southwest, involving the removal of the Mescalero Apache and Navajo peoples from the District of Arizona. Beginning in October 1862, colonel of volunteers Christopher "Kit" Carson was ordered to move against the Mescalero Apache and Navajo, round them up, and relocate them to the Bosque Redondo Reservation in the eastern part of the New Mexico territory. The forced removal was deemed necessary for white settlement and development in Arizona. Carson was encouraged to embark on a scorched earth policy in order to move the Natives as quickly as possible.

By the winter of 1863, most of the Mescalero Apache had been captured and moved to the reservation; most went peacefully. However, the Navajo proved more troublesome, and when a December 1862 delegation of Navajo was rebuffed by American officials, they vowed not to surrender and began a running fight with Carson's forces. Throughout most of 1863, Carson employed brutal tactics to subdue the Navajo, including the destruction of most of their villages and crops.

By late December 1863, Carson's men had cornered the remaining Navajo fighters in Arizona's Canyon de Chelly. On January 6, 1864, with the remaining Navajo trapped in a frigid and snowy canyon, Carson led his men in a brutal assault against them. The Canyon de Chelly Campaign, which ended on January 16, resulted in 23 Navajos killed and 34 captured. An additional 200 capitulated. By March 1, 1864, some 11,500 Navajo had been rounded up, held at Fort Canby, and then force-marched 400 miles to the reservation. As many as 3,000 Navajo died of starvation, disease, and abuse along the way, and another 2,000 were dead within two years on the tiny reservation.

The legacy of Native American participation in the American Civil War was generally a tragic one. For the Cherokee, Creek, Chickasaw, Choctaw, and Seminole—collectively referred to as the "Five Civilized Tribes"—treaties signed after the war provided for huge territorial concessions, and the continued erosion of tribal authority and the physical integrity of their nations. Even though many Cherokees had fought for the Union, the provisions of a July 19, 1866, treaty with the federal government required the tribe to cede parcels of land as railroad right-of-ways, relinquish a four-mile-wide strip of land that ran the entire length of that nation's border with Kansas, and to allow the U.S. government to settle "friendly Indians" west of 96 degrees longitude without the permission of the Cherokee National Council.

Other tribes signed treaties with similar provisions that produced a growing Native American dependence on the federal government. At the conclusion of the war, the U.S. Army could devote even greater efforts to supporting pacification, detribalization, and assimilation policies in regard to all Native Americans. Indeed, the U.S. government pursued these policies generally without regard for the affiliations Native Americans had expressed during the Civil War.

Deborah Kidwell

Further Reading

Abel, Annie. *The American Indian in the Civil War, 1862–1865.* Lincoln: University of Nebraska Press, 1992.

Colton, Ray C. *The Civil War in the Western Territories.* Norman: University of Oklahoma Press, 1984.

Fischer, Leroy H. *The Civil War Era in Indian Territory.* Los Angeles: L. L. Morrison, 1974.

Confederate ordnance consisted mostly of prewar U.S. Navy guns, a large number of which were captured at the Norfolk Navy Yard. With only a small number of ships, Confederate requirements in this area were far more modest than those of the Union. The South did produce an ordnance designer of genius in Lieutenant John Mercer Brooke. His rifled guns were probably the best of their type in the war.

At the start of the war, the Confederacy announced its intention to send out privateers. But decisions by the European states, led by Great Britain, denied the Confederacy the right to bring prizes into their ports, so any captures would necessarily have to be returned to the South. Getting them through the Union blockade would not be easy. Soon the Union Navy rounded up the few privateers that got to sea. Mallory wanted not private ships but government cruisers, and these carried the brunt of the war against Union commerce. Although he never gave up commerce raiding altogether, increasingly Mallory shifted to a more defensive strategy that involved smaller ironclads and increasing use of torpedoes and the means to deliver them.

The four best-known Confederate high seas commerce raiders were the *Sumter* (the first Confederate raider), *Florida* (*Oreto*), *Alabama*, and *Shenandoah*. During the period August 1862 to June 1864, the *Alabama*, captained by Raphael Semmes, cruised the Atlantic, Caribbean, and the Pacific all the way to India. It sailed 75,000 miles, took 66 prizes, and sank the Union warship *Hatteras* off Galveston. Two dozen Union warships were diverted to search for it, and its exploits were a considerable boost to Confederate morale. In June 1864 off Cherbourg, France, the *Alabama* fought one of the war's more dramatic naval battles but was sunk by the U.S. Navy screw steam sloop *Kearsarge*. The *Shenandoah* continued its depredations after the end of the war, devastating the Union whaling fleet. Captain James Waddell eventually sailed the *Shenandoah* to England, the only Confederate warship to circumnavigate the globe.

Although commerce raiders exacted a toll on Union merchant shipping, in the end the Confederacy benefited from it only in a negative and indirect way. The Union Navy was forced to divert some naval assets into hunting down the raiders, but Secretary of the Navy Gideon Welles resisted pressures to dilute the blockade. Confederate commerce raiding, therefore, succeeded mainly in contributing to the decline of the U.S. merchant marine, as many ships were transferred to foreign flag registry. Most did not return after the war.

Above all, Mallory embraced ironclads, but this was a contest that the South could not win. Securing iron plate was a constant problem, as was transporting it over the inadequate Confederate railroad system. Most Confederate ironclads built during the war followed the design of the casemated *Virginia*, the ex-U.S. steam frigate *Merrimack* that had been scuttled at the Norfolk Navy Yard by withdrawing Union forces, then raised and rebuilt by the Confederates as an ironclad ram. Mallory arranged for the building of 34 casemated ironclads, of which only 21 were actually commissioned. There were also some 20 cruisers, of which the most famous were the *Alabama*, *Florida*, *Nashville*, *Shenandoah*, and *Sumter*; a dozen spar torpedo boats; 43 government-owned blockade runners; and a large number of river and coastal defense vessels. In addition, the Confederacy arranged for the purchase abroad of 5 seagoing ironclads (although only the *Stonewall* was ever commissioned).

Significant naval warfare occurred on the great inland rivers, especially the Mississippi, but also notably the Cumberland, Tennessee, and Red Rivers. Throughout, the Confederacy found itself outnumbered and outgunned. After the Union capture of Vicksburg on July 4, 1863, however, the river war in the West was all but over. The North did make a major foray up the Red River the next year. It turned out to be a major Union fiasco, but not because of any Confederate naval activity.

Although the Confederates did win some naval battles along the Gulf Coast, most notably at Galveston, Texas on January 1, 1863, for the most part it was a pattern of steady defeat. Along the Atlantic Seaboard, Mallory's hopes that the *Virginia* might be able to break the Union blockade and even threaten Northern ports proved illusory. Ultimately, most Confederate naval activity was defensive in nature to contest Union amphibious operations but also to attempt to drive the blockaders off station. Blockade running centered on such ports as Wilmington, Charleston, Savannah, and Galveston. As the North gained increasing control of key coastal points, however, such activity became increasingly problematic.

The record of the Confederate States Navy during the Civil War was a mixed one, yet its contributions were significant. The Confederate navy never succeeded in its chief aim of breaking the blockade, which indeed became more effective as the war progressed. Nonetheless, the Confederacy certainly made effective use of the meager resources it did possess. As with the army, it was simply overwhelmed by Union numbers and manufacturing advantage.

Kenneth J. Blume and Spencer C. Tucker

Further Reading

Brooke, George M., Jr., ed. *John M. Brooke: Naval Scientist and Educator*. Charlottesville: University Press of Virginia, 1980.

Bulloch, James D. *The Secret Service of the Confederate States in Europe, or How the Confederate Cruisers were Equipped*. New York: Modern Library, 2001.

Dalzell, George W. *The Flight from the Flag: The Continuing Effect of the Civil War upon the American Carrying Trade*. Chapel Hill: University of North Carolina Press, 1940.

Luraghi, Raimondo. *A History of the Confederate Navy*. Translated by Paolo D. Coletta. Annapolis, MD: Naval Institute Press, 1996.

Scharf, J. Thomas. *History of the Confederate States Navy*. New York: Gramercy Books, 1996. [Reprint]

Still, William N., Jr., ed. *The Confederate Navy: The Ships, Men and Organization, 1861–65*. Annapolis, MD: Naval Institute Press, 1997.

Still, William N., Jr. *Iron Afloat: The Story of the Confederate Armorclads*. Columbia: University of South Carolina Press, 1985.

Tucker, Spencer C. *Blue and Gray Navies: The Civil War Afloat*. Annapolis, MD: Naval Institute Press, 2006.

Navy, Union

Naval power played a central role in Federal planning from the beginning of the war and contributed substantially to the Union's defeat of the Confederacy. "At all the watery margins," President Abraham Lincoln commented in referring to the men of the navy, "they have been present. Not only on the deep sea, the broad bay, the rapid river, but also up the narrow muddy bayou, and wherever the ground was a little damp, they have made their tracks."

Secretary of the Navy Gideon Welles headed the Union naval effort. Welles, who was from Connecticut, had during 1846–1849 been chief of the Naval Bureau of Provisions and Clothing. An efficient administrator, he turned out to be one of Lincoln's best cabinet choices. Welles had the final decision on ship construction, purchases, and conversions. He also determined the broad outlines of naval policy, and he oversaw the conduct of operations. President Lincoln was interested in naval matters, as he was in all activities of the federal government, but his chief preoccupation was with the army and he rarely interfered in naval matters. Welles and able Assistant Secretary of the Navy Gustavus Vasa Fox (a new position created early in the war) worked well together, with Welles making all major decisions regarding strategy. Fox's day-to-day management of the department kept it functioning smoothly.

A major part of the story of the U.S. Navy during the Civil War is its growth in terms of ships, materiel, and personnel. The navy began the war in April 1861 with but 90 ships on the Navy Register, of which 21 were unseaworthy, 27 were laid up in naval yards for extensive repairs or not yet launched, and 28 were on foreign stations, far from the rivers, harbors, and coastlines of the United States. Only 14 ships were actually on Home Station: seven screw steamers, three sailing frigates, one side-wheeler, two store ships, and one steam tender. During the war, the Navy Department ordered some 200 new warships (not all were completed during the war) but it also purchased or leased another

The North's industrial and technological prowess came to the fore with the design of the revolutionary ironclad, the *Monitor*. This photograph shows dents in the *Monitor*'s turret inflicted by the *Virginia*'s shot. (National Archives)

418 vessels. By the end of 1861, the fleet had swelled to 264 ships, and by the end of the war, it numbered 671, the largest navy in the world next to that of Great Britain.

The Civil War occurred during a period of great change in naval technology. Steam power, ironclad warships, and more powerful ordnance were transforming naval warfare. To meet the crisis of secession, the U.S. Navy not only expanded rapidly but also built many technologically advanced or innovative warships. Most famous of these was the revolutionary *Monitor*. Although successful for its purpose, it had only limited use outside coastal waters, but nonetheless became the model for subsequent Union ironclad construction. Other noteworthy designs were the *Unadilla*-class "90-day gunboats"; the "double-enders" (side-wheel gunboats with rudders at each end so that the vessel could operate backward or forward in narrow rivers); the experimental ironclad *New Ironsides* (patterned on the French La *Gloire* and a far more practical design for coastal operations than the monitors); and the monster ram *Dunderberg,* which was not completed until after the war's end and was then sold to France.

In addition to a rapid expansion of the fleet, the numbers of personnel swelled rapidly, from 7,600 in 1861 to 51,000 in 1865. The war, in effect, solved the long-standing promotion bottleneck that had plagued the antebellum navy but, in turn, created a postbellum "hump." Among noteworthy officers, whose fame was reinforced or ensured as a result of the war, were David Glasgow Farragut, Andrew Hull Foote, Samuel F. Du Pont, David Dixon Porter, and John Dahlgren.

The navy's tripartite strategic mission was shaped by geographical realities, military necessities, political and diplomatic limitations, and Confederate policies. Lincoln followed the broad outlines of Lieutenant General Winfield Scott's so-called Anaconda Plan to starve the South into submission by controlling the Confederacy's three main maritime borders and then bisecting it with large Union armies. Welles concentrated the bulk of Union naval resources on the naval blockade of the South.

The distances and problems presented by the blockade were considerable. From Alexandria, Virginia to the Rio Grande in Texas, the Southern coastline extended more than 3,500 miles. Indeed, for much of this distance, the outer banks presented a double coastline. There were 189 harbors, river mouths, or indentations that would have to be guarded. The Mississippi and its tributary rivers counted 3,615 miles and sounds, bayous, rivers, and inlets along the Atlantic and Gulf coasts constituted another 2,000 miles. The Union blockaders were also handicapped by the fact that the largest Southern ports boasted substantial defensive works of stone or brick.

Apart from the blockade, the navy's chief duties would be to support army operations ashore and to hunt down and destroy Confederate privateers (at the beginning of the war) and commerce raiders on the high seas. Union navy riverine operations were a crucial part of the Anaconda Plan. River duties typically included operations against Confederate gunboats, the reduction of Confederate forts and batteries, transportation of troops, and amphibious raids against Confederate lines of communication. Important naval support of army operations occurred on the James, York, Potomac, Ohio, Tennessee, Cumberland, Mississippi, and Red Rivers. Strategically, the most critical riverine operations took place on the Mississippi, and securing control of that great river was a central Union military objective, as this would cut off the trans-Mississippi west from the remainder of the Confederacy.

Union naval operations in the West were initially under the army, which paid for the first warships there. However, naval officers provided overall command. Flag Officer Foote, who worked well with his army counterpart Brigadier General Ulysses S. Grant, won the first big Union victory in the West, at Fort Henry on the Tennessee River in February 1862. After the follow-on Union victory (essentially won by Grant) at Fort Donelson on the Cumberland, Foote operated on the upper Mississippi, attempting to push through to Nashville.

At the same time, Flag Officer Farragut led Union naval forces in assaulting the Mississippi's mouth. His squadron ran past the Confederate forts and took New Orleans in April 1862. Securing Vicksburg proved more difficult. It resisted Union efforts until July 1863, but ships under Rear Admiral David D. Porter played a key role in Grant's land victory there. Army-Navy cooperation in the West had, for the most part been excellent, especially between Grant and Foote and Grant and Porter, Foote's successor. Fighting continued in the West and along the Gulf coasts, however. The 1864 campaign up the Red River, a fiasco hatched in Washington, was marked by poor army-navy coordination. Union operations against Galveston and other points along the Texas coast were also largely unsuccessful. In August 1964, Farragut won the last great contest on the Gulf coast, and the most sanguinary naval battle of the war, Mobile Bay.

The best-known Civil War naval battle was that in the East, in Hampton Roads, part of the 1862 Peninsular Campaign against Richmond. In the first clash between two ironclad ships in history, on March 9, 1862, the *Monitor* fought to a draw with the CSS *Virginia*. Both sides claimed victory. The battle was not renewed and both ships were soon lost, the *Monitor* to a severe storm and

the *Virginia* scuttled to prevent capture. The battle had tremendous significance for subsequent warship construction with each side building ironclad ships of their type.

Most Union naval assets were devoted to blockade duties. Ultimately the blockaders were divided into four separate naval commands: the North Atlantic, South Atlantic, East Gulf, and West Gulf Blockading Squadrons. From mid-1861 until the end of the war in April 1865, Union blockading operations focused systematically on closing off centers of Confederate blockade running and trade. Important blockade-related naval operations included Hatteras Inlet in August 1861; Port Royal in November 1861; the capture of New Orleans in April 1862; the battle of Mobile Bay in August 1864; and amphibious operations against Charleston (1863–1865) and Fort Fisher (December 1864–January 1865). Although blockade runners continued to get through to the end of the war, the Union blockade was nonetheless an important factor in the Union victory. It starved the South with its poor manufacturing base of such essential supplies as railroad iron and steam engines, leading to the breakdown of the Southern transportation and distribution systems. This adversely impacted Southern soldiers and civilians alike. For the Union sailors involved, blockade duties typically saw extended periods of tedium broken only by the occasional chase or engagement.

Although Welles came under considerable criticism from Northern business interests for what was perceived to be his lack of attention to the problem, the navy did send out warships to sink or capture the Confederate commerce raiders. Necessarily this effort was the lowest Union naval priority. Confederate Secretary of the Navy Stephen Mallory had hoped that Southern commerce raiding would draw off substantial numbers of Union warships from the blockade, but Welles refused to take the bait. Nonetheless, dozens of Union warships were committed to the effort. Unfortunately for them, the Atlantic and Pacific were vast areas in which the raiders could hide. Although Confederate commerce raiding did force large numbers of Union merchant ships into foreign ownership and drove up shipping rates, it did not have the effect that the Confederates had hoped. Eventually, Union warships hunted down such raiders as the *Florida* and *Alabama*. The most spectacular of these engagements occurred on June 19, 1864, when the Union screw steam sloop *Kearsarge* sank the Confederate raider *Alabama* off Cherbourg, France.

Union efforts on the high seas occasionally had unfortunate effects. In November 1861 overzealous U.S. Navy Captain Charles Wilkes of the USS *San Jacinto* precipitated a major diplomatic crisis by overhauling the British mail steamer *Trent* and removing two Confederate envoys, James Mason and John Slidell. War with Britain loomed but Lincoln was determined to avoid it, and the so-called *Trent* Affair was ultimately resolved peacefully with the release of the two commissioners.

Finally, mention should be made of the tremendous Union naval logistical effort, both to support its own blockading efforts and to supply the army in amphibious operations. Critical in this was the decision taken by Washington early in the war to secure bases from which the blockading squadrons could operate. The Union Navy demonstrated great ability in setting up and maintaining repair and supply facilities as well as putting together the vast logistics network supplying coal, food, and essential military supplies. This impressive effort goes largely unmentioned in most histories of the war.

Kenneth J. Blume and Spencer C. Tucker

Further Reading

Anderson, Bern. *By Sea and by River: The Naval History of the Civil War*. New York: Knopf, 1962.

Canney, Donald L. *Lincoln's Navy: The Ships, Men and Organization, 1861–65*. Annapolis, MD: Naval Institute Press, 1997.

Musicant, Ivan. *Divided Waters: The Naval History of the Civil War*. New York: HarperCollins, 1995.

Niven, John. *Gideon Welles, Lincoln's Secretary of the Navy*. New York: Oxford University Press, 1973.

Porter, David D. *The Naval History of the Civil War*. New York: Sherman, 1886 (reprint, Secaucus, NJ: Castle, 1984).

Roberts, William H. *Civil War Ironclads: The U.S. Navy and Industrial Mobilization*. Baltimore, MD: Johns Hopkins University Press, 2002.

Tucker, Spencer C. *Blue and Gray Navies: The Civil War Afloat*. Annapolis, MD: Naval Institute Press, 2006.

News of the War

Civilians eagerly awaited news from the front, whether by mail or newspaper. The national newspapers reported on the conduct of the war and the results of each engagement, but the casualty lists printed in the local papers held the greatest interest. Soldiers, too, looked to newspapers to get a wider perspective on what they had experienced on the battlefield.

Northern newspapers did not hesitate to criticize Union officers in print, or to publish details about the size and location of the armies, and many editors saw it as their duty to do so. Confederate generals had access to smuggled northern newspapers and benefited from this widely available intelligence. General William T. Sherman vehemently objected to the carping presence of reporters near his army. He complained in a letter to his brother: "I cannot pick up a paper but tells of our situation here . . . the busy agents of the press follow up and proclaim to the world the whole thing, . . . and all the real effects of surprise are lost." However, the same newspapers published stories lionizing Sherman when his fortunes turned.

Southern newspapers, beset by paper shortages, could not publish as many copies or issues as the Northern papers. Nor could they afford the quality of illustrations published by such Northern weeklies as *Harper's* and *Frank Leslie's Illustrated Newspaper*. Foreign correspondents, such as William Russell of the *London Times*, were frequently sympathetic to the South, although not answerable to the Confederate government.

More than 30 military artists traveled with both Union and Confederate armies to create eyewitness drawings of the battles. Newspaper publishers made woodcut engravings from the drawings, which allowed them to be mass-produced. In their haste to record the action, some artists and publishers resorted to repetition, and one can find the same faces or scenes appearing in pictures of supposedly different battles.

Alfred Waud and Winslow Homer became famous for the pictures they drew for the weekly Northern newspapers. Also well known were Alfred Waud's brother William and Thomas Nast.

An English artist, Frank Vizetelly, traveled with both the Union and the Confederate armies to draw scenes for a London newspaper.

The *New York Herald's* wagon in the field near Bealton, Virginia, in August 1863. Newspapers played a vital role for both the Union and the Confederacy during the Civil War. Whether they were agitating for or against slavery or reporting battlefield details, newspapers served as lightning rods for public opinion, informing both the public and government leaders alike. (Library of Congress)

Although photography had been possible since the late 1830s, the technology did not yet exist to mass-produce photographs for publication. Mathew Brady and his many assistants, including Timothy O'Sullivan and Alexander Gardner, were among the first photographers to travel with the Union armies, hauling their heavy equipment in horse-drawn wagons. Civil war photographers traveled with bulky cameras and portable darkrooms, which existed in the form of tents mounted on wagons. The cameras and plates of the era required at least 30 seconds of exposure time, during which the subject had to remain motionless. Photographers rushed to develop the plates before the images faded away.

Although photography was too slow to capture battle action on film, thousands of Civil War photographs show camps and buildings, individual or group portraits, posed scenes, and corpses on the battlefields. Mathew Brady and his assistants took more than 3,500 photographs. Traveling with the army to record the war was dangerous work. Brady later said, "No one will ever know what I went through to secure those negatives." His vivid photographs of the battlefield carnage brought the reality of war home to the civilian population for the first time in history. Most of Brady's photographs are preserved at the Library of Congress and the National Archives.

Finally, Civil War soldiers left an unprecedented number of letters and journals, many of which have been preserved and published.

Roberta Wiener

Further Reading

Coopersmith, Andrew S. *Fighting Words: An Illustrated History of Newspaper Accounts of the Civil War.* New York: W. W. Norton & Co., 2004.

Meredith, Roy. *Mr. Lincoln's Camera Man: Mathew B. Brady.* New York: Charles Scribner's Sons, 1946.

Russell, William H. *My Diary North and South.* Philadelphia: Temple University Press, 1987.

Sherman, William T. *The Sherman Letters: Correspondence between General and Senator Sherman from 1837 to 1891.* New York: Charles Scribner's Sons, 1894.

Officer Corps

When war began in the spring of 1861, neither side was ready to fight. Professional soldiers understood this fact. Civilians and politicians did not. The young northern and southern volunteers needed time to make the change from civilian to soldier. They needed time to learn how to march and to fight. There were hardly enough professionals to teach them these fundamentals.

In 1861, there were only about 16,000 professional, or regular, soldiers in the entire United States Army. Most of them were in the west where they fought the Indians. About 15,000 of the regular soldiers were enlisted men. Only 26 of them deserted to join the Confederate Army. The rest stayed loyal to the United States. They represented a valuable cadre of professional soldiers who could train the volunteers. Instead, the Federal government blundered by keeping the existing regular units intact and not using the professional enlisted men as trainers.

There were 1,080 army officers on active duty when the war began. Six hundred and twenty were from the North and 460 from the South. All but 16 of the Northern-born officers stayed loyal to the Union. The 16 who left the U.S. Army were all married to Southern women. Of the officers from the South, about two-thirds of them left the U.S. Army to join the Confederacy while one-third remained loyal to the Union side. The Union-loyal, Southern-born officers, such as the gifted George Thomas, had to overcome prejudice from the War Department to gain promotion.

Both sides employed retired West Point graduates to help meet the huge demand for experienced officers. These proved a mixed blessing. For example, the 34-year-old George McClellan had resigned in 1857 to pursue business opportunities. Thus his knowledge of war was up to date when he returned to the army. In contrast, Leonidas Polk had graduated from West Point in 1827, gone on furlough, and decided to discard his uniform to become an Episcopal minister. Since that time he had neither studied war nor seen a battle. Yet, when "Bishop" Polk offered his services to the Confederacy, Davis made him a general and assigned him to command the defense of the Mississippi River. Polk's subsequent strategic blundering unhinged the entire Confederate defense of the west.

To help make up the shortfall in experienced officers, both sides used foreign trained officers. They, too, proved a mixed blessing. Some showed great merit. Irish-born Patrick Cleburne served as a noncommissioned officer in the Royal Army before emigrating to Arkansas. He developed into one of the South's outstanding combat generals. Alfred Duffié was a St. Cyr graduate and combat veteran. He came to the United States at war's onset and secured the rank of captain in the 2nd New York Cavalry. Duffié's impressive resume eventually led to divisional command, yet he never exhibited any notable leadership qualities. Cleburne and Duffié illustrate the variety of talent provided by foreign-educated officers.

Moreover, for every capable foreign-trained leader there were two or three like

Vicksburg and skillfully foiled all of Grant's attempts during those months.

Then, in April 1863, Grant launched a new campaign, sending his gunboats and transports past Vicksburg, then crossing his army into Mississippi below the town and marching for Jackson, squarely in Vicksburg's rear. Despite his advantage in overall numbers within the state of Mississippi, Pemberton was distracted by diversions Grant planned and was unprepared for the speed and boldness of his opponent's campaign. Pemberton's response was confused and hesitant. Ordered by Johnston to pull all his troops out of fortresses and combine them for an open-field battle against Grant in the interior of the state, Pemberton started to do so. Then he received a cryptic telegram from Davis that Pemberton interpreted to mean he was not to leave Vicksburg or Port Hudson ungarrisoned at any time. Returning the garrisons, he set out to meet Grant with a reduced field army. Grant met and defeated him at the Battle of Champion Hill, May 16, 1863, and defeated him again the next day at Big Black River Bridge. What was left of Pemberton's field army fled back into the fortifications of Vicksburg. Grant followed and laid siege. On July 4, 1863, Pemberton was forced to surrender.

With no suitable command available at his rank, Pemberton resigned his lieutenant general's commission and became a colonel in the artillery. After the war, he retired near Warrenton, Virginia, and then returned to Pennsylvania, where he died at Penllyn on July 31, 1881.

Steven E. Woodworth

Further Reading

Ballard, Michael B. *Pemberton: A Biography*. Jackson: University Press of Mississippi, 1991.

Shea, William L., and Terrence J. Winschel. *Vicksburg Is the Key: The Struggle for the Mississippi River*. Lincoln: University of Nebraska Press, 2003.

Peninsula Campaign

After winning a minor success at Rich Mountain, in western Virginia, authorities in Washington summoned 35-year-old George B. McClellan to the capital to assume command of the Division of the Potomac. Soon thereafter, McClellan replaced the aged and infirm Winfield Scott as commander of all Union armies. McClellan ably undertook the complex task of organizing and training the Army of the Potomac. When Confederate General Joseph E. Johnston's army withdrew from Manassas Junction, McClellan received permission to begin what became known as the Peninsula Campaign. McClellan's plan called for moving his army by water to Fort Monroe of the tip of the so-called peninsula between the York and James Rivers. From there he would advance up the Peninsula and capture the Confederate capital at Richmond. On March 17, 1862, the movement began.

On April 4, McClellan's infantry began a cautious advance up the Peninsula until they encountered Confederate defenses at the Warwick River. Although Union forces outnumbered the Confederates by at least four to one, McClellan refused to press his advantage and instead began siege operations. His caution allowed Confederate reinforcements to arrive on the Peninsula. By May 3 McClellan had assembled some 112,000 men. Johnston had slightly over 60,000. Confronting such daunting odds, Johnston decided to retreat to the fortifications on the outskirts of Richmond. Two days later, McClellan began a cautious pursuit that led to a inconclusive fight, the Battle of Williamsburg, against the Confederate rear guard. More importantly, Johnston's retreat compelled the Confederates to evacuate Norfolk and scuttle the ironclad *Virginia*.

McClellan had expected additional reinforcements from the forces operating in northern Virginia. Instead, Confederate General Thomas "Stonewall" Jackson conducted a masterful diversionary offensive in the Shenandoah Valley that caused Union authorities to retain units earmarked to assist McClellan for the defense of Washington. The absence of these reinforcements increased McClellan's caution. His slow pursuit finally brought the Army of the Potomac to Johnston's defensive position protecting Richmond by the end of May.

Because McClellan expected General John Pope's army to advance from Fredericksburg and join him outside of Richmond, McClellan occupied a position straddling the Chickahominy River. Johnston, in turn,

saw that McClellan could be attacked and defeated in detail. He conceived a good plan, but in the ensuing Battle of Fair Oaks, also called Seven Pines (May 31, 1862), poor Confederate staff work undid his plan. The result was a frustrating series of blunders that cost the attacking Confederates about 6,000 men while McClellan lost about 5,000. Most importantly, Johnston was severely wounded during the battle. Robert E. Lee replaced him.

During June, McClellan reverted to a methodical approach against the Confederate fortifications. Lee, in turn, summoned Jackson from the Shenandoah Valley. Even though he was still badly outnumbered, when Jackson arrived, Lee began a ferocious series of attacks against McClellan.

The ensuing combats became known as the Seven Days' Battles: Oak Grove, June 25; Mechanicsville, June 26; Gaines's Mill,

A 12-pound howitzer gun captured by Butterfield's Brigade near Hanover Court House, during the Peninsula Campaign, May 27, 1862. (Library of Congress)

opposing lines diverged, often with a mile or more of no man's land between them. This region featured a tangle of woods, swamps, and streams. It was in this area that Grant made repeated attempts to turn Lee's right flank and cut the Confederate rail communications. These attempts produced a series of fierce encounters that lasted until the onset of winter.

One notable Union attempt to break through the Confederate center came on July 30, 1864. Union miners had dug a tunnel underneath the Confederate defenses and filled it with gunpowder. When the mine exploded, Union troops attacked. The ensuing Battle of the Crater was another Union debacle, featuring poor leadership and bad staff work. It cost Grant's army about 4,400 casualties.

On August 18–19, 1864, Grant continued to extend his siege lines around Petersburg in order to cut Lee's lines of communication. When Grant occupied the Weldon Railroad, the Confederates unsuccessfully counterattacked. The occupation of the Weldon Railroad meant that only one rail line, the Southside Railroad, remained to supply Petersburg. On August 25, 1864, Grant's effort to cut the Southside Railroad collapsed in the face of a determined Confederate attack at the Battle of Reams's Station. It was becoming ever clearer that the offensive capacity of Grant's army was much reduced due to the accumulation of casualties and the brilliance of Lee's defensive measures. However, as the Union line slowly extended to the west, Lee had to extend his line to match it. With almost all his available manpower tied to the

Railroad gun and crew in Petersburg, Virginia, ca. 1864–1865. (Library of Congress)

fortifications of Richmond and Petersburg, Lee had nothing left with which to deliver one of his famous offensive strikes. In addition, relentless Union pressure caused steady attrition within the Confederate ranks.

Grant's next effort to turn Lee's left flank produced the Battle of Peeble's Farm (September 30–October 2) followed by Hatcher's Run (October 27). Neither of these offensives produced decisive results. The two armies largely suspended operations for the winter months, although there was another battle along Hatcher's Run at Dabney's Mills on February 5–7, 1865. Aggressive until the end, Lee attempted a surprise offensive against Fort Stedman on March 25, 1865, but he simply had too few resources to support such an effort. The end came for Petersburg on April 1, when General Phil Sheridan defeated the Confederate forces at Five Forks, a strategic crossroads located west of the city. The next day, Grant launched his final assault against Petersburg, but Lee had already concluded that he had to evacuate. The entire Petersburg Campaign from June 1864 to April 1865 cost the Union about 42,000 casualties and the Confederates about 28,000. The fall of Petersburg led to Grant's vigorous pursuit and Lee's surrender at Appomattox Court House on April 9, 1865.

James R. Arnold

Further Reading

Arnold, James R. *The Armies of U.S. Grant.* London: Arms and Armour Press, 1995.

Boatner, Mark M., III. *The Civil War Dictionary.* New York: David McKay Co., 1959.

Catton, Bruce. *The Army of the Potomac: A Stillness at Appomattox.* Garden City, NY: Doubleday & Company, Inc., 1953.

Hess, Earl J. *In the Trenches at Petersburg: Field Fortifications and Confederate Defeat.* Chapel Hill: University of North Carolina Press, 2009.

U.S. Military Academy. *The West Point Atlas of American Wars, Volume I, 1689–1900.* New York: Frederick A. Praeger Publishers, 1959.

Polk, Leonidas (1806–1864)

Leonidas Polk was born on April 10, 1806, in Raleigh, North Carolina, into a socially, politically, and militarily prestigious family. Polk's third cousin, James K. Polk, was president of the United States. Polk attended the U.S. Military Academy, West Point. His roommate was Albert Sidney Johnston and he also knew cadets Jefferson Davis and Robert E. Lee. Six months following his graduation in 1827, Polk resigned his commission as a second lieutenant to enter the Virginia Theological Seminary.

Following his ordination and because of his social position and family name, Polk rose quickly in the Episcopal Church, becoming missionary bishop to the Southwest in 1837. In 1841 he was named bishop of Louisiana. Polk played a key role in the establishment of the Episcopal University of the South in Sewanee, Tennessee. With the secession of the Deep South, Polk was instrumental in the Louisiana Convention leaving the Episcopal Church of the United States. In June 1861 Polk secured from Davis, now president of the Confederacy, a commission as a major general, despite the fact that he had never held a command and had been out of the army for more than 30 years. Polk proved an extraordinarily poor choice.

Many Northern newspapers ran stories expressing outrage that a man of the cloth would be engaging in active warfare, but Polk never had any difficulty combining his religious beliefs with a willingness to fight. Indeed he relished his title of "the Fighting Bishop."

Although Union forces repulsed Jackson at Chantilly on September 1, 1862, Pope had been totally out-maneuvered during the campaign. Pope then compounded his failure and unpopularity by blaming his defeat at Second Bull Run on officers who were still loyal to McClellan and by searching for a scapegoat. He found one in General Fitz John Porter, who in Pope's mind had failed to attack Jackson's flank as ordered. Porter was subsequently court-martialed and cashiered in a celebrated trial. Lincoln, however, faced with Lee's impending invasion of Maryland, had little recourse but to remove Pope from command and reappoint McClellan.

In the fall of 1862, Pope was reassigned to the Department of the Northwest, and he arrived in Minnesota to direct operations against the Santee Sioux under Little Crow. Subsequent moves by Henry H. Sibley and Alfred Sully eventually crushed the Sioux uprising and restored peace to the region. By January 1865, Pope was in charge of the Department of the Mississippi, and two months later, he received a brevet promotion to major general of regulars for the capture of Island No. 10.

After the war, Pope gained a measure of notoriety during Reconstruction by championing civil rights for former African American slaves. While commanding the Third Military District, encompassing Alabama, Georgia, and Florida, he restricted press activity to silence anti-Reconstruction criticism. Eventually, Pope's talent for military administration asserted itself, and he redeemed his reputation as a general. Over the next two decades, he held a variety of commands throughout the West and participated in several successful Indian wars. His forces enjoyed considerable success against the Apache under Geronimo, but he also labored incessantly to keep land-hungry white settlers, or "boomers," out of the Indian Territory.

Pope also ignited controversy by condemning the Bureau of Indian Affairs for its treatment of Native Americans. He argued that the reservation system should be a military jurisdiction and therefore less susceptible to corruption and inefficiency. Pope also felt that gifts and annuities for the tribes were little more than bribery for good behavior. A better solution would be to deal fairly with Indians on reservations and educate them with a view toward assimilation. Pope retired from the army in March 1886 and died in Sandusky, Ohio, on September 23, 1892.

A fine administrator, John Pope's abrasive personality alienated subordinates and masked his leadership abilities.

John C. Fredriksen

Further Reading

Cozzens, Peter, and Robert I. Girandi, eds. *Abandoned by Lincoln: A Military Biography of Major General John Pope*. Urbana, IL: University of Illinois Press, 1990.

Cozzens, Peter, and Robert I. Girandi, eds. *The Military Memoirs of General John Pope*. Chapel Hill: University of North Carolina Press, 1998.

Porter, David Dixon (1813–1891)

U.S. Navy admiral David Dixon Porter was born in Chester, Pennsylvania, on June 8, 1813, the third of 10 children of Commodore David Porter, who had distinguished himself in the War of 1812. Porter's adopted brother was David G. Farragut. Porter first went to sea with his father at age 10. After brief service as a midshipman in the Mexican Navy serving under his father, in which he was wounded and briefly a prisoner of war of the Spanish, Porter joined the U.S. Navy as a midshipman in February 1829. He became a passed midshipman in July 1835 and made lieutenant in February 1841. Routine assignments included service in the Mediterranean.

Porter distinguished himself during the Mexican-American War (1846–1848), especially in operations against Tabasco. Frustrated by the slow rate of advancement in the U.S. Navy, Porter took leave of absence to captain merchant vessels.

Returning to duty with the navy in 1855, he received command of the steamer *Supply* and then served ashore at the Portsmouth Navy Yard during 1857–1860. He was on the verge of a second leave of absence from the navy when the secessionist crisis occurred.

On April 1, 1861, Porter received command of the powerful sidewheel frigate *Powhatan*. He circumvented both Secretary of the Navy Gideon Welles and commander of the Brooklyn Navy Yard Captain Andrew H. Foote in carrying out Secretary of War William H. Seward's plan to relieve Fort Pickens in Florida. This removed the *Powhatan* from participation in the effort to relieve Fort Sumter but probably did not in itself scuttle that operation. Despite his having disobeyed orders, Porter received promotion to commander on April 22.

The *Powhatan* then conducted operations in the Gulf. Early in 1862 Porter returned to Washington, where he convinced Welles and Assistant Secretary of the Navy Gustavus V. Fox that bombardment of the two Confederate forts on the lower Mississippi by a flotilla of mortar boats would be essential to the success of a plan to capture the port of New Orleans. He pledged that both forts would be rendered ineffective by shelling from 13-inch mortars within 48 hours.

Receiving command of the mortar flotilla under the overall command of his foster brother and commander of the West Gulf Coast Blockading Squadron Flag Officer David Farragut, Porter carried out a six-day

bombardment of Forts Jackson and St. Philip, which failed to reduce the forts. Farragut then ran past the forts with the ships of his squadron, while Porter supplied gunfire support. With the two forts then cut off by the Union ships and troops, Porter took their surrender on April 28.

On October 15, 1862, now an acting rear admiral, Porter assumed command of the Mississippi Flotilla, now designated the Mississippi Squadron. Naval activity then sharply increased with the initiation of joint operations against Vicksburg. In January 1863 Porter helped secure Arkansas Post. Porter worked closely and effectively with Major General Ulysses S. Grant and Brigadier General William T. Sherman. Porter was rewarded for his role in the surrender of Vicksburg with advancement to permanent rear admiral over many other more senior officers, with a date of rank of July 4, 1863.

In the spring of 1864, Porter commanded the naval phase of the Red River Expedition, supporting army troops ashore under Major General Nathaniel P. Banks in an effort to capture Shreveport. Banks and Porter did not get along but low water levels in the Red, in part caused by Confederate efforts, was the most serious problem to plague Porter. Despite myriad problems, Porter succeeded in extraditing his ships and was not blamed for the fiasco. Still, the abortive Red River Campaign was one of the great military blunders of the war.

In September 1864 Porter assumed command of the North Atlantic Blockading Squadron. That December he assembled the most powerful naval force to that point in U.S. history: 61 warships, including 5 ironclads, mounting a total of 635 guns for an attack on Fort Fisher in an effort to close off the port of Wilmington to Confederate blockade runners. The initial assault went poorly, thanks to ineffective cooperation on the part of the pools. Ten percent of the prisoners perished in a single winter month.

The worst prison in the North was at Elmira, New York. It often flooded and a pool of sewage stood at the center of the prison. There was only one stove to warm each group of 200 prisoners. At its peak occupancy, the prison held over 12,000 men. Ten prisoners died each day.

Over all, about 25,976 Confederate and 30,218 Union soldiers died while being held prisoner. About 2,000 on each side managed to escape from prison, often by digging tunnels.

Roberta Wiener

Further Reading

Katcher, Philip. *The American Civil War Source Book*. London: Arms and Armour Press, 1992.

Pickenpaugh, Roger. *Captives in Grey: The Civil War Prisons of the Union*. Tuscaloosa: University of Alabama Press, 2009.

Ransom, John L. *Andersonville Diary*. Middlebury, VT: P.S. Eriksson, 1986.

R

Railroads

On the eve of the Civil War, there were more than 200 railroads in the United States, most of which were located in the states remaining loyal to the Union. In 1860, the United States had 30,626 miles of track and two-thirds of this was in the North. Many of these lines served to connect the essentially agricultural western states with the East, helping to cement the west economically and politically with the Union cause.

Most northern railroads were interconnected and had converted to a standard rail gauge (4′ 8.5″ in width), enabling trains from different companies to use the same tracks. The South, in contrast, had gauges that varied widely from one railroad company to another, impeding long-distance transport of goods and people. The existence of more extensive and efficient northern rail lines meant that the Union could transport many more troops and supplies to more places and with far fewer transfers than could the Confederacy.

Railroads proved to be of great strategic importance during the Civil War in the supply of the large field armies. Trains traveled at least five times faster than mule-drawn or horse-drawn wagons, which meant that men or supplies moving by train usually arrived at the front in timely fashion as well as in good condition. Also, trains were far less affected by poor weather, and were rarely waylaid by rain or snow storms. By contrast, wagons mired down on unpaved roads if the weather was wet, and the mules that pulled the wagons were themselves consumers of the fodder that was one of the chief items needed to supply a Civil War army. Beyond a certain distance, wagons became useless as supply vehicles since their teams would, in effect, have eaten their entire payload. Railroads suffered from none of these drawbacks.

Railroads expanded the geographical range of military operations and allowed warfare on a near-continental scale. Now armies could conduct campaigns that would have not have been possible with wagon-train logistics. With increased ease of resupply, field forces could also grow in size.

Leaders on both sides in the war realized the importance of the railroads to their own operations and to those of the enemy. The July 21, 1861, First Battle of Bull Run (Manassas) was precipitated by the Union desire to control the important southern rail center at Manassas Junction, Virginia, as a first step in an advance on the Confederate capital of Richmond. Union Brigadier General Irvin McDowell, commanding a large and ill-prepared Union force, moved southwest from Washington D.C. toward Manassas, where an equally untrained Confederate force under Brigadier General P.G.T. Beauregard awaited him. Fortunately for Beauregard, Confederate Brigadier General Joseph E. Johnston was able to elude Union troops under Brigadier General Robert Patterson and bring 10,000 men to Manassas from the Shenandoah Valley in a movement that was partially effected with the aid of rail transport. It was the first such rail-borne troop movement in U.S. history. Johnston joined Beauregard the day before the battle, and his troops played a decisive role in its outcome.

destroyed Southern railroad facilities everywhere they went. Indeed railroads were one of Sherman's chief targets, and the smoke of bonfires made of crossties marked his progress across the southeastern states. Sherman's men used the standard Civil War procedure for destroying track. After tearing up a section, the men piled the ties and set fire to them. Then they heated the rails over the blazing bonfires until the middles of the rails were red-hot and pliable. Finally teams of men took each end of the heated rail and bent it double around a tree or telegraph pole, forming the famous "Sherman neckties."

Railroads were beyond doubt an invaluable strategic resource that helped to secure the Northern victory in thee war. Without them, the war would have lasted longer and been even more costly in terms of lives lost.

Kathleen Warnes

Further Reading

Angevine, Robert G. *The Railroad and the State: War, Politics, and Technology in Nineteenth Century America.* Stanford, CA: Stanford University Press, 2004.

Pickenpaugh, Roger. *Rescue by Rail: Troop Transfer and the Civil War in the West, 1863.* Lincoln: University of Nebraska Press, 1998.

Turner, George E. *Victory Rode the Rails: The Strategic Place of the Railroads in the Civil War.* Indianapolis, IN: Bobbs-Merrill, 1953.

Weber, Thomas. *The Northern Railroads in the Civil War, 1861–1865.* Bloomington: Indiana University Press, 1999.

Reconstruction

Reconstruction refers to the post–Civil War policies of the U.S. government toward the former Confederate states of the South. These policies dictated the terms by which Southern states could rejoin the Union and reassert their full political and civil rights under the U.S. Constitution.

The Reconstruction period was divided into two phases. Presidential Reconstruction, during 1865–1867, was the period when President Abraham Lincoln and his successor, President Andrew Johnson, guided the federal government's policy toward the South. Both Lincoln and Johnson favored a moderate policy that would allow the Southern states to rejoin the Union quickly and without enacting substantial changes to their political, economic, or social structures.

After Lincoln's assassination in April 1865, Johnson was unable to maintain sufficient congressional or public support for those policies. Presidential Reconstruction ended in March 1867, when a newly elected Congress, dominated by Radical Republicans, opened its session. This second phase, which was known as Radical Reconstruction and lasted from 1867 to 1877, was guided by such vengeful congressional leaders as Thaddeus Stevens and Charles Sumner. The Radical Republicans' goal was to punish white Southerners for rebelling against the Union and to elevate African Americans in the South to alleviate the effects of slavery. By passing several substantial pieces of legislation, Congress hoped to enact significant political, economic, and social change in the South and restructure Southern society.

The federal government had only limited success with its plans, primarily because of political infighting in the North among Radical Republicans, Republicans, and Democrats. In addition, white Southerners worked diligently to undermine the effects of legislation and exert local control over Southern society. Reconstruction paved the way for blacks to be enfranchised for the first time, but it generated enormous anger among whites. Largely as a result of compromises surrounding the presidential election of 1876, by 1877, all the former Confederate states had been readmitted to the Union and federal troops withdrew from the South. Thus the Reconstruction Era came to an end.

James R. Arnold

Further Reading

Donald, David, and J. G. Randall. *The Civil War and Reconstruction*. New York: W. W. Norton: 2001.

McKitrick, Eric L. *Andrew Johnson and Reconstruction*. 1988. Reprint, New York: Oxford University Press, 2002.

Simpson, Brooks D. *The Reconstruction Presidents*. Lawrence: University of Kansas Press, 1998.

Rosecrans, William Starke (1819–1898)

Born in Delaware County, Ohio, on September 6, 1819, William Starke Rosecrans graduated from the U.S. Military Academy at West Point in 1842. He entered the Corps of Engineers, but in 1854 he left the army to pursue a career in business and engineering.

In 1861, Rosecrans joined the staff of Major General George B. McClellan. He rose to the rank of brigadier general in May 1861, and as McClellan's chief subordinate was the real author of most of the success in the fall 1861 campaign in western Virginia, although McClellan appropriated all of the credit. An embittered Rosecrans then sought transfer to the western theater.

Assigned to the Army of the Mississippi, Rosecrans participated in the slow advance toward Corinth, Mississippi. After the capture of Corinth, May 30, 1862, Rosecrans rose to command the Army of the Mississippi,

which remained in northern Mississippi under the overall command of Major General Ulysses S. Grant. Rosecrans waged a partly successful operation at Iuka (September 19).

In October, Major General Sterling Price's army, combined with one of similar size under Major General Earl Van Dorn, moved to recapture Corinth, which Grant had charged Rosecrans with defending. The Confederate attack came October 7–8, 1862. Rosecrans handled his troops poorly and showed signs of panic. Nevertheless, the stubbornness of his troops secured victory. Rosecrans made no attempt to pursue the defeated Confederates until it was too late, and Grant never forgave Rosecrans for this second lapse within a month.

Seeing Corinth as a victory, President Abraham Lincoln tapped Rosecrans to take over the army that Major General Don Carlos Buell had mismanaged during the just-concluded Kentucky Campaign. On October 27, 1862, Rosecrans assumed command and christened it the Army of the Cumberland.

Rosecrans knew Lincoln expected aggressive action. A few weeks later, when he learned from a Chattanooga newspaper that a Confederate army under General Braxton Bragg had been weakened by the transfer of one-fourth of its infantry to Mississippi, Rosecrans determined to attack. He met Bragg's army just outside Murfreesboro, Tennessee, along the banks of Stones River, on December 31, 1862. Bragg moved first, seizing the initiative and nearly defeating the Army of the Cumberland at the Battle of Stones Rivers. Rosecrans responded with an inspiring performance. His refusal to acknowledge defeat earned Rosecrans victory. Following the battle, the Confederates retreated about 40 miles to Tullahoma.

The victory, coming in the midst of Union defeats, was a political godsend for Lincoln,

When the Civil War began, Gen. Winfield Scott was head of the U.S. Army. He contributed to overall federal strategy during the war's early days, but proved too old to continue as general-in-chief. (Historic Print & Map Company)

enjoyed the status of his military rank and dressed accordingly in suitably ornate uniforms. His nickname also indicates Scott's temperament. Along with the status of rank Scott expected similar deference from those under his command. An ambitious man, Scott was easy to insult, hesitant to put past differences behind him, and made enemies easily, including his political superiors (whom he viewed as meddlers in military affairs) and military colleagues (whom he viewed as potential competitors). Scott had lengthy feuds with Andrew Jackson, as both general and president, and with several high-ranking army officers. These feuds, however, did not prevent Scott from becoming commanding general of the army

in 1841 when, as senior officer, he assumed the post on the death of Major General Alexander Macomb.

Scott's greatest military achievements came during the Mexican-American War. Triggered by American interest in securing Mexico's territory of California, the American annexation of Texas, and a subsequent dispute over the Texas-Mexico border, the war provided President James K. Polk an opportunity to fulfill his manifest destiny campaign pledges. Scott, however, already had personality clashes with the president. Polk kept Scott in Washington, D.C., as his personal military adviser instead of letting him take command of the U.S. Army in the field, lest he become a war hero. That job went to Brigadier General Zachary Taylor. To his credit Scott assisted Taylor in his early campaigns while at the same time constantly agitating to get a field command himself. In time, however, Taylor's victories made him a potential political rival to Polk as well, and when a plan developed to invade central Mexico, Polk was left with the distasteful choice of appointing either Taylor or Scott to lead it. Polk decided the best political course of action was to get Scott out of Washington, and in November 1846 Scott headed for New Orleans to take command of the invasion force.

In March 1847, Scott began his Mexican campaign with a major amphibious landing at Veracruz. He seized the city and prepared to move out of the coastal lowlands before the malarial season began. The Mexican Army, however, tried to contain Scott in the lowlands by blocking the road to Mexico City at Cerro Gordo with a force half again as large as Scott's 8,000-man force. Scott used a diversionary action to hold the Mexicans while the bulk of his force looped to the north and fell upon the Mexican left flank, forcing the enemy to retreat in disarray and leave most of their artillery behind. Consolidating his army at the town of Puebla, Scott was confronted with the reality that the term of service of seven of his volunteer regiments was to end in June, and most of the men were determined to leave. Scott let them go and waited for reinforcements, which arrived in the form of future president Franklin Pierce's division in early August.

Scott then pressed forward toward Mexico City. Though he had managed to avoid major battles to this point, now Scott had to destroy the Mexican Army before he could enter the city itself. Clashing with Antonio López de Santa Anna at the Battle of Contreras, the Battle of Churubusco, and the Battle of Molino del Rey, Scott achieved major victories but with high casualties. Santa Anna retreated into Mexico City and prepared a last-ditch defense, leaving Scott to ponder which heavily defended causeway he wanted to attack in order to gain access to the city. Scott chose the most direct route, opting to attack the fortified Mexican position at Chapultepec, on high ground overlooking Mexico City from the southwest. On September 13, Scott began a confused and violent assault upon Chapultepec that left 103 Americans dead and 703 wounded but forced the Mexicans from the heights. Scott immediately rushed into Mexico City and claimed it as Santa Anna retreated to the north. The loss of Mexico City forced the Mexicans to recognize that the war was over, and peace negotiations, supervised by Scott and Polk's negotiator Nicholas Trist, began some weeks later. The subsequent Treaty of Guadalupe Hidalgo ended the war on March 10, 1848, and Scott led the last U.S. troops out of Mexico in mid-June.

In the meantime, however, Scott had to assume the duties of military occupation, setting an example for occupation duties in the future. Scott cracked down on common crime by U.S. soldiers and Mexican civilians alike, placed an assessment on the city to pay for civil services, and courted the favor of the Catholic Church in order to placate the Mexican populace. His administration of occupied Mexico was so successful that a group of Mexican landowners wanted to make Scott dictator of Mexico; Scott declined. This time of victory, however, was ruined by squabbling over the glory and credit for success. The controversy centered on General Gideon Pillow, one of Polk's political appointees whom Scott hated (Pillow had been Polk's prewar law partner), who sent reports to the president and secretary of war that claimed most of the credit for the victory for himself. Incensed, Scott ordered Pillow to amend his reports, but Pillow refused. Even worse, the "Leonidas letter," an anonymous letter that seemed to support Pillow's version of events, appeared in various newspapers. Scott, as it turned out correctly, presumed that Pillow was behind the note and moved to prefer charges of court-martial against Pillow. Scott charged Pillow with violating army regulations against officer correspondence with newspapers, plus the theft of two small Mexican howitzers that Pillow appropriated as personal war trophies. Pillow and other officers with Democratic allegiances countered with charges against Scott. The resulting court of inquiry proved an embarrassment, and, when the court dismissed the most serious charges against all involved, the whole sorry affair came to an end.

Scott spent his last years in the military service of his country writing, lecturing, and trying to secure the legacy of his victory in Mexico. In 1852, the Whig Party persuaded him to run for president against his former subordinate, the Democrat Franklin Pierce, but Scott lost the election by a generous

Assuming command of a division in Grant's Army of the Tennessee, Sherman distinguished himself in the Battle of Shiloh, where he was slightly wounded. Promoted to major general of volunteers in May, he developed a close friendship with Grant and by that summer was Grant's principal subordinate. Sherman participated in Halleck's Corinth Campaign and then the effort to take Vicksburg, where he was rebuffed in fighting north of the city at Chickasaw Bluffs. Sherman then led XV Corps of the Army of the Mississippi and took part in the capture of Arkansas Post. After his corps transferred to the Army of the Tennessee, Sherman aided Grant in the capture of Vicksburg, for which he was promoted to regular army brigadier general in July.

When Grant took charge in the western theater, he assigned Sherman command of the Army of the Tennessee in October 1863. Sherman then led the Union left wing in the Battle of Chattanooga. When Grant became Union Army general-in-chief, Sherman took command of the Military Division of the Mississippi in March 1864, for all practical purposes overall command of the western theater.

With his armies of the Cumberland, the Tennessee, and the Ohio, Sherman launched a campaign against General Joseph E. Johnston's Confederate Army of the Tennessee in May 1864, driving toward Atlanta. Sherman made steady, if slow (100 miles in 74 days), progress against the able delaying tactics of Johnston. Then, General John Bell Hood replaced Johnston and launched a series of attacks. Sherman defeated all of them and then captured Atlanta on September 2. His capture of Atlanta had immense strategic consequences and assured Lincoln's reelection. For this accomplishment, Sherman received the thanks of Congress and a promotion to regular army major general.

Destroying such military stocks as would not be of use to him and detaching part of his force to deal with Hood in Tennessee, Sherman began his March to the Sea on November 16, 1864. He was very much a modern general in the sense that he practiced total war. He believed that destroying property would likely bring the war to a speedier end than would the taking of lives. He encouraged his armies to forage liberally off the land, cutting a wide swath of destruction through Georgia. Reaching the coast, his forces occupied Savannah on December 21, 1864.

Turning northward, Sherman began a drive through the Carolinas in mid-January 1865, taking Columbia, South Carolina, on February 17. The city was burned, but retreating Confederate troops rather than Sherman were probably to blame. Sherman then accepted the surrender of the last Confederate field army under General Johnston, near Durham Station, North Carolina, on April 26.

Following the war, in June 1865, Sherman took command of the Division of the Missouri. When Grant was promoted to general in July 1866, Sherman was advanced to lieutenant general, and when Grant became president in March 1869, Sherman moved up to become commanding general of the army as a full general. During his years in command, the army successfully ended many of the wars with Native Americans in the West. Here a chief concern was to protect the railroads. He also practiced against the Native Americans the same sort of war he had in 1864–1865, seeking to destroy food stocks and other resources in order to bring the fighting to a speedier conclusion. At the same time, however, he strongly opposed speculators and corrupt Indian agents who profited at Native American expense.

On June 19, 1879, Sherman delivered his "War Is Hell" speech at West Point. As commanding general, he took a deep interest in professionalism and in military education, establishing the School of Application for Infantry and Cavalry (today the Command and General Staff College) at Fort Leavenworth, Kansas, in 1881. He also encouraged the publication of military journals. He stepped down as commanding general on November 1, 1883. He retired from the army on February 8, 1884, and lived in New York City. His two volumes of memoirs, *The Memoirs of General William T. Sherman*, are, like the man who wrote them, plain-spoken and direct. Sherman refused to run for president on the Republican ticket in 1884 and died in New York City on February 14, 1891. An intelligent and aggressive commander who is often credited with originating modern total war, Sherman was also an able administrator and a notable military reformer.

Spencer C. Tucker

Further Reading

Kenneth, Lee. *Sherman: A Soldier's Life*. New York: HarperCollins, 2001.

Marszalek, John F. *Sherman: A Soldier's Passion for Order*. New York: Free Press, 1993.

Sherman, William T. *Memoirs of General William T. Sherman*. 2 vols. Reprint. Bloomington: Indiana University Press, 1957.

Shiloh, Battle of

The Battle of Shiloh (also known as the Battle of Pittsburg Landing) took place along the banks of the Tennessee River at Pittsburg Landing, some 23 miles north of the strategic town of Corinth, Mississippi. The battle derived its name from a small Baptist church named Shiloh.

The battle followed a string of Union victories along the Mississippi, Cumberland, and Tennessee Rivers. Stung by defeats at Fort Henry (February 6, 1862) and at Fort Donelson (February 13–16) and the loss of Nashville (February 25), commander of Confederate Department No. 2 General Albert Sidney Johnston was determined to engage and defeat the Federals. He called for a concentration of forces so he could attack and reclaim the initiative.

The strategy promulgated by his counterpart, Major General Henry Halleck, was to send forces down the Mississippi but also sever Confederate railroad lines across the region and take the town of Corinth, Mississippi, a key railhead. Halleck ordered Major General Ulysses S. Grant and his army (soon to be named the Army of the Tennessee) to link up with Major General Don Carlos Buell's Army of the Ohio, which was marching from Nashville. The two would then operate together in a joint offensive south against Corinth. Seizing the town would sever two important Confederate railroads: the west-east Memphis & Charleston, which connected Mississippi, Memphis, and Richmond, and the north-south Mobile–Ohio Railroad.

Grant's six divisions of nearly 39,000 men arrived at Pittsburg Landing. Grant pushed his men two miles inland on the west bank of the river, where they set up camp and waited for Buell's forces. Buell, in turn, was delayed by heavy rains. Grant's troops were loosely arrayed near Shiloh Church. Grant, however, had neglected to send any reconnaissance parties to ascertain Confederate strength. Here and later, Grant was more preoccupied with his own offensive plans. As a result, defensive arrangements had been largely ignored. By early April, Grant's 39,830 men were scattered throughout the area, with no attempt having been made to form any sort of battle line or even throw up rudimentary earthworks.

Federal perspective, although criticized for his lack of preparation, Grant had proven himself an aggressive commander. (When asked to sack Grant, President Abraham Lincoln retorted, "I cannot spare this man; he fights.") Along with Antietam, Vicksburg, and Gettysburg, Shiloh was one of the key battles of the entire war.

Rick Dyson

Further Reading

Daniel, Larry J. *Shiloh, the Battle That Changed the Civil War*. New York: Simon and Schuster, 1997.

Frank, Joseph A. *Seeing the Elephant: Raw Recruits at the Battle of Shiloh*. Westport, CT: Greenwood, 1989.

Roland, Charles P. *Albert Sidney Johnston: Soldier of Three Republics*. Austin: University of Texas Press, 1964.

Smith, Timothy B. *The Untold Story of Shiloh: The Battle and the Battlefield*. Knoxville: University of Tennessee Press, 2006.

Slavery

The most brutal institution in American history, slavery existed in the United States from the early 17th century until 1865, when Congress enacted the Thirteenth Amendment shortly after the Union victory over the Confederacy in the Civil War. By that point, more than four million African American slaves lived in the United States. Although their communities thrived and multiplied, these people were subject to harsh living conditions and enjoyed none of the rights or freedoms so fiercely protected by white Americans.

Native Americans were the first enslaved people in North America. Many aboriginal societies had practiced different forms of slavery for thousands of years before they had ever seen Europeans. The practice, how-ever, represented a temporary condition and was used more as a badge of status than a moneymaking enterprise. Most Indian slaves were women and children either purchased or captured as prizes in warfare. Some were adopted into their new tribe over time, their offspring being free persons who could even rise to positions of leadership. Slavery, therefore, was not a hereditary condition, nor was it based on race.

Europeans continued the practice of enslaving Indians after their arrival in the New World in the late 15th century. Spanish, English, and French colonists broadened the scope of Indian slavery by selling Indians, including men, into bondage in other colonies as punishment for warfare or rebellion. The Spanish in particular erected a vast system of slave labor in its colonies in Latin America.

The English and French enslaved Native Americans much less frequently and seldom held Indian slaves to labor among them. Rather, they sold Indian captives south to the West Indies, as Connecticut colonists did to surviving Native American women and children following the Pequot War of 1636–1637, which virtually annihilated the Pequots from New England. The system of chattel slavery that developed in the New World and focused on African Americans was different than the slavery practiced against Native Americans. The first group of African slaves, numbering four men and women, arrived aboard a Dutch ship at Jamestown, Virginia in 1619.

English planters like John Rolfe quickly realized the enormous profits to be had from importing unfree laborers. Rolfe's introduction of a viable tobacco plant in Virginia served as a major impetus for the adoption of African slavery as the region's main labor system. Tobacco was an extremely labor-intensive crop, requiring field hands to spend long hours bending over plants under the blazing hot sun. Some white indentured servants were forced to work in the fields, but as the 17th century progressed, it proved more and more difficult to convince Europeans to immigrate under these conditions.

African slaves solved many of these problems. Physically, Africans were more used to such brutal weather conditions and capable of laboring in them for longer periods than whites. As African slaves represented a diversity of nations and spoke a wide variety of languages, they also found it difficult to communicate with one another and organize resistance to their forced bondage. And unlike the Native Americans, Africans were too far from their homeland to run away from their white masters. Finally, some West African leaders proved extremely receptive to the idea of selling other Africans into slavery for profit, so that most of the kidnapping of Africans and forcing them into bondage was actually done by other Africans, requir-

ing even less effort on the part of whites to perpetuate the system. For all these reasons, African slavery quickly emerged as a desirable and profitable labor system.

Throughout the course of the 17th century, the various British North American colonies enacted a series of laws and social conventions that served to entrench African slavery at the heart of colonial society, particularly in the South. Although African slavery spread to all of the colonies, it never took hold in the northern colonies as it did in the southern, primarily because of the nature of the work required. Northern colonies were populated with small family farms, and the rocky terrain proved inhospitable for crops like tobacco. Slaves certainly existed in the northern colonies but not in nearly such large numbers as in their southern counterparts.

During the colonial period, nowhere did slavery become more firmly entrenched than in Virginia, and the slave system that Virginia developed during this period served as a model for all other slave societies in the

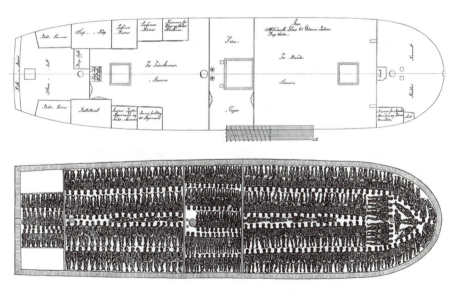

Deck plan of a slave ship, showing how captured Africans were arranged as cargo, 1700s. (North Wind Picture Archives)

were taught such trades as carpentry or blacksmithing. Some slaves even became preachers, presiding over many of the religious aspects of slave life.

Religion, in fact, was a pillar of African American life during this period. Whites had long boasted that slavery allowed them an opportunity to Christianize African "heathens," and many whites actively encouraged the spread of religion among slaves, pushing in particular Biblical injunctions for slaves to obey their masters and accept their condition in life. As with other aspects of slave culture, African Americans accepted Christianity but modified it, combining with it some aspects of traditional African religions. Because slaves were prohibited by law from learning how to read or write, slave preachers played a particularly important role in African American religion and were often the center of slave communities.

In recent years, historians have focused more attention on the dynamics of slave communities and whether or not the majority of slaves accepted their condition in life or worked to undermine their bondage. A series of slave rebellions and revolts throughout American history, most notably the Stono Rebellion of 1739 and Nat Turner's Rebellion of 1831, alarmed whites and illustrated that not all slaves complacently accepted their status. Currently, though, historians have been hypothesizing that a majority of slaves most likely sought to undermine the system through a series of small, passive aggressive acts—like working as slowly as possible in the fields or surreptitiously ruining crops. For many, such acts were the only way to show their discontent without suffering tremendous retribution at the hands of their masters.

Short of fomenting a rebellion, the most common measure to undermine the institution of slavery was for a slave to run away. Some fled to Native American communities in the West, which sometimes offered a haven for African Americans. Others made the arduous journey to Canada. Still others opted to take their chances in the North, hoping to melt into one of the many communities of free African Americans living in Northern cities.

The chance of recapture was extremely high, both for those in flight and those who fled to the North. Slaves caught attempting to run away met with particularly harsh punishments, sometimes even death, at the hands of Southern authorities. Some Southern communities even maintained slave patrols, complete with tracking dogs, to discourage runaways. Slave catchers—privately employed agents who returned slaves to their masters for a fee—were particularly feared among slaves for their brutality.

Despite the often cruel conditions of slavery, American slaves enjoyed a higher standard of living than any other enslaved people, and even higher than many of the laboring, free classes around the world. Natural increase of the American slave population, through high birth rates and relatively low death rates, was marked throughout slavery's existence.

By the outbreak of the American Revolution, more than half a million slaves lived in the British colonies, almost all of them in the South. As tobacco proved less and less profitable, however, slavery seemed to be on the decline. The delegates at the Continental Congress even briefly discussed abolishing slavery, although strenuous objections form Southern delegates, whose constituents had enormous sums tied up in slave property, brought such talk to a close quickly.

The idea that the colonists could be fighting the British for their freedom at the same time they held half a million people in bondage troubled many Americans, but the issue of race played a tremendous role in assuaging their consciences. For centuries, Africans had been seen as an inferior people, and most white Americans, in both the North and South, managed to convince themselves that slaves were better off and better cared for in bondage than they would be with their freedom.

Adhering to the belief that slavery was an important aspect of American life, the delegates of the Constitutional Convention enshrined the institution of slavery in the U.S. Constitution in 1787, ensuring its continuance in the United States despite any qualms Americans might be feeling about it. However, the convention did incorporate a ban on the international slave trade, to be implemented in 1808. This ban on importation did little to lessen the strength of slavery as an institution, however, as the slave population in America was thriving on its own accord, and the lack of new imports served to keep the price of slaves high.

By this point, slavery had geographically split the country, with the Southern states relying on it heavily while many of the Northern states abolished it or passed laws to phase it out. Many Americans in both regions thought that slavery would eventually disappear from the entire country, as it was becoming less profitable for Southern tobacco planters.

In 1793, however, Eli Whitney invented the cotton gin, a labor-saving machine that transformed cotton from a ridiculously high-labor crop into a profitable one. Growing cotton still required a tremendous amount of labor, but its rewards proved greater after the advent of the cotton gin.

Almost immediately, settlers pushed into the southwest to establish large cotton plantations in Mississippi, Louisiana, and Georgia. Into these new regions, they took thousands of slaves, purchased from failing tobacco planters in Virginia who were happy to convert their slave property into ready cash. Suddenly, the institution of slavery was reborn, reestablishing itself as the backbone of Southern financial interests once again. With the South emerging as one of the chief cotton regions of the world, slavery was more entrenched than ever.

The spread of slavery to new states ignited a "fire bell in the night," according to the elderly Thomas Jefferson in 1820. Jefferson in the 1770s had attempted to put slavery on a course of destruction. However, by the first decades of the 19th century, Jefferson, like other leading Southern statesmen, proclaimed the need to protect the institution to save the Southern way of life. Indeed, slavery became the most abiding and powerful symbol of that way of life.

Increasingly, Northern and Southern politicians came to view each other as members of hostile camps, representing two opposing images of American life: one based on free labor and the other based on slave labor. As a result, the issue of admitting new states that either prohibited slavery or allowed it emerged as one of vital political significance. Southerners saw the admission of a free state as a tangible sign of growing Northern political power, and vice versa. The advent of a vocal and controversial abolition movement in the North only heightened Southern fears of a plot to destroy slavery and the South's political power.

The result was increasing sectional tension between the two regions as more and more territories petitioned for statehood in the federal Union during the first half of the 19th century. The adoption of a series of compromises, most notably the Missouri Compromise of 1820 and the Compromise of 1850, only offered temporary relief for these tensions, which eventually culminated in the secession of 11 Southern states and the outbreak of the Civil War in 1861.

During the war, U.S. president Abraham Lincoln adhered to his position that the conflict was not over slavery but rather the issue of states' rights and the sanctity of the federal Union. In 1862, he issued the Emancipation Proclamation, which freed all slaves in the rebelling states. Although abolitionists praised the move, Lincoln still held that it had been a war measure, prompted by the fact that slaves were directly contributing to the South's fighting capabilities by manning the home front and freeing up more whites for service on the battlefield. The wording of the proclamation was also important, as it essentially only freed the slaves in areas not under the federal government's control, while leaving slaves in bondage in other regions.

Nevertheless, by the end of the war, the South's defeat brought slavery to a *de facto* end, as hundreds of thousands of slaves fled to the victorious Union troops. Congress officially declared slavery dead with the passage of the Thirteenth Amendment in 1865.

The struggle for equal rights for African Americans was another issue, and one that most white Americans chose not to tackle in the aftermath of the war. By the end of Reconstruction, white Southerners had reestablished their control over African Americans through a series of laws and restrictions that severely curtailed their rights and opportunities. It was not until the civil rights movement of the 1950s and 1960s that African Americans were truly able to throw off this new form of control, which in many ways proved even more confining than the bondage of slavery.

Jason Newman

Further Reading

Brown, Richard D., ed. *Slavery in American Society*. Lexington, MA: D.C. Heath, 1992.

Fogel, Robert W. *Without Consent of Contract: The Rise and Fall of American Slavery*. New York: Norton, 1989.

Franklin, John H. *From Slavery to Freedom: A History of Negro Americans*. 1996.

Kolchin, Peter. *American Slavery, 1619–1877*. New York: Hill and Wang, 1993.

Ransom, Roger L. *Conflict and Compromise: The Political Economy of Slavery, Emancipation, and the American Civil War*. New York: Cambridge University Press, 1989.

Wayne, Michael. "The Reshaping of Plantation Society Revisited." *Journal of Mississippi History* 54 (1992): 333–48.

Smith, Edmund Kirby (1824–1893)

Edmund Kirby Smith was born in St. Augustine, Florida on May 16, 1824. Smith graduated from the U.S. Military Academy, West Point, in 1845. He served in the Mexican-American War (1846–1848) and was cited for gallantry at the Battle of Cerro Gordo. In 1849, he returned to West Point to teach mathematics, where he remained until 1852. From 1852 to 1858, Smith served in the West as an officer in the 2nd Cavalry Regiment, participating in numerous skirmishes against the Comanches and other Native American tribes of the Southwest.

Smith opposed Southern secession, but when his home state of Florida seceded from the Union on January 10, 1861, Major Smith resigned from the U.S. Army and accepted a commission as a colonel in the Confederate Army. At the outset of the war, Smith was General Joseph E. Johnston's chief of staff and helped to prepare incoming recruits for the Army of the Shenandoah. In June 1861, he was promoted to brigadier general and took command of a brigade. Wounded at the First Battle of Bull Run (July 21, 1861), where he played an important role in the Confederate victory, Smith was next promoted to major general and assigned to work in tandem with General Braxton Bragg in Tennessee in the western theater. Here Smith led an invasion of Kentucky leading to a notable victory in the Battle of Richmond, Kentucky (August 29–30, 1862). Smith's inability to coordinate with Bragg's invading army contributed to Confederate failure at the Battle of Perryville on October 8, 1862.

Thereafter, Smith was appointed lieutenant general and reassigned to command the Trans-Mississippi Department, which included Louisiana, Arkansas, and Texas. Smith energized Confederate operations in the trans-Mississippi. He also proved a surprisingly capable administrator, promoting regional self-sufficiency after his department became isolated from the eastern Confederacy following the Union victory at Vicksburg on July 4, 1863. The fact that the region became known as "Kirby Smithdom" underscores Smith's accomplishments. In 1864, Smith, now a full general, defeated Union efforts to take western Louisiana and Texas. But already the region had become a backwater because the war's decisive operations were taking place in Georgia and Virginia. Smith formally surrendered on May 26, 1865.

Following the war, Smith was affiliated with an insurance company and a telegraph company, both of which failed. From 1870 to 1875, he was president of the University of Nashville. He then taught math at the University of the South in Sewanee, Tennessee from 1875 until his death there on March 28, 1893.

Spencer C. Tucker

Further Reading

Arnold, James R. *Jeff Davis's Own: Cavalry, Comanches, and the Battle for the Texas Frontier.* New York: John Wiley & Sons, Inc, 2000.

Parks, Joseph H. *General Edmund Kirby Smith, C.S.A.* Baton Rouge: Louisiana State University Press, 1992.

Warner, Ezra J. *Generals in Gray: Lives of the Confederate Commanders.* Baton Rouge: Louisiana State University Press, 2006.

Stones River, Battle of

Following the Confederate defeat at Perryville, Kentucky, on October 8, 1862, Union forces moved into central Tennessee, eventually occupying the city of Nashville, the first state capital returned to Federal control. That same month, Major General William S. Rosecrans assumed command of the Union Army of the Cumberland, assigned to conduct operations in Tennessee.

Prodded by his superiors to act, Rosecrans waited until he believed he had accumulated sufficient supplies, departing Nashville on December 26, 1862. His army moved in three columns southeast from Nashville in the direction of Chattanooga. Major General Alexander M. McCook commanded the right wing; Major General George H. Thomas had charge of the center; and Major General Thomas L. Crittenden commanded the left wing. Crittenden's left wing advanced astride the Nashville–Chattanooga Railroad, which crossed Stones River.

The Federal force totaled approximately 47,000 men. From December 26 to 30, the army covered about 30 miles, reaching to just before Murfreesboro, where Confederate general Braxton Bragg and his 38,000-man Army of Tennessee awaited the Federal advance on Stones River. Bragg's army was deployed on a 4-mile front, approximately 1.5 miles west and northwest of Murfreesboro. Lieutenant generals Leonidas Polk and William Hardee commanded Bragg's two corps. Bragg's cavalry consisted of two brigades of experienced horsemen commanded by brigadier generals Joseph Wheeler and John Wharton. As the two armies closed,

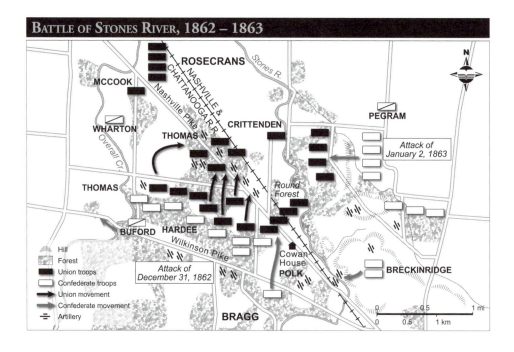

An Ohio soldier-artist's drawing of the Battle of Stones River depicting a charging battle line. (Library of Congress)

both Bragg and Rosecrans planned offensive actions. Ironically, the two commanders came up with approximately the same plan of holding with their right flank and attacking with their left.

Bragg began the battle. At 6:22 a.m., December 31, Major General John P. McCown's division of Hardee's corps, supported by Wharton's cavalry, struck the Union right flank, where McCook's corps was supposed to attack at 7:00 a.m. to extend the Confederate line, but the men were then just finishing breakfast. Major General Patrick R. Cleburne's division moved just behind McCown. These divisions of Hardee's corps drove back McCook's corps. Meanwhile, the Confederate cavalry circled wide to harass the Federal rear.

Brigadier General Philip Sheridan, commanding a division of McCook's corps, rallied his men and repelled three Confederate attacks, briefly holding up the Southern advance. But by mid-morning, the entire Federal flank was in retreat and being driven back into Thomas's corps.

As the Federals fell back on the Nashville Pike, Rosecrans recalled the first Union division sent across Stones River, part of two planned for the Union assault on the Confederate right, held by Major General John C. Breckenridge's single division. Rosecrans shifted two divisions into a defensive posture in front of the massed Federal artillery at the Nashville Pike. The spirited Union defense of Round Forest, a wooded area around the pike and the paralleling Chattanooga and Nashville Railroad that became known as "Hell's Half Acre," bought time for Thomas to construct a new Union defensive line to meet the Confederate attack driving in the Union right. The new line ran perpendicular to the old position and parallel to the Nashville Pike. The Union lines now came to resemble a narrow V. Supported by massed artillery to their rear, the Union defenders beat back numerous Confederate attacks.

Following the initial attack, Bragg did little to influence the battle. Although he had belatedly ordered Polk's forces to join the Confederate attack by striking the Union center, Polk committed his troops piecemeal. By nightfall and the close of the first day's battle, the new Union line had held.

Having now won a tactical victory, Bragg was convinced that Rosecrans would soon withdraw. Throughout New Year's Day as Bragg waited, however, Rosecrans remained in place and each side warily watched the other. With the Federals still holding their positions, at 4:00 p.m. on January 2 Bragg ordered Breckenridge to attack the Union left on the east side of Stones River in order to seize the high ground there. Observing the Confederates to his front massing for the attack, Crittenden ordered his artillery commander, Major John Mendenhall, to mass his guns at the ford where the first Union division had crossed earlier. Although the attacking Confederates drove the Union forces back, at 4:45 p.m. Mendenhall opened up with his 57 massed guns, tearing great holes in the Confederate ranks and driving Breckenridge back to his original position.

On the night of January 2, the commanders of two Confederate divisions that had sustained heavy casualties on the 31st wrote to Bragg asking for a withdrawal. Polk seconded the suggestion. At first Bragg angrily rejected it, but on the morning of January 3, believing falsely that Rosecrans had been reinforced, Bragg ordered a withdrawal for that evening, to Tullahoma, Tennessee. Rosecrans declined to pursue his adversary, contenting himself with occupying Murfreesboro.

The cost of the three-day battle was high for both sides. Union casualties numbered 1,730 dead, 7,802 wounded, and 3,717 missing. Southern losses were almost as great: 1,294 dead, 7,845 wounded, and 1,027 missing.

Stones River came at a time of Union defeats in Virginia. Although technically a Confederate victory, it served to elevate Union morale. Lincoln was particularly grateful to Rosecrans for his stand at Stones River. Lincoln correctly perceived that Rosecrans was now in position to drive on the key Confederate city of Chattanooga. On the Confederate side, many faulted Bragg's conduct of the battle, accelerating a growing lack of confidence of Bragg's qualifications for high command.

Julius Menzoff and Spencer C. Tucker

Further Reading

Connelly, Thomas L. *Autumn of Glory: The Army of Tennessee, 1862–1865*. Baton Rouge: Louisiana State University Press, 1971.

Cozzens, Peter. *No Better Place to Die: The Battle of Stones River*. Champaign: University of Illinois Press, 1991.

McDonough, James L. *Stones River—Bloody River in Tennessee*. Knoxville: University of Tennessee Press, 1980.

Strategy, Confederate

Military strategy is the way national leaders use military resources to achieve political objectives. Effective military strategy efficiently uses battles to craft campaigns that accomplish military objectives, thus achieving a political objective. If war is used as a political instrument, then the nature of the political goal will influence the military strategy selected. The Confederacy's overarching political goal was independence. Once its state governments took over the Federal installations on their soil, all the Confederacy had to do was protect its gains and secure foreign recognition. A defensive military strategy could accomplish that passive political goal. The South did not have to conquer the North, occupy any Union cities, or take any other offensive action. Instead, it needed to stand on the defensive long enough to overcome its relative shortcomings in manufacturing and infrastructure and secure foreign recognition, hoping that the North would tire of the war first.

There was enormous support in the South for the war in the first few months after fighting began at Fort Sumter. Southerners were sure that a single battle would decide the issue and bring independence. Young men rushed to war, but nobody gave much thought as to what to do after the first battle. The strategically indecisive nature of the First Battle of Bull Run/Manassas (despite a tactical victory, it did not end the war) changed that. President Jefferson Davis and his advisors suddenly faced the huge problem of defending the Confederacy.

At the start of the war, the South had few warships, although with the secession of Virginia it did secure the largest prewar U.S. Navy yard in Norfolk, along with a dry dock and large quantities of heavy guns. On the seas, the South adopted the time-honored strategy of weak naval powers. It sent out commerce raiders to create economic pressure in the North for peace. At the same time, the Confederacy sought to protect its own ports and rivers from Union assault. With limited manufacturing resources, the South nonetheless hoped to build, or secure from abroad, a sufficient number of ironclad vessels to enable it to break the Union blockade so that it might sell its cotton in exchange for arms. Davis sought to play the "cotton card" at the beginning of the war, withholding the Southern cotton crop from Europe in the hope of forcing Britain and France to recognize the Confederacy. It turned out to be a serious error, because by the time Davis reversed this unwise policy, the Union blockade was in place and blockade running became progressively more difficult.

Confederate commerce raiding drove up insurance rates for Northern shippers and convinced many owners to register their vessels in foreign countries, but it never proved decisive. Wheat, "King Corn," from the North proved more important than cotton. Confederate efforts to defend the ports and rivers had better success and the South also embraced new technologies at sea, including mines (called torpedoes at the time) and the submarine. Over time, however, the Union Navy still seized or neutralized the major Confederate ports, and the South never could compete with Northern shipbuilding capacity. These factors led it to lose the riverine war as well. Meanwhile, efforts to purchase warships in Europe largely floundered because of Union diplomatic efforts. Blockade running brought large amounts of material into the Confederacy, but poor government control made the effort strategically ineffective. Thus, the Confederacy lost the war at sea.

On land, the Confederates faced an equally daunting challenge. The new nation was vulnerable to invasion all along its northern border and long coastline. Although the Union Army was not large initially, it grew tremendously in size and greatly outnumbered Confederate strength on land. Governors clamored for protection for their states, and Davis sought to satisfy them, as he perceived that he could not afford to have the Union Army successfully invade and occupy any state. He thus chose to defend everywhere, although the western theater did suffer at the expense of the East.

An old military adage holds that to defend everything is to defend nothing—implying that to be successful one should use valu-

able resources to protect vital areas and concede less critical points. However, political necessity trumps even good military theory, and the South deployed its troops in scattered contingents to defend every threatened region. That was not a totally bankrupt strategy. The South hoped to use the advantage of interior lines to be able to concentrate troops from dispersed locations and counter Union offensives. That proved more difficult than expected, but was a reasonable assumption and in line with contemporary military theory. It came apart mainly because of increasing Union control over Confederate rivers and the breakdown of the Confederate rail system from a shortage of rails and steam engines as the war progressed. Additionally, the South adopted what Davis called an offensive-defensive strategy. That is, it opted to conduct occasional offensives to disrupt Union operations.

The Confederacy employed the basic offensive-defensive strategic framework throughout the war. To execute the strategy, Confederate leaders faced a series of decisions about where to concentrate their effort. This resulted in a debate over the relative importance of the eastern and western theaters that continues today. In general, Davis favored the eastern theater, although the South conducted major strategic concentrations in the west in support of both the Shiloh and Chickamauga campaigns. A majority of modern analysts also favor the eastern theater as being the strategic center of the war, based on the proposition that the Confederacy could lose the war in either theater but only win it in the east. A vocal minority supports the decisiveness of the western theater.

In the end the South lost the war, and Confederate military strategy was a failure. Critics propose alternatives, but it is not clear that any would have worked better than the one executed. The South did not have the depth needed to conduct a fighting, scorched-earth withdrawal or the external support and sanctuaries for a long-term insurgency. The South might have targeted better the North's political will, particularly in 1864 when Lincoln faced a challenging reelection bid, but that was a path not taken.

J. Boone Bartholomees, Jr.

Further Reading

Boritt, Gabor S., ed. *Why the Confederacy Lost*. New York: Oxford University Press, 1992.

Connelly, Thomas L. *The Politics of Command: Factions and Ideas in Confederate Strategy*. Baton Rouge: Louisiana State University Press, 1973.

Harsh, Joseph L. *Taken at the Flood: Robert E. Lee and Confederate Strategy in the Maryland Campaign of 1862*. Kent, OH: Kent State University Press, 1999.

Jones, Archer. *Civil War Command and Strategy: The Process of Victory and Defeat*. New York: The Free Press, 1992.

Tanner, Robert G. *Retreat to Victory?: Confederate Strategy Reconsidered*. The American Crisis Series, ed. Steven E. Woodworth. Wilmington, DE: Scholarly Resources Inc., 2002.

Strategy, Union

Since war is a political act, military strategy takes its nature from the political objective of the war. The North's political objective was to force the seceded Southern states to rejoin the Union. That goal required an offensive strategy. The North had to conquer the South to force its surrender and acceptance of reunification. The strategic dilemma was how best to accomplish that.

Commander of the U.S. Army at the beginning of the war, Lieutenant General Winfield Scott recommended a strategy that came to be known as the Anaconda plan, named after the South American snake that strangled its victims to death. Scott thought the North should impose a blockade of the South and then raise and train a large army. Once the latter had been accomplished, the North would use its overwhelming numbers and naval strength to bisect the South. Although prescient, that concept did not fit Northern sentiment, which demanded an immediate military offensive and quick victory. Lincoln ordered such an offensive, but hopes of success evaporated in the Union defeat in the First Battle of Bull Run/Manassas on July 21, 1861.

The North did enjoy tremendous advantages over the South in population and industrial manufacturing capacity. The North had three-quarters of the population and virtually all the manufacturing capacity of the nation in 1860. The task was to translate that into actual military force and then determine how best to use those resources. The Union began pursuing very early, although informally, a military strategy based on abundance. First, the Union Navy would isolate the Confederacy by blockading Southern ports. Next, Union armies would attack all around the periphery of the Confederacy (to include the coastal flank). In the western theater, Union offensives would split the Confederacy along the lines of the great rivers—the Mississippi, Tennessee, and Cumberland. In the eastern theater, the attacks focused on the enemy capital at Richmond, Virginia. Such offensives, if properly coordinated to strike together, would overwhelm the Confederates and negate their theoretical advantage of interior lines. The problem the Union had was coordinating the attacks.

President Lincoln ordered all the Union armies to begin offensive action on February 22, 1862, but Washington's Birthday proved to be a strategic disappointment. Brigadier General Ulysses S. Grant attacked early and seized Forts Henry and Donelson (February 7–16, 1862) in Tennessee, but nobody moved on the appointed day, and some of the Union armies never attacked that spring. That was symptomatic of the Union's problem—it had the troops and supplies but could not employ them effectively. The telegraph and railways had improved strategic communications, but local commanders still made the final decision on their tactical operations. Coordinating them took more than improved communications. The inability to coordinate simultaneous attacks around the periphery of the South allowed the Confederates to exploit their advantage of interior lines. The fact that the North made steady progress, especially in the western theater in 1862, where the South's biggest city (New Orleans) and one of its most important states (Tennessee) fell to Union advances, reflected the size of its armies and control of the rivers more than successful strategy.

Union attempts to exploit its naval superiority by attacking the Confederacy from the sea, like Major General George B. McClellan's Peninsular Campaign in the spring of 1862, offered tremendous strategic promise but produced poor results because of McClellan's cautious style. General Robert E Lee's exceptionally aggressive nature moved the war from the outskirts of Richmond to the outskirts of Washington during the summer of 1862, and only the hard-won Union victory at Antietam (September 17, 1862) stopped a Confederate invasion of Maryland that fall.

The western armies made slow but steady progress in the task of splitting the Confederacy along its major river lines. Ulysses Grant, now a major general in recognition of his victory at Forts Henry and Donelson, worked tirelessly through the winter of 1862 and spring of 1863 to capture Vicksburg, Mississippi, the final major Confederate stronghold on the Mississippi River. The surrender of Vicksburg on July 4, 1863, combined with the nearly simultaneous victory of Major General George G. Meade over Lee at Gettysburg (July 1–3, 1863), signified the turning point of the war. From then on the Union had the strategic initiative, although it could still lose the war.

When President Lincoln selected Ulysses Grant as the new head of the Union army in March 1864 and promoted him to lieutenant general, the general brought with him no new grand strategy. The final campaign that Grant executed from May 1864 to April 1865 was essentially Lincoln's 1862 idea executed effectively. Grant ordered all five major Union armies to attack in May 1864. Even that late in the war, not all the armies complied, and Grant had to relieve some commanders and closely supervise others to achieve the result. Nevertheless, the simultaneous pressure prevented the Confederates from massing to counter any single drive.

Only two major modifications to the Union military strategy occurred during the war. First, President Lincoln became convinced that the insistence of his generals on attacking Richmond was misplaced. He ordered Major General Joseph Hooker, and subsequently Meade, to focus their efforts instead on Lee's Army of Northern Virginia. This shift from trying to take a place to trying to destroy an enemy army was a significant strategic change. Major General William T. Sherman, supported by Grant and Lincoln, among others, added the second new element to Union strategy. He came to believe that Southern morale and support for the war would not break until the Southern people experienced what Sherman called the hard hand of war. Sherman's march to the sea when his army destroyed a wide swath of Georgia is the most famous example of to the commanding general. At length, an exasperated Grant unleashed Union general Philip H. Sheridan with 12,000 veteran troopers on a raid toward Richmond to lure Stuart out into the open and destroy him. An indecisive skirmish occurred at Todd's Tavern on May 9, 1864, but two days later, Stuart confronted Sheridan's legions with less than half his number at Yellow Tavern. In a confused fight only six miles from Richmond, Stuart was shot and mortally wounded. He was painfully conveyed to Richmond, where he died on May 12, 1864. When informed of Stuart's passing, a very sad Lee declared, "He never brought me a piece of false information."

For three years Stuart had served as the eyes and ears of the Army of Northern Virginia and contributed greatly to many of its victories. His only stumble, at the Battle of Gettysburg, was serious and may have cost the Confederacy the war. Nevertheless, Stuart is widely regarded as America's finest cavalry leader.

John C. Fredriksen

Further Reading

Brewer, James D. *The Raiders of 1862*. Westport, CT: Praeger Publishers, 1997.

Nesbitt, Mark. *Saber and Scapegoat: J. E. B. Stuart and the Gettysburg Controversy*. Mechanicsburg, PA: Stackpole Books, 1994.

Rhea, Gordon C. *The Battles for Spotsylvania Court House and the Road to Yellow Tavern, May 7–12, 1864*. Baton Rouge: Louisiana State University Press, 1997.

Thomas, Emory A. *Bold Dragoon: The Life of J. E. B. Stuart*. New York: Harper and Row, 1988.

Trout, Robert J. *They Followed the Plume: The Story of J. E. B. Stuart and His Staff*. Mechanicsburg, PA: Stackpole Books, 1993.

T

Telegraph

The telegraph was immensely important to both sides in the Civil War, allowing rapid communication between field commands and higher headquarters. Around 1830, scientists had determined that messages could be transmitted by means of an electrical impulse through wires. A number of electric telegraphy systems were developed, but American Samuel Morse created a system and a code for it that employed short and long breaks in the electrical current ("dots and dashes"). Morse received a patent for his invention in 1840, and three years later the U.S. Congress appropriated funds to build a pilot forty-mile telegraph line from Baltimore to Washington. In 1844, Morse transmitted his first message over this line— "What hath God wrought?"

The telegraph allowed messages to be transmitted over considerable distances within minutes. Applied initially to the control of railroad traffic, the combination of telegraph and railroad brought about great changes in military operations. The telegraph first proved its great military value during the Crimean War (1853–1856).

During the Civil War there were three major telegraph entities: commercial telegraph companies, the Military Telegraph Service, and the Signal Corps Field Telegraph. At the outbreak of the war, several commercial companies were providing telegraph service. The American Telegraph Company was the principal company to the north of Washington and, in early 1861, it extended its wires to Washington and the War Department. Secretary of War Simon Cameron solicited the aid of several telegraph executives and enlisted the services of Thomas S. Scott of the Pennsylvania Railroad who became general manager of all lines in and around Washington. The government requested that the American Telegraph Company install such telegraph lines and facilities as would be necessary to support the war. Anson Stager from Western Union recommended that the government take control of existing commercial telegraph facilities, and in October 1861, the U.S. Military Telegraph Service came into being. The government assumed control of all telegraphic facilities for use by the Military Telegraph Service, and Stager became its chief with the eventual rank of colonel.

The Military Telegraph Service was in reality a civilian bureau attached to the Quartermaster Department. The supervisors received commissions in the Quartermaster Department, but the operators were civilians. Cameron's replacement as secretary of war, Edwin Stanton, a former telegraph executive, championed the Military Telegraph Service throughout the war. Stager was stationed in Cleveland, Ohio, and his principal subordinate, Major Thomas Eckert, assumed tactical control of the service in the east and accompanied the Army of the Potomac during its various campaigns.

Of some 2,000 telegraph operators working in the country during the war, more than half eventually worked for the Military Telegraph Service. Some women, including Mary E. Smith, Louisa E. Volker, and Ann Marean, served in the Military Telegraph Service, and strategic dead end. A defeated army, whether Union or Confederate, could and did retire from the field to the safety of its capital's fortifications. Protected by these nearly impregnable fortifications, the defeated force refit to fight new battles.

The western theater extended for about 300 miles from the Mississippi River to the Allegheny Mountains. In the West the major rivers—the Mississippi, Tennessee, and Cumberland—ran north to south. This gave the Union natural avenues to follow to invade the South. In the West, there were fewer big cities and fewer railroads. These facts made it harder for western armies to receive logistical support. As soon as they moved away from the rivers, their supply lines became vulnerable to Confederate raiders and guerrillas.

West of the Mississippi lay a vast area stretching all the way to the Pacific Ocean. Although the trans-Mississippi theater provided the Confederacy with manpower, mules and horses, and grain, from a strategic viewpoint it was a backwater region. Both sides invested most of their strength east of the Mississippi. The trans-Mississippi received the leftovers.

The 3,500-mile-long Confederate coastline was another theater of war that included some 189 harbors and navigable river mouths. Because this lengthy coastline was so difficult to blockade effectively, Union strategists decided that the best policy was to capture the ports themselves. Union strategists wisely divided the seacoast into two parts: the Atlantic and the Gulf. In both areas the major southern ports became the focal points of Union army-navy amphibious operations.

Thus, four theaters of war defined the Civil War: the east, the west, the trans-Mississippi, and the Confederate seacoast.

James R. Arnold

Further Reading

Kerby, Robert L. *Kirby Smith's Confederacy: The Trans-Mississippi South, 1863–1865.* New York: Columbia University Press, 1972.

Reed, Rowena. *Combined Operations in the Civil War.* Annapolis, MD: Naval Institute Press, 1978.

U.S. Military Academy. *The West Point Atlas of American Wars, Volume I, 1689–1900.* New York: Frederick A. Praeger Publishers, 1959.

Winters, Harold A. *Battling the Elements: Weather and Terrain in the Conduct of War.* Baltimore, MD: Johns Hopkins University Press, 1998.

Thomas, George Henry (1816–1870)

Born in Southampton County, Virginia on July 31, 1816, George Henry Thomas graduated from the U.S. Military Academy at West Point in 1840. He served in the Second Seminole and Mexican Wars, and saw action against the Comanche in the 1850s while under the command of Robert E. Lee. During this time he was seriously wounded by a Comanche arrow.

When the Civil War began, Thomas remained loyal to the Union and was commissioned a brigadier general in August 1861. While commanding a division in Kentucky, he defeated a Confederate force in the January 19, 1862, Battle of Mill Springs. Thomas's division was part of Brigadier General Don Carlos Buell's Army of the Ohio.

Thomas participated in the Shiloh campaign, although the Battle of Shiloh of April 6–7, 1862, ended before Thomas and his division reached the battlefield. Following Shiloh, western theater commander Major General Henry W. Halleck reorganized Union forces so as to give Thomas command of what had been Major General Ulysses S. Grant's army while Grant was sidelined in a meaningless second-in-command position. No significant action took place during Halleck's subsequent plodding advance toward Corinth, Mississippi. Thereafter, Thomas resumed his accustomed division command in the Army of the Ohio as that force moved east to restore the Memphis & Charleston Railroad.

When the campaign ended with Buell having done nothing to mitigate Washington's frustration, it was not Thomas but rather Brigadier General William S. Rosecrans that the authorities selected to replace the discredited Buell. Thomas was probably passed over because of his southern birth. Thomas thus continued in a subordinate role, commanding a corps-sized force at the Battle of Stones River, December 31, 1862–January 2, 1863. Thomas performed creditably at Stones River to carry on in command of the XIV Corps of the Army of the Cumberland.

Five months passed while the Army of the Cumberland remained idle, and Washington's dissatisfaction now focused on Rosecrans.

Virginia born, Union loyal Gen. George Thomas, one of the Union Army's most able and important leaders. (Library of Congress)

Thomas strongly supported his commander, insisting that the army should not move until it was completely prepared, regardless of the broader strategic situation. When in June 1863 the army did move, Thomas performed well in the campaign that maneuvered Confederate forces under General Braxton Bragg almost completely out of Tennessee. In August Rosecrans resumed the advance, once again turning Bragg and forcing him back. The Confederates had received heavy reinforcements and Bragg counterattacked at the Battle of Chickamauga, September 19–20, 1863. On the second day of the battle Thomas had his finest hour. As the Union right and center broke under Confederate attack, Thomas, with his corps reinforced to about half the army's total strength, continued to hold his position on the left until nightfall. This action covered the rest of the army's escape and Thomas received the sobriquet, the "Rock of Chickamauga."

After Chickamauga, Rosecrans allowed Bragg to besiege his army in Chattanooga. Washington responded by giving Grant overall command of Union forces west of the Appalachians. Grant sacked Rosecrans, elevating Thomas to command of the Army of the Cumberland, although there was no warmth between the two men. Grant brought reinforcements to Chattanooga from the armies of the Tennessee and Potomac and then personally directed the combined force in drubbing Bragg in the November 23–25 Battle of Chattanooga. Although Thomas's troops played a key role in the victory, he had committed them only reluctantly.

The following spring, with Grant's promotion to general-in-chief, Major General William T. Sherman took over command of the army group for the advance from Chattanooga to Atlanta. Thomas continued to serve capably in command of the Army of the Cumberland, but when Sherman wanted rapid movement, he turned to one of the other armies under his command, usually the Army of the Tennessee.

Following the fall of Atlanta on September 2, 1864, Sherman assigned Thomas to the defense of Tennessee, while Sherman took four corps on his November-December March to the Sea. When Hood launched his Invasion of Tennessee, Thomas's army met him at the Battle of Nashville, December 15–16, 1864. Thomas's planning for this battle was masterful. The ensuing victory was decisive and obtained at relatively small cost. Thomas received promotion to major general for his efforts.

Following the Civil War, Thomas remained in the regular U.S. Army, commanding the Division of the Pacific beginning in 1869. He died, still holding the command, in San Francisco on March 28, 1870.

Steven E. Woodworth

Further Reading

Cleaves, Freeman. *Rock of Chickamauga: The Life of General George H. Thomas*. Norman: University of Oklahoma Press, 1948.

McKinney, Francis F. *Education in Violence*. Detroit, MI: Wayne State University Press, 1961.

Woodworth, Steven E., ed. *Grant's Lieutenants: From Chattanooga to Appomattox*. Lawrence: University Press of Kansas, 2008.

Trans-Mississippi Theater

Far from most of the major battles in the Civil War, the trans-Mississippi was a unique theater. Consisting of the territory west of the Mississippi River, the trans-Mississippi theater was home to sizable populations of Mexicans, Germans, and other immigrants, and those who served west of the Mississippi were thus a mixed bunch. Unlike the other theaters, in the trans-Mississippi Native Americans fought on both the Union and Confederate sides, their circumstances before the war determining their loyalties.

Warfare in this theater also differed from that of the East and the West. Most engagements in the trans-Mississippi theater were small cavalry encounters rather than pitched battles. A number of the engagements

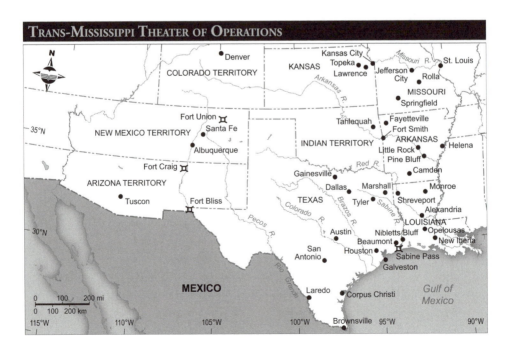

TRANS-MISSISSIPPI THEATER OF OPERATIONS

featured fighting between white settlers and soldiers against raiding Indians. In addition, the theater west of the Mississippi was marked by guerrilla warfare. Two of the most infamous partisan soldiers of the war, William Quantrill and "Bloody" Bill Anderson, fought mainly in the trans-Mississippi.

Early in the war, the Union Army could not threaten most areas of the trans-Mississippi. Since most of the theater was safe from Union invasion, soldiers had some freedom to attempt to fulfill the prewar expansionary ambitions of the South. Before the war, the South harnessed the influence of Manifest Destiny through a paramilitary organization known as the Knights of the Golden Circle. Headquartered in San Antonio, Texas, the organization sought to expand the South's borders into the American southwest, northern Mexico, and the Caribbean in order to create a vast Southern slave empire. With these ideals, Southerners in Texas, New Mexico, and Arizona joined Brigadier General Henry Hopkins Sibley's brigade to conquer New Mexico. They hoped to then move against California, then finally gain the desired territory in Latin America. Sibley's February–March 1862 attempt failed because of its extended logistical lines, however, and the Union forces captured a large share of the Southerners' supplies.

As the war extended into 1862, a major threat to the trans-Mississippi developed on its northern border and coast in New Orleans and northwestern Arkansas. New Orleans, the largest port city in the South, was a major priority for the Union because its capture would help to give the North control of the Mississippi River. The Union navy took control of the city on April 28, 1862. The other threatened area, northwestern Arkansas, was the only area of the theater that bordered Union territory. Tension in the area climaxed on March 6–8, 1862, with the largest land battle of the trans-Mississippi, the Battle of Pea Ridge. Confederate forces under Major

General Earl Van Dorn lost the battle, and with it control of Missouri. On December 7, 1862, another major battle occurred at Prairie Grove, Arkansas. Here Confederate General Thomas Hindman's offensive with a 10,000-man army was defeated by an equal sized force commanded by General James Blunt. At Prairie Grove, men fought with the same tenacity displayed by soldiers east of the Mississippi River. The Confederates lost over 1,300 men while Blunt lost over 1,200.

As 1862 ended, Galveston, Texas, another major city in the trans-Mississippi, fell under Union control. Galveston did not remain in Union hands for long, however; on January 1, 1863, Texas forces, many of them having served in Sibley's brigade, retook the city. The Union Army encroached further into Confederate territory in the trans-Mississippi from the north and east during 1863, slowly taking command of cities along the Mississippi River and even Fort Smith, Arkansas.

With the Union capture of Vicksburg, Mississippi, the "Gibraltar of the West" on July 4, 1863, the Mississippi River fell under Union control and the first major objective in the Union's overall strategy was reached. The Union Army had cut the trans-Mississippi off from the rest of the Confederacy, allowing only limited communication through couriers. Instead of discouragement, however, the isolation bred resolve and independence in the men fighting west of the Mississippi.

Shortly after its isolation from the rest of the Confederacy, the trans-Mississippi received the nickname "Kirby Smithdom," named after the Confederate commander of the theater, General Edmund Kirby Smith. The men had to rely on themselves, unable to count on Confederate forces east of the river for assistance. From March to May 1864 the Union attempted its largest invasion of the trans-Mississippi region, known as the Red River Campaign. Though strategically the region was not as valuable as was the western theater, for the Union, the French intervention in Mexico and the desire to secure cotton made its conquest a major aim.

The Union invasion was a two-pronged attack, the main thrust from Louisiana and the other from Arkansas. Confederates in the trans-Mississippi were successful in repulsing both armies at Mansfield, Louisiana and Camden, Arkansas, defeats that ended Union efforts to organize another major invasion west of the Mississippi.

The final action in the trans-Mississippi theater occurred on May 12–13, 1865, over a month after General Robert E. Lee surrendered at Appomattox, in the Battle of Palmito Ranch near the southern tip of Texas. By mid May, most of the Confederate units disbanded and went home, leaving Kirby Smith a commander without an army. On May 26, Smith finally surrendered. The last Confederate general to surrender to the U.S. Army was, however, Cherokee Brigadier General Stand Watie, who relinquished his sword on June 23, 1865.

Charles D. Grear

Further Reading

Christ, Mark K. *Civil War Arkansas, 1863: The Battle for a State*. Norman: University of Oklahoma Press, 2010.

Frazier, Donald S. *Blood and Treasure: Confederate Empire in the Southwest*. College Station: Texas A & M University Press, 1995.

Kerby, Robert L. *Kirby Smith's Confederacy: The Trans-Mississippi South, 1863–1865*. Tuscaloosa: The University of Alabama Press, 1972.

Oates, Stephen B. *Confederate Cavalry West of the River*. Austin: University of Texas Press, 1961.

Shea, William L., and Earl J. Hess. *Pea Ridge: Civil War Campaign in the West*. Chapel Hill: The University of North Carolina Press, 1992.

Smith, David Paul. *Frontier Defense in the Civil War: Texas Rangers and Rebels*. College Station: Texas A & M University Press, 1992.

Thompson, Jerry D. *Vaqueros in Blue and Gray*. Austin, TX: State House Press, 2000.

V

Vicksburg, Siege of

U.S. Grant's victory at Champion Hill on May 15, 1863, compelled John C. Pemberton's forces to retire inside Vicksburg's fortifications. On May 19 and again on May 22, Grant ordered assaults against the fortifications. Their failure convinced Grant to begin formal siege operations. In contrast to Confederate defenders at the so-called Siege of Petersburg in 1864–1865, Pemberton's defenders were completely isolated with their backs against the Mississippi River and Grant's army positioned in an arc around the city's landward perimeter.

For the next 43 days, Grant's army employed the full range of classic siege techniques. Vicksburg was a powerful position. Confederate engineers had labored for seven months to construct a nine-mile-long defensive system that followed the crest of a steep ridge. The roads leading to Vicksburg provided the easiest access to the city. Accordingly, the Confederates built nine forts to protect these roads. During the siege, both Union and Confederate efforts focused on these forts and on the outworks protecting them.

Because his army had only one battery of six 32-pound siege guns, Grant's army had to improvise a siege train. Admiral David Porter's naval squadron lent a battery of large caliber naval guns to assist siege operations. Still, since Grant's infantry lacked enough heavy artillery to batter down the Confederate fortifications, they worked to dig through and under the Confederate works. After establishing their own twelve-mile-long trench system facing the Confederate works, they began a network of approach trenches leading toward the Confederate line. In addition, the Union infantry dug tunnels underneath key Confederate fortifications. On June 25, an explosive-filled tunnel beneath the Third Louisiana Redan detonated and the Union infantry charged into the crater. An intense, close-range combat ensued, but the Confederates held the position. The setback slowed, but did not halt, the inexorable advance of the Union approach trenches. By the end of June, sapheads all along the front were within 5–120 yards of the Confederate trench lines. Numerous mines had been dug beneath key Confederate fortifications and were ready for detonation.

Inside the city, the defenders and the remaining civilians suffered terribly from hunger. Sickness and wounds had reduced the defenders by some 10,000 men, about half of the Pemberton's total effective strength. From the beginning of the siege, Pemberton's only hope was for a relief army to open an escape avenue. Outside the city, General Joseph E. Johnston commanded a potential relief army. At its peak strength, Johnston managed to assemble about 31,000 men. However, by then Grant's army had 71,000, half of which he used to block any relief effort. Equally important, Johnston was ill-suited for bold offensive operations. As early as June 15, he informed authorities in Richmond that Vicksburg could not be relieved.

With the numerous mines charged, and the saps prepared for the passage of the Union assault troops, Grant planned a final assault

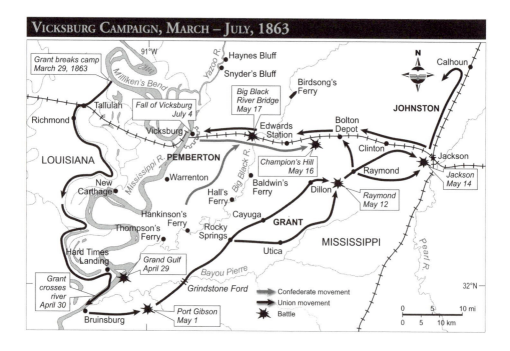

VICKSBURG CAMPAIGN, MARCH – JULY, 1863

Grant breaks camp March 29, 1863

Fall of Vicksburg July 4

Big Black River Bridge May 17

Champion's Hill May 16

Raymond May 12

Jackson May 14

Grand Gulf April 29

Grant crosses river April 30

Port Gibson May 1

Confederate movement
Union movement
Battle

A Currier & Ives print depicting ships of Union rear admiral David Porter's Mississippi Squadron running past the Confederate fortress of Vicksburg, April 16, 1863. (Library of Congress)

for July 6. On the afternoon of July 3, 1863, Pemberton wisely asked for terms. The formal surrender of the city came on July 4. At Vicksburg, Grant's army captured 29,491 men and 172 artillery pieces. The capture of this army reduced the Confederacy to only one remaining major army in the west. As a direct consequence of the fall of Vicksburg, on July 9 the Confederate fortress at Port Hudson also surrendered, thereby opening the Mississippi River to Union commercial trade. Union control of the river also severed the Confederacy in two. This adversely affected Confederate logistics, but its psychological impact was even more important as southerners perceived that the boundaries of their nation were dramatically shrinking. Along with the Union victory at Gettysburg, the fall of Vicksburg marked the beginning of the end for the Confederacy.

James R. Arnold

Further Reading

Arnold, James R. *Grant Wins the War*. New York: James Wiley and Sons, 1997.

Bearss, Edwin C. *The Campaign for Vicksburg*. 3 vols. Dayton, OH: Morningside House, 1986.

Grant, Ulysses S. *Personal Memoirs*. New York: De Capo Press, 1982.

Hoehling, A.A, ed. *Vicksburg: Forty-seven Days of Siege*. Englewood Cliffs, NJ: Prentice-Hall, 1969.

U.S. Military Academy. *The West Point Atlas of American Wars*. Vol. I, 1689–1900. New York: Frederick A. Praeger Publishers, 1959.

Fugitive Slave Acts (1793, 1850)

Passed on February 12, 1793, and signed into law by President George Washington, the Fugitive Slave Act implemented Article IV, Section 2 of the Constitution, which prohibited states from freeing persons "held to Service or Labor" and required states to return fugitive slaves to the state from which they had fled. The Fugitive Slave Act made it a federal offense to assist escapees and permitted the seizure of escaped slaves—as well as any children subsequently born to them—in any state of the union for as long as they lived. The act also specifically recognized the role of agents—known as slave-catchers—in securing escaped slaves, and it authorized judges and magistrates to approve the transfer of slaves. However, northern states passed laws that made the Fugitive Slave Act more difficult to enforce. As part of the Compromise of 1850, Congress strengthened the Fugitive Slave Act. The new act imposed harsh penalties for assisting or failing to return runaway slaves, at the same time stripping free blacks of any legal right to challenge the claims of

$200 Reward.

RANAWAY from the subscriber, on the night of Thursday, the 30th of Sepember,

FIVE NEGRO SLAVES,

To-wit : one Negro man, his wife, and three children.

The man is a black negro, full height, very erect, his face a little thin. He is about forty years of age, and calls himself *Washington Reed,* and is known by the name of Washington. He is probably well dressed, possibly takes with him an ivory headed cane, and is of good address. Several of his teeth are gone.

Mary, his wife, is about thirty years of age, a bright mulatto woman, and quite stout and strong.

The oldest of the children is a boy, of the name of FIELDING, twelve years of age, a dark mulatto, with heavy eyelids. He probably wore a new cloth cap.

MATILDA, the second child, is a girl, six years of age, rather a dark mulatto, but a bright and smart looking child.

MALCOLM, the youngest, is a boy, four years old, a lighter mulatto than the last, and about equally as bright. He probably also wore a cloth cap. If examined, he will be found to have a swelling at the navel.

Washington and Mary have lived at or near St. Louis, with the subscriber, for about 15 years.

It is supposed that they are making their way to Chicago, and that a white man accompanies them, that they will travel chiefly at night, and most probably in a covered wagon.

A reward of $150 will be paid for their apprehension, so that I can get them, if taken within one hundred miles of St. Louis, and $200 if taken beyond that, and secured so that I can get them, and other reasonable additional charges, if delivered to the subscriber, or to THOMAS ALLEN, Esq., at St. Louis, Mo. The above negroes, for the last few years, have been in possession of Thomas Allen, Esq., of St. Louis.

WM. RUSSELL.

ST. LOUIS, Oct. 1, 1847.

An 1847 poster advertises a reward of $200 for the apprehension and return of five runaway slaves. Although slavery was illegal in several Northern states, government officials in the free states were required by the Fugitive Slave Act of 1850 to aid in the capture of runaway slaves and return them to their previous masters. (Library of Congress) slave owners. Under the Fugitive Slave Acts, free blacks were frequently forced into slavery. Abolitionists, now legally required to assist slave owners, defiantly supported the Underground Railroad, organized to help slaves escape to Canada, where they were safe from American laws.

Fugitive Slave Act (1793)

An act respecting fugitives from justice, and persons escaping from the service of their masters.

Section 1. Be it enacted by the Senate and House of Representatives of the United States of America in Congress assembled, That whenever the executive authority of any state in the Union, or of either of the territories northwest or south of the river Ohio, shall demand any person as a fugitive from justice, of the executive authority of any such state or territory to which such person shall have fled, and shall moreover produce the copy of an indictment found, or an affidavit made before a magistrate of any state or territory as aforesaid, charging the person so demanded, with having committed treason, felony or other crime, certified as authentic by the governor or chief magistrate of the state or territory from whence the person so charged fled, it shall be the duty of the executive authority of the state or territory to which such person shall have fled, to cause him or her to be arrested and secured, and notice of the arrest to be given to the executive authority making such demand, or to the agent of such authority appointed to receive the fugitive, and to cause the fugitive to be delivered to such agent when he shall appear: But if no such agent shall appear within six months from the time of the arrest, the prisoner may be discharged. And all costs or expenses incurred in the apprehending, securing, and transmitting such fugitive to the state or territory making such demand, shall be paid by such state or territory.

Sec. 2. And be it further enacted, That any agent, appointed as aforesaid, who shall receive the fugitive into his custody, shall be empowered to transport him or her to the state or territory from which he or she shall have fled. And if any person or persons shall by force set at liberty, or rescue the fugitive from such agent while transporting, as aforesaid, the person or persons so offending shall, on conviction, be fined not exceeding five hundred dollars, and be imprisoned not exceeding one year.

Sec. 3. And be it also enacted, That when a person held to labour in any of the United States, or in either of the territories on the northwest or south of the river Ohio, under the laws thereof, shall escape into any other of the said states or territory, the person to whom such labour or service may be due, his agent or attorney, is hereby empowered to seize or arrest such fugitive from labour, and to take him or her before any judge of the circuit or district courts of the United States, residing or being within the state, or before any magistrate of a county, city or town corporate, wherein such seizure or arrest shall be made, and upon proof to the satisfaction of such judge or magistrate, either by oral testimony or affidavit taken before and certified by a magistrate of any such state or territory, that the person so seized or arrested, doth, under the laws of the state or territory from which he or she fled, owe service or labour to the person claiming him or her, it shall be the duty of such judge or magistrate to give a certificate thereof to such claimant, his agent or attorney, which shall be sufficient warrant for removing the said fugitive from labour, to the state or territory from which he or she fled.

Sec. 4. And be it further enacted, That any person who shall knowingly and willingly obstruct or hinder such claimant, his agent or attorney in so seizing or arresting such fugitive from labour, or shall rescue such fugitive from such claimant, his agent or attorney when so arrested pursuant to the authority herein given or declared; or shall harbor or conceal such person after notice that he or she was a fugitive from labour, as aforesaid, shall, for either of the said offences, forfeit and pay the sum of five hundred dollars. Which penalty may be recovered by and for the benefit of such claimant, by action of debt, in any court proper to try the same; saving moreover to the person claiming such labour or service, his right of action for or on account of the said injuries or either of them.

Approved, February 12, 1793.

Fugitive Slave Act (1850)

Section 1

Be it enacted by the Senate and House of Representatives of the United States of America in Congress assembled, That the persons who have been, or may hereafter be, appointed commissioners, in virtue of any act of Congress, by the Circuit Courts of the United States, and Who, in consequence of such appointment, are authorized to exercise the powers that any justice of the peace, or other magistrate of any of the United States, may exercise in respect to offenders for any crime or offense against the United States, by arresting, imprisoning, or bailing the same under and by the virtue of the thirty-third section of the act of the twenty-fourth of September seventeen hundred and eighty-nine, entitled "An Act to establish the judicial courts of the United States" shall be, and are hereby, authorized and required to exercise and discharge all the powers and duties conferred by this act.

Section 2

And be it further enacted, That the Superior Court of each organized Territory of the United States shall have the same power to appoint commissioners to take acknowledgments of bail and affidavits, and to take depositions of witnesses in civil causes, which is now possessed by the Circuit Court of the United States; and all commissioners who shall hereafter be appointed for such purposes by the Superior Court of any organized Territory of the United States, shall possess all the powers, and exercise all the duties, conferred by law upon the commissioners appointed by the Circuit Courts of the United States for similar purposes, and shall moreover exercise and discharge all the powers and duties conferred by this act.

Section 3

And be it further enacted, That the Circuit Courts of the United States shall from time to time enlarge the number of the commissioners, with a view to afford reasonable facilities to reclaim fugitives from labor, and to the prompt discharge of the duties imposed by this act.

Section 4

And be it further enacted, That the commissioners above named shall have concurrent jurisdiction with the judges of the Circuit and District Courts of the United States, in their respective circuits and districts within the several States, and the judges of the Superior Courts of the Territories, severally and collectively, in term-time and vacation; shall grant certificates to such claimants, upon satisfactory proof being made, with authority to take and remove such fugitives from service or labor, under the restrictions herein contained, to the State or Territory from which such persons may have escaped or fled.

Section 5

And be it further enacted, That it shall be the duty of all marshals and deputy marshals to obey and execute all warrants and precepts issued under the provisions of this act, when to them directed; and should any marshal or deputy marshal refuse to receive such warrant, or other process, when tendered, or to use all proper means diligently to execute the same, he shall, on conviction thereof, be fined in the sum of one thousand dollars, to the use of such claimant, on the motion of such claimant, by the Circuit or District Court for the district of such marshal; and after arrest of such fugitive, by such marshal or his deputy, or whilst at any time in his custody under the provisions of this act, should such fugitive escape, whether with or without the assent of such marshal or his deputy, such marshal shall be liable, on his official bond, to be prosecuted for the benefit of such claimant, for the full value of the service or labor of said fugitive in the State, Territory, or District whence he escaped: and the better to enable the said commissioners, when thus appointed, to execute their duties faithfully and efficiently, in conformity with the requirements of the Constitution of the United States and of this act, they are hereby authorized and empowered, within their counties respectively, to appoint, in writing under their hands, any one or more suitable persons, from time to time, to execute all such warrants and other process as may be issued by them in the lawful performance of their respective duties; with authority to such commissioners, or the persons to be appointed by them, to execute process as aforesaid, to summon and call to their aid the bystanders, or posse comitatus of the proper county, when necessary to ensure a faithful observance of the clause of the Constitution referred to, in conformity with the provisions of this act; and all good citizens are hereby commanded to aid and assist in the prompt and efficient execution of this law, whenever their services may be required, as aforesaid, for that purpose; and said warrants shall run, and be executed by said officers, any where in the State within which they are issued.

Section 6

And be it further enacted, That when a person held to service or labor in any State or Territory of the United States, has heretofore or shall hereafter escape into another State or Territory of the United States, the person or persons to whom such service or labor may be due, or his, her, or their agent or attorney, duly authorized, by power of attorney, in writing, acknowledged and certified under the seal of some legal officer or court of the State or Territory in which the same may be executed, may pursue and reclaim such fugitive person, either by procuring a warrant from some one of the courts, judges, or commissioners aforesaid, of the proper circuit, district, or county, for the apprehension of such fugitive from service or labor, or by seizing and arresting such fugitive, where the same can be done without process, and by taking, or causing such person to be taken, forthwith before such court, judge, or commissioner, whose duty it shall be to hear and determine the case of such claimant in a summary manner; and upon satisfactory proof being made, by deposition or affidavit, in writing, to be taken and certified by such court, judge, or commissioner, or by other satisfactory testimony, duly taken and certified by some court, magistrate, justice of the peace, or other legal officer authorized to administer an oath and take depositions under the laws of the State or Territory from which such person owing service or labor may have escaped, with a certificate of such magistracy or other authority, as aforesaid, with the seal of the proper court or officer thereto attached, which seal shall be sufficient to establish the competency of the proof, and with proof, also by affidavit, of the identity of the person whose service or labor is claimed to be due as aforesaid, that the person so arrested does in fact owe service or labor to the person or persons claiming him or her, in the State or Territory from which such fugitive may have escaped as aforesaid, and that said person escaped, to make out and deliver to such claimant, his or her agent or attorney, a certificate setting forth the substantial facts as to the service or labor due from such fugitive to the claimant, and of his or her escape from the State or Territory in which he or she was arrested, with authority to such claimant, or his or her agent or attorney, to use such reasonable force and restraint as may be necessary, under the circumstances of the case, to take and remove such fugitive person back to the State or Territory whence he or she may have escaped as aforesaid. In no trial or hearing under this act shall the testimony of such alleged fugitive be admitted in evidence; and the certificates in this and the first [fourth] section mentioned, shall be conclusive of the right of the person or persons in whose favor granted, to remove such fugitive to the State or Territory from which he escaped, and shall prevent all molestation of such person or persons by any process issued by any court, judge, magistrate, or other person whomsoever.

Section 7

And be it further enacted, That any person who shall knowingly and willingly obstruct, hinder, or prevent such claimant, his agent or attorney, or any person or persons lawfully assisting him, her, or them, from arresting such a fugitive from service or labor, either with or without process as aforesaid, or shall rescue, or attempt to rescue, such fugitive from service or labor, from the custody of such claimant, his or her agent or attorney,

or other person or persons lawfully assisting as aforesaid, when so arrested, pursuant to the authority herein given and declared; or shall aid, abet, or assist such person so owing service or labor as aforesaid, directly or indirectly, to escape from such claimant, his agent or attorney, or other person or persons legally authorized as aforesaid; or shall harbor or conceal such fugitive, so as to prevent the discovery and arrest of such person, after notice or knowledge of the fact that such person was a fugitive from service or labor as aforesaid, shall, for either of said offences, be subject to a fine not exceeding one thousand dollars, and imprisonment not exceeding six months, by indictment and conviction before the District Court of the United States for the district in which such offence may have been committed, or before the proper court of criminal jurisdiction, if committed within any one of the organized Territories of the United States; and shall moreover forfeit and pay, by way of civil damages to the party injured by such illegal conduct, the sum of one thousand dollars for each fugitive so lost as aforesaid, to be recovered by action of debt, in any of the District or Territorial Courts aforesaid, within whose jurisdiction the said offence may have been committed.

Section 8

And be it further enacted, That the marshals, their deputies, and the clerks of the said District and Territorial Courts, shall be paid, for their services, the like fees as may be allowed for similar services in other cases; and where such services are rendered exclusively in the arrest, custody, and delivery of the fugitive to the claimant, his or her agent or attorney, or where such supposed fugitive may be discharged out of custody for the want of sufficient proof as aforesaid, then such fees are to be paid in whole by such claimant, his or her agent or attorney; and in all cases where the proceedings are before a commissioner, he shall be entitled to a fee of ten dollars in full for his services in each case, upon the delivery of the said certificate to the claimant, his agent or attorney; or a fee of five dollars in cases where the proof shall not, in the opinion of such commissioner, warrant such certificate and delivery, inclusive of all services incident to such arrest and examination, to be paid, in either case, by the claimant, his or her agent or attorney. The person or persons authorized to execute the process to be issued by such commissioner for the arrest and detention of fugitives from service or labor as aforesaid, shall also be entitled to a fee of five dollars each for each person he or they may arrest, and take before any commissioner as aforesaid, at the instance and request of such claimant, with such other fees as may be deemed reasonable by such commissioner for such other additional services as may be necessarily performed by him or them; such as attending at the examination, keeping the fugitive in custody, and providing him with food and lodging during his detention, and until the final determination of such commissioners; and, in general, for performing such other duties as may be required by such claimant, his or her attorney or agent, or commissioner in the premises, such fees to be made up in conformity with the fees usually charged by the officers of the courts of justice within the proper district or county, as near as may be practicable, and paid by such claimants, their agents or attorneys, whether such supposed fugitives from service or labor be ordered to be delivered to such claimant by the final determination of such commissioner or not.

Section 9

And be it further enacted, That, upon affidavit made by the claimant of such fugitive, his agent or attorney, after such certificate has been issued, that he has reason to apprehend that such fugitive will he rescued by force from his or their possession before he can be taken beyond the limits of the State in which the arrest is made, it shall be the duty of the officer making the arrest to retain such fugitive in his custody, and to remove him to the State whence he fled, and there to deliver him to said claimant, his agent, or attorney. And to this end, the officer aforesaid is hereby authorized and required to employ so many persons as he may deem necessary to overcome such force, and to retain them in his service so long as circumstances may require. The said officer and his assistants, while so employed, to receive the same compensation, and to be allowed the same expenses, as are now allowed by law for transportation of criminals, to be certified by the judge of the district within which the arrest is made, and paid out of the treasury of the United States.

Section 10

And be it further enacted, That when any person held to service or labor in any State or Territory, or in the District of Columbia, shall escape therefrom, the party to whom such service or labor shall be due, his, her, or their agent or attorney, may apply to any court of record therein, or judge thereof in vacation, and make satisfactory proof to such court, or judge in vacation, of the escape aforesaid, and that the person escaping owed service or labor to such party. Whereupon the court shall cause a record to be made of the matters so proved, and also a general description of the person so escaping, with such convenient certainty as may be; and a transcript of such record, authenticated by the attestation of the clerk and of the seal of the said court, being produced in any other State, Territory, or district in which the person so escaping may be found, and being exhibited to any judge, commissioner, or other office, authorized by the law of the United States to cause persons escaping from service or labor to be delivered up, shall be held and taken to be full and conclusive evidence of the fact of escape, and that the service or labor of the person escaping is due to the party in such record mentioned. And upon the production by the said party of other and further evidence if necessary, either oral or by affidavit, in addition to what is contained in the said record of the identity of the person escaping, he or she shall be delivered up to the claimant, And the said court, commissioner, judge, or other person authorized by this act to grant certificates to claimants or fugitives, shall, upon the production of the record and other evidences aforesaid, grant to such claimant a certificate of his right to take any such person identified and proved to be owing service or labor as aforesaid, which certificate shall authorize such claimant to seize or arrest and transport such person to the State or Territory from which he escaped: Provided, That nothing herein contained shall be construed as requiring the production of a transcript of such record as evidence as aforesaid. But in its absence the claim shall be heard and determined upon other satisfactory proofs, competent in law.

Source: Fugitive Slave Act. U.S. Statutes at Large 1 (1793): 302; *Fugitive Slave Act. U.S. Statutes at Large* 9 (1850): 462.

Missouri Compromise (March 3, 1820)

Missouri's application for U.S. statehood in 1819 caused considerable controversy because, if it had been admitted as a slave state, Missouri would have tipped the balance in the U.S. Senate toward the slave states. Opponents of slavery wanted Missouri to eliminate the institution prior to being admitted as a state; proponents thought that was a matter for Missouri alone to decide. On March 3, 1820, the Missouri Compromise, hammered out by U.S. congressman Henry Clay, solved the problem at least temporarily by admitting Missouri as a slave state and Maine (formerly part of Massachusetts) as a free state. The law further provided that, with the exception of Missouri, slavery would be prohibited in the Louisiana Territory north of 36° 30′ north latitude and permitted south of that line. The Missouri Compromise, however, did not put an end to sectional conflict. Victory in the Mexican-American War (1846–1848) reignited quarrels over the status of slavery in the vast new territories gained by the United States. The three congressional titans of the antebellum decades—Henry Clay, Daniel Webster, and John C. Calhoun—played a part in crafting the Compromise of 1850, which admitted California as a free state, allowed the other new territories to decide for themselves, and toughened the Fugitive Slave Law.

An Act to authorize the people of the Missouri territory to form a constitution and state government, and for the admission of such state into the Union on an equal footing with the original states, and to prohibit slavery in certain territories.

Be it enacted by the Senate and House of Representatives of the United States of America, in Congress assembled, That the inhabitants of that portion of the Missouri territory included within the boundaries herein after designated, be, and they are hereby, authorized to form for themselves a constitution and state government, and to assume such name as they shall deem proper; and the said state, when formed, shall be admitted into the Union, upon an equal footing with the original states, in all respects whatsoever.

SEC. 2. And be it further enacted, That the said state shall consist of all the territory included within the following boundaries, to wit: Beginning in the middle of the Mississippi river, on the parallel of thirty-six degrees of north latitude; thence west, along that parallel of latitude, to the St. Francois river; thence up, and following the course of that river, in the middle of the main channel thereof, to the parallel of latitude of thirty-six degrees and thirty minutes; thence west, along the same, to a point where the said parallel is intersected by a meridian line passing through the middle of the mouth of the Kansas river, where the same empties into the Missouri river, thence, from the point aforesaid north, along the said meridian line, to the intersection of the parallel of latitude which passes through the rapids of the river Des Moines, making the said line to correspond with the Indian boundary line; thence east, from the point of intersection last aforesaid, along the said parallel of latitude, to the middle of the channel of the main fork of the said river Des Moines; thence down arid along the middle of the main channel of the said river Des Moines, to the mouth of the same, where it empties into the Mississippi river; thence, due east, to the middle of the main channel of the Mississippi river; thence down, and following the course of the Mississippi river, in the middle of the main channel thereof, to the place of beginning: Provided, The said state shall ratify the boundaries aforesaid. And provided also, That the said state shall have concurrent jurisdiction on the river Mississippi, and every other river bordering on the said state so far as the said rivers shall form a common boundary to the said state; and any other state or states, now or hereafter to be formed and bounded by the same, such rivers to be common to both; and that the river Mississippi, and the navigable rivers and waters leading into the same, shall be common highways, and forever free, as well

to the inhabitants of the said state as to other citizens of the United States, without any tax, duty impost, or toll, therefore, imposed by the said state.

SEC. 3. And be it further enacted, That all free white male citizens of the United States, who shall have arrived at the age of twenty-one years, and have resided in said territory: three months previous to the day of election, and all other persons qualified to vote for representatives to the general assembly of the said territory, shall be qualified to be elected and they are hereby qualified and authorized to vote, and choose representatives to form a convention, who shall be apportioned amongst the several counties as follows:

From the county of Howard, five representatives. From the county of Cooper, three representatives. From the county of Montgomery, two representatives. From the county of Pike, one representative. From the county of Lincoln, one representative. From the county of St. Charles, three representatives. From the county of Franklin, one representative. From the county of St. Louis, eight representatives. From the county of Jefferson, one representative. From the county of Washington, three representatives. From the county of St. Genevieve, four representatives. From the county of Madison, one representative. From the county of Cape Girardeau, five representatives. From the county of New Madrid, two representatives. From the county of Wayne, and that portion of the county of Lawrence which falls within the boundaries herein designated, one representative.

And the election for the representatives aforesaid shall be holden on the first Monday, and two succeeding days of May next, throughout the several counties aforesaid in the said territory, and shall be, in every respect, held and conducted in the same manner, and under the same regulations as is prescribed by the laws of the said territory regulating elections therein for members of the general assembly, except that the returns of the election in that portion of Lawrence county included in the boundaries aforesaid, shall be made to the county of Wayne, as is provided in other cases under the laws of said territory.

SEC. 4. And be it further enacted, That the members of the convention thus duly elected, shall be, and they are hereby authorized to meet at the seat of government of said territory on the second Monday of the month of June next; and the said convention, when so assembled, shall have power and authority to adjourn to any other place in the said territory, which to them shall seem best for the convenient transaction of their business; and which convention, when so met, shall first determine by a majority of the whole number elected, whether it be, or be not, expedient at that time to form a constitution and state government for the people within the said territory, as included within the boundaries above designated; and if it be deemed expedient, the convention shall be, and hereby is, authorized to form a constitution and state government; or, if it be deemed more expedient, the said convention shall provide by ordinance for electing representatives to form a constitution or frame of government; which said representatives shall be chosen in such manner, and in such proportion as they shall designate; and shall meet at such time and place as shall be prescribed by the said ordinance; and shall then form for the people of said territory, within the boundaries aforesaid, a constitution and state government: Provided, That the same, whenever formed, shall be republican, and not repugnant to the constitution of the United States; and that the legislature of said state shall never interfere with the primary disposal of the soil by the United States, nor with any regulations Congress may find necessary for securing the title in such soil to the bona fide purchasers; and that no tax shall be imposed on lands the property of the United States; and in no case shall non-resident proprietors be taxed higher than residents.

SEC. 5. And be it further enacted, That until the next general census shall be taken, the said state shall be entitled to one representative in the House of Representatives of the United States.

SEC. 6. And be it further enacted, That the following propositions be, and the same are hereby, offered to the convention of the said territory of Missouri, when formed, for their free acceptance or rejection, which, if accepted by the convention, shall be obligatory upon the United States:

First. That section numbered sixteen in every township, and when such section has been sold, or otherwise disposed of, other lands equivalent thereto, and as contiguous as may be, shall be granted to the state for the use of the inhabitants of such township, for the use of schools.

Second. That all salt springs, not exceeding twelve in number, with six sections of land adjoining to each, shall be granted to the said state for the use of said state, the same to be selected by the legislature of the said state, on or before the first day of January, in the year one thousand eight hundred and twenty-five; and the same, when so selected, to be used under such terms, conditions, and regulations, as the legislature of said state shall direct: Provided, That no salt spring, the right whereof now is, or hereafter shall be, confirmed or adjudged to any individual or individuals, shall, by this section, be granted to the said state: And provided also, That the legislature shall never sell or lease the same, at anyone time, for a longer period than ten years, without the consent of Congress.

Third. That five per cent of the net proceeds of the sale of lands lying within the said territory or state, and which shall be sold by Congress, from and after the first day of January next, after deducting all expenses incident to the same, shall be reserved for making public roads and canals, of which three fifths shall be applied to those objects within the state, under the direction of the legislature thereof; and the other two fifths in defraying, under the direction of Congress, the expenses to be incurred in making of a road or roads, canal or canals, leading to the said state.

Fourth. That four entire sections of land be, and the same are hereby, granted to the said state, for the purpose of fixing their seat of government thereon; which said sections shall, under the direction of the legislature of said state, be located, as near as may be, in one body, at any time, in such townships and ranges as the legislature aforesaid may select, on any of the public lands of the United States: Provided, That such locations shall be made prior to the public sale of the lands of the United States surrounding such location.

Fifth. That thirty-six sections, or one entire township, which shall be designated by the President of the United States, together with the other lands heretofore reserved for that purpose, shall be reserved for the use of a seminary of learning, and vested in the legislature of said state, to be appropriated solely to the use of such seminary by the said legislature: Provided, That the five foregoing propositions herein offered, are on the condition that the convention of the said state shall provide, by an ordinance, irrevocable without the consent or the United States, that every and each tract of land sold by the United States, from and after the first day of January next, shall remain exempt from any tax laid by order or under the authority of the state, whether for state, county, or township, or any other purpose whatever, for the term of five years from and after the day of sale; And further, That the bounty lands granted, or hereafter to be granted, for military services during the late war, shall, while they continue to be held by the patentees, or their heirs remain exempt as aforesaid from taxation for the term of three year; from and after the date of the patents respectively.

SEC. 7. And be it further enacted, That in case a constitution and state government shall be formed for the people of the said territory of Missouri, the said convention or representatives, as soon thereafter as may be, shall cause a true and attested copy of such constitution or frame of state government, as shall be formed or provided, to be transmitted to Congress.

SEC. 8. And be it further enacted. That in all that territory ceded by France to the United States, under the name of Louisiana, which lies north of thirty-six degrees and thirty minutes north latitude, not included within the limits of the state, contemplated by this act, slavery and involuntary servitude, otherwise than in the punishment of crimes, whereof the parties shall have been duly convicted, shall be, and is hereby, forever prohibited: Provided always, That any person escaping into the same, from whom labour or service is lawfully claimed, in any state or territory of the United States, such fugitive may be lawfully reclaimed and conveyed to the person claiming his or her labour or service as aforesaid.

APPROVED, March 6, 1820.

Source: A Century of Lawmaking for a New Nation: U.S. Congressional Documents and Debates, 1774–1875. U.S. Statutes at Large 16 (1820): 545.

Frederick Douglass: "What to the Slave is the Fourth of July?" (July 5, 1852)

African American abolitionist Frederick Douglass (circa 1817–1895) was born in Maryland to a slave and an unknown white father. He was separated from his mother and grandmother in early childhood. His master's wife began teaching him to read, but when her husband ordered her to cease, Douglass covertly studied on his own and taught other slaves. After two failed attempts, he escaped to freedom in 1838 and settled in Massachusetts. He soon joined the Abolition movement and became a well-regarded anti-slavery speaker, even traveling to England to make addresses. On July 5, 1852, in Rochester, New York, Douglass delivered this address to a large crowd at a Fourth of July celebration. His words stirred tremendous debate, but struck a chord with many other abolitionists and African Americans who held that the U.S. Declaration of Independence's promise of liberty and equality had been denied to slaves in the United States. Douglass was also a prolific writer, publisher, supporter of voting rights for women and blacks, and a tireless anti-slavery campaigner. During the Civil War, Douglass helped recruit an African American army regiment, the 54th Massachusetts. After the war, he spoke out against racism and in support of voting rights.

Editor, orator, and abolitionist Frederick Douglass was the foremost African American leader of the 19th century in the United States. He was also an advocate for women's suffrage. (Library of Congress)

Mr. President, Friends, and Fellow Citizens: He who could address this audience without a quailing sensation, has stronger nerves than I have. I do not remember ever to have appeared as a speaker before any assembly more shrinkingly, nor with greater distrust of my ability, than I do this day. A feeling has crept over me, quite unfavorable to the exercise of my limited powers of speech. The task before me is one which requires much previous thought and study for its proper performance. I know that apologies of this sort are generally considered flat and unmeaning. I trust, however, that mine will not be so considered. Should I seem at ease, my appearance would much misrepresent me. The little experience I have had in addressing public meetings, in country school houses, avails me nothing on the present occasion.

The papers and placards say that I am to deliver a 4th July oration. This certainly sounds large, and out of the common way, for it is true that I have often had the privilege to speak in this beautiful Hall, and to address many who now honor me with their presence. But neither their familiar faces, nor the perfect gauge I think I have of Corinthian Hall, seems to free me from embarrassment.

The fact is, ladies and gentlemen, the distance between this platform and the slave plantation, from which I escaped, is considerable—and the difficulties to be overcome in getting from the latter to the former, are by no means slight. That I am here today is, to me, a matter of astonishment as well as of gratitude. You will not, therefore, be surprised, if in what I have to say. I evince no elaborate preparation, nor grace my speech with any high sounding exordium. With little experience and with less learning, I have been able to throw my thoughts hastily and imperfectly together; and trusting to your patient and generous indulgence, I will proceed to lay them before you.

This, for the purpose of this celebration, is the 4th of July. It is the birthday of your National Independence, and of your political freedom. This, to you, is what the Passover was to the emancipated people of God. It carries your minds back to the day, and to the act of your great deliverance; and to the signs, and to the wonders, associated with that act, and that day. This celebration also marks the beginning of another year of your national life; and reminds you that the Republic of America is now 76 years old. I am glad, fellow-citizens, that your nation is so young. Seventy-six years, though a good old age for a man, is but a mere speck in the life of a nation. Three score years and ten is the allotted time for individual men; but nations number their years by thousands. According to this fact, you are, even now, only in the beginning of your national career, still lingering in the period of childhood. I repeat, I am glad this is so. There is hope in the thought, and hope is much needed, under the dark clouds which lower above the horizon. The eye of the reformer is met with angry flashes, portending disastrous times; but his heart may well beat lighter at the thought that America is young, and that she is still in the impressible stage of her existence. May he not hope that high lessons of wisdom, of justice and of truth,

will yet give direction to her destiny? Were the nation older, the patriot's heart might be sadder, and the reformer's brow heavier. Its future might be shrouded in gloom, and the hope of its prophets go out in sorrow. There is consolation in the thought that America is young. Great streams are not easily turned from channels, worn deep in the course of ages. They may sometimes rise in quiet and stately majesty, and inundate the land, refreshing and fertilizing the earth with their mysterious properties. They may also rise in wrath and fury, and bear away, on their angry waves, the accumulated wealth of years of toil and hardship. They, however, gradually flow back to the same old channel, and flow on as serenely as ever. But, while the river may not be turned aside, it may dry up, and leave nothing behind but the withered branch, and the unsightly rock, to howl in the abyss-sweeping wind, the sad tale of departed glory. As with rivers so with nations.

Fellow-citizens, I shall not presume to dwell at length on the associations that cluster about this day. The simple story of it is that, 76 years ago, the people of this country were British subjects. The style and title of your "sovereign people" (in which you now glory) was not then born. You were under the British Crown. Your fathers esteemed the English Government as the home government; and England as the fatherland. This home government, you know, although a considerable distance from your home, did, in the exercise of its parental prerogatives, impose upon its colonial children, such restraints, burdens and limitations, as, in its mature judgement, it deemed wise, right and proper.

But, your fathers, who had not adopted the fashionable idea of this day, of the infallibility of government, and the absolute character of its acts, presumed to differ from the home government in respect to the wisdom and the justice of some of those burdens and restraints. They went so far in their excitement as to pronounce the measures of government unjust, unreasonable, and oppressive, and altogether such as ought not to be quietly submitted to. I scarcely need say, fellow-citizens, that my opinion of those measures fully accords with that of your fathers. Such a declaration of agreement on my part would not be worth much to anybody. It would, certainly, prove nothing, as to what part I might have taken, had I lived during the great controversy of 1776. To say now that America was right, and England wrong, is exceedingly easy. Everybody can say it; the dastard, not less than the noble brave, can flippantly discant on the tyranny of England towards the American Colonies. It is fashionable to do so; but there was a time when to pronounce against England, and in favor of the cause of the colonies, tried men's souls. They who did so were accounted in their day, plotters of mischief, agitators and rebels, dangerous men. To side with the right, against the wrong, with the weak against the strong, and with the oppressed against the oppressor! here lies the merit, and the one which, of all others, seems unfashionable in our day. The cause of liberty may be stabbed by the men who glory in the deeds of your fathers. But, to proceed.

Feeling themselves harshly and unjustly treated by the home government, your fathers, like men of honesty, and men of spirit, earnestly sought redress. They petitioned and remonstrated; they did so in a decorous, respectful, and loyal manner. Their conduct was wholly unexceptionable. This, however, did not answer the purpose. They saw themselves treated with sovereign indifference, coldness and scorn. Yet they persevered. They were not the men to look back.

As the sheet anchor takes a firmer hold, when the ship is tossed by the storm, so did the cause of your fathers grow stronger, as it breasted the chilling blasts of kingly displeasure. The greatest and best of British statesmen admitted its justice, and the loftiest eloquence of the British Senate came to its support. But, with that blindness which seems to be the unvarying characteristic of tyrants, since Pharaoh and his hosts were drowned in the Red Sea, the British Government persisted in the exactions complained of.

The madness of this course, we believe, is admitted now, even by England; but we fear the lesson is wholly lost on our present rulers.

Oppression makes a wise man mad. Your fathers were wise men, and if they did not go mad, they became restive under this treatment. They felt themselves the victims of grievous wrongs, wholly incurable in their colonial capacity. With brave men there is always a remedy for oppression. Just here, the idea of a total separation of the colonies from the crown was born! It was a startling idea, much more so, than we, at this distance of time, regard it. The timid and the prudent (as has been intimated) of that day, were, of course, shocked and alarmed by it.

Such people lived then, had lived before, and will, probably, ever have a place on this planet; and their course, in respect to any great change, (no matter how great the good to be attained, or the wrong to be redressed by it), may be calculated with as much precision as can be the course of the stars. They hate all changes, but silver, gold and copper change! Of this sort of change they are always strongly in favor.

These people were called tories in the days of your fathers; and the appellation, probably, conveyed the same idea that is meant by a more modern, though a somewhat less euphonious term, which we often find in our papers, applied to some of our old politicians.

Their opposition to the then dangerous thought was earnest and powerful; but, amid all their terror and affrighted vociferations against it, the alarming and revolutionary idea moved on, and the country with it.

On the 2nd of July, 1776, the old Continental Congress, to the dismay of the lovers of ease, and the worshipers of property, clothed that dreadful idea with all the authority of national sanction. They did so in the form of a resolution; and as we seldom hit upon resolutions, drawn up in our day, whose transparency is at all equal to this, it may refresh your minds and help my story if I read it.

"Resolved, That these united colonies are, and of right, ought to be free and Independent States; that they are absolved from all allegiance to the British Crown; and that all political connection between them and the State of Great Britain is, and ought to be, dissolved."

Citizens, your fathers made good that resolution. They succeeded; and to-day you reap the fruits of their success. The freedom gained is yours; and you, therefore, may properly celebrate this anniversary. The 4th of July is the first great fact in your nation's history, the very ring-bolt in the chain of your yet undeveloped destiny.

Pride and patriotism, not less than gratitude, prompt you to celebrate and to hold it in perpetual remembrance. I have said that the Declaration of Independence is the ring-bolt to the chain of your nation's destiny; so, indeed, I regard it. The principles contained in that instrument are saving principles. Stand by those principles, be true to them on all occasions, in all places, against all foes, and at whatever cost.

From the round top of your ship of state, dark and threatening clouds may be seen. Heavy billows, like mountains in the distance, disclose to the leeward huge forms of flinty rocks! That bolt drawn, that chain broken, and all is lost. Cling to this day—cling to it, and to its principles, with the grasp of a storm-tossed mariner to a spar at midnight.

The coming into being of a nation, in any circumstances, is an interesting event. But, besides general considerations, there were peculiar circumstances which make the advent of this republic an event of special attractiveness.

The whole scene, as I look back to it, was simple, dignified and sublime.

The population of the country, at the time, stood at the insignificant number of three millions. The country was poor in the munitions of war. The population was weak and scattered, and the country a wilderness unsubdued. There were then no means of concert and combination, such as exist now. Neither steam nor lightning had then been reduced to order and discipline. From the Potomac to the Delaware was a journey of many days. Under these, and innumerable other disadvantages, your fathers declared for liberty and independence and triumphed.

Fellow Citizens, I am not wanting in respect for the fathers of this republic. The signers of the Declaration of Independence were brave men. They were great men too— great enough to give fame to a great age. It does not often happen to a nation to raise, at one time, such a number of truly great men. The point from which I am compelled to view them is not, certainly, the most favorable; and yet I cannot contemplate their great deeds with less than admiration. They were statesmen, patriots and heroes, and for the good they did, and the principles they contended for, I will unite with you to honor their memory.

They loved their country better than their own private interests; and, though this is not the highest form of human excellence, all will concede that it is a rare virtue, and that when it is exhibited, it ought to command respect. He who will, intelligently, lay down his life for his country, is a man whom it is not in human nature to despise. Your fathers staked their lives, their fortunes, and their sacred honor, on the cause of their country. In their admiration of liberty, they lost sight of all other interests.

They were peace men; but they preferred revolution to peaceful submission to bondage. They were quiet men; but they did not shrink from agitating against oppression. They showed forbearance; but that they knew its limits. They believed in order; but not in the order of tyranny. With them, nothing was "settled" that was not right. With them, justice, liberty and humanity were "final"; not slavery and oppression. You may well cherish the memory of such men. They were great in their day and generation. Their solid manhood stands out the more as we contrast it with these degenerate times.

How circumspect, exact and proportionate were all their movements! How unlike the politicians of an hour! Their statesmanship looked beyond the passing moment, and stretched away in strength into the distant future. They seized upon eternal principles, and set a glorious example in their defence. Mark them!

Fully appreciating the hardship to be encountered, firmly believing in the right of their cause, honorably inviting the scrutiny of an on-looking world, reverently appealing to heaven to attest their sincerity, soundly comprehending the solemn responsibility they were about to assume, wisely measuring the terrible odds against them, your fathers, the fathers of this republic, did, most deliberately, under the inspiration of a glorious patriotism, and with a sublime faith in the great principles of justice and freedom, lay deep the corner-stone of the national superstructure, which has risen and still rises in grandeur around you.

Of this fundamental work, this day is the anniversary. Our eyes are met with demonstrations of joyous enthusiasm. Banners and pennants wave exultingly on the breeze. The din of business, too, is hushed. Even Mammon seems to have quitted his grasp on this day. The ear-piercing fife and the stirring drum unite their accents with the ascending peal of a thousand church bells. Prayers are made, hymns are sung, and sermons are preached in honor of this day; while the quick martial tramp of a great and multitudinous nation, echoed back by all the hills, valleys and mountains of a vast continent, bespeak the occasion one of thrilling and universal interests nation's jubilee.

Friends and citizens, I need not enter further into the causes which led to this anniversary. Many of you understand them better than I do. You could instruct me in regard to them. That is a branch of knowledge in which you feel, perhaps, a much deeper interest than your speaker. The causes which led to the separation of the colonies from the British crown have never lacked for a tongue. They have all been taught in your common schools, narrated at your firesides, unfolded from your pulpits, and thundered from your legislative halls, and are as familiar to you as household words. They form the staple of your national poetry and eloquence.

I remember, also, that, as a people, Americans are remarkably familiar with all facts which make in their own favor. This is esteemed by some as a national trait—perhaps a national weakness. It is a fact, that whatever makes for the wealth or for the reputation of Americans, and can be had cheap! will be found by Americans. I shall not be charged with slandering Americans, if I say I think the American side of any question may be safely left in American hands.

I leave, therefore, the great deeds of your fathers to other gentlemen whose claim to have been regularly descended will be less likely to be disputed than mine!

THE PRESENT.

My business, if I have any here to-day, is with the present. The accepted time with God and his cause is the ever-living now.

> "Trust no future, however pleasant,
> Let the dead past bury its dead;
> Act, act in the living present,
> Heart within, and God overhead."

We have to do with the past only as we can make it useful to the present and to the future. To all inspiring motives, to noble deeds which can be gained from the past, we are welcome. But now is the time, the important time. Your fathers have lived, died, and have done their work, and have done much of it well. You live and must die, and you must do your work. You have no right to enjoy a child's share in the labor of your fathers, unless your children are to be blest by your labors. You have no right to wear out and waste the hard-earned fame of your fathers to cover your indolence. Sydney Smith tells us that men seldom eulogize the wisdom and virtues of their fathers, but to excuse some folly or wickedness of their own. This truth is not a doubtful one. There are illustrations of it near and remote, ancient and modern. It was fashionable, hundreds of years ago, for the children of Jacob to boast, we have "Abraham to our father," when they had long lost Abraham's faith and spirit. That people contented themselves under the shadow of Abraham's great name, while they repudiated the deeds which made his name great. Need I remind you that a similar thing is being done all over this country to-day? Need I tell you that the Jews are not the only people who built the tombs of the prophets, and garnished the sepulchres of the righteous? Washington could not die

fill he had broken the chains of his slaves. Yet his monument is built up by the price of human blood, and the traders in the bodies and souls of men, shout—"We have Washington to our father." Alas! that it should be so; yet so it is.

> "The evil that men do, lives after them,
> The good is oft' interred with their
> bones."

Fellow-citizens, pardon me, allow me to ask, why am I called upon to speak here to-day? What have I, or those I represent, to do with your national independence? Are the great principles of political freedom and of natural justice, embodied in that Declaration of Independence, extended to us? and am I, therefore, called upon to bring our humble offering to the national altar, and to confess the benefits and express devout gratitude for the blessings resulting from your independence to us?

Would to God, both for your sakes and ours, that an affirmative answer could be truthfully returned to these questions! Then would my task be light, and my burden easy and delightful. For who is there so cold, that a nation's sympathy could not warm him? Who so obdurate and dead to the claims of gratitude, that would not thankfully acknowledge such priceless benefits? Who so stolid and selfish, that would not give his voice to swell the hallelujahs of a nation's jubilee, when the chains of servitude had been torn from his limbs? I am not that man. In a case like that, the dumb might eloquently speak, and the "lame man leap as an hart."

But, such is not the state of the case. I say it with a sad sense of the disparity between us. I am not included within the pale of this glorious anniversary! Your high independence only reveals the immeasurable distance between us. The blessings in which you, this day, rejoice, are not enjoyed in common. The rich inheritance of justice, liberty, prosperity and independence, bequeathed by your fathers, is shared by you, not by me. The sunlight that brought life and healing to you, has brought stripes and death to me. This Fourth July is yours, not mine. You may rejoice, I must mourn. To drag a man in fetters into the grand illuminated temple of liberty, and call upon him to join you in joyous anthems, were inhuman mockery and sacrilegious irony. Do you mean, citizens, to mock me, by asking me to speak to-day? If so, there is a parallel to your conduct. And let me warn you that it is dangerous to copy the example of a nation whose crimes, lowering up to heaven, were thrown down by the breath of the Almighty, burying that nation in irrecoverable ruin! I can to-day take up the plaintive lament of a peeled and woe-smitten people!

Fellow-citizens; above your national, tumultuous joy, I hear the mournful wail of millions! whose chains, heavy and grievous yesterday, are, to-day, rendered more intolerable by the jubilee shouts that reach them. If I do forget, if I do not faithfully remember those bleeding children of sorrow this day, "may my right hand forget her cunning, and may my tongue cleave to the roof of my mouth!" To forget them, to pass lightly over their wrongs, and to chime in with the popular theme, would be treason most scandalous and shocking, and would make me a reproach before God and the world. My subject, then fellow-citizens, is AMERICAN SLAVERY. I shall see, this day, and its popular characteristics, from the slave's point of view. Standing, there, identified with the American bondman, making his wrongs mine, I do not hesitate to declare, with all my soul, that the character and conduct of this nation never looked blacker to me than on this 4th of July! Whether we turn to the declarations

of the past, or to the professions of the present, the conduct of the nation seems equally hideous and revolting. America is false to the past, false to the present, and solemnly binds herself to be false to the future. Standing with God and the crushed and bleeding slave on this occasion, I will, in the name of humanity which is outraged, in the name of liberty which is fettered, in the name of the constitution and the Bible, which are disregarded and trampled upon, dare to call in question and to denounce, with all the emphasis I can command, everything that serves to perpetuate slavery—the great sin and shame of America! "I will not equivocate; I will not excuse;" I will use the severest language I can command; and yet not one word shall escape me that any man, whose judgement is not blinded by prejudice, or who is not at heart a slaveholder, shall not confess to be fight and just.

But I fancy I hear some one of my audience say, it is just in this circumstance that you and your brother abolitionists fail to make a favorable impression on the public mind. Would you argue more, and denounce less, would you persuade more, and rebuke less, your cause would be much more likely to succeed. But, I submit, where all is plain there is nothing to be argued. What point in the anti-slavery creed would you have me argue? On what branch of the subject do the people of this country need light? Must I undertake to prove that the slave is a man? That point is conceded already. Nobody doubts it. The slaveholders themselves acknowledge it in the enactment of laws for their government. They acknowledge it when they punish disobedience on the part of the slave. There are seventy-two crimes in the State of Virginia, which, if committed by a black man, (no matter how ignorant he be), subject him to the punishment of death; while only two of the same crimes see one of these human flesh-jobbers, armed with pistol, whip and bowie-knife, driving a company of a hundred men, women, and children, from the Potomac to the slave market at New Orleans. These wretched people are to be sold singly, or in lots, to suit purchasers. They are food for the cotton-field, and the deadly sugar-mill. Mark the sad procession, as it moves wearily along, and the inhuman wretch who drives them. Hear his savage yells and his blood-chilling oaths, as he hurries on his affrighted captives! There, see the old man, with locks thinned and gray. Cast one glance, if you please, upon that young mother, whose shoulders are bare to the scorching sun, her briny tears falling on the brow of the babe in her arms. See, too, that girl of thirteen, weeping, yes! weeping, as she thinks of the mother from whom she has been torn! The drove moves tardily. Heat and sorrow have nearly consumed their strength; suddenly you hear a quick snap, like the discharge of a rifle; the fetters clank, and the chain rattles simultaneously; your ears are saluted with a scream, that seems to have torn its way to the centre of your soul! The crack you heard, was the sound of the slave-whip; the scream you heard, was from the woman you saw with the babe. Her speed had faltered under the weight of her child and her chains! that gash on her shoulder tells her to move on. Follow this drove to New Orleans. Attend the auction; see men examined like horses; see the forms of women rudely and brutally exposed to the shocking gaze of American slave-buyers. See this drove sold and separated forever; and never forget the deep, sad sobs that arose from that scattered multitude. Tell me citizens, WHERE, under the sun, you can witness a spectacle more fiendish and shocking. Yet this is but a glance at the American slave-trade, as it exists, at this moment, in the ruling part of the United States.

I was born amid such sights and scenes. To me the American slave-trade is a terrible reality. When a child, my soul was often pierced with a sense of its horrors. I lived on Philpot Street, Fell's Point, Baltimore, and have watched from the wharves, the slave ships in the Basin, anchored from the shore, with their cargoes of human flesh, waiting for favorable winds to waft them down the Chesapeake. There was, at that time, a grand slave mart kept at the head of Pratt Street, by Austin Woldfolk. His agents were sent into every town and county in Maryland, announcing their arrival, through the papers, and on flaming "hand-bills," headed CASH FOR NEGROES. These men were generally well dressed men, and very captivating in their manners. Ever ready to drink, to treat, and to gamble. The fate of many a slave has depended upon the turn of a single card; and many a child has been snatched from the arms of its mother by bargains arranged in a state of brutal drunkenness.

The flesh-mongers gather up their victims by dozens, and drive them, chained, to the general depot at Baltimore. When a sufficient number have been collected here, a ship is chartered, for the purpose of conveying the forlorn crew to Mobile, or to New Orleans. From the slave prison to the ship, they are usually driven in the darkness of night; for since the antislavery agitation, a certain caution is observed.

In the deep still darkness of midnight, I have been often aroused by the dead heavy footsteps, and the piteous cries of the chained gangs that passed our door. The anguish of my boyish heart was intense; and I was often consoled, when speaking to my mistress in the morning, to hear her say that the custom was very wicked; that she hated to hear the rattle of the chains, and the heart-rending cries. I was glad to find one who sympathised with me in my horror.

Fellow-citizens, this murderous traffic is, to-day, in active operation in this boasted republic. In the solitude of my spirit, I see clouds of dust raised on the highways of the South; I see the bleeding footsteps; I hear the doleful wail of fettered humanity, on the way to the slave-markets, where the victims are to be sold like horses, sheep, and swine, knocked off to the highest bidder. There I see the tenderest ties ruthlessly broken, to gratify the lust, caprice and rapacity of the buyers and sellers of men. My soul sickens at the sight.

> "Is this the land your Fathers loved,
> The freedom which they toiled to win?
> Is this the earth whereon they moved?
> Are these the graves they slumber in?"

But a still more inhuman, disgraceful, and scandalous state of things remains to be presented.

By an act of the American Congress, not yet two years old, slavery has been nationalized in its most horrible and revolting form. By that act, Mason & Dixon's line has been obliterated; New York has become as Virginia; and the power to hold, hunt, and sell men, women, and children as slaves remains no longer a mere state institution, but is now an institution of the whole United States. The power is co-extensive with the star-spangled banner and American Christianity. Where these go, may also go the merciless slave-hunter. Where these are, man is not sacred. He is a bird for the sportsman's gun. By that most foul and fiendish of all human decrees, the liberty and person of every man are put in peril. Your broad republican domain is hunting ground for men. Not for thieves and robbers, enemies of society, merely, but for men guilty of no crime. Your lawmakers

have commanded all good citizens to engage in this hellish sport. Your President, your Secretary of State, your lords, nobles, and ecclesiastics, enforce, as a duty you owe to your free and glorious country, and to your God, that you do this accursed thing. Not fewer than forty Americans have, within the past two years, been hunted down and, without a moment's warning, hurried away in chains, and consigned to slavery and excruciating torture. Some of these have had wives and children, dependent on them for bread; but of this, no account was made. The right of the hunter to his prey stands superior to the right of marriage, and to all rights in this republic, the rights of God included! For black men there are neither law, justice, humanity, not religion. The Fugitive Slave Law makes MERCY TO THEM, A CRIME; and bribes the judge who tries them. An American JUDGE GETS TEN DOLLARS FOR EVERY VICTIM HE CONSIGNS to slavery, and five, when he fails to do so. The oath of any two villains is sufficient, under this hell-black enactment, to send the most pious and exemplary black man into the remorseless jaws of slavery! His own testimony is nothing. He can bring no witnesses for himself. The minister of American justice is bound by the law to hear but one side; and that side, is the side of the oppressor. Let this damning fact be perpetually told. Let it be thundered around the world, that, in tyrant-killing, king-hating, people-loving, democratic, Christian America, the seats of justice are filled with judges, who hold their offices under an open and palpable bribe, and are bound, in deciding in the case of a man's liberty, hear only his accusers!

In glaring violation of justice, in shameless disregard of the forms of administering law, in cunning arrangement to entrap the defenceless, and in diabolical intent, this Fugitive Slave Law stands alone in the annals

Boston, the DEWEYS of Washington, and other great religious lights of the land, have, in utter denial of the authority of Him, by whom they professed to he called to the ministry, deliberately taught us, against the example or the Hebrews and against the remonstrance of the Apostles, they teach "that we ought to obey man's law before the law of God."

My spirit wearies of such blasphemy; and how such men can be supported, as the "standing types and representatives of Jesus Christ," is a mystery which I leave others to penetrate. In speaking of the American church, however, let it be distinctly understood that I mean the great mass of the religious organizations of our land. There are exceptions, and I thank God that there are. Noble men may be found, scattered all over these Northern States, of whom Henry Ward Beecher of Brooklyn, Samuel J. May of Syracuse, and my esteemed friend on the platform, are shining examples; and let me say further, that upon these men lies the duty to inspire our ranks with high religious faith and zeal, and to cheer us on in the great mission of the slave's redemption from his chains.

Religion in England and Religion in America

One is struck with the difference between the attitude of the American church towards the anti-slavery movement, and that occupied by the churches in England towards a similar movement in that country. There, the church, true to its mission of ameliorating, elevating, and improving the condition of mankind, came forward promptly, bound up the wounds of the West Indian slave, and restored him to his liberty. There, the question of emancipation was a high religious question. It was demanded, in the name of humanity, and according to the law of the living God. The Sharps, the Clarksons, the Wilberforces, the Buxtons, and Burchells and the Knibbs, were alike famous for their piety, and for their philanthropy. The anti-slavery movement there was not an anti-church movement, for the reason that the church took its full share in prosecuting that movement: and the anti-slavery movement in this country will cease to be an anti-church movement, when the church of this country shall assume a favorable, instead or a hostile position towards that movement. Americans! your republican politics, not less than your republican religion, are flagrantly inconsistent. You boast of your love of liberty, your superior civilization, and your pure Christianity, while the whole political power of the nation (as embodied in the two great political parties), is solemnly pledged to support and perpetuate the enslavement of three millions of your countrymen. You hurl your anathemas at the crowned headed tyrants of Russia and Austria, and pride yourselves on your Democratic institutions, while you yourselves consent to be the mere tools and bodyguards of the tyrants of Virginia and Carolina. You invite to your shores fugitives of oppression from abroad, honor them with banquets, greet them with ovations, cheer them, toast them, salute them, protect them, and pour out your money to them like water; but the fugitives from your own land you advertise, hunt, arrest, shoot and kill. You glory in your refinement and your universal education; yet you maintain a system as barbarous and dreadful as ever stained the character of a nation—a system begun in avarice, supported in pride, and perpetuated in cruelty. You shed tears over fallen Hungary, and make the sad story of her wrongs the theme of your poets, statesmen and orators, till your gallant sons are ready to fly to arms to vindicate her cause against her oppressors; but, in regard to the ten thousand wrongs of the American slave, you would enforce the strictest silence, and would hail him as an enemy of the nation who dares to make those wrongs the subject of public discourse! You are all on fire at the mention of liberty for France or for Ireland; but are as cold as an iceberg at the thought of liberty for the enslaved of America. You discourse eloquently on the dignity of labor; yet, you sustain a system which, in its very essence, casts a stigma upon labor. You can bare your bosom to the storm of British artillery to throw off a threepenny tax on tea; and yet wring the last hard-earned farthing from the grasp of the black laborers of your country. You profess to believe "that, of one blood, God made all nations of men to dwell on the face of all the earth," and hath commanded all men, everywhere to love one another; yet you notoriously hate, (and glory in your hatred), all men whose skins are not colored like your own. You declare, before the world, and are understood by the world to declare, that you "hold these truths to be self evident, that all men are created equal; and are endowed by their Creator with certain inalienable rights; and that, among these are, life, liberty, and the pursuit of happiness;" and yet, you hold securely, in a bondage which, according to your own Thomas Jefferson, "is worse than ages of that which your fathers rose in rebellion to oppose," a seventh part of the inhabitants of your country.

Fellow-citizens! I will not enlarge further on your national inconsistencies. The existence of slavery in this country brands your republicanism as a sham, your humanity as a base pretence, and your Christianity as a lie. It destroys your moral power abroad; it corrupts your politicians at home. It saps the foundation of religion; it makes your name a hissing, and a by word to a mocking earth. It is the antagonistic force in your government, the only thing that seriously disturbs and endangers your Union. It fetters your progress; it is the enemy of improvement, the deadly foe of education; it fosters pride; it breeds insolence; it promotes vice; it shelters crime; it is a curse to the earth that supports it; and yet, you cling to it, as if it were the sheet anchor of all your hopes. Oh! be warned! be warned! a horrible reptile is coiled up in your nation's bosom; the venomous creature is nursing at the tender breast of your youthful republic; for the love of God, tear away, and fling from you the hideous monster, and let the weight of twenty millions crush and destroy it forever!

The Constitution

But it is answered in reply to all this, that precisely what I have now denounced is, in fact, guaranteed and sanctioned by the Constitution of the United States; that the right to hold and to hunt slaves is a part of that Constitution framed by the illustrious Fathers of this Republic.

Then, I dare to affirm, notwithstanding all I have said before, your fathers stooped, basely stooped,

> "To palter with us in a double sense:
> And keep the word of promise to the ear,
> But break it to the heart."

And instead of being the honest men I have before declared them to be, they were the veriest imposters that ever practised on mankind. This is the inevitable conclusion, and from it there is no escape. But I differ from those who charge this baseness on the framers of the Constitution of the United States. It is a slander upon their memory, at least, so I believe. There is not time now to argue the constitutional question at length—nor have I the ability to discuss it as it ought to be discussed. The subject has been handled with masterly power by Lysander Spooner, Esq., by William Goodell, by Samuel E. Sewall, Esq., and last, though not least, by Gerritt of secession. The document repudiated the U.S. Constitution, and dissolved the union among the states, thus severing South Carolina's ties to the United States. Four days later, South Carolina issued a declaration in which it justified its secession, asserted that the Constitution guaranteed the right of states to self-government, and argued that the federal government was illegally interfering in the institution of slavery. South Carolina was the first state to secede from the union and the site of the first shots fired in the Civil War, on April 12, 1861, at Fort Sumter. Ten other Southern states seceded between January and June of 1861: Mississippi, Florida, Alabama, Georgia, Louisiana, Texas, Virginia, Arkansas, North Carolina, and Tennessee. The first six of these states met in Alabama and formed the Confederate States of America in February 1861.

The people of the State of South Carolina, in Convention assembled, on the 26th day of April, A.D., 1852, declared that the frequent violations of the *Constitution of the United States*, by the Federal Government, and its encroachments upon the reserved rights of the States, fully justified this State in then withdrawing from the Federal Union; but in deference to the opinions and wishes of the other slaveholding States, she forbore at that time to exercise this right. Since that time, these encroachments have continued to increase, and further forbearance ceases to be a virtue.

And now the State of South Carolina having resumed her separate and equal place among nations, deems it due to herself, to the remaining United States of America, and to the nations of the world, that she should declare the immediate causes which have led to this act.

In the year 1765, that portion of the British Empire embracing Great Britain, undertook to make laws for the government of that portion composed of the thirteen American Colonies. A struggle for the right

of self-government ensued, which resulted, on the *4th of July, 1776, in a Declaration*, by the Colonies, "that they are, and of right ought to be, FREE AND INDEPENDENT STATES; and that, as free and independent States, they have full power to levy war, conclude peace, contract alliances, establish commerce, and to do all other acts and things which independent States may of right do."

They further solemnly declared that whenever any "form of government becomes destructive of the ends for which it was established, it is the right of the people to alter or abolish it, and to institute a new government." Deeming the Government of Great Britain to have become destructive of these ends, they declared that the Colonies "are absolved from all allegiance to the British Crown, and that all political connection between them and the State of Great Britain is, and ought to be, totally dissolved."

In pursuance of this *Declaration of Independence*, each of the thirteen States proceeded to exercise its separate sovereignty; adopted for itself a Constitution, and appointed officers for the administration of government in all its departments—Legislative, Executive and Judicial. For purposes of defense, they united their arms and their counsels; and, in 1778, they entered into a League known as the *Articles of Confederation*, whereby they agreed to entrust the administration of their external relations to a common agent, known as the Congress of the United States, expressly declaring, in the *first Article* "that each State retains its sovereignty, freedom and independence, and every power, jurisdiction and right which is not, by this Confederation, expressly delegated to the United States in Congress assembled."

Under this Confederation, the war of the Revolution was carried on, and on the 3rd of September, 1783, the contest ended, and a *definite Treaty* was signed by Great

Britain, in which she acknowledged the independence of the Colonies in the following terms: "*ARTICLE 1*—His Britannic Majesty acknowledges the said United States, viz: New Hampshire, Massachusetts Bay, Rhode Island and Providence Plantations, Connecticut, New York, New Jersey, Pennsylvania, Delaware, Maryland, Virginia, North Carolina, South Carolina and Georgia, to be FREE, SOVEREIGN AND INDEPENDENT STATES; that he treats with them as such; and for himself, his heirs and successors, relinquishes all claims to the government, propriety and territorial rights of the same and every part thereof."

Thus were established the two great principles asserted by the Colonies, namely: the right of a State to govern itself; and the right of a people to abolish a Government when it becomes destructive of the ends for which it was instituted. And concurrent with the establishment of these principles, was the fact, that each Colony became and was recognized by the mother Country a FREE, SOVEREIGN AND INDEPENDENT STATE.

In *1787, Deputies were appointed by the States to revise the Articles of Confederation*, and on 17th September, 1787, these Deputies recommended for the adoption of the States, the Articles of Union, known as the *Constitution of the United States*.

The parties to whom this *Constitution* was submitted, were the several sovereign States; they were to agree or disagree, and when nine of them agreed the compact was to take effect among those concurring; and the General Government, as the common agent, was then invested with their authority.

If only nine of the thirteen States had concurred, the other four would have remained as they then were—separate, sovereign States, independent of any of the provisions of the *Constitution*. In fact, two of the States did not accede to the *Constitution* until long after it had gone into operation among the other eleven; and during that interval, they each exercised the functions of an independent nation.

By this *Constitution*, certain duties were imposed upon the several States, and the exercise of certain of their powers was restrained, which necessarily implied their continued existence as sovereign States. But to remove all doubt, an *amendment* was added, which declared that the powers not delegated to the United States by the Constitution, nor prohibited by it to the States, are reserved to the States, respectively, or to the people. On the 23nd May, 1788, South Carolina, by a Convention of her People, passed an Ordinance assenting to this Constitution, and afterwards altered her own Constitution, to conform herself to the obligations she had undertaken.

Thus was established, by compact between the States, a Government with definite objects and powers, limited to the express words of the grant. This limitation left the whole remaining mass of power subject to the clause reserving it to the States or to the people, and rendered unnecessary any specification of reserved rights.

We hold that the Government thus established is subject to the two great principles asserted in the *Declaration of Independence*; and we hold further, that the mode of its formation subjects it to a third fundamental principle, namely: the law of compact. We maintain that in every compact between two or more parties, the obligation is mutual; that the failure of one of the contracting parties to perform a material part of the agreement, entirely releases the obligation of the other; and that where no arbiter is provided, each party is remitted to his own judgment to determine the fact of failure, with all its consequences.

In the present case, that fact is established with certainty. We assert that fourteen of the

States have deliberately refused, for years past, to fulfill their constitutional obligations, and we refer to their own Statutes for the proof.

The Constitution of the United States, in its *fourth Article*, provides as follows: "No person held to service or labor in one State, under the laws thereof, escaping into another, shall, in consequence of any law or regulation therein, be discharged from such service or labor, but shall be delivered up, on claim of the party to whom such service or labor may be due."

This stipulation was so material to the compact, that without it that compact would not have been made. The greater number of the contracting parties held slaves, and they had previously evinced their estimate of the value of such a stipulation by making it a condition in the *Ordinance* for the government of the territory ceded by Virginia, which now composes the States north of the Ohio River.

The same *article of the Constitution* stipulates also for rendition by the several States of fugitives from justice from the other States.

The General Government, as the common agent, passed laws to carry into effect these stipulations of the States. For many years these laws were executed. But an increasing hostility on the part of the non-slaveholding States to the institution of slavery, has led to a disregard of their obligations, and the laws of the General Government have ceased to effect the objects of the Constitution. The States of Maine, New Hampshire, Vermont, Massachusetts, Connecticut, Rhode Island, New York, Pennsylvania, Illinois, Indiana, Michigan, Wisconsin and Iowa, have enacted laws which either nullify the Acts of Congress or render useless any attempt to execute them. In many of these States the fugitive is discharged from service or labor

claimed, and in none of them has the State Government complied with the stipulation made in the Constitution. The State of New Jersey, at an early day, passed a law in conformity with her constitutional obligation; but the current of anti-slavery feeling has led her more recently to enact laws which render inoperative the remedies provided by her own law and by the laws of Congress. In the State of New York even the right of transit for a slave has been denied by her tribunals; and the States of Ohio and Iowa have refused to surrender to justice fugitives charged with murder, and with inciting servile insurrection in the State of Virginia. Thus the constituted compact has been deliberately broken and disregarded by the non-slaveholding States, and the consequence follows that South Carolina is released from her obligation.

The ends for which the *Constitution* was framed are declared by itself to be "to form a more perfect union, establish justice, insure domestic tranquility, provide for the common defence, promote the general welfare, and secure the blessings of liberty to ourselves and our posterity."

These ends it endeavored to accomplish by a Federal Government, in which each State was recognized as an equal, and had separate control over its own institutions. The right of property in slaves was recognized by giving to free persons distinct political rights, by giving them the right to represent, and burthening them with direct taxes for three-fifths of their slaves; by authorizing the importation of slaves for twenty years; and by stipulating for the rendition of fugitives from labor.

We affirm that these ends for which this Government was instituted have been defeated, and the Government itself has been made destructive of them by the action of the non-slaveholding States. Those States have assume the right of deciding upon the propriety of our domestic institutions; and have denied the rights of property established in fifteen of the States and recognized by the *Constitution*; they have denounced as sinful the institution of slavery; they have permitted open establishment among them of societies, whose avowed object is to disturb the peace and to eloign the property of the citizens of other States. They have encouraged and assisted thousands of our slaves to leave their homes; and those who remain, have been incited by emissaries, books and pictures to servile insurrection.

For twenty-five years this agitation has been steadily increasing, until it has now secured to its aid the power of the common Government. Observing the *forms* of the *Constitution*, a sectional party has found within that *Article* establishing the Executive Department, the means of subverting the Constitution itself. A geographical line has been drawn across the Union, and all the States north of that line have united in the election of a man to the high office of President of the United States, whose opinions and purposes are hostile to slavery. He is to be entrusted with the administration of the common Government, because he has declared that that "Government cannot endure permanently half slave, half free," and that the public mind must rest in the belief that slavery is in the course of ultimate extinction.

This sectional combination for the submersion of the *Constitution*, has been aided in some of the States by elevating to citizenship, persons who, by the supreme law of the land, are incapable of becoming citizens; and their votes have been used to inaugurate a new policy, hostile to the South, and destructive of its beliefs and safety.

On the 4th day of March next, this party will take possession of the Government. It has announced that the South shall be excluded from the common territory, that the judicial

tribunals shall be made sectional, and that a war must be waged against slavery until it shall cease throughout the United States.

The guaranties of the *Constitution* will then no longer exist; the equal rights of the States will be lost. The slaveholding States will no longer have the power of self-government, or self-protection, and the Federal Government will have become their enemy.

Sectional interest and animosity will deepen the irritation, and all hope of remedy is rendered vain, by the fact that public opinion at the North has invested a great political error with the sanction of more erroneous religious belief.

We, therefore, the People of South Carolina, by our delegates in Convention assembled, appealing to the Supreme Judge of the world for the rectitude of our intentions, have solemnly declared that the Union heretofore existing between this State and the other States of North America, is dissolved, and that the State of South Carolina has resumed her position among the nations of the world, as a separate and independent State; with full power to levy war, conclude peace, contract alliances, establish commerce, and to do all other acts and things which independent States may of right do.

Adopted December 24, 1860

Source: Confederate States of America—Declaration of the Immediate Causes Which Induce and Justify the Secession of South Carolina from the Federal Union. Avalon Project, Yale Law Library: http://avalon.law.yale.edu/20th_century/decade19.asp.

Jefferson Davis: Inaugural Address (February 18, 1861)

Meeting in Montgomery, Alabama, delegates from Mississippi, Florida, Alabama, Georgia, and Louisiana formed the Confederate States of America on February 8, 1861, and adopted a provisional constitution based on the U.S. Constitution. The following day, they elected Jefferson Davis (1808–1889)—who was at home in Mississippi—to a six-year term as president of the new nation. A West Point graduate, Davis had served in the frontier army, became a planter in Mississippi, was elected to the U.S. Congress, and resigned to serve in the Mexican-American War. Wounded in the war, he was elected U.S. senator, and then appointed U.S. Secretary of War in 1853. He left U.S. government service when Mississippi seceded from the Union. Davis had expected to serve the Confederate cause as commander of his state militia. In her memoir, Davis's wife described his dismay at receiving the telegram calling him to Montgomery to assume the presidency, writing that he told her the news "as a man might speak of a sentence of death." On February 18, 1861, Davis delivered this speech, his one and only inaugural address. In it, he expressed hope for peace but called for the establishment of an army and navy to protect the new nation from northern aggression.

Gentlemen of the Congress of the Confederate States of America, Friends, and Fellow-citizens:

Called to the difficult and responsible station of Chief Magistrate of the Provisional Government which you have instituted, I approach the discharge of the duties assigned to me with humble distrust of my abilities, but with a sustaining confidence in the wisdom of those who are to guide and aid me in the administration of public affairs, and an abiding faith in the virtue and patriotism of the people. Looking forward to the speedy establishment of a permanent government to take the place of this, which by its greater moral and physical power will be better able to combat with many difficulties that arise from the conflicting interests of separate nations, I enter upon the duties of the office to which I have been chosen with the hope that the beginning of our career, as a Confederacy,

may not be obstructed by hostile opposition to our enjoyment of the separate existence and independence we have asserted, and which, with the blessing of Providence, we intend to maintain.

Our present political position has been achieved in a manner unprecedented in the history of nations. It illustrates the American idea that governments rest on the consent of the governed, and that it is the right of the people to alter or abolish them at will whenever they become destructive of the ends for which they were established. The declared purpose of the compact of the Union from which we have withdrawn was to "establish justice, insure domestic tranquility, provide for the common defense, promote the general welfare, and secure the blessings of liberty to ourselves and our posterity;" and when, in the judgment of the sovereign States composing this Confederacy, it has been perverted from the purposes for which it was ordained, and ceased to answer the ends for which it was established, a peaceful appeal to the ballot box declared that, so far as they are concerned, the Government created by that compact should cease to exist. In this they merely asserted the right which the Declaration of Independence of July 4, 1776, defined to be "inalienable." Of the time and occasion of its exercise they as sovereigns were the final judges, each for itself. The impartial and enlightened verdict of mankind will vindicate the rectitude of our conduct; and He who knows the hearts of men will judge of the sincerity with which we have labored to preserve the Government of our fathers in its spirit.

The right solemnly proclaimed at the birth of the United States, and which has been solemnly affirmed and reaffirmed in the Bills of Rights of the States subsequently admitted into the Union of 1789, undeniably recognizes in the people the power to resume the authority delegated for the purposes of government. Thus the sovereign States here represented have proceeded to form this Confederacy; and it is by abuse of language that their act has been denominated a revolution. They formed a new alliance, but within each State its government has remained; so that the rights of person and property have not been disturbed. The agent through which they communicated with foreign nations is changed, but this does not necessarily interrupt their international relations. Sustained by the consciousness that the transition from the former Union to the present Confederacy has not proceeded from a disregard on our part of just obligations, or any, failure to perform every constitutional duty, moved by no interest or passion to invade the rights of others, anxious to cultivate peace and commerce with all nations, if we may not hope to avoid war, we may at least expect that posterity will acquit us of having needlessly engaged in it. Doubly justified by the absence of wrong on our part, and by wanton aggression on the part of others, there can be no cause to doubt that the courage and patriotism of the people of the Confederate States will be found equal to any measure of defense which their honor and security may require. An agricultural people, whose chief interest is the export of commodities required in every manufacturing country, our true policy is peace, and the freest trade which our necessities will permit. It is alike our interest and that of all those to whom we would sell, and from whom we would buy, that there should be the fewest practicable restrictions upon the interchange of these commodities. There can, however, be but little rivalry between ours and any manufacturing or navigating community, such as the Northeastern States of the American Union. It must follow, therefore, that mutual interest will invite to good will and kind offices on both parts. If, however, passion or lust of dominion should cloud the judgment or inflame the ambition of those States, we must prepare to meet the emergency and maintain, by the final arbitrament of the sword, the position which we have assumed among the nations of the earth.

We have entered upon the career of independence, and it must be inflexibly pursued. Through many years of controversy with our late associates of the Northern States, we have vainly endeavored to secure tranquility and obtain respect for the rights to which we were entitled. As a necessity, not a choice, we have resorted to the remedy of separation, and henceforth our energies must be directed to the conduct of our own affairs, and the perpetuity of the Confederacy which we have formed. If a just perception of mutual interest shall permit us peaceably to pursue our separate political career, my most earnest desire will have been fulfilled. But if this be denied to us, and the integrity of our territory and jurisdiction be assailed, it will but remain for us with firm resolve to appeal to arms and invoke the blessing of Providence on a just cause.

As a consequence of our new condition and relations, and with a vicar to meet anticipated wants, it will be necessary to provide for the speedy and efficient organization of branches of the Executive department having special charge of foreign intercourse, finance, military affairs, and the postal service. For purposes of defense, the Confederate States may, under ordinary circumstances, rely mainly upon the militia; but it is deemed advisable, in the present condition of affairs, that there should be a well-instructed and disciplined army, more numerous than would usually be required on a peace establishment. I also suggest that, for the protection of our harbors and commerce on the high seas, a navy adapted to those objects will be required. But this, as well as other subjects appropriate to our necessities, have doubtless engaged the attention of Congress.

With a Constitution differing only from that of our fathers in so far as it is explanatory of their well-known intent, freed from sectional conflicts, which have interfered with the pursuit of the general welfare, it is not unreasonable to expect that States from which we have recently parted may seek to unite their fortunes to ours under the Government which we have instituted. For this your Constitution makes adequate provision; but beyond this, if I mistake not the judgment and will of the people, a reunion with the States from which we have separated is neither practicable nor desirable. To increase the power, develop the resources, and promote the happiness of the Confederacy, it is requisite that there should be so much of homogeneity that the welfare of every portion shall be the aim of the whole. When this does not exist, antagonisms are engendered which must and should result in separation.

Actuated solely by the desire to preserve our own rights, and promote our own welfare, the separation by the Confederate States has been marked by no aggression upon others, and followed by no domestic convulsion. Our industrial pursuits have received no check, the cultivation of our fields has progressed as heretofore, and, even should we be involved in war, there would be no considerable diminution in the production of the staples which have constituted our exports, and in which the commercial world has an interest scarcely less than our own. This common interest of the producer and consumer can only be interrupted by exterior force which would obstruct the transmission of our staples to foreign markets—a course of conduct which would be as unjust, as it would be detrimental, to manufacturing and commercial interests abroad.

Should reason guide the action of the Government from which we have separated, a policy so detrimental to the civilized world, the Northern States included, could not be dictated by even the strongest desire to inflict injury upon us; but, if the contrary should prove true, a terrible responsibility will rest upon it, and the suffering of millions will bear testimony to the folly and wickedness of our aggressors. In the meantime there will remain to us, besides the ordinary means before suggested, the well-known resources for retaliation upon the commerce of an enemy.

Experience in public stations, of subordinate grade to this care and disappointment are the price of official elevation. You will see many errors to forgive, many deficiencies to tolerate; but you shall not find in me either want of zeal or fidelity to the cause that is to me the highest in hope, and of most enduring affection. Your generosity has bestowed upon me an undeserved distinction, one which I neither sought nor desired. Upon the continuance of that sentiment, and upon your wisdom and patriotism, I rely to direct and support me in the performance of the duties required at my hands.

We have changed the constituent parts, but not the system of government. The Constitution framed by our fathers is that of these Confederate States. In their exposition of it, and in the judicial construction it has received, we have a light which reveals its true meaning.

Thus instructed as to the true meaning and just interpretation of that instrument, and ever remembering that all offices are but trusts held for the people, and that powers delegated are to be strictly construed, I will hope by due diligence in the performance of my duties, though I may disappoint your expectations, yet to retain, when retiring, something of the good will and confidence which welcome my entrance into office.

It is joyous in the midst of perilous times to look around upon a people united in heart, where one purpose of high resolve animates and actuates the whole; where the sacrifices to be made are not weighed in the balance against honor and right and liberty and equality. Obstacles may retard, but they cannot long prevent, the progress of a movement sanctified by its justice and sustained by a virtuous people. Reverently let us invoke the God of our fathers to guide and protect us in our efforts to perpetuate the principles which by his blessing they were able to vindicate, establish, and transmit to their posterity. With the continuance of his favor ever gratefully acknowledged, we may hopefully look forward to success, to peace, and to prosperity.

Source: James D. Richardson, *A Compilation of the Messages and Papers of the Confederacy Including the Diplomatic Correspondence 1861–1865.* Nashville: United States Publishing Company, 1905, 32–36.

Robert Edward Lee (1807–1870) American general and leader of the Confederate forces in the American Civil War. (Getty Images)

Robert E. Lee: Resignation from the U.S. Army (April 20, 1861) and correspondence regarding his command of Virginia forces

The prominent Virginian, Robert E. Lee (1807–1870), was a highly esteemed career soldier when the Civil War broke out. He had graduated second in his class at West Point in 1829, served in the Army Corps of Engineers, distinguished himself in the Mexican American War, returned to West Point as superintendent, and accepted a commission as lieutenant colonel of a cavalry regiment assigned to serve on the Texas frontier. As Texas plunged into open rebellion early in 1861, Lee made plans to lead his regiment north in defiance of secessionist demands to surrender. Although he intended to resign his commission and offer his services to Virginia, he refused to abandon his duty while still a U.S. soldier. General Winfield Scott, whom Lee had thoroughly impressed while serving in Mexico, recalled Lee to Washington and offered him command of all federal armies on April 18, 1861. Two days later, with the following letter, Lee graciously expressed his esteem for Scott and his fellow soldiers as he resigned from the U.S. army. Within days, Lee assumed command of Virginia forces with the rank of major general.

Letter from Robert E. Lee to Winfield Scott

ARLINGTON, VA, April 20, 1861.

GENERAL: Since my interview with you on the 18th inst. I have felt that I ought not longer to retain my commission in the army. I therefore tender my resignation, which I request you will recommend for acceptance. It would have been presented at once, but for the struggle it has cost me to separate myself from a service to which I have devoted the best years of my life and all the ability I possessed. During the whole of that time—more than a quarter of a century—I have experienced nothing but kindness from my superiors and a most cordial friendship from my comrades. To no one, general, have I been as much indebted as to yourself for uniform kindness and consideration, and it has always been my ardent desire to merit your approbation. I shall carry to the grave the most grateful recollections of your kind consideration, and your name and fame will always be dear to me.

Save in the defence of my native State, I never desire again to draw my sword. Be pleased to accept my most earnest wishes for the continuance of your happiness and prosperity, and believe me most truly yours,

R. E. LEE

Letter from Confederate Secretary of State George W. Munford to President Jefferson Davis

RICHMOND, VA., April 22, 1861.

His Excellency JEFFERSON DAVIS, President of the Confederate States of America:

I am directed by the Governor to inform you that Colonel Lee is here. The Governor has sent in his nomination as commander of the land and naval forces of Virginia, with rank of major-general. Nomination will be confirmed. . . .

GEORGE W. MUNFORD,
Secretary of State.

Robert E. Lee's General Orders, No. 1

HEADQUARTERS, Richmond, Va., April 23, 1861.

In obedience to orders from his excellency John Letcher, governor of the State, Maj. Gen. Robert E. Lee assumes command of the military and naval forces of Virginia.

R. E. LEE,
Major-General.

Source: Paper. L 32.7, W 29.3 cm. Arlington House, The Robert E. Lee Memorial, ARHO 5623; U.S. War Department, *War of the Rebellion: A Compilation of the Official Records of the Union and Confederate Armies*, Ser. I, Vols. II and LI.

Ulysses S. Grant: Excerpt from autobiography, events of 1861

The early career of Ulysses S. Grant (1822–1885) gave little indication of the qualities that would make him the essential victorious general of the Civil War and propel him to the presidency of the United States. A West Point graduate and combat veteran of the Mexican-American War, Grant struggled with alcoholism and repeated business failures. He volunteered for duty as the Civil War began and assumed command of an Illinois regiment. Independent field command involves great responsibility. Not every officer is equal to the challenge. In this excerpt from his autobiography, Grant describes a formative experience as he faced the anxieties associated with independent command for the first time. When Grant and his regiment found that the Confederates had abandoned their camp in Missouri, he realized that the enemy had suffered the same anxieties that had induced his own fears. This realization taught Grant a valuable lesson. Henceforth, he showed the confidence and determination that so distinguished his conduct for the remainder of the war. Grant began writing of his experiences long after the war because a failed business venture had left him destitute and he needed to earn money. He finished his memoirs in 1885, shortly before his death from cancer. His book sold well and allowed his widow to live in comfort.

My sensations as we approached what I supposed might be "a field of battle" were anything but agreeable. I had been in all the engagements in Mexico that it was possible for one person to be in; but not in command. If some one else had been colonel and I had been lieutenant-colonel I do not think I would have felt any trepidation. Before we were prepared to cross the Mississippi River at Quincy my anxiety was relieved; for the men of the besieged regiment came straggling into town. I am inclined to think both sides got frightened and ran away.

I took my regiment to Palmyra and remained there for a few days, until relieved by the 19th Illinois infantry. From Palmyra I proceeded to Salt River, the railroad bridge over which had been destroyed by the enemy. Colonel John M. Palmer at that time commanded the 13th Illinois, which was acting as a guard to workmen who were engaged in rebuilding this bridge. Palmer was my senior and commanded the two regiments as long as we remained together. The bridge was finished in about two weeks, and I received orders to move against Colonel Thomas Harris, who was said to be encamped at the little town of Florida, some twenty-five miles south of where we then were.

At the time of which I now write we had no transportation and the country about Salt River was sparsely settled, so that it took some days to collect teams and drivers enough to move the camp and garrison equipage of a regiment nearly a thousand strong, together with a week's supply of provision and some ammunition. While preparations for the move were going on I felt quite comfortable; but when we got on the road and found every house deserted I was anything but easy. In the twenty-five miles we had to march we did not see a person, old or young, male or female, except two horsemen who were on a road that crossed ours. As soon as they saw us they decamped as fast as their horses could carry them. I kept my men in the ranks and forbade their entering any of the deserted houses or taking anything from them. We halted at night on the road and proceeded the next morning at an early hour. Harris had been encamped in a creek bottom for the sake of being near water. The hills on either side of the creek extend to a considerable height, possibly more than a hundred feet. As we approached the brow of the hill from which it was expected we could see Harris' camp, and possibly find his men ready formed to meet us, my heart kept getting higher and higher until it felt to me as though it was in my throat. I would have given anything then to have been back in Illinois, but I had not the moral courage to halt and consider what to do; I kept right on. When we reached a point from which the valley below was in full view I halted. The place where Harris had been encamped a few days before was still there and the marks of a recent encampment were plainly visible, but the troops were gone. My heart resumed its place. It occurred to me at once that Harris had been as much afraid of me as I had been of him. This was a view of the question I had never taken before; but it was one I never forgot afterwards. From that event to the close of the war, I never experienced trepidation upon confronting an enemy, though I always felt more or less anxiety. I never forgot that he had as much reason to fear my forces as I had his. The lesson was valuable.

Inquiries at the village of Florida divulged the fact that Colonel Harris, learning of my intended movement, while my transportation was being collected took time by the forelock and left Florida before I had started from Salt River. He had increased the distance between us by forty miles. The next day I started back to my old camp at Salt River bridge. The citizens living on the line of our march had returned to their houses after we passed, and finding everything in good order, nothing carried away, they were at their front doors ready to greet us now. They had evidently been led to believe that the National troops carried death and devastation with them wherever they went.

Source: Ulysses Grant, *Personal Memoirs of U.S. Grant.* New York: Charles L. Webster & Co., 1885, vol. 1, 249–50.

Abraham Lincoln: Address to Congress (July 4, 1861)

Abraham Lincoln's (1809–1865) opposition to the expansion of slavery prompted him to join the newly formed Republican Party in 1856. After a political career as an Illinois state legislator and U.S. congressman, Lincoln ran for U.S. senator and lost to the incumbent Stephen A. Douglas. In the famous debates leading up to that election, Lincoln set forth his moral opposition to slavery while noting his willingness to tolerate slavery's existence in the South for the sake of preserving national unity. Following his victory as the Republican candidate for the U.S. presidency, Lincoln stated in his inaugural address his arguments against secession and his intention to exhaust all peaceful means of resolving the conflict with the South before resorting to war. President Lincoln called a special session of Congress on July 4, 1861, and delivered an address, excerpted here, in which he explained his reasons for waging war against the seceded Southern states and asked Congress to appropriate the funding for war. By calling forth patriotic symbols and articulating his goals in such plain language, Lincoln not only inspired the assembled congressmen to support the war but the public as well, as the text of the speech was widely circulated and reprinted in newspapers around the North.

At the beginning of the present presidential term, four months ago, the functions of the Federal government were found to be generally suspended within the several states of South Carolina, Georgia, Alabama, Mississippi, Louisiana, and Florida, excepting only those of the Post Office Department.

Within these states all the forts, arsenals, dockyards, customhouses, and the like, including the movable and stationary property in and about them, had been seized and were held in open hostility to this government, excepting only Forts Pickens, Taylor, and Jefferson, on and near the Florida coast, and Fort Sumter, in Charleston Harbor, South Carolina. The forts thus seized had been put in improved condition, new ones had been built, and armed forces had been organized and were organizing, all avowedly with the same hostile purpose.

The forts remaining in the possession of the Federal government in and near those states were either besieged or menaced by warlike preparations, and especially Fort Sumter was nearly surrounded by well-protected hostile batteries, with guns equal in quality to the best of its own and outnumbering the latter as perhaps ten to one. A disproportionate share of the Federal muskets and rifles had somehow found their way into these states, and had been seized to be used against the government. Accumulations of the public revenue lying within them had been seized for the same object. The Navy was scattered in distant seas, leaving but a very small part of it within the immediate reach of the government. Officers of the Federal Army and Navy had resigned in great numbers, and, of those resigning, a large proportion had taken up arms against the government. Simultaneously and in connection with all this the purpose to sever the Federal Union was openly avowed. In accordance with this purpose, an ordinance had been adopted in each of these states declaring the states respectively to be separated from the national Union. A formula for instituting a combined government of these states had been promulgated, and this illegal organization, in the character of Confederate States, was already invoking recognition, aid, and intervention from foreign powers.

Finding this condition of things and believing it to be an imperative duty upon the incoming executive to prevent, if possible, the consummation of such attempt to destroy the Federal Union, a choice of means to that end became indispensable. This choice was made and was declared in the inaugural address. The policy chosen looked to the exhaustion of all peaceful measures before a resort to any stronger ones. It sought only to hold the public places and property not already wrested from the government and to collect the revenue, relying for the rest on time, discussion, and the ballot box. It promised a continuance of the mails at government expense to the very people who were resisting the government, and it gave repeated pledges against any disturbance to any of the people or any of their rights. Of all that which a President might constitutionally and justifiably do in such a case, everything was forborne without which it was believed possible to keep the government on foot.

On the 5th of March, the present incumbent's first full day in office, a letter of Major Anderson, commanding at Fort Sumter, written on the 28th of February and received at the War Department on the 4th of March, was by that department placed in his hands. This letter expressed the professional opinion of the writer that reenforcements could not be thrown into that fort within the time for his relief rendered necessary by the limited supply of provisions, and with a view of holding possession of the same, with a force of less than 20,000 good and well-disciplined men. This opinion was concurred in by all the officers of his command, and their memoranda on the subject were made enclosures of Major Anderson's letter.

The whole was immediately laid before Lieutenant General Scott, who at once concurred with Major Anderson in opinion. On reflection, however, he took full time, consulting with other officers, both of the Army and the Navy, and at the end of four days came reluctantly, but decidedly, to the same conclusion as before. He also stated at the same time that no such sufficient force was then at the control of the government or

could be raised and brought to the ground within the time when the provisions in the fort would be exhausted. In a purely military point of view this reduced the duty of the administration in the case to the mere matter of getting the garrison safely out of the fort.

It was believed, however, that to so abandon that position under the circumstances would be utterly ruinous; that the necessity under which it was to be done would not be fully understood; that by many it would be construed as a part of a voluntary policy; that at home it would discourage the friends of the Union, embolden its adversaries, and go far to insure to the latter a recognition abroad; that, in fact, it would be our national destruction consummated. This could not be allowed. Starvation was not yet upon the garrison, and ere it would be reached, Fort Pickens might be reenforced. This last would be a clear indication of policy, and would better enable the country to accept the evacuation of Fort Sumter as a military necessity.

An order was at once directed to be sent for the landing of the troops from the steamship Brooklyn into Fort Pickens. This order could not go by land but must take the longer and slower route by sea. The first return news from the order was received just one week before the fall of Fort Sumter. The news itself was that the officer commanding the Sabine, to which vessel the troops had been transferred from the Brooklyn, acting upon some quasi-armistice of the late administration (and of the existence of which the present administration, up to the time the order was dispatched, had only too vague and uncertain rumors to fix attention), had refused to land the troops. To now reenforce Fort Pickens before a crisis would be reached at Fort Sumter was impossible, rendered so by the near exhaustion of provisions in the latter named fort. In precaution against such a conjuncture, the government had a few days before commenced preparing an expedition, as well-adapted as might be, to relieve Fort Sumter, which expedition was intended to be ultimately used or not, according to circumstances. The strongest anticipated case for using it was now presented, and it was resolved to send it forward.

As had been intended in this contingency, it was also resolved to notify the governor of South Carolina that he might expect an attempt would be made to provision the fort, and that if the attempt should not be resisted there would be no effort to throw in men, arms, or ammunition without further notice, or in case of an attack upon the fort. This notice was accordingly given, whereupon the fort was attacked and bombarded to its fall, without even awaiting the arrival of the provisioning expedition.

It is thus seen that the assault upon and reduction of Fort Sumter was in no sense a matter of self-defense on the part of the assailants. They well knew that the garrison in the fort could by no possibility commit aggression upon them. They knew—they were expressly notified—that the giving of bread to the few brave and hungry men of the garrison was all which would on that occasion be attempted, unless themselves, by resisting so much, should provoke more. They knew that this government desired to keep the garrison in the fort, not to assail them but merely to maintain visible possession, and thus to preserve the Union from actual and immediate dissolution, trusting, as hereinbefore stated, to time, discussion, and the ballot box for final adjustment; and they assailed and reduced the fort for precisely the reverse object—to drive out the visible authority of the Federal Union, and thus force it to immediate dissolution.

That this was their object the executive well understood; and having said to them in the inaugural address, "You can have no

conflict without being yourselves the aggressors," he took pains not only to keep this declaration good but also to keep the case so free from the power of ingenious sophistry as that the world should not be able to misunderstand it. By the affair at Fort Sumter, with its surrounding circumstances, that point was reached. Then and thereby the assailants of the government began the conflict of arms, without a gun in sight or in expectancy to return their fire, save only the few in the fort, sent to that harbor years before for their own protection, and still ready to give the protection in whatever was lawful. In this act, discarding all else, they have forced upon the country the distinct issue: "Immediate dissolution or blood."

And this issue embraces more than the fate of the United States. It presents to the whole family of man the question whether a constitutional republic, or democracy—a government of the people by the same people—can or cannot maintain its territorial integrity against its own domestic foes. It presents the question whether discontented individuals, too few in numbers to control administration according to organic law in any case, can always, upon the pretenses made in this case, or on any other pretenses, or arbitrarily without any pretense, break up their government and thus practically put an end to free government upon the earth. It forces us to ask—Is there in all republics this inherent and fatal weakness? Must a government of necessity be too strong for the liberties of its own people, or too weak to maintain its own existence?

So viewing the issue, no choice was left but to call out the war power of the government and so to resist force employed for its destruction by force for its preservation. . . .

It might seem at first thought to be of little difference whether the present movement at the South be called "secession" or "rebellion." The movers, however, well understand the difference. At the beginning they knew they could never raise their treason to any respectable magnitude by any name which implies violation of law. They knew their people possessed as much of moral sense, as much of devotion to law and order, and as much pride in and reverence for the history and government of their common country as any other civilized and patriotic people. They knew they could make no advancement directly in the teeth of these strong and noble sentiments. Accordingly, they commenced by an insidious debauching of the public mind. They invented an ingenious sophism, which, if conceded, was followed by perfectly logical steps through all the incidents to the complete destruction of the Union. The sophism itself is that any state of the Union may consistently with the national Constitution, and therefore lawfully and peacefully, withdraw from the Union without the consent of the Union or of any other state. The little disguise that the supposed right is to be exercised only for just cause, themselves to be the sole judge of its justice, is too thin to merit any notice.

With rebellion thus sugarcoated, they have been drugging the public mind of their section for more than thirty years, and until at length they have brought many good men to a willingness to take up arms against the government the day after some assemblage of men have enacted the farcical pretense of taking their state out of the Union who could have been brought to no such thing the day before.

This sophism derives much, perhaps the whole, of its currency from the assumption that there is some omnipotent and sacred supremacy pertaining to a state—to each state of our Federal Union. Our states have neither more nor less power than that reserved to them in the Union by the Constitution, no one of them ever having been a state out of the Union. The original ones passed into the Union even before they cast off their British colonial dependence, and the new ones each came into the Union directly from a condition of dependence, excepting Texas; and even Texas, in its temporary independence, was never designated a state. The new ones only took the designation of states on coming into the Union, while that name was first adopted for the old ones in and by the Declaration of Independence. Therein the "United Colonies" were declared to be "free and independent states"; but even then the object plainly was not to declare their independence of one another or of the Union, but directly the contrary, as their mutual pledge and their mutual action before, at the time, and afterward abundantly show.

The express plighting of faith by each and all of the original thirteen in the Articles of Confederation, two years later, that the Union shall be perpetual is most conclusive. Having never been states, either in substance or in name, outside of the Union, whence this magical omnipotence of "state rights," asserting a claim of power to lawfully destroy the Union itself? Much is said about the "sovereignty" of the states, but the word even is not in the national Constitution, nor, as is believed, in any of the state constitutions. What is a "sovereignty" in the political sense of the term? Would it be far wrong to define it "a political community without a political superior"? Tested by this, no one of our states, except Texas, ever was a sovereignty; and even Texas gave up the character on coming into the Union, by which act she acknowledged the Constitution of the United States and the laws and treaties of the United States made in pursuance of the Constitution to be for her the supreme law of the land.

The states have their status in the Union, and they have no other legal status. If they break from this, they can only do so against law and by revolution. The Union, and not themselves separately, procured their independence and their liberty. By conquest or purchase the Union gave each of them whatever of independence and liberty it has. The Union is older than any of the states, and, in fact, it created them as states. Originally some dependent colonies made the Union, and in turn the Union threw off their old dependence for them and made them states, such as they are. Not one of them ever had a state constitution independent of the Union. Of course it is not forgotten that all the new states framed their constitutions before they entered the Union, nevertheless dependent upon and preparatory to coming into the Union.

Unquestionably the states have the powers and rights reserved to them in and by the national Constitution; but among these surely are not included all conceivable powers, however mischievous or destructive, but at most such only as were known in the world at the time as governmental powers; and certainly a power to destroy the government itself had never been known as a governmental—as a merely administrative—power. This relative matter of national power and state rights, as a principle, is no other than the principle of generality and locality. Whatever concerns the whole should be confided to the whole—to the general government—while whatever concerns only the state should be left exclusively to the state. This is all there is of original principle about it. Whether the national Constitution in defining boundaries between the two has applied the principle with exact accuracy is not to be questioned. We are all bound by that defining without question.

What is now combated is the position that secession is consistent with the Constitution—is lawful and peaceful. It is not contended that there is any express law for it, and nothing should ever be implied as law which leads to unjust or absurd consequences. . . .

The seceders insist that our Constitution admits of secession. They have assumed to make a national constitution of their own, in which of necessity they have either discarded or retained the right of secession, as they insist it exists in ours. If they have discarded it, they thereby admit that on principle it ought not to be in ours. If they have retained it, by their own construction of ours they show that to be consistent they must secede from one another whenever they shall find it the easiest way of settling their debts or effecting any other selfish or unjust object. The principle itself is one of disintegration and upon which no government can possibly endure.

If all the states save one should assert the power to drive that one out of the Union, it is presumed the whole class of seceder politicians would at once deny the power and denounce the act as the greatest outrage upon state rights. But suppose that precisely the same act, instead of being called "driving the one out," should be called "the seceding of the others from that one," it would be exactly what the seceders claim to do, unless, indeed, they make the point that the one, because it is a minority, may rightfully do what the others, because they are a majority, may not rightfully do. These politicians are subtle and profound on the rights of minorities. They are not partial to that power which made the Constitution and speaks from the Preamble, calling itself "We, the people."

It may well be questioned whether there is today a majority of the legally qualified voters of any state, except, perhaps, South Carolina, in favor of disunion. There is much reason to believe that the Union men are the majority in many, if not in every other one, of the so-called seceded states. The contrary has not been demonstrated in any one of them. It is ventured to affirm this even of Virginia and Tennessee; for the result of an election held in military camps, where the bayonets are all on one side of the question voted upon, can scarcely be considered as demonstrating popular sentiment. At such an election all that large class who are at once for the Union and against coercion would be coerced to vote against the Union. . . .

This is essentially a people's contest. On the side of the Union it is a struggle for maintaining in the world that form and substance of government whose leading object is to elevate the condition of men; to lift artificial weights from all shoulders; to clear the paths of laudable pursuit for all; to afford all an unfettered start and a fair chance in the race of life. Yielding to partial and temporary departures, from necessity, this is the leading object of the government for whose existence we contend. . . .

Our popular government has often been called an experiment. Two points in it our people have already settled—the successful establishing and the successful administering of it. One still remains: its successful maintenance against a formidable internal attempt to overthrow it. It is now for them to demonstrate to the world that those who can fairly carry an election can also suppress a rebellion; that ballots are the rightful and peaceful successors of bullets, and that when ballots have fairly and constitutionally decided, there can be no successful appeal back to bullets; that there can be no successful appeal except to ballots themselves at succeeding elections. Such will be a great lesson of peace, teaching men that what they cannot take by an election neither can they take it by a war; teaching all the folly of being the beginners of a war.

Lest there be some uneasiness in the minds of candid men as to what is to be the course of the government toward the Southern states after the rebellion shall have been suppressed, the executive deems it proper to say it will be his purpose then, as ever, to be guided by the Constitution and the laws, and that he probably will have no different understanding of the powers and duties of the Federal government relatively to the rights of the states and the people under the Constitution than that expressed in the inaugural address.

He desires to preserve the government, that it may be administered for all as it was administered by the men who made it. Loyal citizens everywhere have the right to claim this of their government, and the government has no right to withhold or neglect it. It is not perceived that in giving it there is any coercion, any conquest, or any subjugation in any just sense of those terms.

The Constitution provides, and all the states have accepted the provision, that "the United States shall guarantee to every state in this Union a republican form of government." But if a state may lawfully go out of the Union, having done so it may also discard the republican form of government, so that to prevent its going out is an indispensable means to the end of maintaining the guaranty mentioned; and when an end is lawful and obligatory, the indispensable means to it are also lawful and obligatory.

It was with the deepest regret that the executive found the duty of employing the war power in defense of the government forced upon him. He could but perform this duty or surrender the existence of the government. No compromise by public servants could in this case be a cure; not that compromises are not often proper, but that no popular government can long survive a marked precedent that those who carry an election can only save the government from immediate destruction by giving up the main point upon which the people gave the election. The people themselves, and not their servants, can safely reverse their own deliberate decisions.

As a private citizen the executive could not have consented that these institutions shall perish; much less could he in betrayal of so vast and so sacred a trust as these free people had confided to him. He felt that he had no moral right to shrink, not even to count the chances of his own life, in what might follow. In full view of his great responsibility he has so far done what he has deemed his duty. You will now, according to your own judgment, perform yours. He sincerely hopes that your views and your action may so accord with his as to assure all faithful citizens who have been disturbed in their rights of a certain and speedy restoration to them under the Constitution and the laws.

And having thus chosen our course, without guile and with pure purpose, let us renew our trust in God and go forward without fear and with manly hearts.

Source: James D. Richardson, *A Compilation of the Messages and Papers of the Presidents 1789–1897*. Washington D.C.: Government Printing Office, 1897, vol. 6, 20–31.

"The Battle Hymn of the Republic" (1862)

Julia Ward Howe (1819–1910) wrote the lyrics to "The Battle Hymn of the Republic" while visiting U.S. army camps around Washington, D.C., in November 1861 with her husband, Massachusetts abolitionist Samuel Gridley Howe. Mrs. Howe set her new lyrics to music composed in the 1850s and originally intended for a spiritual. The original tune became a popular marching and camp song among Union soldiers, who often substituted irreverent words such as "John Brown's body lies a-mouldering in the grave," or "We'll hang old Jeff Davis from a sour apple tree." Mrs. Howe hoped to provide a more inspirational song befitting the cause for which the Union soldiers fought. She published the lyrics in the *Atlantic Monthly*, receiving the fee of five dollars from editor James T. Fields, who supposedly gave the song its name. It became an instant hit with the public and one of the most popular songs of the Civil War, and remains a well-known and loved patriotic song.

Mine eyes have seen the glory of the
    coming of the Lord
He is trampling out the vintage where
    the grapes of wrath are stored,
He has loosed the fateful lightening
    of His terrible swift sword
His truth is marching on.

Glory! Glory! Hallelujah!
Glory! Glory! Hallelujah!
Glory! Glory! Hallelujah!
His truth is marching on.
I have seen Him in the watch-fires of
    a hundred circling camps
They have builded Him an altar in the
    evening dews and damps
l can read His righteous sentence by
    the dim and flaring lamps
His day is marching on.

Glory! Glory! Hallelujah!
Glory! Glory! Hallelujah!
Glory! Glory! Hallelujah!
His truth is marching on.

I have read a fiery gospel writ in
    burnish'd rows of steel,
"As ye deal with my contemners, So
    with you my grace shall deal;"

Let the Hero, born of woman, crush
   the serpent with his heel
Since God is marching on.

Glory! Glory! Hallelujah!
Glory! Glory! Hallelujah!
Glory! Glory! Hallelujah!
His truth is marching on.

He has sounded forth the trumpet that
   shall never call retreat
He is sifting out the hearts of men
   before His judgment-seat
Oh, be swift, my soul, to answer
   Him! be jubilant, my feet!
Our God is marching on.

Glory! Glory! Hallelujah!
Glory! Glory! Hallelujah!
Glory! Glory! Hallelujah!
His truth is marching on.

He has sounded form the trumpet that
   shall never call retreat
He is sifting out the hearts of men
   before His judgment-seat
Oh, be swift, my soul, to answer
   Him! be jubilant, my feet!
Our God is marching on.
Glory! Glory! Hallelujah!
Glory! Glory! Hallelujah!
Glory! Glory! Hallelujah!
His truth is marching on.

In the beauty of the lilies Christ was
   born across the sea,
With a glory in His bosom that trans-
   figures you and me:
As He died to make men holy, let us
   die to make men free,
While God is marching on.

Glory! Glory! Hallelujah!
Glory! Glory! Hallelujah!
Glory! Glory! Hallelujah!
His truth is marching on.

Source: Julia Ward Howe, "Battle Hymn of the Republic." *The Atlantic Monthly* 9, no. 52 (1862): 10.

Conscription Acts (April 16, 1862, and March 3, 1863)

The enormous manpower demands of the Civil War led both sides to institute a nationwide draft, the first in U.S. history. The thinly stretched Confederacy acted first on April 16, 1862. Although public support for the war was strong in the South, this law met with mixed reactions, in part because it was subject to a series of exemptions for wealthy slave owners and in part because a nationwide draft seemed to override traditional states' rights positions whereby the states would raise their own troop levies. By early 1864, the Confederate draft extended to men from ages 17 to 50. State governors in the northern states were unable to raise sufficient numbers of volunteer troops, so on March 3, 1863, a joint session of the U.S. Congress passed the hotly debated Enrollment Act authorizing nationwide conscription. This act permitted the hiring of substitutes or payment of $300 for an exemption, thus giving the wealthy a legal way to avoid service. On June 15, 1863, three months after passage of the Enrollment Act, President Abraham Lincoln issued a call for 100,000 troops to counter a feared invasion of the north. So controversial was the draft that riots broke out in several locations— most notably in New York—during the month of July 1863, and a number of people were killed before the states accepted federal authority.

An Act to Further Provide for the Public Defence, April 16, 1862

Preamble.

In view of the exigencies of the country, and the absolute necessity of keeping in the service our gallant army, and of placing in the field a large additional force to meet the advancing columns of the enemy now invading our soil: Therefore

Rioters sack the brownstone houses in New York during the draft riots of 1863. The riots erupted during the Union Army's attempt at drafting individuals (primarily poor immigrants) during the American Civil War. Illustration from *The New York Illustrated News*, July 25, 1863. (Library of Congress)

The Congress of the Confederate States of America do enact, That the President be, and he is hereby authorized to call out and place in the military service of the Confederate States, for three years, unless the war shall have been sooner ended, all white men who are residents of the Confederate States, between the ages of eighteen and thirty-five years at the time the call or calls may be made, who are not legally exempted from military service. All of the persons aforesaid who are now in the armies of the Confederacy, and whose term of service will expire before the end of the war, shall be continued in the service for three years from the date of their original enlistment, unless the war shall have been sooner ended: Provided, however, That all such companies, squadrons, battalions, and regiments, whose term of original

enlistment was for twelve months, shall have the right, within forty days, on a day to be fixed by the Commander of the Brigade, to re-organize said companies, battalions, and regiments, by electing all their officers, which they had a right heretofore to elect, who shall be commissioned by the President: Provided further, That furloughs not exceeding sixty days, with transportation home and back, shall be granted to all those retained in the service by the provisions of this Act beyond the period of their original enlistment, and who have not heretofore received furloughs under the provisions of an Act entitled "An Act providing for the granting of bounty and furloughs to privates and non-commissioned officers in the Provisional Army," approved eleventh December, eighteen hundred and sixty-one, said furloughs to be granted at such times and in such numbers as the Secretary of War may deem most compatible with the public interest: and Provided, further, That in lieu of a furlough the commutation value in money of the transportation herein above granted, shall be paid to each private, musician, or non-commissioned officer who may elect to receive it, at such time as the furlough would otherwise be granted: Provided further, That all persons under the age of eighteen years or over the age of thirty-five years, who are now enrolled in the military service of the Confederate States, in the regiments, squadrons, battalions, and companies hereafter to be re-organized, shall be required to remain in their respective companies, squadrons, battalions and regiments for ninety days, unless their places can be sooner supplied by other recruits not now in the service, who are between the ages of eighteen and thirty-five years; and all laws and parts of laws providing for the re-enlistment of volunteers and the organization thereof into companies, squadron, battalions, or regiments, shall be and the same are hereby repealed.

SEC. 2. Be it further enacted, That such companies, squadrons, battalions, or regiments organized, or in process of organization by authority from the Secretary of War, as may be within thirty days from the passage of this Act, so far completed as to have the whole number of men requisite for organization actually enrolled, not embracing in said organization any persons now in service, shall be mustered into the service of the Confederate States as part of the land forces of the same, to be received in that arm of the service in which they are authorized to organize, and shall elect their company, battalion, and regimental officers.

SEC. 3. Be it further enacted, That for the enrollment of all persons comprehended within the provisions of this Act, who are not already in service in the armies of the Confederate States, it shall be lawful for the President, with the consent of the Governors of the respective States, to employ State officers, and on failure to obtain such consent, he shall employ Confederate officers, charged with the duty of making such enrollment in accordance with rules and regulations to be prescribed by him.

SEC. 4. Be it further enacted, That persons enrolled under the provisions of the preceding Section, shall be assigned by the Secretary of War, to the different companies now in the service, until each company is filled to its maximum number, and the persons so enrolled shall be assigned to companies from the States from which they respectively come.

SEC. 5. Be it further enacted, That all Seamen and ordinary Seamen in the land forces of the Confederate States, enrolled under the provisions of this Act, may, on application of the Secretary of the Navy, be transferred from the land forces to the Naval service.

SEC. 6. Be it further enacted, That in all cases where a State may not have in the army a number of Regiments, Battalions, Squadrons or Companies, sufficient to absorb the number of persons subject to military service under this Act, belonging to such State, then the residue or excess thereof, shall be kept as a reserve, under such regulations as may be established by the Secretary of War, and that at stated periods of not greater than three months, details, determined by lot, shall be made from said reserve, so that each company shall, as nearly as practicable, be kept full: Provided, That the persons held in reserve may remain at home until called into service by the President: Provided, also, That during their stay at home, they shall not receive pay: Provided, further, That the persons comprehended in this Act, shall not be subject to the Rules and Articles of War, until mustered into the actual service of the Confederate States; except that said persons, when enrolled and liable to duty, if they shall wilfully refuse to obey said call, each of them shall be held to be a deserter, and punished as such, under said Articles: Provided, further, That whenever, in the opinion of the President, the exigencies of the public service may require it, he shall be authorized to call into actual service the entire reserve, or so much as may be necessary, not previously assigned to different companies in service under provision of section four of this Act; said reserve shall be organized under such rules as the Secretary of War may adopt: Provided, The company, battalion and regimental officers shall be elected by the troops composing the same: Provided, The troops raised in any one State shall not be combined in regimental, battalion, squadron or company organization with troops raised in any other States.

SEC. 7. Be it further enacted, That all soldiers now serving in the army or mustered in the military service of the Confederate States, or enrolled in said service under the authorizations heretofore issued by the Secretary of War, and who are continued in the service by virtue of this Act, who have not received the bounty of fifty dollars allowed by existing laws, shall be entitled to receive said bounty.

SEC. 8. Be it further enacted, That each man who may hereafter be mustered into service, and who shall arm himself with a musket, shot-gun, rifle or carbine, accepted as an efficient weapon, shall be paid the value thereof, to be ascertained by the mustering officer under such regulations as may be prescribed by the Secretary of War, if he is willing to sell the same, and if he is not, then he shall be entitled to receive one dollar a month for the use of said received and approved musket, rifle, shot-gun or carbine.

SEC. 9. Be it further enacted, That persons not liable for duty may be received as substitutes for those who are, under such regulations as may be prescribed by the Secretary of War.

SEC. 10. Be it further enacted, That all vacancies shall be filled by the President from the company, battalion, squadron, or regiment in which such vacancies shall occur, by promotion according to seniority, except in case of disability or other incompetency: Provided, however, That the President may, when in his opinion, it may be proper, fill such vacancy or vacancies by the promotion of any officer or officers, or private or privates from such company, battalion, squadron or regiment who shall have been distinguished in the service by exhibition of valor and skill; and that whenever a vacancy shall occur in the lowest grade of the commissioned officers of a company, said vacancy shall be filled by election: Provided, That all appointments made by the President shall be by and with the advice and consent of the Senate.

SEC. 11. Be it further enacted, That the provisions of the first section of this Act, relating to the election of officers, shall apply to those regiments, battalions, and squadrons which are composed of twelve months and war companies combined in the same organization, without regard to the manner in which the officers thereof were originally appointed.

SEC. 12. Be it further enacted, That each company of infantry shall consist of one hundred and twenty-five, rank and file; each company of field artillery of one hundred and fifty, rank and file; each of cavalry, of eighty, rank and file.

SEC. 13. Be it further enacted, That all persons, subject to enrollment, who are not now in the service, under the provisions of this Act, shall be permitted, previous to such enrollment, to volunteer in companies now in the service.

APPROVED April 16, 1862.

An Act for Enrolling and Calling Out the National Forces, and for Other Purposes, March 3, 1863

Whereas there now exist in the United States an insurrection and rebellion against the authority thereof, and it is, under the Constitution of the United States, the duty of the government to suppress insurrection and rebellion, to guarantee to each State a republican form of government, and to preserve the public tranquility; and whereas, for these high purposes, a military force is indispensable, to raise and support which all persons ought willingly to contribute; and whereas no service can be more praiseworthy and honorable than that which is rendered for the maintenance of the Constitution and Union, and the consequent preservation of free government: Therefore—

Be it enacted by the Senate and House of Representatives of the United States of America in Congress assembled, That all able-bodies male citizens of the United States, and persons of foreign birth who shall have declared on oath their intention to become citizens under and in pursuance of the laws thereof, between the ages of twenty and forty-five years, except as hereinafter excepted, are hereby declared to constitute the national forces, and shall be liable to perform military duty in the service of the United States when called out by the President for that purpose.

SEC. 2. And be it further enacted, That the following persons be, and they are hereby, excepted and exempt from the provisions of this act, and shall not be liable to military duty under the same, to wit: Such as are rejected as physically or mentally unfit for the service; also, First the Vice-President of the United States, the judges of the various courts of the United States, the heads of the various executive departments of the government, and the governors of the several States. Second, the only son liable to military duty of a widow dependent upon his labor for support. Third, the only son of aged or infirm parent or parents dependent upon his labor for support. Fourth, where there are two or more sons of aged or infirm parents subject to draft, the father, or, if he be dead, the mother, may elect which son shall be exempt. Fifth, the only brother of children not twelve years old, having neither father nor mother dependent upon his labor for support. Sixth, the father of motherless children under twelve years of age dependent upon his labor for support. Seventh, where there are a father and sons in the same family and household, and two of them are in the military service of the United States as non-commissioned officers, musicians, or privates, the residue of such family and household, not exceeding two, shall be exempt. And no persons but such as are herein excepted shall be exempt: Provided, however, That no person who has been convicted of any felony shall be enrolled or permitted to serve in said forces.

SEC. 3. And be it further enacted, That the national forces of the United States not now in the military service, enrolled under this act, shall be divided into two classes: the first of which shall comprise all persons subject to do military duty between the ages of twenty and thirty-five years, and all unmarried persons subject to do military duty above the age of thirty-five and under the age of forty-five; the second class shall comprise all other persons subject to do military duty, and they shall not, in any district, be called into the service of the United States until those of the first class hall have been called.

SEC. 4. And be it further enacted, That, for greater convenience in enrolling, calling out, and organizing the national forces, and for the arrest of deserters and spies of the enemy, the United States shall constitute one or more, as the President shall direct, and each congressional district of the respective states, as fixed by a law of the state next preceding the enrolment, shall constitute one: Provided, That in states which have not by their laws been divided into two or more congressional districts, the President of the United States shall divide the same into so many enrolment districts as he may deem fit and convenient.

SEC. 8. And be it further enacted, That in each of said districts there shall be a board of enrolment, to be composed of the provost-marshal, as president, and two other persons, to be appointed by the President of the United States, one of whom shall be a licensed and practising physician and surgeon.

SEC. 10. And be it further enacted, That the enrolment of each class shall be made separately, and shall only embrace those whose ages shall be on the first day of July thereafter between twenty and forty-five years.

SEC. 11. And be it further enacted, That all persons thus enrolled shall be subject, for two years after the first day of July succeeding the enrolment, to be called into the military service of the United States, and to continue in service during the present rebellion, not, however, exceeding the term of three years; and when called into service shall be placed on the same footing, in all respects, as volunteers for three years, or during the war, including advance pay and bounty as now provided by law.

SEC. 12. And be it further enacted, That whenever it may be necessary to call out the national forces for military service, the President is hereby authorized to assign to each district the number of men to be furnished by said district; and thereupon the enrolling board shall, under the direction of the President, make a draft of the required number, and fifty per cent, in addition, and shall make an exact and complete roll of the names of the person so drawn, and of the order in which they drawn, so that the first drawn may stand first upon the said roll and the second second may stand second, and so on; and the persons so drawn shall be notified of the same within ten days thereafter, by a written or printed notice, to be served personally or by leaving a copy at the last place of residence, requiring them to appear at a designated rendezvous to report for duty. In assigning to the districts the number of men to be furnished therefrom, the President shall take into consideration the number of volunteers and militia furnished by and from the several states in which said districts are situated, and the period of their service since the commencement of the present rebellion, and shall so make said assignment as to equalize the numbers among the districts of the several states, considering and allowing for the numbers already furnished as aforesaid and the time of their service.

SEC. 13. And be it further enacted, That any person drafted and notified to appear as aforesaid, may, on or before the day fixed for his appearance, furnish an acceptable substitute to take his place in the draft; or he may pay to such person as the Secretary of War may authorize to receive it, such sum, not exceeding three hundred dollars, as the Secretary may determine, for the procuration of such substitute; which sum shall be fixed at a uniform rate by a general order made at the time of ordering a draft for any state or territory; and thereupon such person so furnishing the substitute, or paying the money, shall be discharged from further liability under that draft. And any person failing to report after due service of notice, as herein prescribed, without furnishing a substitute, or paying the required sum therefor, shall be deemed a deserter, and shall be arrested by the provost-marshal and sent to the nearest military post for trial by court-martial, unless, upon proper showing that he is not liable to do military duty, the board of enrolment shall relive him from the draft.

SEC. 16. And be it further enacted, That as soon as the required number of able-bodied men liable to do military duty shall be obtained from the list of those drafted, the remainder shall be discharged; and all drafted persons reporting at the place of rendezvous shall be allowed travelling pay from their places of residence; and all persons discharged at the place of rendezvous shall be allowed travelling pay to their places of residence; and all expenses connected with the enrolment and draft, including subsistence while at the rendezvous, shall be paid form the appropriation for enrolling and drafting, under such regulations as the President of the United States shall prescribe; and all expenses connected with the arrest and return of deserters to their regiments, or such other duties as the provost-marshal shall be called upon to perform, shall be paid from the appropriation for arresting deserters, under such such regulations as the President of the United States shall prescribe: Provided, The provost-marshals shall in no case receive commutation for transportation or for fuel and quarters, but only for forage, when not furnished by the government, together with actual expenses of postage, stationery, and clerk hire authorized by the provost-marshal-general.

SEC. 17. And be it further enacted, That any person enrolled and drafted according to the provisions of this act who shall furnish an acceptable substitute, shall thereupon receive from the board of enrolment a certificate of discharge from such draft, which shall exempt him from military duty during the time for which he was drafted; and such substitute shall be entitled to the same pay and allowances provided by law as if he had been originally drafted into the service of the United States.

SEC. 18. And be it further enacted, That such of the volunteers and militia now in the service of the United States as may reenlist to serve one year, unless sooner discharged, after the expiration of their present term of service, shall be entitled to a bounty of fifty dollars, one half of which to be paid upon such reenlistment, and the balance at the expiration of the term of reenlistment; and such as may reenlist to serve for two years, unless sooner discharged, after the expiration of their present term of enlistment, shall receive, upon such reenlistment, twenty-five dollars of the one hundred dollars bounty for enlistment provided by the fifth section of the act approved twenty-second of July, eighteen hundred and sixty-one, entitled "An act to authorize the employment of volunteers to aid in enforcing the laws and protecting public property."

SEC. 25. And be it further enacted, That if any person shall resist any draft of men enrolled under this act into the service of the United States, or shall counsel or aid any person to resist any such draft; or shall counsel or aid any person to resist any such draft; or shall assault or obstruct any officer in making such draft, or in the performance of any service in relation thereto; or shall counsel any person to assault or obstruct any such officer, or shall counsel any drafted men not to appear at the place of rendezvous, or wilfully dissuade them from the performance of military duty as required by law, such person shall be subject to summary arrest by the provost-marshal, and shall be forthwith delivered to the civil authorities, and upon conviction thereof, be punished by a fine not exceeding five hundred dollars, or by imprisonment not exceeding two years, or by both of said punishments.

SEC. 33. And be it further enacted, That the President of the United States is hereby authorized and empowered, during the present rebellion, to call forth the national forces, by draft, in the manner provided for in this act.

Sources: The Statutes at Large of the Confederate States of America, Commencing with the First Session of the First Congress; Public Laws of the Confederate States of America, Passed at the First Session of the First Congress, 1862. Richmond: R.M. Smith, Printer to Congress, 1862; *An Act for enrolling and calling out the national Forces, and for other Purposes, Congressional Record.* 37th Cong., 3d. Sess. Ch. 74, 75, 1863.

Emancipation Proclamation (September 22, 1862)

The following is the text of the Emancipation Proclamation, a decree signed by President Abraham Lincoln on September 22, 1862, shortly after the Union success at Antietam. Effective on January 1, 1863, the Emancipation Proclamation freed the slaves in all areas rebelling against the Union at that point in time. Technically, therefore, the proclamation did not free any slaves, as slaves from conquered Confederate territory had already been freed under a series of Confiscation Acts regarding captured contraband, while slaves in areas still controlled by the Confederacy were not affected by the proclamation, nor were slaves residing in the border states that had remained loyal to the Union. Despite the limited practical impact of the proclamation, however, it had an enormous psychological impact. It elevated the abolition of slavery to one of the North's stated war aims, gained the support of European nations that had long ago abolished slavery, and

undercut Confederate hopes for foreign support. The proclamation also set a precedent for the adoption of the Thirteenth Amendment—which banned slavery—after the war ended in Union victory in 1865.

Whereas on the 22nd day of September, A.D. 1862, a proclamation was issued by the President of the United States, containing, among other things, the following, to wit:

"That on the 1st day of January, A.D. 1863, all persons held as slaves within any State or designated part of a State the people whereof shall then be in rebellion against the United States shall be then, thenceforward, and forever free; and the executive government of the United States, including the military and naval authority thereof, will recognize and maintain the freedom of such persons and will do no act or acts to repress such persons, or any of them, in any efforts they may make for their actual freedom.

"That the executive will on the 1st day of January aforesaid, by proclamation, designate the States and parts of States, if any, in which the people thereof, respectively, shall then be in rebellion against the United States; and the fact that any State or the people thereof shall on that day be in good faith represented in the Congress of the United States by members chosen thereto at elections wherein a majority of the qualified voters of such States shall have participated shall, in the absence of strong countervailing testimony, be deemed conclusive evidence that such State and the people thereof are not then in rebellion against the United States."

Now, therefore, I, Abraham Lincoln, President of the United States, by virtue of the power in me vested as Commander-In-Chief of the Army and Navy of the United States in time of actual armed rebellion against the authority and government of the

United States, and as a fit and necessary war measure for supressing said rebellion, do, on this 1st day of January, A.D. 1863, and in accordance with my purpose so to do, publicly proclaimed for the full period of one hundred days from the first day above mentioned, order and designate as the States and parts of States wherein the people thereof, respectively, are this day in rebellion against the United States the following, to wit:

Arkansas, Texas, Louisiana (except the parishes of St. Bernard, Palquemines, Jefferson, St. John, St. Charles, St. James, Ascension, Assumption, Terrebone, Lafourche, St. Mary, St. Martin, and Orleans, including the city of New Orleans), Mississippi, Alabama, Florida, Georgia, South Carolina, North Carolina, and Virginia (except the forty-eight counties designated as West Virginia, and also the counties of Berkeley, Accomac, Morthhampton, Elizabeth City, York, Princess Anne, and Norfolk, including the cities of Norfolk and Portsmouth), and which excepted parts are for the present left precisely as if this proclamation were not issued.

And by virtue of the power and for the purpose aforesaid, I do order and declare that all persons held as slaves within said designated States and parts of States are, and henceforward shall be, free; and that the Executive Government of the United States, including the military and naval authorities thereof, will recognize and maintain the freedom of said persons.

And I hereby enjoin upon the people so declared to be free to abstain from all violence, unless in necessary self-defence; and I recommend to them that, in all case when allowed, they labor faithfully for reasonable wages.

And I further declare and make known that such persons of suitable condition will be received into the armed service of the United States to garrison forts, positions, stations, and other places, and to man vessels of all sorts in said service.

And upon this act, sincerely believed to be an act of justice, warranted by the Constitution upon military necessity, I invoke the considerate judgment of mankind and the gracious favor of Almighty God.

Source: Abraham Lincoln, *Emancipation Proclamation, January 1, 1863.* Presidential Proclamations, 1791–1991, Record Group 11, General Records of the United States Government, National Archives.

Sam R. Watkins: Book excerpt, Confederate reaction to conscription

Confederate Private Sam Watkins (1839–1901) of the Maury Grays (Company H), First Tennessee Regiment, first published his Civil War memoir as a newspaper serial in 1881. After enlisting at the age of 21, he fought in numerous major battles in Mississippi, Kentucky, Tennessee, and Georgia. Of some 3,200 recruits who joined his unit throughout the war, only 65 remained in the ranks by the final surrender. Watkins's account spares no detail, ranging from the hundreds of men he killed in battle to the suffering of the wounded and his contempt for many of the officers. In this excerpt, he describes the Confederate enlisted men's reaction to the conscription act of 1862, as well as to the subsequent act exempting from service any man who owned at least twenty slaves. While the conscription act destroyed the hopes of 12-month enlistees who had expected to return home, the exemption in particular demonstrated to the common soldiers the nature of the Confederacy's class system. Desertion became more common, and deserters, when captured, were shot or flogged in front of their comrades. Fear and resentment grew and morale plummeted as a result. At this time, Watkins served under General Braxton Bragg and described Bragg's regime as a "tyrannical holocaust."

Chapter III

Corinth

Well, here we were, again "reorganizing," and after our lax discipline on the road to and from Virginia, and after a big battle, which always disorganizes an army, what wonder is it that some men had to be shot, merely for discipline's sake? And what wonder that General Bragg's name became a terror to deserters and evil doers? Men were shot by scores, and no wonder the army had to be reorganized. Soldiers had enlisted for twelve months only, and had faithfully complied with their volunteer obligations; the terms for which they had enlisted had expired, and they naturally looked upon it that they had a right to go home. They had done their duty faithfully and well. They wanted to see their families; in fact, wanted to go home anyhow. War had become a reality; they were tired of it. A law had been passed by the Confederate States Congress called the conscript act. A soldier had no right to volunteer and to choose the branch of service he preferred. He was conscripted.

From this time on till the end of the war, a soldier was simply a machine, a conscript. It was mighty rough on rebels. We cursed the war, we cursed Bragg, we cursed the Southern Confederacy. All our pride and valor had gone, and we were sick of war and the Southern Confederacy.

A law was made by the Confederate States Congress about this time allowing every person who owned twenty negroes to go home. It gave us the blues; we wanted twenty negroes. Negro property suddenly became very valuable, and there was raised the howl of "rich man's war, poor man's fight." The glory of the war, the glory of the South, the glory and the pride of our volunteers had no charms for the conscript.

Source: Sam R. Watkins, *Company Aytch: Or, a Side Show of the Big Show.* Nashville, Tenn.: Cumberland Presbyterian Pub. House, 1882, 46–49.

Clement Vallandigham: Speech before Congress (February 23, 1863) and letter from prison (May 5, 1863)

On March 3, 1863, the U.S. Congress passed the controversial Enrollment Act, which instituted the nation's first military draft. Clement Vallandigham (1820–1871), an Ohio congressman and leader of the anti-war movement in the north, made the following speech before Congress on February 23 during the debate over the act. He argued that the proposed law violated the Constitution, also making reference to Lincoln's suspension of the right of habeus corpus (which required an arrested individual to be brought before a court and formally charged). This was Vallandigham's last speech before he left Congress to run for governor of Ohio. Two months later, he courted arrest by making an anti-war speech in Columbus. General Ambrose Burnside, commander of the Military District of Ohio, had recently issued an order prohibiting statements of sympathy for the enemy. Vallandigham was held at a military prison, denied the right of habeus corpus, and found guilty by a military tribunal. A visitor smuggled out the following letter, in which Vallandigham urged his supporters to stand firm in the face of "military despotism." Vallandigham was sentenced to two years in prison, but Lincoln instead banished him to the Confederacy. After escaping to Canada, he continued his ultimately unsuccessful campaign for governor from his headquarters in Ontario. Vallandigham's defiant return to Ohio and politics in 1864 went unpunished, as the authorities no longer viewed him as dangerous.

The Conscription Bill

SPEECH DELIVERED IN THE HOUSE OF REPRESENTATIVES, FEBRUARY 23, 1863.

IN the last days of the late Congress, a law was enacted which gives the President power to call into the military service every man between the ages of eighteen and forty-five. No exceptions on the ground of color; and only a few special exemptions, at the head of which is the President. The Bill virtually admits that the war is no longer one to which the people give, freely, themselves and their substance; but a war whose further prosecution must be enforced by arbitrary power. The Constitution makes a distinction between the army and the militia; to the States, it reserves the right to control, officer, and discipline the latter, until mustered into the service of the United States. This reserved right of the States the Conscription Bill disregards, and clothes the President with power to convert the entire militia into a Federal army, under his immediate direction and command; leaving out those who are able and willing to commute by paying three hundred dollars.

The Bill passed the Senate without much opposition: went through at midnight, when Democrats and Conservatives were not there to oppose it, or even record their votes against it. On coming to the House, the Chairman of the Military Committee gave notice of their intention to bring the Bill to a final vote, without debate. Its opponents could not muster more than thirty fighting men, but had such men as VALLANDIGHAM and VOOR-HEES for leaders, and determined to give all the resistance parliamentary rules would permit. By perseverance and management, they brought the majority to a discussion of the Bill, and the war opened in earnest. A debate ensued which, for power, eloquence, strength of argument, and bold defense of constitutional rights, has not often been equalled. Inspired with the courage always given to those who are right, VALLAN-DIGHAM, VOORHEES, PENDLETON, and the others, standing unmoved against the strong current of despotism, boldly assailed the most dangerous and vulnerable features of the Bill. Its friends faltered, relaxed their hold upon one after another of their favorite despotic measures. They had determined to give the provost marshals power to arrest and hold civilians, but were compelled to insert a provision that persons arrested should be handed over to the civil authorities for trial. All that related to "treasonable practices" was stricken out, though retained in the "Indemnity Bill." Other important concessions were made; thus, by fearless, and manly courage, a few sacred constitutional rights were wrested from the hard grasp of despotism. At the most exciting moment of the conflict, Mr. V. addressed the House. BINGHAM, of Ohio, thought his "assumptions unworthy of any man who had grown to man's estate under the shelter of the Constitution." VOORHEES replied he "had held the House spell-bound with one of the ablest arguments he had ever heard."

Mr. VALLANDIGHAM said:

Mr. SPEAKER: I do not propose to discuss this bill at any great length in this House. I am satisfied that there is a settled purpose to enact it into a law, so far as it is possible for the action of the Senate and House, and the President, to make it such. I appeal, therefore, from you, from them, directly to the country; to a forum where there is no military committee, no previous question, no hour rule, and where the people themselves are the masters. I commend the spirit in which this discussion was commenced by the chairman of the military committee, (Mr. Olin,) and I do it the more cheerfully because, unfortunately, he is not always in so good a temper as he was to-day; and I trust, that throughout the debate, and on its close, he will exhibit that same disposition which characterized his opening remarks. Only let me caution him that he can not dictate to the minority here what course they shall pursue. But, sir, I regret that I can not extend the commendation to the gentleman from Pennsylvania, (Mr. Campbell,) who addressed the House a little while ago. His speech was extremely offensive, and calculated to stir up a spirit of bitterness and strife, not at all consistent with that in which debates in this House should be conducted. If he, or any other gentleman of the majority, imagines that any one here is to be deterred by threats, from the expression of his opinions, or from giving such votes as he may see fit to give, he has utterly misapprehended the temper and determination of those who sit on this side of the Chamber. His threat I hurl back with defiance into his teeth. I spurn it. I spit upon it. That is not the argument to be addressed to equals here; and I, therefore, most respectfully suggest, that hereafter, all such be dispensed with, and that we shall be spared personal denunciation, and insinuations against the loyalty of men who sit with me here; men whose devotion to the Constitution, and attachment to the Union of these States is as ardent and immoveable as yours, and who only differ from you as to the mode of securing the great object nearest their hearts.

Mr. CAMPBELL. The gentleman will allow me—

Mr. VALLANDIGHAM. I yield for explanation.

Mr. CAMPBELL. Mr. Speaker: It is a significant fact, that the gentleman from Ohio has applied my remarks to himself, and others on his side of the House. Why was this done? I was denouncing *traitors* here, and I will denounce them while I have a place upon this floor. It is my duty and my privilege to do so. And if the gentleman from Ohio chooses to give my remarks a personal application, he can so apply them.

Mr. VALLANDIGHAM. That is enough.

Mr. CAMPBELL. One moment.

Mr. VALLANDIGHAM. Not another moment after that. I yielded the floor in the spirit of a gentleman, and not to be met in the manner of a blackguard. (Applause and hisses in the galleries.)

Mr. CAMPBELL. The member from Ohio is a blackguard. (Renewed hisses and applause in the galleries.)

Mr. ROBINSON. I rise to a question of order. I demand that the galleries be cleared. We have been insulted time and again by contractors and plunderers of the Government, in these galleries, and I ask that they be now cleared.

Mr. COX. I hope my friend from Illinois will not insist on that. Only a very small portion of those in the galleries take part in these disturbances. The fool killer will take care of them.

The SPEAKER *pro tem*. The chair will have to submit the question to the House.

Mr. COX. I hope the demand will be withdrawn.

The SPEAKER *pro tem*. The Chair will state, that if disorder is repeated, whether by applause or expressions of disapprobation, he will feel called upon himself to order the galleries to be cleared, trusting that the House will sustain him in so doing.

Mr. ROBINSON. I desire the order to be enforced now, and the galleries to be cleared, excepting the ladies gallery.

Mr. ROSCOE CONKLING. I was going to say that I hoped the order would not be extended to that portion of the galleries

Mr. ROBINSON. The galleries were cautioned this afternoon.

Mr. JOHNSON. And it is the same men who have been making this disturbance now. I know their faces well.

Mr. VALLANDIGHAM. I think, Mr. Speaker, that this lesson has not been lost; and that it is sufficiently impressed now upon the minds of the audience that this is a legislative, and is supposed to be a deliberative, assembly, and that no breach of decorum or order should occur among them, whatever may be the conduct of any of us on the floor. I trust, therefore, that my friends on this side will withdraw the demand for the enforcement of the rule of the House.

Mr. ROBINSON. I withdraw the demand.

Mr. VERREE. I raise the point of order, that members here, in debating questions before the House, are not at liberty to use language that is unparliamentarily, and unworthy of a member.

The SPEAKER. That is the rule of the House.

Mr. VERREE. I hope it will be enforced.

Mr. VALLANDIGHAM. And I hope that it will be enforced, also, against members on the other side of the Chamber. We have borne enough, more than enough of such language, for two years past.

The SPEAKER. The gentleman from Illinois withdraws his demand to have the galleries cleared. The Chair desires to say to gentlemen in the galleries, that this being a deliberative body, it is not becoming this House, or the character of American citizens, to disturb its deliberations by any expression of approval or disapproval.

Mr. VALLANDIGHAM. The member from Pennsylvania (Mr. Campbell) alluded to-day, generally, to gentlemen on this side of the House. There was no mistaking the application. The language and gesture were both plain enough. He ventured also, approvingly, to call our attention to the opinions and course of conduct of some Democrats in the State of New York, as if we were to learn our lessons in Democracy, or in any thing else, from that quarter. I do not know, certainly, to whom he alluded. Perhaps it was to a gentleman who spoke, not long since, in the city of New York, and advocated on that

occasion, what is called in stereotype phrase "the vigorous prosecution of the war," and who, but two months previously, addressed assemblages in the same State and city, in which he proposed only to take Richmond, and then let the "wayward sisters depart in peace." Now I know of no one on this side of the Chamber occupying such a position; and I, certainly, will not go to that quarter to learn lessons in patriotism or Democracy.

I have already said, that it is not my purpose to debate the general merits of this Bill at large, and for the reason, that I am satisfied that argument is of no avail here. I appeal, therefore, to the people. Before them, I propose to try this great question— the question of constitutional power, and of the unwise and injudicious exercise of it in this Bill. We have been compelled, repeatedly, since the 4th of March, 1861, to appeal to the same tribunal. We appealed to it at the recent election. And the people did pronounce judgment upon our appeal. The member from Pennsylvania ought to have heard their sentence, and I venture to say that he did hear it, on the night of the election. In Ohio they spoke as with the voice of many waters. The very question, of summary and arbitrary arrests, now sanctioned in this Bill, was submitted, as a direct issue, to the people of that State, as also of other States, and their verdict was rendered upon it. The Democratic Convention of Ohio, assembled on the 4th of July in the city of Columbus, the largest and best, ever held in the State, among other resolutions, of the same temper and spirit, adopted this without a dissenting voice:

"And we utterly condemn and denounce the repeated and gross violation, by the Executive of the United States, of the rights thus secured by the Constitution; and we also utterly repudiate and condemn the monstrous dogma, that in time of war the Constitution is suspended, or its power in any respect enlarged beyond the letter and true meaning of that instrument.

"And we view, also, with indignation and alarm, the illegal and unconstitutional seizure and imprisonment, for alleged political offenses, of our citizens, without judicial process, in States where such process is unobstructed, but by Executive order by telegraph, or otherwise, and call upon all who uphold the Union, the Constitution and the laws, to unite with us, in denouncing and repelling such flagrant violation of the State and Federal Constitutions, and tyrannical infraction of the rights and liberties of American citizens; and that the people of this State CAN NOT SAFELY, AND WILL NOT, SUBMIT to have the freedom of speech and freedom of the press, the two great and essential bulwarks of civil liberty, put down by unwarranted and despotic exertion of power."

On that, the judgment of the people was given at the October elections, and the party candidates nominated by the convention which adopted that resolution, were triumphantly elected. So, too, with the candidates of the same party in the States of Wisconsin, Illinois, Indiana, Pennsylvania, New Jersey, and New York. And, sir, that "healthy reaction," recently, of which the member from Pennsylvania (Mr. Campbell) affected to boast, has escaped my keenest sense of vision. I see only that hand-writing on the wall which the fingers of the people wrote against him and his party, and this whole Administration, at the ballot-box, in October and November last. Talk to me, indeed, of the leniency of the Executive! too few arrests! too much forbearance by those in power! Sir,

it is the people who have been too lenient. They have submitted to your oppressions and wrongs as no free people ought ever to submit. But the day of patient endurance has gone by at last. Mistake them not. They will be lenient no longer. Abide by the Constitution, stand by the laws, restore the Union, if *you* can restore it—not by force—you have tried that and failed. Try some other method now—the ancient, the approved, the reasonable way—the way in which the Union was first made. Surrender it not now—not yet—never. But unity is not Union; and attempt not, at your peril—I warn you—to coerce unity by the utter destruction of the Constitution and of the rights of the States and the liberties of the people. Union is liberty and consent: unity is despotism and force. For what was the Union ordained? As a splendid edifice, to attract the gaze and admiration of the world? As a magnificent temple— a stupendous superstructure of marble and iron, like this Capitol, upon whose lofty dome the bronzed image—hollow and inanimate—of Freedom is soon to stand erect in colossal mockery, while the true spirit, the living Goddess of Liberty, veils her eyes and turns away her face in sorrow, because, upon the altar established here, and dedicated by our fathers to her worship—you, a false and most disloyal priesthood, offer up, night and morning, the mingled sacrifices of servitude and despotism? No, sir. It was for the sake of the altar, the service, the religion, the devotees, that the temple of the Union was first erected; and when these are all gone, let the edifice itself perish. Never—never—never will the people consent to lose their own personal and political rights and liberties, to the end that you may delude and mock them with the splendid unity of despotism.

Sir, what are the bills which have passed, or are still before the House? The bill to give the

President entire control of the currency—the purse—of the country. A tax-bill to clothe him with power over the whole property of the country. A bill to put all power in his hands over the personal liberties of the people. A bill to indemnify him, and all under him, for every act of oppression and outrage already consummated. A bill to enable him to suspend the writ of habeas corpus in order to justify or protect him, and every minion of his, in the arrests which he or they may choose to make—arrests, too, for mere opinions' sake. Sir, some two hundred years ago, men were burned at the stake, subjected to the horrors of the Inquisition, to all the tortures that the devilish ingenuity of man could invent—for what? For opinions on questions of religion—of man's duty and relation to his God. And now, to-day, for opinions on questions political, under a free government, in a country whose liberties were purchased by our fathers by seven years' out-pouring of blood, and expenditure of treasure—we have lived to see men, the born heirs of this precious inheritance, subjected to arrest and cruel imprisonment at the caprice of a President, or a secretary, or a constable. And, as if that were not enough, a bill is introduced here, to-day, and pressed forward to a vote, with the right of debate, indeed—extorted from you by the minority—but without the right to amend, with no more than the mere privilege of protest—a bill which enables the President to bring under his power, as commander-in-chief, every man in the United States between the ages of twenty and forty-five—three millions of men. And, as if not satisfied with that, this bill provides, further, that every other citizen, man, woman, and child, under twenty years of age and over forty-five, including those that may be exempt between these ages, shall be also, at the mercy—so far as his personal liberty is concerned—of some miserable "provost marshal" with the rank of a captain of cavalry, who is never to see service in the field; and every Congressional district in the United States is to be governed—yes, governed—by this petty satrap—this military eunuch—this Baba—and he even may be black—who is to do the bidding of your Sultan, or his Grand Vizier. Sir, you have but one step further to go—give him the symbols of his office—the Turkish bow-string and the sack.

What is it, sir, but a bill to abrogate the Constitution, to repeal all existing laws, to destroy all rights, to strike down the judiciary, and erect, upon the ruins of civil and political liberty, a stupendous superstructure of despotism. And for what? To enforce law? No, sir. It is admitted now, by the legislation of Congress, and by the two proclamations of the President; it is admitted by common consent, that the war is for the abolition of negro slavery, to secure freedom to the black man. You tell me, some of you, I know, that it is so prosecuted because this is the only way to restore the Union; but others openly and candidly confess that the purpose of the prosecution of the war is to abolish slavery. And thus, sir, it is that the freedom of the negro is to be purchased, under this bill, at the sacrifice of every right of the white men of the United States.

Sir, I am opposed—earnestly, inexorably opposed—to this measure. If there were not another man in this House to vote against it—if there were none to raise his voice against it—I, at least, dare stand here alone in my place, as a Representative, undismayed, unseduced, unterrified, and heedless of the miserable cry of "disloyalty," of sympathy with the rebellion, and with rebels, to denounce it as the very consummation of the conspiracy against the Constitution and the liberties of my country.

Sir, I yield to no man in devotion to the Union. I am for maintaining it upon the principles on which it was first formed; and I would have it, at every sacrifice, except of honor, which is "the life of the nation." I have stood by it in boyhood and in manhood, to this hour; and I will not now consent to yield it up; nor am I to be driven from an earnest and persistent support of the only means by which it can be restored, either by the threats of the party of the Administration here, or because of affected sneers and contemptuous refusals to listen, now, to re-union, by the party of the Administration at Richmond. I never was weak enough to cower before the reign of terror inaugurated by the men in power here, nor vain enough to expect favorable responses now, or terms of settlement, from the men in power, or the presses under their control, in the South. Neither will ever compromise this great quarrel, nor agree to peace on the basis of re-union: but I repeat it—stop fighting, and let time and natural causes operate— uncontrolled by military influences— and the ballot there, as the ballot here, will do its work. I am for the Union of these States; and but for my profound conviction that it can never be restored by force and arms; or, if so restored, could not be maintained, and would not be worth maintaining, I would have united, at first—even now would unite, cordially—in giving, as I have acquiesced, silently, in your taking, all the men and all the money you have demanded. But I did not believe, and do not now believe, that the war could end in any thing but final defeat; and if it should last long enough, then in disunion; or, if successful upon the principles now proclaimed, that it must and would end in the establishment of an imperial military despotism—not only in the South but in the North and West. And to that I never will submit. No, rather, first I am ready to yield up property, and liberty— nay, life itself.

Sir, I do not propose to discuss now the question of the constitutionality of this measure. The gentleman from Ohio, who preceded me, (Mr. White,) has spared me the necessity of an argument on that point. He has shown that, between the army of the United States, of which, by the Constitution, the President of the United States is the commander-in-chief, and the militia, belonging to the States, there is a wide, and clearly marked line of distinction. The distinction is fully and strongly defined in the Constitution; and has been recognized in the entire legislation and practice of the Government from the beginning. The States have the right, and have always exercised it, of appointing the officers of their militia, and you have no power to take it away. Sir, this bill was originally introduced in the Senate as a militia bill, and as such, it recognized the right of the States to appoint the officers; but finding it impossible, upon that basis, to give to the Executive of the United States the entire control of the millions thus organized into a military force, as the conspirators against State rights and popular liberty desire, the original bill was abandoned; and to-day behold here a stupendous Conscription Bill, for a standing army of more than three millions of men, forced from their homes, their families, their fields, and their workshops—an army organized, officered, and commanded by the servant President, now the master Dictator, of the United States. And for what? Foreign war? Home defense? No; but for coercion, invasion, and the abolition of negro slavery by force. Sir, the conscription of Russia is mild and merciful and just, compared with this. And yet, the enforcement of that conscription has just stirred again the slumbering spirit of insurrection in Poland, though the heel of despotic power has trodden upon the necks of her people for a century.

Where now are your taunts and denunciations, heaped upon the Confederate Government for its conscription, when you, yourselves, become the humble imitators of that government, and bring in here a Conscription Act, more odious even than that passed by the Confederate Congress at Richmond? Sir, the chairman of the military committee rejoiced that for the last two years the army had been filled up by voluntary enlistments. Yes, your army has hitherto been thus filled up by the men of the North and West. One million two hundred and thirty-seven thousand men—for most of the drafted men enlisted, or procured substitutes—have voluntarily surrendered their civil rights, subjected themselves to military law, and thus passed under the command and within the control of the President of the United States. It is not for me to complain of that. It was their own act—done of their own free will and accord—unless bounties, promises, and persuasion may be regarded as coercion. The work you proposed was gigantic, and your means proportionate to it. And what has been the result? What do you propose now? What is this bill? A confession that the people are no longer ready to enlist: that they are not willing to carry on this war longer, until some effort has been made to settle this great controversy in some other way than by the sword. And yet, in addition to the 1,237,000 men who have voluntarily enlisted, you propose now to force the entire body of the people, between the ages of twenty and forty-five, under military law, and within the control of the President, as commander-in-chief of the army, for three years, or during the war—which is to say "for life;" aye, sir, for life, and half your army has already found, or will yet find, that their enlistment was for life too.

I repeat it, sir, this bill is a confession that the people of the country are against this war. It is a solemn admission, upon the record in the legislation of Congress, that they will not voluntarily consent to wage it any longer. And yet, ignoring every principle upon which the Government was founded, this measure is an attempt, by compulsion, to carry it on against the will of the people. Sir, what does all this mean? You were a majority at first, the people were almost unanimously with you, and they were generous and enthusiastic in your support. You abused your power, and your trust, and you failed to do the work which you promised. You have lost the confidence, lost the hearts of the people. You are now in a minority at home. And yet, what a spectacle is exhibited here to-night! You, an accidental, temporary majority, condemned and repudiated by the people, are exhausting the few remaining hours of your political life, in attempting to defeat the popular will, and to compel, by the most desperate and despotic of expedients ever resorted to, the submission of the majority of the people, at home, to the minority, their servants, here. Sir, this experiment has been tried before, in other ages and countries, and its issue always, among a people born free, or fit to be free, has been expulsion or death to the conspirators and tyrants.

I make no threats. They are not arguments fit to be addressed to equals in a legislative assembly; but there is truth, solemn, alarming truth, in what has been said, to-day, by gentlemen on this side of the Chamber. Have a care, have a care, I entreat you, that you do not press these measures too far. I shall do nothing to stir up an already excited people—not because of any fear of your contemptible petty provost marshals, but because I desire to see no violence or revolution in the North or West. But I warn you now, that whenever, against the will of the people, and to perpetuate power and office in a popular government which they have taken from you, you undertake to enforce this bill, and, like the destroying angel in Egypt, enter every house for the first-born sons of the people—remember Poland. You can not, and will not be permitted to, establish a military despotism. Be not encouraged by the submission of other nations. The people of Austria, of Russia, of Spain, of Italy, have never known the independence and liberty of freemen. France, in seventy years, has witnessed seven principal revolutions—the last brought about in a single day, by the arbitrary attempt of the king to suppress freedom of speech and of the press, and next the free assembling of the people; and when he would have retraced his steps and restored these liberties, a voice from the galleries, not filled with clerks and plunderers and place-men, uttered the sentiments and will of the people of France, in words now historic: "It is too late." The people of England never submitted, and would not now submit, for a moment, to the despotism which you propose to inaugurate in America. England can not, to-day, fill up her standing armies by conscription. Even the "press gang," unknown to her laws, but for a time acquiesced in, has long since been declared illegal; and a sweeping conscription like this now, would hurl not only the ministry from power, but the queen from her throne.

Sir, so far as this bill is a mere military measure, I might have been content to have given a silent vote against it; but there are two provisions in it hostile, both to the letter and spirit of the Constitution, and inconsistent with the avowed scope and purpose of the bill itself; and, certainly, as I read them in the light of events which have occurred in the past two years, of a character which demands that the majority of this House shall strike them out. There is nothing in the argument, that we have no time to send the bill back to the Senate, lest it should be lost. The presiding officers of both Houses are friends of the bill, and will constitute committees of conference of men favorable to it. They will agree at once, and can at any moment, between this and the 4th of March, present their report as a question of the highest privilege; and you have a two-thirds majority in both branches to adopt it.

With these provisions of the bill stricken out, leaving it simply as a military measure, to be tested by the great question of peace or war, I would be willing that the majority of the House should take the responsibility of passing it without further debate; although, even then, you would place every man in the United States, between the ages of twenty and forty-five, under military law, and within the control, everywhere, of the President, except the very few who are exempt; but you would leave the shadow, at least, of liberty to all men not between these ages, or not subject to draft under this bill, and to the women and children of the country too.

Sir, these two provisions propose to go a step further, and include every one, man, woman and child, and to place him or her under the arbitrary power, not only of the President and his cabinet, but of some two hundred and fifty other petty officers, captains of cavalry, appointed by him. There is no distinction of sex, and none of age. These provisions, sir, are contained in the seventh and twenty-fifth sections of the bill. What are they? I comment not on the appointment of a general provost marshal of the United States, and provost marshals in every Congressional District. Let that pass. But what do you propose to make the duty of each provost marshal in carrying out the draft? Among other things, that he shall "inquire into, and report to the provost marshal general"—what? Treason? No. Felony? No. Breach of the peace, or violation of law of any kind ? No; but "treasonable practices;" yes, TREASONABLE PRACTICES. What mean you by these strange, ominous words? Whence come they? Sir, they are no more new or original than any other of the cast-off rags filched by this Administration from the lumber-house of other and more antiquated despotisms. The history of European tyranny has taught us somewhat of this doctrine of constructive treason. Treasonable practices! Sir, the very language is borrowed from the old proclamations of the British monarchs, some hundreds of years ago. It brings up the old, identical quarrel of the fourteenth century. Treasonable practices! It was this that called forth that English Act of Parliament of twenty-fifth Edward III, from which we have borrowed the noble provision against constructive treason, in the Constitution of the United States. Arbitrary arrests, for no crime known, defined or limited by law, but for pretended offenses, herded together under the general and most comprehensive name of "treasonable practices," had been so frequent, in the worst periods of English history, that in the language of the act of Henry the Fourth, "no man knew how to behave himself, or what to do or say, for doubt of the pains of treason." The statute of Edward the Third, had cut all these fungous, toadstool treasons up by the root; and yet, so prompt is arbitrary power to denounce all opposition to it as treasonable, that, as Lord Hale observes.

"Things were so carried by parties and factions, in the succeeding reign of Richard the Second, that this statute was but little observed, but as this or that party got the better. So the crime of high treason was, in a manner, arbitrarily imposed and adjudged *to the disadvantage of the party which was to be judged;* which by various vicissitudes and revolutions, mischiefed all parties, first and last, and left a great unsettledness and unquietness in the minds of the people, and was one of the occasions of the unhappiness of the king."

And he adds that,

"It came to pass that almost every offense that was, *or seemed to be,* a breach of the faith and allegiance due to the king, was, by *construction, consequence and interpretation*, raised into the offense of high treason."

Richard the Second procured an Act of Parliament—even he did not pretend to have power to do it by proclamation—declaring that the bare purpose to depose the king, and to place another in his stead, without any overt act, was treason; and yet, as Blackstone remarks, so little effect have over-violent laws to prevent crime, that within two years afterward this very prince was both deposed and put to death. Still the struggle for arbitrary and despotic power continued; and up to the time of Charles the First, at various periods, almost every conceivable offense relating to the government, and every form of opposition to the king, was declared high treason. Among these were execrations against the king; calling him opprobrious names by public writing; refusing to abjure the Pope; marrying without license certain of the king's near relatives; derogating from his royal style or title; impugning his supremacy, or assembling riotously to the number of twelve, and refusing to disperse on proclamation. But steadily, in better times, the people and the Parliament of England returned to the spirit and letter of the act of Edward the Third, passed by a Parliament which now, for five hundred years, has been known and honored as *parliamentum benedictum*, the "blessed Parliament"—just as this Congress will be known, for ages to come, as "the accursed Congress"—and among many other acts, it was declared by a statute, in the first year of the Fourth Henry's reign, that "*in no time to come* any treason be judged, otherwise than as ordained by the statute of king Edward the Third." And for nearly two hundred years, it has been the aim of the lawyers and judges of England to adhere to the plain letter, spirit, and intent of that act, "to be extended," in the language of Erskine, in his noble defense of Hardy, "by no new or occasional constructions—to be strained by no fancied analogies—to be measured by no rules of political expediency—to be judged of by no theory—to be determined by the wisdom of no individual, however wise—but to be expounded by the simple, genuine letter of the law."

Such, sir, is the law of treason in England to-day; and so much of the just and admirable statute of Edward as is applicable to our form of government, was embodied in the Constitution of the United States. The men of 1787 were well read in history and in English constitutional law. They knew that monarchs and governments, in all ages, had struggled to extend the limits of treason, so as to include all opposition to those in power. They had learned the maxim that, miserable is the servitude where the law is either uncertain or unknown, and had studied and valued the profound declaration of Montesquieu, that "if the crime of treason be indeterminate, that alone is sufficient to make any government degenerate into arbitrary power." Hear Madison, in the Federalist:

> "As *new-fangled and artificial treasons* have been the great engines by which violent factions, the natural offspring of free

governments, have usually *wreaked their alternate malignity on each other*, the convention have, with great judgment, opposed a barrier to this peculiar danger, by inserting a constitutional definition of the crime, fixing the proof necessary for conviction of it, and restraining the Congress, even in punishing it, from extending the consequences of guilt beyond the person of its author."

And Story, not foreseeing the possibility of such a party or Administration as is now in power, declared it "*an impassable barrier* against arbitrary constructions, either by the courts or by Congress, upon the crime of treason." "Congress"—that, sir, is the word, for he never dreamed that the President, or, still less, his clerks, the cabinet ministers, would attempt to declare and punish treasons. And yet, what have we lived to hear in America daily, not in political harangues, or the press only, but in official proclamations and in bills in Congress! Yes, your high officials talk now of "treasonable practices," as glibly "as girls of thirteen do of puppy dogs." Treasonable practices! Disloyalty! Who imported these precious phrases, and gave them a legal settlement here? Your Secretary of War. He it was who, by command of our most noble President, authorized every marshal, every sheriff, every township constable, or city police man, in every State in the Union, to fix, in his own imagination, what he might choose to call a treasonable or disloyal practice, and then to arrest any citizen at his discretion, without any accusing oath, and without due process, or any process of law. And now, sir, all this monstrous tyranny, against the whole spirit and the very letter of the Constitution, is to be deliberately embodied in an Act of Congress! Your petty provost marshals are to determine what treasonable practices are, and "inquire into," detect, spy out, eavesdrop, ensnare, and then inform, report to the chief spy at Washington. These, sir, are now to be our American liberties under your Administration. There is not a crowned head in Europe who dare venture on such an experiment. How long think you this people will submit? But words, too—conversation or public speech—are to be adjudged "treasonable practices." Men, women, and children are to be hauled to prison for free speech. Whoever shall denounce or oppose this Administration—whoever may affirm that war will not restore the Union, and teach men the gospel of peace, may be reported and arrested, upon some old grudge, and by some ancient enemy, it may be, and imprisoned as guilty of a treasonable practice.

Sir, there can be but one treasonable practice, under the Constitution, in the United States. Admonished by the lessons of English history, the framers of that instrument defined what treason is. It is the only offense defined in the Constitution. We know what it is. Every man can tell whether he has committed treason. He has only to look into the Constitution, and he knows whether he has been guilty of the offense. But neither the Executive, nor Congress, nor both combined, nor the courts, have a right to declare, either by pretended law, or by construction, that any other offense shall be treason, except that defined and limited in this instrument. What is treason? It is the highest offense known to the law—the most execrable crime known to the human heart—the crime of *loesce majestatis*; of the parricide who lifts his hand against the country of his birth or his adoption. "Treason against the United States," says the Constitution, "shall consist ONLY in levying war against them, or in adhering to their enemies, giving them aid and comfort." (Here a Republican member nodded several times and smiled, and Mr. V. said.) Ah, sir,

I understand you. But was Lord Chatham guilty of legal treason, treasonable aid and comfort, when he denounced the war against the Colonies, and rejoiced that America had resisted? Was Burke, or Fox, or Barré guilty, when defending the Americans, in the British Parliament, and demanding conciliation and peace? Were even the Federalists guilty of treason, as defined in the Constitution, for "giving aid and comfort" to the enemy, in the war of 1812? Were the Whigs in 1846? Was the Ohio Senator liable to punishment, under the Constitution, and by law, who said, sixteen years ago, in the Senate Chamber, when we were at war in Mexico, "If I were a Mexican as I am an American, I would greet your volunteers with bloody hands, and welcome them to hospitable graves?" Was Abraham Lincoln guilty, because he denounced that same war, while a Representative on the floor of this House ? Was all this "adhering to the enemy, giving him aid and comfort," within the meaning of this provision?

A MEMBER. The Democratic papers said so.

Mr. VALLANDIGHAM. Sir, I am speaking now as a lawyer, and as a legislator, to legislators and lawyers acting under oath and the other special and solemn sanctions of this Chamber, and not in the loose language of the political canvass. And I repeat, sir, that if such had been the intent of the Constitution, the whole Federal party, and the whole Whig party, and their Representatives in this and the other Chamber, might have been indicted and punished as traitors. Yet, not one of them was ever arrested. And shall they, or their descendants, undertake now to denounce and to punish, as guilty of treason, every man who opposes the policy of this Administration, or is against this civil war; and for peace upon honorable terms? I hope, in spite of the hundreds of your provost marshals, and all your threats, that there will be so much of opposition to the war as will compel the Administration to show a decent respect for, and yield some sort of obedience to, the Constitution and laws, and to the rights and liberties of the States and of the people.

But to return; the Constitution not only defines the crime of treason, but, in its jealous care to guard against the abuses of tyrannic power, it expressly ascertains the character of the proof, and the number of witnesses necessary for conviction, and limits the punishment to the person of the offender, thus going beyond both the statute of Edward, and the common law. And yet every one of these provisions is ignored or violated by this bill.

"No person," says the Constitution, "shall be convicted of treason"—as just defined—"unless on the testimony of two witnesses."

Where, and when, and by whom, sir, are the two witnesses to be examined, and under what oath? By your provost marshals, your captains of cavalry? By the jailors of your military bastilles, and inside of Forts Warren and Lafayette? Before arrest, upon arrest, while in prison, when discharged, or at any time at all? Has any witness ever been examined in any case heretofore? What means the Constitution by declaring that no person shall be *convicted* of treason "unless on the *testimony of two witnesses*?" Clearly, conviction in a judicial court, upon testimony openly given under oath, with all the sanctions and safeguards of a judicial trial to the party accused. And if any doubt there could be upon this point, it is removed by the sixth article of the amendments.

But the Constitution proceeds:

"Unless on the testimony of two witnesses *to the same overt act*."

But words, and still less, thoughts or opinions, sir, are not acts; and yet, nearly every case of arbitrary arrest and imprisonment, in the wholly loyal States, at least, has been for words spoken or written, or for thoughts, or opinions supposed to be entertained by the party arrested. And that, too, sir, is precisely what is intended by this bill.

But further:

"The testimony of two witnesses to the same overt act, or *confession in open court*."

What, court? The court of some deputy provost marshal at home, or of your provost marshal general, or Judge Advocate General, here in Washington? The court of a military bastille, whose gates are shut day and night against every officer of the law, and whose very casemates are closed to the light and air of heaven? Call you that "open court?" Not so the Constitution. It means judicial court, law court, with judge and jury and witnesses and counsel; and to speak of it as any thing else, is a confusion of language, and an insult to intelligence and common sense. Yet, to-night, you deliberately propose to enact the illegal and unconstitutional executive orders, or proclamations, of last summer, into the semblance and form of law.

"To inquire into treasonable practices," says the bill. So, then, your provost-marshals are to be deputy spies to the grand spy, holding his secret inquisitions here in Washington, upon secret reports, sent by telegraph perhaps, or through the mails, both under the control of the Executive. What right has he to arrest and hold me without a hearing, because some deputy spy of his chooses to report me guilty of "disloyalty," or of "treasonable practices?" Is this the liberty secured by the Constitution? Sir, let me tell you, that if the purpose of this bill be to crush out all opposition to the Administration and the party in power, you have no constitutional right to enact it, and not force enough to compel the people, your masters, to submit.

But the enormity of the measure does not stop here. Says the Constitution:

"Congress shall make no law abridging the freedom of speech, or of the press."

And yet speech—mere words, derogatory to the President, or in opposition to his Administration, and his party and policy, have, over and over again, been reported by the spies and informers and shadows, or other minions, of the men in power, to be "disloyal practices," for which hundreds of free American citizens, of American, not African, descent, have been arrested and imprisoned for months, without public accusation, and without trial by jury, or trial at all. Even upon pretence of guilt of that most vague and indefinite, but most comprehensive of all offenses, "discouraging enlistments," men have been seized at midnight, and dragged from their beds, their homes, and their families, to be shut up in the stone casements of your military fortresses, as felons. And now, by this bill, you propose to declare, in the form and semblance of law, that whoever "counsels or dissuades" any one from the performance of the military duty required under this conscription, shall be summarily arrested by your provost marshals, and held, without trial, till the draft shall have been completed. Sir, even the "Sedition Law" of '98 was constitutional, merciful and just, compared with this execrable enactment. Wisely did Hamilton ask, in the *Federalist*, "What signifies a declaration that the liberty of the press (or of speech) shall be inviolably preserved, when its security must altogether depend on public opinion, *and on the general spirit of the people*, and of the Government."

But this extraordinary bill does not stop here.

"No person," says the Constitution, "*no person shall be held to answer for a capital or otherwise infamous crime, unless on a presentment or indictment of a grand jury, except in cases arising in the land and naval force, or in the militia when in actual service in time of war or public danger; nor be deprived of life, liberty, or property, without due process of law.*"

Note the exception. Every man not in the military service, is exempt from arrest, except by due process of law; or, being arrested without it, is entitled to demand immediate inquiry and discharge, or bail; and if held, then presentment or indictment by a grand jury in a civil court, and according to the law of the land. And yet you now propose, by this Bill, in addition to the 1,237,000 men who have voluntarily surrendered that great right of freemen, second only to the ballot—and, indeed, essential to it—to take it away forcibly, and against their consent, from three millions more, whose only crime is that they happen to have been so born as to be now between the ages of twenty and forty-five. Do it, if you can, under the Constitution; and when you have thus forced them into the military service, they will be subject to military law, and not entitled to arrest only upon due process of law, nor to indictment by a grand jury in a civil court. But you can not, you shall not—because the Constitution forbids it—deprive the whole people, also, of the United States, of these rights, "inestimable to them, and formidable to tyrants only," under "the war power," or upon pretense of "military necessity," and by virtue of an act of Congress creating and defining new treasons, new offenses, not only unknown to the Constitution, but expressly excluded by it. But again:

"In all criminal prosecutions,"—

and wherever a penalty is to be imposed, imprisonment or fine inflicted, it is a criminal prosecution—

"In all criminal prosecutions," says the Constitution, "the accused shall enjoy the right to a speedy and public trial, by an impartial jury of the State and district wherein the crime shall have been committed, which district shall have been previously ascertained by law; and to be informed of the nature and cause of the accusation; to be confronted with the witnesses against him; to have compulsory process for obtaining witnesses in his favor, and to have the assistance of counsel, for his defense."

Do you propose to allow any of these rights? No, sir—none—not one; but, in the twenty-fifth section, you empower these provost marshals of yours to arrest any man—men not under military law—whom he may charge, or any one else may charge before him, with "counseling or dissuading" from military service, and to hold him in confinement indefinitely, until the draft has been completed. Sir, has it been completed in Connecticut yet? Is it complete in New York? Has it been given up? If so now, nevertheless it was in process of pretended execution for months. In any event, you propose, now, to leave to the discretion of the Executive the time during which all persons arrested, under the provisions of this Bill, shall be held in confinement upon that summary and arbitrary arrest; and when

he sees fit, and then only, shall the accused be delivered over to the civil authorities for trial. And is this the speedy and public trial by jury, which the Constitution secures to every citizen not in the military service?

"The State and district wherein the crime"—

Yes, crime, for crime it must be, known to and defined by law, to justify the arrest—

"Shall have been committed, which district shall have been previously ascertained by law."

Do you mean to obey that, and to observe State lines, or district lines, in arrests and imprisonments? Has it ever been done? Were not Keyes, and Olds, and Mahoney, and Sheward, and my friend here to the left, (Mr. Allen, of Illinois,) and my other friend from Maryland, (Mr. May,) dragged from their several States and districts, to New York, or Massachusetts, or to this city? The pirate, the murderer, the counterfeiter, the thief—you would have seized by due and sworn process of law, and tried forthwith, by jury, at home; but honorable and guiltless citizens, members of this House, your peers upon this floor, were thrust, and may, again, under this bill, be thrust into distant dungeons and bastilles, upon the pretence of some crawling, verminous spy and informer, that they have "dissuaded" some one from obedience to the draft, or are otherwise guilty of some "treasonable practice."

"And to be informed of the nature and cause of the accusation."

How? By presentment or indictment of a grand jury. When? "Speedily," says the

Constitution. "When the draft is completed," says this bill; and the President shall determine that. But who is to limit and define, "counseling or dissuading" from military service? Who shall ascertain and inform the accused of the "nature and cause" of a "treasonable practice?" Who, of all the thousand victims of arbitrary arrests, within the last twenty-two months, even to this day, has been informed of the charge against him, although long since released? Yet even the Roman pro-consul, in a conquered province, refused to send up a prisoner, without signifying the crimes with which he was charged.

"To be confronted with the witnesses against him."

Witnesses, indeed! Fortunate will be the accused if there be any witnesses against him. But is your deputy provost marshal to call them? O, no; he is only to "inquire into, and report." Is your provost marshal general? What! call witnesses from the remotest parts of the Union, to a secret inquisition here in Washington. Has any "prisoner of State," hitherto, been confronted with witnesses, at any time? Has he even been allowed to know so much as the names of his accusers? Yet, Festus could boast, that it was not the manner of the Romans, to punish any man, "before that he, which is accused, have the accusers face to face."

"To have compulsory process for obtaining witnesses in his favor."

Sir, the compulsory process will be, under this bill, as it has been from the first, to compel the absence rather, of not only the witnesses, but the friends and nearest relatives of the accused; even the wife of his bosom, and his children—the inmates of his own household. Newspapers, the bible, letters from home, except under surveillance, a breath of air, a sight of the waves of the sea, or of the mild, blue sky, the song of birds, whatever was denied to the prisoner of Chillon, and more too; yes, even a solitary lamp in the case-mate, where a dying prisoner struggled with death, all have been refused to the American citizen accused of disloyal speech or opinions, by this most just and merciful Administration.

And, finally, says the Constitution:

"To have the assistance of counsel for his defense."

And yet your Secretary of State, the "conservative" Seward—the confederate of Weed, that treacherous, dissembling foe to constitutional liberty, and the true interests of his country—forbade his prisoners to employ counsel, under penalty of prolonged imprisonment. Yes, charged with treasonable practices, yet the demand for counsel was to be dealt with as equal to treason itself. Here is an order, signed by a minion of Mr. Seward, and read to the prisoners at Fort Lafayette, on the 3d of December, 1861:

"I am instructed, by the Secretary of State, to inform you, that the Department of State, of the United States, *will not recognize any one as an attorney for political prisoners*, and will look with distrust upon all applications for release through such channels; and that such applications *will be regarded as additional reasons for declining to release the prisoners*."

And here is another order to the same effect, dated "Department of State, Washington, November 27, 1861," signed by

William H. Seward himself, and read to the prisoners at Fort Warren, on the 29th of November, 1861:

"Discountenancing and repudiating all such practices."

The disloyal practice, forsooth, of employing counsel:

"The Secretary of State desires that all the State prisoners may understand *that they are expected to revoke all such engagements now existing, and avoid any hereafter*, as they can only lead to new complications and embarrassments to the cases of prisoners, on whose *behalf the Government might be disposed to act with liberality*."

Most magnanimous Secretary! Liberality toward men guilty of no crime, but who, though they had been murderers or pirates, were entitled, by the plain letter of the Constitution, to have "the assistance of counsel for their defense." Sir, there was but one step further possible, and that short step was taken some months later, when the prisoners of State were required to make oath, as the condition of their discharge, that they would not seek their constitutional and legal remedy in Court, for the wrongs and outrages inflicted upon them.

Sir, incredible as all this will seem some years hence, it has happened, all of it, and more yet untold, within the last twenty months, in the United States. Under executive usurpation, and by virtue of presidential proclamations and cabinet orders, it has been done without law and against Constitution; and now it is proposed, I repeat, to sanction and authorize it all, by an equally unconstitutional and void act of Congress. Sir, legislative tyranny is no more tolerable than executive tyranny. It is a vain thing to seek to cloak all this under the false semblance of law. Liberty is no more guarded or secured, and arbitrary power no more hedged in and limited here, than under the executive orders of last summer. We know what has already been done, and we will submit to it no longer. Away, then, with your vain clamor about disloyalty, your miserable mockery of: treasonable practices. We have read, with virtuous indignation, in history, ages ago, of an Englishman executed for treason, in saying that he would make his son heir to the crown, meaning of his own tavern-house, which bore the sign of the crown; and of that other Englishman, whose favorite buck the king had killed, and who suffered death as a traitor, for wishing, in a fit of vexation, that the buck, horns and all, were emboweled in the body of the king. But what have we not lived to see in our own time? Sir, not many months ago, this Administration, in its great and tender mercy toward the six hundred and forty prisoner of State, confined, for treasonable practices, at Camp Chase, near the capital of Ohio, appointed a commissioner, an extra-judicial functionary, unknown to the Constitution and laws, to hear and determine the cases of the several parties accused, and with power to discharge at his discretion, or to banish to Bull's Island, in Lake Erie. Among the political prisoners called before him, was a lad of fifteen, a newsboy upon the Ohio River, whose only offense proved, upon inquiry, to be, that he owed fifteen cents, the unpaid balance of a debt due to his washer-woman—possibly a woman of color—who had him arrested by the provost marshal, as guilty of "disloyal practices." And yet, for four weary months the lad had lain in that foul and most loathsome prison, under military charge, lest, peradventure, he should overturn the Government of the United States; or, at least, the Administration of Abraham Lincoln!

SEVERAL MEMBERS ON THE DEM-OCRATIC SIDE OF THE HOUSE. Oh no; the case can not be possible.

Mr. VALLANDIGHAM. It is absolutely true, and it is one only among many such cases. Why, sir, was not the hump-back carrier of the New York Daily News, a paper edited by a member of this House, arrested in Connecticut, for selling that paper, and hurried off out of the State, and imprisoned in Fort Lafayette ? And yet, Senators and Representatives, catching up the brutal cry of a blood thirsty but infatuated partisan press, exclaim "the Government has been too lenient, there ought to have been more arrests!"

Well did Hamilton remark, that "arbitrary imprisonments have been, in all ages, the favorite and most formidable instruments of tyranny;" and not less truly, Blackstone declares, that they are "a less public, a less striking, and therefore *a more dangerous engine* of arbitrary government," than executions upon the scaffold. And yet, to-night, you seek here, under cloak of an act of Congress, to authorize these arrests and imprisonments, and thus to renew again that reign of terror which smote the hearts of the stoutest among us, last summer, as "the pestilence which walketh in darkness."

But the Constitution provides further that,

"The right of the people to be secure in their persons, houses, papers, and effects, against unreasonable searches and seizures, shall not be violated, and no warrants shall issue, but upon probable cause, supported by oath or affirmation, and particularly describing the place to be searched, and the persons or things to be seized."

Sir, every line, letter, and syllable of this provision has been repeatedly violated, under pretence of securing evidence of disloyal or treasonable practices; and now you propose, by this bill, to sanction the past violations, and authorize new and continued infractions in future. Your provost marshals, your captains of cavalry, are to "inquire into treasonable practices." How? In any way, sir, that they may see fit; and of course, by search and seizure of person, house, papers or effects; for, sworn and appointed spies and informers as they are, they will be and can be of no higher character, and no more scrupulous of law, or right, or decency, than their predecessors of last summer, appointed under executive proclamations of no more or less validity than this bill, which you seek now to pass into a law. Sir, there is but one step farther to take. Put down the peaceable assembling of the people; the right of petition for redress of grievances; the "right of the people to keep and bear arms;" and finally, the right of suffrage and elections, and then these United States, this Republic of ours, will have ceased to exist. And that short step you will soon take, if the States and the people do not firmly and speedily check you in your headlong plunge into despotism. What yet remains? The Constitution declares that:

"The enumeration in the Constitution, of certain rights, shall not be construed to deny or disparage others retained by the people,"

And again:

"The powers not delegated to the United States by the Constitution, nor prohibited by it to the States, are reserved to the States respectively, or to the people."

And yet, under the monstrous doctrine, that in war the Constitution is suspended, and that the President as commander-in-chief, not of the military forces only, but of the whole people of the United States, may, under "the war power," do whatever he shall think necessary and proper to be done, in any State or part of any State, however remote from the scene of warfare, every right of the people is violated or threatened, and every power of the States, usurped. Their last bulwark, the militia, belonging solely to the States, when not called, as such, into the actual service of the United States, you now deliberately propose, by this bill, to sweep away, and to constitute the President supreme military dictator, with a standing army of three millions and more at his command. And for what purpose are the militia to be thus taken from the power and custody of the States? Sir, the opponents of the Constitution anticipated all this, and were denounced as raving incendiaries or distempered enthusiasts. The Federal Government, said Patrick Henry, in the Virginia Convention,

"Squints towards monarchy. Your President may easily become a king. If ever he violates the laws, *will not the recollection of his crimes teach him to make one bold push for the American throne*? Will not the immense difference between being master of everything, and being ignominiously tried and punished, powerfully excite him to make this bold push? But, sir, where is the existing force to punish him? Can he not, at the head of his army, beat down all opposition? What then will become of you and your rights? Will not absolute despotism ensue?"

And yet, for these apprehensions, Henry has been the subject of laughter and pity for seventy years. Sir, the instinctive love of liberty is wiser and more far-seeing than any philosophy.

Hear, now, Alexander Hamilton, in the *Federalist*. Summing up what he calls the exaggerated and improbable suggestions respecting the power of calling for the services of the militia, urged by the opponents of the Constitution, whose writings he compares to some ill-written tale, or romance full of frightful and distorted shapes, he says:

"The militia of New Hampshire (they allege) is to be marched to Georgia; of Georgia to New Hampshire; of New York to Kentucky; and of Kentucky to Lake Champlain. Nay, the debts due to the French and Dutch, are to be paid in militia-men, instead of Louis d'ors and ducats. At one moment, there is to be a large army to lay prostrate the liberties of the people; at another moment, the militia of Virginia are to be dragged from their homes, five or six hundred miles, to tame the republican contumacy of Massachusetts; *and that of Massachusetts is to be transported an equal distance, to subdue the refractory haughtiness of the aristocratic Virginians.* Do persons who rave at this rate, imagine that their eloquence can impose any conceits or absurdities upon the people of America, for infallible truths?"

And yet, sir, just three-quarters of a century later, we have lived to see these raving conceits and absurdities practiced, or attempted, as calmly and deliberately as though the power and the right had been expressly conferred.

And now, sir, listen to the answer of Hamilton to all this—himself the friend of a strong government, a Senate for life, and an Executive for life, with the sole and exclusive power over the militia, to be held by the National Government; and the Executive of each State to be appointed by that Government:

"If there should be an army to be made use of as the engine of despotism, what need of the militia? If there should be no army, *whither would the militia, irritated at being required to undertake a distant and distressing expedition, for the purpose of riveting the chains of slavery upon a part of their countrymen*

And the reporter, unable to follow the vehement orator of the Revolution, adds:

"Here, Mr. Henry strongly and pathetically expatiated on the probability of the President's enslaving America, and the horrid consequences that must result."

direct their course, BUT TO THE SEATS OF THE TYRANTS WHO HAD MEDITATED SO FOOLISH, AS WELL AS SO WICKED, A PROJECT; TO CRUSH THEM IN THEIR IMAGINED INTRENCHMENTS OF POWER, AND MAKE THEM AN EXAMPLE OF THE VENGEANCE OF AN ABUSED AND INCENSED PEOPLE? Is this the way in which usurpers stride to dominion over a numerous and enlightened nation?"

Sir, Mr. Hamilton was an earnest, sincere man, and, doubtless, wrote what he believed: he was an able man also, and a philosopher; and yet how little did he foresee, that just seventy-five years later, that same Government, which he was striving to establish, would, in desperate hands, attempt to seize the whole militia of the Union, and convert them into a standing army, indefinite as to the time of its service, and for the very purpose of not only beating down State sovereignties, but of abolishing even the domestic and social institutions of the States.

Sir, if your objects are constitutional, you have power abundantly under the Constitution, without infraction or usurpation. The men who framed that instrument, made it both for war and peace. Nay, more, they expressly provide for the cases of insurrection and rebellion. You have ample power to do all that of right you ought to do—all that the people, your masters, permit under their supreme will, the Constitution. Confine, then, yourselves within these limits, and the rising storm of popular discontent will be hushed.

But I return, now, again, to the arbitrary arrests sanctioned by this Bill, and by that other consummation of despotism, the Indemnity and Suspension Bill, now in the Senate. Sir, this is the very question which, as I said a little while ago, we made a chief issue before the people in the late elections. You did, then, distinctly claim—and you found an Attorney-General and a few other venal or very venerable lawyers to defend the monstrous claim—that the President had the right to suspend the writ of habeas corpus; and that every one of these arrests was legal and justifiable. We went before the people with the Constitution and the laws in our hands, and the love of liberty in our hearts; and the verdict of the people was rendered against you. We insisted that Congress alone could suspend the writ of habeas corpus when, in cases of rebellion or invasion, the public safety might require it. And to-day, sir, that is beginning to be again the acknowledged doctrine. The Chief Justice of the Supreme Court of the United States so ruled in the Merriman case; and the Supreme Court of Wisconsin, I rejoice to say, has rendered a like decision; and if the question be ever brought before the Supreme Court of the United States, undoubtedly it will be so decided, finally and forever. You yourselves now admit it; and at this moment, your "Indemnity Bill," a measure more execrable than even this Conscription, and liable to every objection which I have urged against it, undertakes to authorize the President to suspend the writ all over, or in any part of, the United States.

Sir, I deny that you can thus delegate your right to the Executive. Even your own power is conditional. You can not suspend the writ except where the public safety requires it, and then only in cases of rebellion or invasion. A foreign war, not brought home by invasion, to our own soil, does not authorize the suspension, in any case. And who is to judge whether and where there is rebellion or invasion, and whether and when the public safety requires that the writ be suspended? Congress alone, and they can not substitute the judgment of the President for their own. Such, too, is the opinion of Story: "The right to judge," says he, "whether exigency has arisen, must *exclusively* belong to that body." But not so under the bill which passed this House the other day.

Nor is this all. Congress alone can suspend the writ. When and where? In cases of rebellion or invasion. Where rebellion? Where invasion? Am I to be told, that because there is rebellion in South Carolina, the writ of habeas corpus can be suspended in Pennsylvania and Massachusetts where there is none? Is that the meaning of the Constitution? No, sir; the writ can be suspended only where the rebellion or invasion exists—in States, or parts of States alone, where the enemy, foreign or domestic, is found in arms; and moreover, the public safety can require its suspension only where there is rebellion or invasion. Outside of these conditions, Congress has no more authority to suspend the writ, than the President—and least of all, to suspend it without limitation as to time, and generally all over the Union, and in States not invaded or in rebellion. Such an act of Congress is of no more validity, and no more entitled to obedience, than an Executive proclamation; and in any just and impartial court, I venture to affirm that it will be so decided.

But, again, sir, even though the writ be constitutionally suspended, there is no more power in the President to make arbitrary arrests than without it. The gentleman from Rhode Island, (Mr. Sheffield,) said, very justly—and I am sorry to see him lend any support to this bill—that the suspension of the writ of habeas corpus does not authorize arrests, except upon sworn warrant, charging some offence known to the law, and dangerous to the public safety. He is right. It does not; and this was so admitted in the bill which passed the Senate, in 1807. The suspension only denies release upon bail, or a discharge without trial, to parties thus arrested. It suspends no other right or privilege under the Constitution—certainly not the right to a speedy public trial, by jury, in a civil Court. It dispenses with no "due process of law," except only that particular writ. It does not take away the claim for damages to which a party illegally arrested, or legally arrested, but without probable cause, is entitled.

And yet, everywhere, it has been assumed, that a suspension of the writ of habeas corpus, is a suspension of the entire Constitution, and of all laws, so far as the personal rights of the citizen are concerned, and that, therefore, the moment it is suspended, either by the President, as heretofore asserted, or by Congress, as now about to be authorized, arbitrary arrests, without sworn warrant, or other due process of law, may be made at the sole pleasure or discretion of the Executive. I tell you no; and that, although we may not be able to take the body of the party arrested from the provost marshal by writ of habeas corpus, every other right and privilege of the Constitution and of the common law remains intact, including the right to resist the wrong-doer or trespasser, who without due authority, would violate your person, or enter your house, which is your castle; and, after all this, the right also to prosecute on indictment, or for damages, as the nature or aggravation of the case may demand. And yet, as claimed by you of the party in power, the suspension of this writ is a total abrogation of the Constitution and of the liberties of the citizen, and the rights of the States. Why, then, sir, stop with arbitrary arrests and imprisonments? Does any man believe that it will end here? Not so have I learned history. The guillotine! the guillotine! the guillotine follows next.

Sir, when one of those earliest confined in Fort Lafayette—I had it from his own lips—made complaint to the Secretary of State of the injustice of his arrest, and the severity of the treatment to which he had been subjected in the exercise of arbitrary power, no offence being alleged against him, "Why, sir," said the Secretary, with a smile of most significant complacency, "my dear, sir, you ought not to complain; *we might have gone further*." Light flashed upon the mind of the gentleman, and he replied: "Ah! that is true, sir; you had just the same right to behead, as to arrest and imprison me." And shall it come to this? Then, sir, let us see who is beheaded first. It is horrible enough to be imprisoned without crime, but when it becomes a question of life or death, remember the words of the book of Job—"All that a man hath will he give for his life."

Sir, it is this which makes revolutions. A gentleman upon the other side asked, this afternoon, which party was to rise now in revolution. The answer of the able and gallant gentleman from Pennsylvania, (Mr. Biddle,) was pertinent arid just—"No party, but an outraged people." It is not, let me tell you, the leaders of parties who begin revolutions. Never. Did any one of the distinguished characters of the Revolution of 1776, participate in the throwing of the tea into Boston harbor? Who was it? Who, to-day, can name the actors in that now historic scene? It was not Hancock, nor Samuel Adams, nor John Adams, nor Patrick Henry, nor Washington; but men unknown to fame. Good men agitate; obscure men begin real revolutions; great men finally direct and control them. And if, indeed, we are about to pass through the usual stages of revolution, it will not be the leaders of the Democratic party, not I, not the men with me here, to-night—but some man among the people, now unknown and unnoted, who will hurl your tea into the harbor; and it may even be in Boston once again; for the love of liberty, I would fain believe, lingers still under the shadow of the monument on Bunker Hill. But sir, we seek no revolution except through the ballot-box. The conflict to which we challenge you, is not of arms but of argument. Do you believe in the virtue and intelligence of the people? Do you admit their capacity for self-government? Have they not intelligence enough to understand the right, and virtue enough to pursue it? Come then: meet us through the press, and with free speech, and before the assemblages of the people, and we will argue these questions, as we and our fathers have done from the beginning of the Government—"Are we right, or you right, we wrong or you wrong?" And by the judgment of the people, we will, one and all, abide.

Sir, I have done now with my objections to this bill. I have spoken as though the Constitution survived, and was still the supreme law of the land. But if, indeed, there be no Constitution any longer, limiting and restraining the men in power, then there is none binding upon the States or the people. God forbid. We have a Constitution yet, and laws yet. To them I appeal. Give us our rights; give us known and fixed laws; give us the judiciary; arrest us only upon due process of law; give us presentment or indictment by grand juries; speedy and public trial; trial by jury and at home; tell us the nature and. cause of the accusation; confront us with witnesses; allow us witnesses in our behalf, and the assistance of counsel for our defense; secure us in our persons, our houses, our papers, and our effects; leave us arms, not for resistance to law or against rightful authority, but to defend ourselves from outrage and violence; give us free speech and a free press; the right peaceably to assemble; and above all, free and undisturbed elections and the ballot—take our sons, take our money, our property, take all else, and we will wait a little, till at the time and in the manner appointed by Constitution and law, we shall eject you from the trusts you have abused, and the seats of power you have dishonored, and other and better men shall reign in your stead.

C. L. Vallandigham Letter from Prison (May 5, 1863)

"To the Democracy of Ohio:

"I am here in a military bastille for no other offence than my political opinions, and the defence of them and of the rights of the people, and of your constitutional liberties. Speeches made in the hearing of thousands of you in denunciation of the usurpations of power, infractions of the Constitution and laws, and of military despotism, were the sole cause of my arrest and imprisonment. I am a Democrat—for Constitution, for law, for the Union, for liberty—this is my only 'crime.' For no disobedience to the Constitution; for no violation of law; for no word, sign or gesture of sympathy with the men of the South, who are for disunion and Southern independence, but in obedience to *their* demand as well as the demand of Northern Abolition disunionists and traitors, I am here in bonds to-day; but

"Time, at last, sets all things even!"

Meanwhile, Democrats of Ohio, of the Northwest, of the United States, be firm, be true to your principles, to the Constitution, to the Union, and all will yet be well. As for myself, I adhere to every principle, and will make good through imprisonment and life itself every pledge and declaration which I have ever made, uttered or maintained from the beginning. To you, to the whole people, to TIME, I again appeal. Stand firm! Falter not an instant!

C. L. Vallandigham."

Source: James L. Vallandigham, *A Life of Clement L. Vallandigham.* Baltimore: Turnbull Brothers, 1872, 229–30, 260–61.

Mary Loughborough: Book excerpt, siege of Vicksburg

After the brutally costly Union assault of May 22, 1863, against the Confederate defensive works around Vicksburg, General U.S. Grant decided to besiege the town until it surrendered. Union artillery rained shells on Vicksburg from the landward side, while Union vessels fired from the Mississippi River. The continuous shelling forced many of the town's civilian inhabitants to vacate their houses and take refuge underground, yet even the hastily dug caves presented the danger of burial alive if a shell hit the ground directly overhead. Mary Ann Webster Loughborough, the 27-year-old wife of Confederate major James M. Loughborough, had—along with their two-year-old daughter—left their home in St. Louis to follow her husband's army. She kept a diary of her experiences under siege, which she published in 1864 as *My Cave Life in Vicksburg*. These excerpts paint a vivid picture of, first, evacuating a town before an advancing Union army, then, in Vicksburg, the terror of incoming shells and sudden deaths, and the effects of starvation on herself and her child. Vicksburg surrendered on July 4, 1863.

At the start of the siege, about 2,500 civilians lived in Vicksburg. Many took shelter in makeshift cave homes dug into the river bluff in order to escape the Union bombardment. Civilian diarists recalled how they used prayer to endure. (Library of Congress)

CHAPTER IX.
JACKSON THREATENED COLONEL GRIERSON
GENERAL PEMBERTON DEPARTS
MY MIND IS MADE UP TO GO ALSO
RIDE ON THE CARS
VICKSBURG AGAIN.

OUR quiet was destined to be of short duration. We were startled one morning by hearing that Colonel Grierson, of the Federal army, was advancing on Jackson. The citizens applied to General Pemberton to protect them. He answered that there was no danger. Suddenly, the ladies' carriage and saddle horses were pressed, and the clerks and young men of the town were mounted on them, and started out to protect us (1). I was told that the first time they met the Federal troops, most of them were captured, and we heard of them no more. "We need not have feared, for Colonel Grierson was spoken of everywhere (so some ladies from the district through which he passed, afterward told me) as a gentle man who would not allow his men to treat anyone with the slightest disrespect, or take the least article from a citizen's house; and they all treated ladies courteously. There was not one instance of unkindness to any human being, so far as I could learn. He should have the thanks of every brave man and Southern woman. This man, though an avowed enemy, scorned to torture or wage war on God's weaker creation.

Again the rumor came that from Canton a large Federal force was advancing on Jackson. Jackson was to be defended!! Which I doubted. Soon General Pemberton left and went to Vicksburg Mrs. Pemberton to Mobile. Batteries were being erected in different parts of the town, one directly opposite the house I was in. I stood considering one morning where it was best to go, and what it was best to do, when a quick gallop sounded on the drive, and a friend rode hastily up and said, "Are you going to leave?" "Yes," I answered," but I have not yet decided where to go." "Well, I assure you there is no time for deliberation; I shall take my family to Vicksburg, as the safest place, and, if you will place yourself under my charge, I will see you safely to your husband." So the matter was agreed upon, and we were to leave that evening. Still, I was in doubt; the Federal army was spreading all over the country, and I feared to remain where I was. Yet I thought, may I not be in danger in Vicksburg? Suppose the gunboats should make an attack? Still, it was true, as my friend had said, we were in far more danger here from the rabble that usually followed a large army, and who might plunder, insult, and rob us.

No; to Vicksburg we must go!

Very hurriedly we made our arrangements, packing with scarcely a moment to lose, not stopping to discuss our sudden move and the alarming news. Our friends, also, were in as great a panic and dismay as ourselves. Mrs. A. had some chests of heavy silver. Many of the pieces were such that it would have taken some time to bury them. Her husband was absent, and she feared to trust the negro men with the secret. Another friend feared to bury her diamonds, thinking in that case she might never see them more; feared, also, to retain them, lest, through negroes' tales, the cupidity of the soldiers might become excited, and she be a sufferer in consequence. Every tumult in the town caused us to fly to the doors and windows, fearing a surprise at any time; and not only ladies, with pale faces and anxious

eyes, met us at every turn, but gentlemen of anti-military dispositions were running hither and thither, with carpet bags and little valises, seeking conveyances, determined to find a safe place, if one could be found, where the sound of a gun or the smell of powder might never disturb them any more; and, as they ran, each had an alarming report to circulate; so that with the rush and roar of dray, wagon, and carriage, the distracting reports of the rapid advance of the Federal army, and the stifling clouds of dust that arose with all, we were in a fair way to believe ourselves any being or object but ourselves.

The depot was crowded with crushing and elbowing human beings, swaying to and fro baggage being thrown hither and thither horses wild with fright, and negroes with confusion; and so we found ourselves in a car, amid the living stream that flowed and surged along seeking the Mobile cars seeking the Vicksburg cars seeking anything to bear them away from the threatened and fast depopulating town.

CHAPTER X.
GROUNDLESS FEAR OF AN ATTACK
BY GUNBOATS
SHELLS FALL
THE BOMBARDMENT BEGINS
CAVE SHELTER
GARRISON FORCE
CAVES AND CAVE LIFE.

FROM gentlemen who called on the evening of the attack in the rear of the town, we learned that it was quite likely, judging from the movements on the river, that the gunboats would make an attack that night. "We remained dressed during the night; once or twice we sprang to our feet, startled by the report of a cannon; but after waiting in the darkness of the veranda for some time, the perfect quiet of the city convinced us that our alarm was needless.

Next day, two or three shells were thrown from the battle field, exploding near the house. This was our first shock, and a severe one. "We did not dare to go in the back part of the house all day.

Some of the servants came and got down by us for protection, while others kept on with their work as if feeling a perfect contempt for the shells.

In the evening we were terrified and much excited by the loud rush and scream of mortar shells; we ran to the small cave near the house, and were in it during the night, by this time wearied and almost stupefied by the loss of sleep.

The caves were plainly becoming a necessity, as some persons had been killed on the street by fragments of shells. The room that I had so lately slept in had been struck by a fragment of a shell during the first night, and a large hole made in the ceiling. I shall never forget my extreme fear during the night, and my utter hopelessness of ever seeing the morning light. Terror stricken, we remained crouched in the cave, while shell after shell followed each other in quick succession. I endeavored by constant prayer to prepare myself for the sudden death I was almost certain awaited me. My heart stood still as we would hear the reports from the guns, and the rushing and fearful sound of the shell as it came toward us. As it neared, the noise became more deafening; the air was full of the rushing sound; pains darted through my temples; my ears were full of the confusing noise; and, as it exploded, the report flashed through my head like an electric shock, leaving me in a quiet state of terror the most painful that I can imagine cowering in a corner, holding my child to my heart, the only feeling of my life being the choking throbs of my heart, that rendered me almost breathless. As singly they fell short, or beyond the cave, I was aroused by a feeling of thankfulness that was of short duration. Again and again the terrible fright came over us in that night.

I saw one fall in the road without the mouth of the cave, like a flame of fire, making the earth tremble, and, with a low, singing sound, and the fragments sped on in their work of death.

Morning found us more dead than alive, with blanched faces and trembling lips. "We were not reassured on hearing, from a man who took refuge in the cave, that a mortar shell in falling would not consider the thickness of earth above us a circumstance.

Some of the ladies, more courageous by day light, asked him what he was in there for, if that was the case. He was silenced for an hour, when he left. As the day wore on, and we were still preserved, though the shells came as ever, we were somewhat encouraged.

The next morning, we heard that Vicksburg would not in all probability hold out more than a week or two, as the garrison was poorly provisioned; and one of General Pemberton's staff officers told us that the effective force of the garrison, upon being estimated, was found to be fifteen thousand men; General Loring having been cut off after the battle of Black River, with probably ten thousand. The ladies all cried, "Oh, never surrender!" but after the experience of the night, I really could not tell what I wanted, or what my opinions were.

How often I thought of M upon the battle field, and his anxiety for us in the midst of this unanticipated danger, wherein the safety lay entirely on the side of the belligerent gentlemen, who were shelling us so furiously, at least two miles from the city, in the bend of the river near the canal. So constantly dropped the shells around the city, that the inhabitants all made preparations to live under the ground during the siege. M sent over and had a cave made in a hill near by. We seized the opportunity one evening, when the gunners were probably at their supper, for we had a few moments of quiet, to go over and take pos session. We were under the care of a friend of M, who was paymaster on the staff of the same General with whom M was Adjutant.

We had neighbors on both sides of us; and it would have been an amusing sight to a spectator to witness the domestic scenes presented without by the number of servants preparing the meals under the high bank containing the caves.

Our dining, breakfasting, and supper hours were quite irregular. When the shells were falling fast, the servants came in for safety, and our meals waited for completion some little time; again they would fall slowly, with the lapse of many minutes between, and out would start the cooks to their work. Some families had light bread made in large quantities, and subsisted on it with milk (provided their cows were not killed from one milking time to another), without any more cooking, until called on to replenish. Though most of us lived on corn bread and bacon, served three times a day, the only luxury of the meal consisting in its warmth, I had some flour, and frequently had some hard, tough biscuit made from it, there being no soda or yeast to be procured. At this time we could, also, procure beef. A gentleman friend was kind enough to offer me his camp bed, a narrow spring mattress, which fitted within the contracted cave very comfortably; another had his tent fly stretched over the mouth of our residence to shield us from the sun; and thus I was the recipient of many favors, and under obligations to many gentlemen of the army for delicate and kind attentions; and, in looking back to my trials at that time, I shall ever remember with gratitude the kindness with which they strove to ward off

every deprivation. And so, I went regularly to work, keeping house under ground. Our new habitation was an excavation made in the earth, and branching six feet from the entrance, forming a cave in the shape of a T. In one of the wings my bed fitted; the other I used as a kind of a dressing room; in this the earth had been cut down a foot or two below the floor of the main cave; I could stand erect here; and when tired of sitting in other portions of my residence, I bowed myself into it, and stood impassively resting at full height one of the variations in the still shell-expectant life. M's servant cooked for us under protection of the hill. Our quarters were close, indeed; yet I was more comfortable than I expected I could have been made under the earth in that fashion.

"We were safe at least from fragments of shell and they were flying in all directions; though no one seemed to think our cave any protection, should a mortar shell happen to fall directly on top of the ground above us. We had our roof arched and braced, the supports of the bracing taking up much room in our confined quarters. The earth was about five feet thick above, and seemed hard and compact; yet, poor M, every time he came in, examined it, fearing, amid some of the shocks it sustained, that it might crack and fall upon us.

CHAPTER XXIV.
DEATH OF A FAITHFUL SERVANT
BLOWING UP OF A FORT
LOSS OF PROMINENT OFFICERS
SURRENDER OF VICKSBURG.

THE next day, the families were invited up to our cave; and the lady told me, with tears, of the death of the faithful old man, who had served her mother before her. The morning of the day he died, he called her to him, and said: "Mistress, I feel like I ain't gwin to live much longer. Tell young master, when you see him, that I've been praying for him dis day; tell him it smites my heart mightily to think I won't see his young face dis day with the childern. Please tell the young folks, mistress, to come; and let me pray with them."

"Oh! Uncle! "The mistress answered, "don't talk that way; you will live many years yet, I hope." The young ladies were called, and knelt, while he prayed for them and all he loved, shaking hands with them, and speaking to each one separately, as they left. His cave was next his mistress's. That night he sat smoking his pipe near the entrance, when a mortar shell, exploding near, sent a fragment into the old mans side, rending it open, and tearing away his hip. He lived a few moments, and was carried into the cave. Turning to his mistress, while he shook his head, he said: "Don't stay here, mistress. I said the Lord wanted me." And so the good old Christian died. When he had breathed his last, a sudden panic seized them, for shell after shell fell near them; and they all ran. Some of the gentlemen, hearing them cry, brought them to headquarters.

The next day, the news came that one of the forts to the left of us had been undermined and blown up, killing sixty men; then of the death of the gallant Colonel Irwin, of Missouri; and again, the next day, of the death of the brave old General Green, of Missouri.

"We were now, swiftly nearing the end of our siege life: the rations had nearly all been given out. For the last few days I had been sick; still I tried to overcome the languid feeling of utter prostration. My little one had swung in her hammock, reduced in strength, with a low fever flushing in her face. M was all anxiety, I could plainly see. A soldier brought up, one morning, a little jaybird, as a plaything for the child. After playing with it for a short time, she turned wearily away.

"Miss Mary," said the servant," she s hungry; let me make her some soup from the bird." At first I refused: the poor little plaything should not die; then, as I thought of the child, I half consented. With the utmost haste, Cinth disappeared; and the next time she appeared, it was with a cup of soup, and a little plate, on which laid the white meat of the poor little bird.

On Saturday a painful calm prevailed: there had been a truce proclaimed; and so long had the constant firing been kept up, that the stillness now was absolutely oppressive.

At ten o'clock General Bowen passed by, dressed in full uniform, accompanied by Colonel Montgomery, and proceeded by a courier bearing a white flag. M came by, and asked me if I would like to walk out; so I put on my bonnet and sallied forth beyond the terrace, for the first time since I entered. On the hill above us, the earth was literally covered with fragments of shell Parrott, shrapnel, and canister; besides lead in all shapes and forms, and a long kind of solid shot, shaped like a small Parrott shell. Minie balls lay in every direction, flattened, dented, and bent from the contact with trees and pieces of wood in their flight. The grass seemed deadened the ground ploughed into furrows in many places; while scattered over all, like giant's pepper, in numberless quantity, were the shrapnel balls.

I could now see how very near to the rifle pits my cave laid: only a small ravine between the two hills separated us. In about two hours, General Bowen returned. No one knew, or seemed to know, why a truce had been made; but all believed that a treaty of surrender was pending. Nothing was talked about among the officers but the all-engrossing theme. Many wished to cut their way out and make the risk their own; but I secretly hoped that no such bloody hazard would be attempted.

The next morning, M came up, with a pale face, saying: "It s all over! The white flag floats from our forts! Vicksburg has surrendered! "

He put on his uniform coat, silently buckled on his sword, and prepared to take out the men, to deliver up their arms in front of the fortification.

I felt a strange unrest; the quiet of the day was so unnatural. I walked up and down the cave until M returned. The day was extremely warm; and he came with a violent headache. He told me that the Federal troops had acted splendidly; they were stationed opposite the place where the Confederate troops marched up and stacked their arms; and they seemed to feel sorry for the poor fellows who had defended the place for so long a time. Far different from what he had expected, not a jeer or taunt came from any one of the Federal soldiers. Occasionally, a cheer would be heard; but the majority seemed to regard the poor unsuccessful soldiers with a generous sympathy.

After the surrender, the old gray-headed soldier, in passing on the hill near the cave, stopped, and, touching his hat, said: "It s a sad day this, madam; I little thought we d come to it, when we first stopped in the entrenchments. I hope you'll yet be happy, madam, after all the trouble you've seen."

To which I mentally responded, "Amen." The poor, hunchback soldier, who had been sick, and who, at home in Southern Missouri, is worth a million of dollars, I have been told, yet within Vicksburg has been nearly starved, walked out to-day in the pleasant air, for the first time for many days.

I stood in the doorway and caught my first sight of the Federal uniform since the surrender. That afternoon the road was filled with them, walking about, looking at the forts and the head quarter horses: wagons also filled the road, drawn by the handsome United States horses. Poor M, after keeping his horse upon mulberry leaves during the forty-eight days, saw him no more! After the surrender in the evening, George rode into the city on his mule: thinking to "shine," as the negroes say, he rode M s handsome, silver-mounted dragoon-saddle. I could not help laughing when he returned, with a sorry face, reporting himself safe, but the saddle gone.

M questioned and .re-questioned him, aghast at his loss; for a saddle was a valuable article in our little community; and George, who felt as badly as any one, said: "I met a Yankee, who told me: * Git down off dat mule; I'm gwin to hab dat saddle. I said: No; I ain't gwin to do no such thing. He took out his pistol, and I jumped down."

So Mister George brought back to M a saddle that better befitted his mule than the one he rode off on, a much worn, common affair, made of wood. I felt sorry for M.

That evening George brought evil news again: another horse had been taken. His remaining horse and his only saddle finished the news of the day.

The next morning, Monday, as I was passing through the cave, I saw something stirring at the base of one of the supports of the roof: taking a second look, I beheld a large snake curled between the earth and the upright post. I went out quickly and sent one of the servants for M, who, coming up immediately, took up his sword and fastened one of the folds of the reptile to the post. It gave one quick dart toward him, with open jaws. Fortunately, the length of the sword was greater than the upper length of body; and the snake fell to the earth a few inches from M, who set his heel firmly on it, and severed the head from the body with the sword. I have never seen so large a snake; it was fully as large round the body as the bowl of a good-sized glass tumbler, and over two yards long.

Source: Mary Loughborough, *My Cave Life in Vicksburg*. Little Rock: Kellogg Printing Co., 1882, 26–28, 56–58, 60–63, 136–37.

Abraham Lincoln: Gettysburg Address (November 19, 1863)

The three-day battle of Gettysburg, July 1–3, 1863, when Robert E. Lee's army invaded Pennsylvania, is often regarded as the high-water mark of the Confederacy and the turning point of the Civil War. Lee's army began retreating on July 4, after a battle in which total losses for both sides numbered more than 40,000 men killed, wounded, or missing. On November 19, 1863, Abraham Lincoln attended the dedication of a national cemetery at Gettysburg. His brief address to an estimated crowd of 15,000 followed a two-hour oration by the popular speaker Edward Everett. Lincoln's political enemies mocked the speech's brevity, but its eloquent prose was soon widely quoted. Later a legend grew up around the speech saying that Lincoln had scribbled it on the back of an envelope while on the train from Washington. In fact, the president had prepared his speech in advance, working though several drafts. Americans have looked to this address as representing the noblest vision of America and the sacrifice that is often called upon to attain that vision.

Fourscore and seven years ago our fathers brought forth on this continent a new nation, conceived in liberty and dedicated to the proposition that all men are created equal. Now we are engaged in a great civil war, testing whether that nation or any nation so conceived and so dedicated can long endure. We are met on a great battlefield of that war. We have come to dedicate a portion of that field as a final resting-place for those who here gave their lives that that nation might live. It is altogether fitting and proper that we should do this. But in a larger sense, we cannot dedicate, we cannot consecrate, we cannot hallow this ground. The brave men, living and dead who struggled here have consecrated it far above our poor power to add or detract. The world will little note nor long remember what we say here, but it can never forget what they did here.

It is for us the living rather to be dedicated here to the unfinished work which they who fought here have thus far so nobly advanced. It is rather for us to be here dedicated to the great task remaining before us that from these honored dead we take increased devotion to that cause for which they gave the last full measure of devotion that we here highly resolve that these dead shall not have died in vain, that this nation under God shall have a new birth of freedom, and that government of the people, by the people, for the people shall not perish from the earth.

Source: Abraham Lincoln, *Gettysburg Address*, 1863. Manuscript Division, Library of Congress.

Robert McAllister: Letter, Union account of battle of May 12, 1864

General Robert McAllister (1813–1891) began his Civil War service at age 47 as lieutenant colonel of a New Jersey regiment and eventually advanced to brigadier general in the Army of the Potomac. Unassuming in manner, devoutly sober, and fearless in battle, the little-known McAllister fought tirelessly for the duration or the war, yet wrote more than nine hundred letters and numerous official reports over the course of the Civil War. The letter excerpted here, however, is dated January 24, 1882, and addressed to McAllister's divisional commander at the time of the action at Spotsylvania Court House, Virginia, on May 12, 1864. In it McAllister recounts the actions of his own brigade on that day. Lee's army had constructed elaborate field works, including a horseshoe-shaped entrenchment called the Salient, which commanded the open ground across which attackers had to charge. At dawn on May 12, Grant sent 20,000 Union troops against the Salient, which McAllister's troops were first to penetrate. More than twenty hours of close-range combat ensued in what became known as the "Bloody Angle." Fighting in a drenching rain, the Union army lost 6,800 men, and Lee's army, with estimated losses of perhaps 3,000, retired a short distance to a new line of trenches.

Many officers without men, and many men without officers—all of whom had been driven from our line to the right—came to our assistance here and fought nobly. Here we had representatives from many regiments. Brigades and Divisions were all inspired with one serious thought: we must hold this point or lose all we had gained in the morning. The contest was life or death.

These massed columns pressed forward to the Salient. The Stars and Stripes and the Stars and Bars nearly touched each other across these works. Here, on both sides of these breastworks, were displayed more individual acts of bravery and heroism than I had yet seen in the war. The graycoats and bluecoats would spring with rifles in hand on top of the breastworks, take deadly aim, fire, and then fall across into the trenches below. This I saw repeated again and again. More troops came to our aid and took a hand in the fight. A new line of troops was formed at an obtuse angle from this fighting line to stay the progress of the enemy on the right. But they no sooner formed than they were swept away by the enemy's deadly fire. . .

The fighting lasted all day, and the rain poured down. Many of our men sunk down exhausted in the mud. Ammunition would give out, and more would be brought up. The rifles would become foul. We sent men back by companies to wash them out, after which they would return and renew the fight. . .

Night closed in upon us. The minute we could slack fire, the enemy, determined to gain this point, would close in on us. Had they succeeded in driving us from there, all

we had gained would have been lost. But at 3 a.m. the battle was over and our victory complete. I need not describe to you the scenes of battle, the horrible sight the next morning of the dead and dying mass of humanity that lay in the trenches on the Rebel side of the works, and the dead that covered the ground on our side. . .

Source: Robert McAllister Papers, Special Collections and University Archives, Rutgers University Libraries.

Theodore Lyman: Letter of Union soldier (May 18, 1864)

Colonel Theodore Lyman (1833–1897) of Massachusetts served on the headquarters staff of General George Meade, commander of the Army of the Potomac. A Harvard graduate and naturalist, Lyman met Meade—then an army engineer—in 1856 while collecting specimens in Florida. He served with Meade from September 1863 until the end of the Civil War. Lyman's wartime letters to his wife were collected and published in the book, *Meade's Headquarters.* The excerpt presented here is from a letter dated May 18, 1864, in which he describes the importance of earthworks in the Spotsylvania campaign. The Confederates, as the defenders, could, within a day, construct works that provided an effective barrier against bullets and shells. They could defend these earthworks while inflicting heavy casualties on their attackers. Civil War field works changed the nature of warfare, giving the defender an ascendency that persisted until World War II. The trench warfare of the Civil War—with its piles of corpses traded for a few yards of ground—also foreshadowed the trench warfare of World War I.

HEADQUARTERS, ARMY OF THE POTOMAC

Wednesday, May 18, 1864

I have no right to complain: I have less hardship, more ease, and less exposure than most officers, and, if I must be with the army in the field, I have as good a place as one can well expect. I did hope (though there was no proper ground for it) that we might have the great blessing of an overwhelming victory. Such things you read of in books, but they do not happen often, particularly with such armies to oppose as those of the Rebels. . .

The great feature of this campaign is the extraordinary use made of earthworks. When we arrive on the ground, it takes of course a considerable time to put troops in position for attack, in a wooded country; then skirmishers must be thrown forward and an examination made for the point of attack, and to see if there be any impassable obstacles, such as streams or swamps. Meantime what does the enemy? Hastily forming a line of battle, they then collect rails from fences, stones, logs and all other materials, and pile them along the line; bayonets with a few picks and shovels, in the hands of men who work for their lives, soon suffice to cover this frame with earth and sods; and within one hour, there is a shelter against bullets, high enough to cover a man kneeling, and extending often for a mile or two. When our line advances, there is the line of the enemy, nothing showing but the bayonets, and the battle-flags stuck on the top of the work. It is a rule that, when the Rebels halt, the first day gives them a good rifle pit; the second, a regular infantry parapet with artillery in position; and the third a parapet with an abatis in front and entrenched batteries behind. Sometimes they put this three days work into the first twenty -four hours. Our men can, and do, do the same; but remember, our object is offense to advance. You would be amazed to see how this country is intersected with field-works, extending for miles and miles in different directions and marking the different strategic lines taken up by the two armies, as they warily move about each other.

The newspapers would be comic in their comments, were not the whole thing so tragic. More absurd statements could not be. Lee is not retreating: he is a brave and skilful soldier and he will fight while he has a division or a day's rations left. These Rebels are not half -starved and ready to give up a more sinewy, tawny, formidable-looking set of men could not be. In education they are certainly inferior to our native-born people; but they are usually very quick-witted within their own sphere of comprehension; and they know enough to handle weapons with terrible effect. Their great characteristic is their stoical manliness; they never beg, or whimper, or complain; but look you straight in the face, with as little animosity as if they had never heard a gun.

Now I will continue the history a little. But first I will remark that I had taken part in two great battles, and heard the bullets whistle both days, and yet I had scarcely seen a Rebel save killed, wounded, or prisoners ! I remember how even line officers, who were at the battle of Chancellorsville, said: "Why, we never saw any Rebels where we were; only smoke and bushes, and lots of our men tumbling about"; and now I appreciate this most fully. The great art is to conceal men; for the moment they show, bang, bang, go a dozen cannon, the artillerists only too pleased to get a fair mark. Your typical "great white plain," with long lines advancing and maneuvering, led on by generals in cocked hats and by bands of music, exist not for us. Here it is, as I said: "Left face prime forward!"—and then wrang, wr-r-rang, for three or four hours, or for all day, and the poor, bleeding wounded streaming to the rear. That is a great battle in America.

Well! to our next day Saturday, May 7th. At daylight it would be hard to say what opinion was most held in regard to the enemy, whether they would attack, or stand

1. For the purpose of military operations, this army is divided into two wings, viz.: The right wing, Major-General O. O. Howard, commanding, composed of the Fifteenth and Seventeenth Corps; the left wing, major-General H. W. Slocum commanding, composed of the Fourteenth and Twentieth Corps.

2. The habitual order of march will be, wherever practicable, by four roads, as nearly parallel as possible, and converging at points hereafter to be indicated in orders. The cavalry, Brigadier-General Kilpatrick commanding, will receive special orders from the commander-in-chief.

3. There will be no general train of supplies, but each corps will have its ammunition-train and provision-train, distributed habitually as follows: Behind each regiment should follow one wagon and one ambulance; behind each brigade should follow a due proportion of ammunition-wagons, provision-wagons, and ambulances. In case of danger, each corps commander should change this order of march, by having his advance and rear brigades unencumbered by wheels. The separate columns will start habitually at 7 a.m., and make about fifteen miles per day, unless otherwise fixed in orders.

4. The army will forage liberally on the country during the march. To this end, each brigade commander will organize a good and sufficient foraging party, under the command of one or more discreet officers, who will gather, near the route traveled, corn or forage of any kind, meat of any kind, vegetables, cornmeal, or whatever is needed by the command, aiming at all times to keep in the wagons at least ten days' provisions for his command, and three days' forage. Soldiers must not enter the dwellings of the inhabitants, or commit any trespass; but, during a halt or camp, they may be permitted to gather turnips, potatoes, and other vegetables, and to drive in stock in sight of their camp. To regular foraging-parties must be intrusted the gathering of provisions and forage, at any distance from the road traveled.

5. To corps commanders alone is intrusted the power to destroy mills, houses, cotton-gins, etc.; and for them this general principle is laid down: In districts and neighborhoods where the army is unmolested, no destruction of such property should be permitted; but should guerrillas or bushwhackers molest our march, or should the inhabitants burn bridges, obstruct roads, or otherwise manifest local hostility, then army commanders should order and enforce a devastation more or less relentless, according to the measure of such hostility.

6. As for horses, mules, wagons, etc., belonging to the inhabitants, the cavalry and artillery may appropriate freely and without limit; discriminating, however, between the rich, who are usually hostile, and the poor and industrious, usually neutral or friendly. Foraging-parties may also take mules or horses, to replace the jaded animals of their trains, or to serve as pack-mules for the regiments of brigades. In all foraging, of whatever kind, the parties engaged will refrain abusive or threatening language, and may, where the officer in command thinks proper, given written certificates of the facts, but no receipts; and they will endeavor to leave with each family a reasonable portion for their maintenance.

7. Negroes who are able-bodied and can be of service to the several columns may be taken along; but each army commander will bear in mind that the question of supplies is a very important one, and this

his first duty is to see to those who bear arms.

8. The organization, at once, of a good pioneer battalion for each army corps, composed if possible of Negroes, should be attended to. This battalion should follow the advance-guard, repair roads and double them if possible, so that the columns will not be delayed after reaching bad places. Also, army commanders should practice the habit of giving the artillery and wagons the road, marching their troops on one side, and instruct their troops to assist wagons at steep hills or bad crossings of streams.

9. Captain O. M. Poe, chief-engineer, will assign to each wing of the army a pontoon-train, fully equipped and organized; and the commanders thereof will see to their being properly protected at all times.

By order of Major-General W. T. Sherman,

L. M. Dayton, Aide-de-Camp.

Source: U.S. War Department, *The War of the Rebellion: A Compilation of the Official Records of the Union and Confederate Armies.* Series I, Vol. XLIV. Washington, D.C.: GPO, 1880–1901.

Robert E. Lee: Surrender at Appomattox and farewell to troops (April 1865)

General Robert E. Lee surrendered his Army of Northern Virginia at Appomattox, Virginia, on April 9, 1865. Over the previous two days, Lee had exchanged several letters with Union Lieutenant General Ulysses S. Grant negotiating the terms of surrender. The surrender terms allowed the Confederate officers and men to retain their sidearms, personal possessions, and horses and to return to their homes under parole. The parole bound them to the promise not to take up arms against the government of the United States unless exchanged. On April

10, the day after the surrender, Lee wrote the following public letter of farewell to his men. On April 12, Lee wrote to Confederate President Jefferson Davis recounting in detail the events that led him to conclude that surrender was necessary. The surrenders of other Confederate armies took place between April 26, when Joseph E. Johnston surrendered to William T. Sherman, and May 31, when John Bell Hood surrendered in Mississippi. After the war, Lee returned to private life as the president of Washington College in Lexington, Virginia.

HDQRS. ARMY OF NORTHERN VIRGINIA, April 10, 1865.

After four years of arduous service, marked by unsurpassed courage and fortitude, the Army of Northern Virginia has been compelled to yield to overwhelming numbers and resources. I need not tell the brave survivors of so many hard-fought battles, who have remained steadfast to the last, that I have consented to the result from no distrust of them. But, feeling that valor and devotion could accomplish nothing that could compensate for the loss that must have attended the continuance of the contest, I determined to avoid the useless sacrifice of those whose past services have endeared them to their countrymen.

By the terms of the agreement officers and men can return to their homes and remain until exchanged. You will take with you the satisfaction that proceeds from the consciousness of duty faithfully performed; and I earnestly pray that a merciful God will extend to you his blessing and protection.

With an increasing admiration of your constancy and devotion to your country, and a grateful remembrance of your kind and generous considerations for myself, I bid you all an affectionate farewell.

R. E. LEE, General.

* * *

Confederate general Robert E. Lee surrenders to Union general Ulysses S. Grant at Appomattox Courthouse, Virginia on April 9, 1865. The surrender effectively ended the Civil War. (Library of Congress)

NEAR APPOMATTOX COURT-HOUSE, VA., April 12, 1865.

His Excellency JEFFERSON DAVIS.

Mr. PRESIDENT: It is with pain that I announce to Your Excellency the surrender of the Army of Northern Virginia. The operations which preceded this result will be reported in full. I will therefore only now state that, upon arriving at Amelia Court House on the morning of the 4th with the advance of the army, on the retreat from the lines in front of Richmond and Petersburg, and not finding the supplies ordered to be placed there, nearly twenty-four hours were lost in endeavoring to collect in the country subsistence for men and horses. This delay was fatal, and could not be retrieved. The troops, wearied by continual fighting and marching for several days and nights, obtained neither rest nor refreshment; and on moving, on the 5th, on the Richmond and Danville Railroad, I found at Jetersville the enemy's cavalry, and learned the approach of his infantry and the general advance of

his army toward Burkeville. This deprived us of the use of the railroad, and rendered it impracticable to procure from Danville the supplies ordered to meet us at points of our march. Nothing could be obtained from the adjacent country. Our route to the Roanoke was therefore changed, and the march directed upon Farmville, where supplies were ordered from Lynchburg. The change of route threw the troops over the roads pursued by the artillery and wagon trains west of the railroad, which impeded our advance and embarrassed our movements. On the morning of the 6th, General Longstreet's corps reached Rice's Station, on the Lynchburg railroad. It was followed by the commands of Generals R. H. Anderson, Ewell, and Gordon, with orders to close upon it as fast as the progress of the trains would permit or as they could be directed on roads farther west. General Anderson, commanding Pickett's and B. R. Johnson's divisions, became disconnected with Mahone's division, forming the rear of Longstreet. The enemy's cavalry penetrated the line of march through the interval thus left and attacked the wagon train moving toward Farmville. This caused serious delay in the march of the center and rear of the column, and enabled the enemy to mass upon their flank. After successive attacks Anderson's and Ewell's corps were captured or driven from their position. The latter general, with both of his division commanders, Kershaw and Custis Lee, and his brigadiers, were taken prisoners. Gordon, who all the morning, aided by General W. H. F. Lee's cavalry, had checked the advance of the enemy on the road from Amelia Springs and protected the trains, became exposed to his combined assaults, which he bravely resisted and twice repulsed; but the cavalry having been withdrawn to another part of the line of march, and the enemy massing heavily on his front and both flanks, renewed the attack about 6 p.m., and drove him from the field in much confusion.

The army continued its march during the night, and every effort was made to reorganize the divisions which had been shattered by the day's operations; but the men being depressed by fatigue and hunger, many threw away their arms, while others followed the wagon trains and embarrassed their progress. On the morning of the 7th rations were issued to the troops as they passed Farmville, but the safety of the trains requiring their removal upon the approach of the enemy all could not be supplied. The army, reduced to two corps, under Longstreet and Gordon, moved steadily on the road to Appomattox Court House; thence its march was ordered by Campbell Court House, through Pittsylvania, toward Danville. The roads were wretched and the progress slow. By great efforts the head of the column reached Appomattox Court House on the evening of the 8th, and the troops were halted for rest. The march was ordered to be resumed at

1 a.m. on the 9th. Fitz Lee, with the cavalry, supported by Gordon, was ordered to drive the enemy from his front, wheel to the left, and cover the passage of the trains; while Longstreet, who from Rice's Station had formed the rear guard, should close up and hold the position. Two battalions of artillery and the ammunition wagons were directed to accompany the army, the rest of the artillery and wagons to move toward Lynchburg. In the early part of the night, the enemy attacked Walker's artillery train near Appomattox Station, on the Lynchburg railroad, and were repelled. Shortly afterward their cavalry dashed toward the Court-House, till halted by our line. During the night there were indications of a large force massing on our left and front. Fitz Lee was directed to ascertain its strength, and to suspend his advance till daylight if necessary. About 5 a.m. on the 9th, with Gordon on his left, he moved forward and opened the way. A heavy force of the enemy was discovered opposite Gordon's right, which, moving in the direction of Appomattox Court-House, drove back the left of the cavalry and threatened to cut off Gordon from Longstreet, his cavalry at the same time threatening to envelop his left flank. Gordon withdrew across the Appomattox River, and the cavalry advanced on the Lynchburg road and became separated from the army.

Learning the condition of affairs on the lines, where I had gone under the expectation of meeting General Grant to learn definitely the terms he proposed in a communication received from him on the 8th, in the event of the surrender of the army, I requested a suspension of hostilities until these terms could be arranged. In the interview, which occurred with General Grant in compliance with my request, terms having been agreed on, I surrendered that portion of the Army of Northern Virginia which was on the field, with its arms, artillery, and wagon trains, the officers and men to be paroled, retaining their sidearms and private effects. I deemed this course the best under all the circumstances by which we were surrounded. On the morning of the 9th, according to the reports of the ordnance officers, there were 7,892 organized infantry with arms, with an average of seventy-five rounds of ammunition per man. The artillery, though reduced to sixty-three pieces, with ninety-three rounds of ammunition, was sufficient. These comprised all the supplies of ordnance that could be relied on in the State of Virginia. I have no accurate report of the cavalry, but believe it did not exceed 2,100 effective men. The enemy were more than five times our numbers. If we could have forced our way one day longer, it would have been at a great sacrifice of life, and at its end I did not see how a surrender could have been avoided. We had no subsistence for man or horse, and it could not be gathered in the country. The supplies ordered to Pamplin's Station from Lynchburg could not reach us, and the men, deprived of food and sleep for many days, were worn out and exhausted.

With great respect, your obedient servant, R. E. LEE, General.

Source: U.S. War Department, *The War of the Rebellion: A Compilation of the Official Records of the Union and Confederate Armies.* Series I, Vol. XLIV. Washington, D.C.: GPO, 1880–1901.

Reconstruction Acts (1867)

In the spring and summer of 1867, Congress passed a series of three acts to govern Reconstruction in the South after the Civil War. The first act was passed on March 2, over the veto of President Andrew Johnson, and established military authority over the government of the former Confederate states. The act required these states to submit their constitutions to Congress for approval. The second act, passed on March 23, called for the registration of all eligible voters—which included all men of age 21 or older, regardless of race or former slave status. The voters were to take the oath prescribed by the act and to elect delegates to formulate state constitutions. The third act, passed on July 19, sought to define further the military and civil lines of authority and voter eligibility established in the first two acts. Congress also passed three Reconstruction amendments to the U.S. Constitution. The Thirteenth Amendment banning slavery was adopted by Congress early in 1865 and ratified in December. The Fourteenth Amendment, which extended U.S. citizenship to all races, was passed by Congress in 1866 and became law in 1868. The Fifteenth Amendment, passed by Congress in 1869 and ratified in 1870, extended the right to vote to all male citizens regardless of race or former condition of slavery. Each of these amendments is notable for extending federal law over matters formerly governed by the states.

An Act to provide for the more efficient Government of the Rebel States

Whereas no legal State governments or adequate protection for life or property now exists in the rebel States of Virginia, North Carolina, South Carolina, Georgia, Mississippi, Alabama, Louisiana, Florida. Texas and Arkansas; and whereas it is necessary that peace and good order should be enforced in said States until loyal and republican State governments can be legally established: Therefore,

Be it enacted by the Senate and House of Representatives of the United States of America in Congress assembled, That said rebel States shall be divided into military districts and made subject to the military authority of the United States as hereinafter prescribed, and for that purpose Virginia shall constitute the first district; North Carolina and South Carolina the second district; Georgia, Alabama and Florida the third district;

Mississippi and Arkansas the fourth district; and Louisiana and Texas the fifth district.

Section 2. And be it further enacted, That it shall be the duty of the President to assign to the command of each of the said districts an officer of the army, not below the rank of brigadier-general, and to detail a sufficient military force to enable such officer to perform his duties and enforce his authority within the district to which he is assigned.

Section 3. And be it further enacted, That it shall be the duty of each officer assigned as aforesaid, to protect all persons in their rights of person and property, to suppress insurrection, disorder, and violence, and to punish, or cause to be punished, all disturbers of the public peace and criminals; and to this end he may allow local civil tribunals to take jurisdiction of and to try offenders, or, when in his judgment it may be necessary for the trial of offenders, he shall have power to organize military commissions or tribunals for that purpose, and all interference under color of State authority with the exercise of military authority under this act, shall be null and void.

Section 4. And be it further enacted, That all persons put under military arrest by virtue of this act shall be tried without unnecessary delay, and no cruel or unusual punishment shall be inflicted, and no sentence of any military commission or tribunal hereby authorized, affecting the life or liberty of any person, shall be executed until it is approved by the officer in command of the district, and the laws and regulations for the government of the army shall not be affected by this act, except in so far as they conflict with its provisions: Provided, That no sentence of death under the provisions of this act shall be carried into effect without the approval of the President.

Section 5. And be it further enacted, That when the people of any one of said rebel States shall have formed a constitution of government in conformity with the Constitution of the United States in all respects, framed by a convention of delegates elected by the male citizens of said State, twenty-one years old and upward, of whatever race, color, or previous condition, who have been resident in said State for one year previous to the day of such election, except such as may be disfranchised for participation in the rebellion or for felony at common law, and when such constitution shall provide that the elective franchise shall be enjoyed by all such persons as have the qualifications herein stated for electors of delegates, and when such constitution shall be ratified by a majority of the persons voting on the question of ratification who are qualified as electors for delegates, and when such constitution shall have been submitted to Congress for examination and approval, and Congress shall have approved the same, and when said State, by a vote of its legislature elected under said constitution, shall have adopted the amendment to the Constitution of the United States, proposed by the Thirty-ninth Congress, and known as article fourteen, and when such article shall have become a part of the Constitution of the United States, said State shall be declared entitled to representation in Congress, and senators and representatives shall be admitted therefrom on their taking the oath prescribed by law, and then and thereafter the preceding sections of this act shall be inoperative in said State: Provided, That no person excluded from the privilege of holding office by said proposed amendment to the Constitution of the United States, shall be eligible to election as a member of the convention to frame a constitution for any of said rebel States, nor shall any such person vote for members of such convention.

Section 6. And be it further enacted, That, until the people of said rebel States shall be by law admitted to representation in the Congress of the United States, any civil governments which may exist therein shall be deemed provisional only, and in all respects subject to the paramount authority of the United States at any time to abolish, modify, control, or supersede the same; and in all elections to any office under such provisional governments all persons shall be entitled to vote, and none others, who are entitled to vote under the provisions of the fifth section of this act; and no person shall be eligible to any office under any provisional governments who would be disqualified from holding office under the provisions of the third article of said constitutional amendment.

An Act supplementary to an Act entitled "An Act to provide for the more efficient Government of the Rebel States," passed March second, eighteen hundred and sixty-seven, and to facilitate Restoration.

Be it enacted by the Senate and House of Representatives of the United States of America in Congress assembled, That before the first day of September, eighteen hundred and sixty-seven, the commanding general in each district defined by an act entitled "An act to provide for the more efficient government of the rebel States," passed March second, eighteen hundred and sixty-seven, shall cause a registration to be made of the male citizens of the United States, twenty-one years of age and upwards, resident in each county or parish in the State or States included in his district, which registration shall include only those persons who are qualified to vote for delegates by the act aforesaid, and who shall have taken and subscribed the following oath or affirmation:

"I, _____, do solemnly swear (or affirm), in the presence of Almighty God, that I am a citizen of the State of _____; that I have resided in said State for _____ months next preceding this day, and now reside in the county of _____ or the parish of _____, in said State (as the case may be); that I am twenty-one years old; that I have not be disfranchised for participation in any rebellion or civil war against the United States, nor for felony committed against the laws of any State or of the United States; that I have never been a member of any State legislature, nor held any executive or judicial office in any State and afterwards engaged in insurrection or rebellion against the United States, or given aid or comfort to the enemies thereof; that I have never taken an oath as a member of Congress of the United States, or as an officer of the United States, or as a member of any State legislature, or as an executive or judicial officer of any State, to support the Constitution of the United States, and afterwards engaged in insurrection or rebellion against the United States, or given aid or comfort to the enemies thereof; that I will faithfully support the Constitution and obey the laws of the United States, and will to the best of my ability, encourage others so to do, so help me God" which oath or affirmation may be administered by any registering officer.

Section 2. And be it further enacted, That after the completion of the registration hereby provided for in any State, at such time and places therein as the commanding general shall appoint and direct, of which at least thirty days' public notice shall be given, an election shall be held of delegates to a convention for the purpose of establishing a constitution and civil government for such State loyal to the Union, said convention in each State, except Virginia, to consist of the same number of members as the most numerous branch of the State legislature of such State in the year eighteen hundred and sixty, to be apportioned among the several districts, counties, or parishes of such State by the commanding general, giving to each representation in the ratio of voters registered as aforesaid as nearly as may be. The convention in Virginia shall consist of the same number of members as represented the territory now constituting Virginia in the most numerous branch of the legislature of said State in the year eighteen hundred and sixty, to be apportioned as aforesaid.

Section 3. And be it further enacted, That at said election the registered voters of each State shall vote for or against a convention to form a constitution therefore under this act. Those voting in favor of such a convention shall have written or printed on the ballots by which they vote for delegates, as aforesaid, the words "For a convention," and those voting against such a convention shall have written or printed on such ballots the words "Against a convention." The persons appointed to superintend said election, and to make return of the votes given thereat, as herein provided, shall count and make return of the votes given for and against a convention; and the commanding general to whom the same shall have been returned shall ascertain and declare the total vote in each State for and against a convention. If a majority of the votes given on that question shall be for a convention, then such convention shall be held as hereinafter provided; but if a majority of said votes shall be against a convention, then no such convention shall be held under this act: Provided, That such convention shall not be held unless a majority of all such registered voters shall have voted on the question of holding such convention.

Section 4. And be it further enacted, That the commanding general of each district shall appoint as many boards of registration as may be necessary, consisting of three loyal officers or persons, to make and com-

plete the registration, superintend the election, and make return to him of the votes, list of voters, and of the persons elected as delegates by a plurality of the votes cast at said election; and upon receiving said returns he shall open the same, ascertain the persons elected as delegates, according to the returns of the officers who conducted said election, make proclamation thereof; and if a majority of the votes given on that question shall be for a convention, the commanding general, within sixty days from the date of election, shall notify the delegates to assemble in convention, at a time and place to be mentioned in the notification, and said convention, when organized, shall proceed to frame a constitution and civil government according to the provisions of this act, and the act to which it is supplementary; and when the same shall have been so framed, said constitution shall be submitted by the convention for ratification to the persons registered under the provisions of this act at an election to be conducted by the officers or persons appointed or to be appointed by the commanding general, as hereinbefore provided, and to be held after the expiration of thirty days from the date of notice thereof, to be given by said convention; and the returns thereof shall be made to the commanding general of the district.

Section 5. And be it further enacted, That if, according to said returns, the constitution shall be ratified by a majority of the votes of the registered electors qualified as herein specified, cast at said election, at least one half of all the registered voters voting upon the question of such ratification, the president of the convention shall transmit a copy of the same, duly certified, to the President of the United States, who shall forthwith transmit the same to Congress, if then in session, and if not in session, then immediately upon its next assembling; and if it shall moreover appear to Congress that the election was one at which all the registered and qualified electors in the State had an opportunity to vote freely and without restraint, fear, or the influence of fraud, and if the Congress shall be satisfied that such constitution meets the approval of a majority of all the qualified electors in the State, and if the said constitution shall be declared by Congress to be in conformity with the provisions of the act to which this is supplementary, and the other provisions of said act shall have been complied with, and the said constitution shall be approved by Congress, the State shall be declared entitled to representation, and senators and representatives shall be admitted therefrom as therein provided.

Section 6. And be it further enacted, That all elections in the States mentioned in said "Act to provide for the more efficient government of the rebel States," shall, during the operation of said act, be by ballot; and all officers making the said registration of voters and conducting said elections shall, before entering upon the discharge of their duties, take and subscribe the oath prescribed by the act approved July second, eighteen hundred and sixty-two entitled "An act to prescribe an oath of office": Provided, That if any person shall knowingly and falsely take and subscribe any oath in this act prescribed, such person so offending and being thereof duly convicted shall be subject to the pains, penalties, and disabilities which by law are provided for the punishment of the crime of willful and corrupt perjury.

Section 7. And be it further enacted, That all expenses incurred by the several commanding generals or by virtue of any orders issued, or appointments made, by them, under or by virtue of this act, shall be paid out of any moneys in the treasury not otherwise appropriated.

Section 8. And be it further enacted, That the convention for each State shall prescribe the fees, salary, and compensation to be paid to all delegates and other officers and agents herein authorized or necessary to carry into effect the purposes of this act not herein otherwise provided for, and shall provide for the levy and collection of such taxes on the property in such State as may be necessary to pay the same.

Section 9. And be it further enacted, That the word "article," in the sixth section of the act to which this is supplementary, shall be construed to mean "section."

An Act supplementary to an Act entitled "An Act to provide for the more efficient Government of the Rebel States," passed on the second day of March, eighteen hundred and sixty-seven, and the Act supplementary thereto, passed on the twenty-third day of March, eighteen hundred and sixty-seven.

Be it enacted by the Senate and House of Representatives of the United States of America in Congress assembled, That it is hereby declared to have been the true intent and meaning of the act of the second day of March, one thousand eight hundred and sixty-seven, entitled "An act to provide for the more efficient government of the rebel States," and of the act supplementary thereto, passed on the twenty-third day of March, in the year one thousand eight hundred and sixty-seven, that the governments then existing in the rebel States of Virginia, North Carolina, South Carolina, Georgia, Mississippi, Alabama, Louisiana, Florida, Texas, and Arkansas were not legal State governments; and that thereafter said governments, if continued, were to be continued subject in all respects to the military commanders of the respective districts, and to the paramount authority of Congress.

Section 2. And be it further enacted, That the commander of any district named in said act shall have power, subject to the disapproval of the General of the army of the United States, and to have effect till disapproved, whenever in the opinion of such commander the proper administration of said act shall require it, to suspend or remove from office, or from the performance of official duties and the exercise of official powers, any officer or person holding or exercising, or professing to hold or exercise, any civil or military office or duty in such district under any power, election, appointment or authority derived from, or granted by, or claimed under, any so-called State or the government thereof, or any municipal or other division thereof, and upon such suspension or removal such commander, subject to the disapproval of the General as aforesaid, shall have power to provide from time to time for the performance of the said duties of such officer or person so suspended or removed, by the detail of some competent officer or soldier of the army, or by the appointment of some other person, to perform the same, and to fill vacancies occasioned by death, resignation, or otherwise.

Section 3. And be it further enacted, That the General of the army of the United Sates shall be invested with all the powers of suspension, removal, appointment, and detail granted in the preceding section to district commanders.

Section 4. And be it further enacted, That the acts of the officers of the army already done in removing in said districts persons exercising the functions of civil officers, and appointing others in their stead, are hereby confirmed: Provided, That any person heretofore or hereafter appointed by any district commander to exercise the functions of any civil office, may be removed either by the military officer in command of the district, or by the General of the army. And it shall be the duty of such commander to remove from office as aforesaid all persons who are disloyal to the government of the United States, or who use their official influence in any manner to hinder, delay, prevent, or obstruct the due and proper administration of this act and the acts to which it is supplementary.

Section 5. And be it further enacted, That the boards of registration provided for in the act entitled "An act supplementary to an act entitled "An act to provide for the more efficient government of the rebel States," passed March two, eighteen hundred and sixty-seven, and to facilitate restoration," passed March twenty-three, eighteen hundred and sixty-seven, shall have power, and it shall be their duty before allowing the registration of any person, to ascertain, upon such facts or information as they can obtain, whether such person is entitled to be registered under said act, and the oath required by said act shall not be conclusive on such question, and no person shall be registered unless such board shall decide that he is entitled thereto; and such board shall also have power to examine, under oath, (to be administered by any member of such board,) any one touching the qualification of any person claiming registration; but in every case of refusal by the board to register an applicant, and in every case of striking his name from the list as hereinafter provided, the board shall make a note or memorandum, which shall be returned with the registration list to the commanding general of the district, setting forth the grounds of such refusal or such striking from the list: Provided, That no person shall be disqualified as member of any board of registration by reason of race or color.

Section 6. And be it further enacted, That the true intent and meaning of the oath prescribed in said supplementary act is, (among other things,) that no person who has been a member of the legislature of any State, or who has held any executive or judicial office in any State, whether he has taken an oath to support the Constitution of the United Sates or not, and whether he was holding such office at the commencement of the rebellion, or had held it before, and who has afterwards engaged in insurrection or rebellion against the United States, or given aid or comfort to the enemies thereof, is entitled to be registered or to vote; and the words "executive or judicial office in any State" in said oath mentioned shall be construed to include all civil offices created by law for the administration of any general law of a State, or for the administration of justice.

Section 7. And be it further enacted, That the time for completing the original registration provided for in said act may, in the discretion of the commander of any district be extended to the first day of October, eighteen hundred and sixty-seven; and the boards of registration shall have power, and it shall be their duty, commencing fourteen days prior to any election under said act, and upon reasonable public notice of the time and place thereof, to revise, for a period of five days, the registration lists, and upon being satisfied that any person not entitled thereto has been registered, to strike the name of such person from the list, and such person shall not be allowed to vote. And such board shall also, during the same period, add to such registry the names of all persons who at that time possess the qualifications required by said act who have not been already registered; and no person shall, at any time, be entitled to be registered or to vote by reason of any executive pardon or amnesty for any act or thing which, without such pardon or amnesty, would disqualify him from registration or voting.

Section 8. And be it further enacted, That section four of said last-named act shall be construed to authorize the commanding general named therein, whenever he shall deem it needful, to remove any member of a board of registration and to appoint another in his stead, and to fill any vacancy in such board.

Section 9. And be it further enacted, That all members of said boards of registration and all persons hereafter elected or appointed to office in said military districts, under any so-called State or municipal authority, or by detail or appointment of the district commanders, shall be required to take and to subscribe the oath of office prescribed by law for officers of the United States.

Section 10. And be it further enacted, That no district commander or member of the board of registration, or any of the officers or appointees acting under them shall be bound in his action by any opinion of any civil officer of the United States.

Section 11. And be it further enacted, That all the provisions of this act and of the acts to which this is supplementary shall be construed liberally, to the end that all intents thereof may be fully and perfectly carried out.

APPENDIX: HISTORICAL DILEMMAS IN THE AMERICAN CIVIL WAR

Leadership in the Civil War

As in any armed conflict, leadership was a key factor in the outcome of the Civil War. From commander in chief to company commander, leaders on various levels provided the direction and the motivation that kept the armies in the field and contending for final victory. In some ways, the demands of leadership in the Civil War were much the same as those in any major war. In other ways, however, the Civil War presented a very different set of leadership challenges.

In the first place, to state the obvious, the Civil War was a war within a single society. The rival armies spoke the same language, celebrated many of the same holidays, and shared many of the same cultural memories. To a degree that often amazed soldiers on both sides, they shared the same religion. Many soldiers had relatives in the ranks of the opposing army. All of these factors presented challenges for those whose task it was to motivate men to march, fight, and endure the boredom and discomfort of camp life. These difficulties were compounded by the fact that the opposing soldiers would fraternize easily. Informal enlisted men's truces often sprang up along the picket lines, with soldiers in blue and gray sitting down to discuss anything from politics to army life to their distant homes or to swap Rebel tobacco for Union coffee. Such confabs not infrequently concluded with the mutual agreement that if

the matter was left up to the enlisted soldiers, peace would be concluded at once. In reality, that was almost certainly never the case, but the participants no doubt sincerely believed it at the time, and their belief would have heightened the challenges for officers—or for the commander in chief—who had to motivate such men to soldier on through month after month of war. Fraternization also made operational secrecy unlikely.

At the highest level, Lincoln had to motivate Northerners to fight what turned out to be the bloodiest war in American history for the abstract causes of maintaining the Union, preserving representative self-government, and freeing slaves—when at least a large minority of Northerners at the outset of the war did not at all wish to see the slaves freed. That Lincoln was able to accomplish these motivational tasks is no small measure of why he deserves to be considered one of the greatest statesmen and presidents in U.S. history.

This was certainly not the only war, nor was Lincoln the only commander in chief who faced such a challenge, but it was definitely a difficulty that did not confront Lincoln's opponent, Jefferson Davis. Davis's soldiers could fight for readily understandable goals. Because the majority of rank and file southern soldiers did not own slaves, their motivation came from simply resisting

Yankee invaders. Their more prosperous leaders and officers fought to keep their slaves, or at least to keep blacks in general in a subordinate position in society.

Another facet of Civil War leadership that was unusual, at least relative to the size of the conflict and to later conflicts, was the degree to which citizen-soldiers exercised leadership at relatively high levels of command. It was the only time in U.S. history that forces of such size were commanded to that extent by men who had come directly out of civilian life with little or no military training. Naturally, the Revolutionary War, the War of 1812, and the Mexican War had seen a great many civilians elevated to various levels of command, but the armies in those wars were much smaller. During the Civil War, bankers, lawyers, and farmers not infrequently went straight from civilian life to the rank of colonel commanding a regiment, and a few months' success and survival in that job could very well bring further promotion.

In other cases, politicians parlayed political leverage into appointments directly to general officer rank. Both Lincoln and Davis appointed such "political generals," so called because simply having those men in uniform, with a general's insignia on their shoulders, was something that the rival presidents believed would enhance popular support for the war. In most cases, political generals were military disasters. On the other hand, a surprising number of the citizen-soldiers who worked their way up from field- and company-grade turned out to be excellent generals. Perhaps the most striking example of that type was Union major general John A. Logan. Though his previous military experience was limited to a year as a lieutenant in a volunteer regiment in the Mexican War, Logan rose during the Civil War from command of the 31st Illinois at the

war's outset to command of XV Corps by 1864, and, on the death of Army of the Tennessee commander James B. McPherson, Logan led that army to victory in the hard-fought Battle of Atlanta on July 22, 1864.

It was naturally purely civilian leadership that made the decisions that initially brought on the Civil War. The movement toward secession between November 1860 and April 1861 was neither accidental nor a spontaneous outpouring of popular enthusiasm. Rather, it was carefully organized and relentlessly agitated by the Fire-eaters. Even with all of the secessionists' hard political work, most of the Southern states to secede before Fort Sumter did so by slim margins in the popular votes that ratified the radical step.

By the time Lincoln took office, the secession of the seven Deep South states was a fait accompli, which the outgoing James Buchanan administration had done next to nothing to combat. The Upper and Border South states were threatening a similar course of action, especially if the federal government should make any effort to interfere with the already seceded states. Lincoln was determined to maintain the Union but eager to avoid an armed outbreak if possible. Choosing his path cautiously, the president announced that the federal government would not be the aggressor but that it would continue to hold its remaining forts and outposts in the South. By this time, only three such remained: Fort Pickens, outside the harbor of Pensacola, Florida; Fort Jefferson in the Dry Tortugas; and Fort Sumter, on a mud bar in the harbor of Charleston, South Carolina. Few cared about Fort Pickens; fewer about Fort Jefferson. All eyes were fixed on Fort Sumter, which presently began to run low on supplies. Lincoln determined to send food supplies only and so notified the rebellious governor of South Carolina, promising that if no resistance was made from the South

Carolina—now Confederate—forces ringing the harbor, no aggressive action would be taken by the Union fleet and no troops or ammunition would be sent into the fort. Pickens notified Jefferson Davis, president of the eight-week-old Confederacy, and Davis ordered his military commander on location, Brigadier General Pierre G. T. Beauregard, to reduce the fort before the Union supply convoy could arrive.

Beauregard sent Colonel James Chesnut, lately a U.S. senator from South Carolina, and Major Stephen D. Lee, a career military man, to demand the surrender of the fort. When their demand was refused, Chesnut and Lee went directly to the nearest Confederate battery and gave the order to open fire. Thus the immediate decision for the opening shot of the war devolved on a field officer, albeit one with extensive political experience.

One account has it that when the Confederate cabinet met to discuss the question of whether or not to fire on Fort Sumter, then Secretary of State Robert Toombs of Georgia argued strongly against such a step, maintaining that it would put the Confederacy in the wrong in the eyes of world opinion and awaken the great mass of the Northern population to fight for their flag and country. Other cabinet members, however, argued that a brief armed conflict was exactly what was needed to persuade the slave states then remaining in the Union that their own interest lay in joining the Deep South states in the Confederacy. As for the possibility of bloodshed, Davis's secretary of war, Leroy Pope Walker of Alabama, offered to wipe up, with his pocket-handkerchief, every drop of blood that would be shed as a result of secession. In the end, Walker proved to be completely wrong—although his prediction held up for the duration of the Fort Sumter fight, where there were no casualties.

The Confederate firing on Fort Sumter did indeed rally the North to the Union cause in a way that little else could have done, as tens of thousands of men flocked to volunteer for the Northern army. At the same time, four Upper South states—Arkansas, Tennessee, North Carolina, and all-important Virginia—reacted to the outbreak of hostilities by casting their lots with the Confederacy, drastically increasing its size, wealth, population, and manufacturing capacity. Only the outcome of several years of struggle would reveal the wisdom, or lack thereof, in the decision to fire on Fort Sumter.

Throughout the war, civilian and military leaders interacted in efforts to maximize the achievement of desired political goals by military means. The president who at the outset seemed most likely to be successful in such efforts was clearly Jefferson Davis. An 1828 graduate of the U.S. Military Academy, West Point, Davis had served seven years in the regular army and then had returned to military service for the Mexican War, serving as colonel of the 1st Mississippi Rifles Volunteer Regiment. He had also served as an able secretary of war during 1853–1857, when he had helped to modernize the army. He was personally acquainted with many of the men who would be candidates for general officer rank in the Civil War and knew even more of them by reputation. He prided himself on being able to select the most qualified generals and in having a clear understanding of military operations himself so as to be able to advise and direct his generals.

Davis's first promotions to general officer rank were of necessity limited to men from the first seven states to secede. Notable among them were Louisianans Braxton Bragg and Pierre G. T. Beauregard. Both had been highly regarded in the old army. Beauregard had been an engineer officer on

Jefferson Davis and his cabinet with General Lee in the Council Chamber at Richmond. At left: Benjamin and Mallory (seated); Walker (standing) Jefferson Davis; Robert E. Lee; Regan (seated front); Memminger (in back standing); Toombs (standing); Stephens (seated). (Library of Congress)

the staff of Winfield Scott during the Mexican War. He presided over the bloodless Confederate victory at Fort Sumter and then commanded the Confederate army at Manassas Junction, Virginia. By the late spring of 1861, Davis was free to appoint generals from the second wave of seceding states, including most notably Virginia. Once again, the men Davis selected had held enviable reputations in the prewar U.S. Army. Robert E. Lee and Joseph E. Johnston had led parallel careers, from their 1829 West Point graduation to their Mexican War service, whereas Lee had served as an engineer on Scott's staff and Johnston had commanded a temporary regiment of light infantry, to their parallel appointments as lieutenant colonels, Johnston of the 1st U.S. Cavalry and Lee of the 2nd. Davis was among the many informed observers who thought Lee the more bookish and intellectual and Johnston the

more aggressive combat leader of the two. He had known both men since West Point.

Somehow, despite all of Davis's prewar knowledge, Beauregard and Johnston turned out to be some of the Confederacy's most problematic generals, and after their joint victory at the First Battle of Bull Run, they fell into almost uninterrupted squabbling with Davis. Beauregard turned out to be an inveterate publicity-seeker, and his report on the battle included an unrelated section about how he had, several weeks earlier, proposed a plan that would have won the war—had Davis not nixed it. In fact, Beauregard's plan had been completely unrealistic. From there, the relationship went rapidly downhill. Davis, who would earn a reputation for pride and willfulness during the war, treated Beauregard with remarkable patience and showed considerable humility—all to no avail. The general engaged in increasingly obnoxious grandstanding, writing anti-Davis letters to newspaper editors, heading one of them "within hearing of the enemy's guns," and teaming up with anti-administration members of the Confederate Congress to embarrass the president. Finally, Davis transferred him to the western theater, where his narcissistic tendencies might perhaps find fewer avenues for pernicious expression.

Johnston presented the president with a different set of problems. Like Beauregard, Johnston possessed an overweening pride that made Jefferson Davis appear humble by comparison. When in September, 1861, he learned that Davis had named him fourth in rank on the list of men promoted that summer to full general, Johnston wrote the president a 15-page abusive letter. Misconstruing a Confederate law to his own advantage, the general claimed that he was legally entitled to be the Confederacy's highest-ranking officer, regardless of what the president and Congress might say. Surprisingly, Davis retained Johnston in his command, but relations between the president and his top-ranking general in Virginia were never the same. Johnston's other shortcomings as a general became apparent when the enemy advanced the following spring. Again and again Johnston retreated, giving up important Confederate assets without offering battle. He also showed an almost neurotic reluctance to inform the administration of his plans or even of his current operations. On one occasion, with Johnston's army on the outskirts of Richmond, Davis rode out to consult with the general. Had Confederate soldiers not called out to warn the president, he would have ridden beyond the Rebel outposts because Johnston had retreated once again the preceding night, and, true to form, had not informed Davis. Wounds removed Johnston from duty in May 1862. On his return, Davis assigned him to the western

theater. There, his performance was no better than it had been in the East.

In Lee, Davis finally found the general he was looking for in Virginia. Davis gave Lee the command only after Johnston's wounding, and the president seems to have harbored suspicions that Lee, the highly cerebral engineer officer, would perform timidly in command. In that judgment, Davis could not have been more mistaken, as he very quickly discovered. "His name might be audacity," said a staff officer of Lee, and the general lived up to the claim. He led the Army of Northern Virginia skillfully and extremely aggressively throughout the rest of the war. Indeed, Lee's propensity for the long chance considerably exceeded Davis's own risk tolerance. Nevertheless, Lee was superb in handling Davis. He kept the president thoroughly informed, and from time to time he stroked Davis's military vanity. The Lee-Davis relationship was almost unfailingly pleasant, warm, and mutually trusting.

Davis had more difficulty with his western generals. The high command of the Confederate Army of Tennessee became a snake pit of bitter rivals and seething discontent. Davis's trusted friend and the first overall commander in the West, Albert Sidney Johnston, might have changed all this, though history will never be sure of it, since he died in battle in April 1862. Beauregard, who inherited the western command, had never had a good relationship with Davis. He accomplished little besides a clever retreat and then removed himself from command due to an illness that many believed to have been brought on by nerves.

Davis's replacement for Beauregard, Braxton Bragg, was a skillful strategist, organizer, and disciplinarian, and no worse than an average tactician. Unfortunately for the Confederacy, he was much worse than an average politician, and he had scant gifts

THE OLD BULL DOG ON THE RIGHT TRACK.

A Currier & Ives cartoon from 1864 showing Lincoln and his Democratic opponent in the presidential election, George McClellan. (Library of Congress)

in chief, Grant continued in like manner, moving rapidly and aggressively against the Confederates and ultimately engineering Union victory.

At the far extreme from the level of leadership exercised by Davis, Lincoln, and their top generals was that which fell to the lower-ranking officers whose duty it was to lead troops into battle. It proved to be a particularly dangerous job. In no war prior to the Civil War had weaponry been as lethal. The famous minie ball, fired from the percussion cap rifled musket, made infantry fire far more deadly than before, and the foot soldiers became the chief executioners during the conflict. In no war since the Civil War have officers been expected to expose themselves quite so recklessly to enemy fire. Such exposure to danger was not simply for the purpose of controlling and directing their troops, although that was a very significant concern. Beyond that, however, was the importance of

inspiring the men and proving one's courage by conspicuous display of calmness under enemy fire. The expectation of such exposure could reach as high as general officer ranks. Officer casualties were correspondingly high. Albert Sidney Johnston, who became the highest-ranking officer on either side to die in battle, received his fatal wound while leading a charge. Nor was inspiration the only reason for high losses among officers. After the Battle of Gettysburg, officers of Confederate major general Lafayette McLaws's division noted the high casualties among mounted officers and decided to go into action dismounted in their next battle. They did, but at that battle, Chickamauga, many of them found that they could not direct their troops, resulting in the division becoming immobilized during the latter stages of the battle. In short, tactical leadership in the Civil War was at best a very dangerous proposition.

Steven E. Woodworth

Congress and the War

How Did Congressional Legislation Impact the U.S. Economy During the Civil War?

When the American Civil War erupted in April 1861, Abraham Lincoln's administration had to find a way to finance a conflict that was going to prove to be very expensive, while not completely alienating public support. Raising taxes would have been difficult and potentially very unpopular in the economic and political climate of the time, prompting the government to look for other ways to pay for the war. After the first several campaigns against the Confederates went poorly for the Union, the need for the government to finance the conflict, while also bolstering public support for the war in the North, became even more critical.

In the Defining Moments that follow, Dr. Lee Eysturlid examines some of the actions the U.S. Congress took to fund the war. In the first Defining Moment, he discusses how Congress passed several important laws that aided farmers and improved the health of the North's economy. One of the most significant pieces of legislation was the passage of the Morrill Act, which greatly increased access to higher education and made major improvements in American scientific and agricultural practices. In the second Defining Moment, Dr. Eysturlid reveals how paper money, which became known as "greenbacks," was used by the Federal government as a significant aid in underwriting the cost of the war. Since the greenbacks were not tied to the gold standard, they improved the means of investment, which benefited businesses, banks, and overall industrial growth.

Defining Moment 1: Morrill Land Grant Act

The American Civil War was a boon to land legislation, and the U.S. Congress passed important laws that aided farmers. The Morrill Land Grant Act was part of a greater act that established the Department of Agriculture and the Homestead Act. The intention was the expansion of American natural and intellectual resources. Before the war, American higher education had been based on the classical European model. White males from families that could afford the tuition studied to become lawyers, clergymen, and physicians. Most farmers viewed higher education as a place where Latin and other unimportant, inapplicable topics were taught. The general population, increasingly industrial workers who were often excluded, started to clamor for access.

The antebellum United States had immense land holdings and resources, but few had any real training in how to make the best use of them. Most colleges, which were

Presidential Politics

What Role Did Politics and Slavery Play during the Civil War?

The American Civil War was, in many ways, a political struggle. Begun over the issue of states' rights, politics continued to play a crucial role throughout the conflict. For the Union, the main task at hand was achieving political solidarity. Although the absence of Southern Democrats made it possible for Congress to pass far-reaching legislation, Northern Democrats remained a strong political force. For the South, the major issue facing Confederate politicians—many of whom ran unopposed in one-party elections—was the guiding of a war effort that would succeed without infringing on the very principles for which the South was fighting.

In the Defining Moments that follow, Dr. Lee Eysturlid takes an in-depth look at two important political events during the Civil War. In the first, he examines Lincoln's issuance of the Emancipation Proclamation, which declared that the slaves in any state still in rebellion after 100 days would be made "forever free." This document, today considered the hallmark of Lincoln's presidency, proved a brilliant political maneuver for both moral and practical reasons. It generated additional support for the war from both Northern abolitionists and Great Britain and France, both of which opposed slavery. In the second Defining Moment, Dr. Eysturlid explores the presidential election of 1864. The election, a clear referendum on the president's handling of the war, resulted in Lincoln's reelection and landslide majorities for the Republican Party at all levels of government. The election also dashed Northern Democrats' hopes for an immediate end to hostilities and a negotiated settlement with the South.

Defining Moment 1: Emancipation Proclamation

The bloody battle of Antietam, on September 17, 1862, ended a Confederate invasion of Maryland and forced the Army of Northern Virginia to retreat, making it the first great Union success in the eastern theater. Emboldened by the success, President Abraham Lincoln decided that the time was right to issue his Emancipation Proclamation. This document has been seen by many as the single most far-reaching action taken by the Lincoln administration during the war. It is certainly the most famous. The Emancipation Proclamation gave the rebellious states 100 days to return to the Union and adopt some form of abolition, or else the federal government would declare all slaves in each recalcitrant state "forever free."

The willingness and ability of Lincoln to issue such a potentially politically and socially unpopular decree represented the necessities of the war. It was not at all clear that Union soldiers eager to fight against secession would be eager or even willing to fight against slavery. A large majority of Northerners, including those openly opposed to slavery, feared an influx of freed slaves into their states and communities. Copperhead Democrats played on the fear that African Americans would displace white workers. Lincoln had shown an unwillingness in the first year of the war to advocate abolition, revoking moves by his military commanders in Missouri and the occupied Southern coastal regions to free all slaves belonging to pro-Confederates.

By mid-1862, it had become clear that the war would not end quickly. The large number of slaves then in the South, who worked and farmed the plantations and in some areas built fortifications, freed up thousands of white males for military service. Undermining or removing the slave population as a Southern manpower resource would be a blow to the war effort. The Emancipation Proclamation also gave the Union the moral high ground in the eyes of antislavery Great Britain and France. Active against slavery themselves, such a move all but guaranteed that the Europeans would not diplomatically recognize the South. The final Emancipation Proclamation, issued on New Year's Day 1863, also secured the right to recruit African Americans to serve in the Union Army. This measure was vital because it secured the service of tens of thousands of African American men, who eventually made up 10 percent of total Union manpower.

While the Emancipation Proclamation can be viewed in moral terms as entirely correct, it presented a constitutional dilemma in terms of property. Since slaves were still considered property, the federal government could not legally free them without specific cause against the owner. This explains the warning of the initial document. Anyone not swearing loyalty to the Union was in rebellion, and, as a criminal act, this allowed for the seizure of property. This also explains why slave-owning citizens in the Border States or occupied areas did not, at least initially, have to give up their slaves. An incomplete measure, the Emancipation Proclamation's work was completed by the Thirteenth Amendment in December 1865, which gave all African Americans their freedom.

Lee W. Eysturlid

Defining Moment 2: 1864 U.S. Election

The fall 1864 elections for U.S. president and numerous congressional and gubernatorial positions can be seen, as it was then, as a clear referendum on the war. In the presidential race, incumbent Abraham Lincoln, candidate for the Republican Party—now calling itself the National Union Party—ran against Democrat George B. McClellan. The victory by Lincoln and the Republican Party was important because it meant that the war would be pursued to the bitter end. Lincoln's success dashed Confederate hopes that a Democratic victory would lead to a negotiated peace and independence for the South. Also important was the fact that, for the first time in history, a national election was successfully and fairly held during wartime.

The Republican platform was clear. It pledged full support for the war, a war that would be fought until the South surrendered unconditionally. There would be no peace negotiations. The platform declared slavery to be the cause of the war, creating the impetus for the Thirteenth Amendment. It also endorsed the use of African American troops, encouraged foreign immigration, favored speedy construction of a transcontinental railroad, called for "a vigorous and just system of taxation" and a national

South Carolina made his soon-to-be famous, or perhaps infamous, statement concerning the dominance of cotton on the world textile market: "What would happen if no cotton was furnished for three years?" he threatened. "England would topple headlong and carry the whole civilized world with her, save the South." When the war started, it was an article of faith that cotton would play the great trump card in the Confederacy's quest for recognition, and perhaps military assistance, among the industrialized European states. At the very least, it would break the growing Northern blockade.

Confederate president Jefferson Davis strongly supported the Cotton Embargo of 1861–1862, the result more of a Southern consensus of opinion rather than any single government policy. Newspapers throughout the Confederacy called for planters to hold all of the year's crop back, sending none for shipment to New Orleans or other port cities. The call for an embargo worked, and despite the weakness of the Federal blockade in the first year of the war, little cotton was shipped. In 1862, Great Britain would only receive 3 percent of the amount of cotton it had in 1860. Initial reaction seemed to indicate that the Southern claims were correct. British prime minister Viscount Palmerston and foreign minister Lord John Russell worried aloud that the lack of cotton for the mills would throw millions out of work. French and British diplomats actually talked of the potential for joint action to lift the blockade.

More than any diplomatic action, it was simple economics that conspired to ruin the Southern plan. The immense cotton exports of 1857 through 1860 had filled British warehouses, and even intense production could not turn it all into cloth. Work slowdowns that did occur in 1861 and early 1862 resulted from overproduction rather than a lack of raw materials. Further, by the time the need for cotton had returned, Southern cotton had been replaced by increased production in Egypt and India. Changes in British industry, from primarily textiles to iron, shipbuilding, and armaments, helped compensate as well and made the North, eager to buy, a better trade partner than the South. Finally, crop failures in Western Europe made the British ever more dependent on grain from the North, specifically Midwestern farms. Northerners could now claim that "King Corn" had dethroned "King Cotton." By 1863, the embargo had clearly failed and the South again tried, this time in desperation, to export cotton through the blockade in order to pay for needed war materials.

Lee W. Eysturlid

Defining Moment 2: The *Trent* Affair

In September 1861, the Confederate government decided to send two "ministers plenipotentiary" to Europe. James Mason of Virginia would go to London and John Slidell of Louisiana would be placed in Paris. The new ministers traveled with the hope of capitalizing on the declaration of British neutrality in May. While better, for the North at least, than open diplomatic contact, it gave automatic recognition to the South as a belligerent power. The recognition also came at a disconcerting time for the North because the British foreign minister, Lord Russell, had just met with the Confederate envoys then in London. All this added a sense of paranoia to Union actions in the enforcement of the blockade of the South and in dealings with the British government.

Mason and Slidell departed from Charleston, South Carolina, by way of a blockade runner. This initial escape was a matter of embarrassment for the U.S. Navy because their departure had not been a secret. The

Lithograph of Confederate diplomats James M. Mason and John Slidell being removed from the British ship *Trent* by crew from the USS *San Jacinto* on November 8, 1861. (Bettmann/Corbis)

ministers then sailed to Havana, where they could take a British ship, the steamer *Trent*, on to England. The reason for this was the assumption that the United States could no longer interfere with their travels. This was not to be the case. Captain Charles Wilkes, a 40-year navy veteran and self-proclaimed expert in maritime law, decided he would redeem the service's reputation. Since diplomatic dispatches could legally be seized as contraband of war, Wilkes felt that he could take Mason and Slidell into custody as the "embodiment of dispatches." Commanding the 13-gun sloop USS *San Jacinto*, he stopped the *Trent* on November 8 while at sea and took the two ministers prisoner, but allowed the ship to go.

While the Northern public saw the move as positive, and the House of Representatives voted to laud Wilkes for his actions, it soon became clear that the act was a mistake. British public opinion, egged on by a belligerent press, called for action, even war. Prime Minister Viscount Palmerston and his cabinet voted to send Washington an ultimatum: release the Confederate ministers and apologize. To make their intentions clear, British troops were moved to Canada and the western Atlantic fleet was put on a war-footing. The result was a dive on the American stock market and the inability to sell government bonds.

While American newspapers, always Anglophobic, seemed to welcome war, President Abraham Lincoln thought better of it, reportedly stating: "One war at a time." Also critical was the fact that British India was the sole supplier of Union saltpeter, a key

Print showing Robert E. Lee and 21 Confederate generals, published ca. 1867. (Library of Congress)

to formulate and execute a viable strategic policy.

President Jefferson Davis and Confederate officials maintained that they were fighting for self-defense. Such assertions suggest that the South's logical strategy should have been defensive. The Confederacy's grand strategy, however, was "offensive-defensive." This strategy, designed in an effort to protect the vast territory of the South from a Northern invasion, raised large armies and placed them in defensive postures in the South. This defensive strategy, however, became secondary at times. Whenever circumstances were thought to favor success, Confederate armies launched offensives, as seen in Lee's two invasions of the North in the fall of 1862 and the summer of 1863.

This was not the most effective strategy and, in the midst of the war, Confederate generals debated the merits of the offensive-defensive policy. For example, General Pierre G. T. Beauregard was foremost in criticizing this strategy. After the South's victory at the First Battle of Bull Run (Manassas) on July 21, 1861, Beauregard, eager to maintain the strategic initiative, urged Davis to amass Confederate manpower and drive rapidly toward Washington, D.C. Davis rejected Beauregard's plan, and any momentum gained from victory in the war's first major battle was lost. If Davis had not remained steadfast to the offensive-defensive strategy and had allowed Beauregard to exploit the advantage gained from victory at Bull Run, the war's campaigns might have turned out differently.

To some degree, however, the nature of the rebellion and the expectations of the Southern people dictated the South's military strategy. In *The Confederate War,* Gary Gallagher argues that the key to success lay in maintaining high morale and nationalistic sentiment, which could only be achieved through decisive battlefield victories. Gallagher believes that the adoption of the offensive-defensive strategy fits into this mindset. When Confederate armies earned victories, morale increased; when Southern armies suffered defeats, morale plummeted. Confederate officials, however, failed to appreciate the role of morale and failed to understand that battles, military strategies, and popular support were intrinsically linked.

Perhaps Confederate victories came at too high a cost. In *Attack and Die,* Grady McWhiney and Perry Jamieson contend that in the early stages of the war the "Confederates bled themselves nearly to death" by adhering to archaic tactics, particularly frontal assaults. These historians argue that the South would have benefited by adapting a more defensive strategy that would negate their numerical disadvantage in manpower. McWhiney and Jamieson calculate that "the South lost more than 175,000 soldiers in the first twenty-seven months of the war." Clearly, the South failed to appreciate its most precious resource, the Southern soldier, and should have pursued a strategy such as that employed at Fredericksburg, not Gettysburg.

Another contributing factor to the South's defeat was the failure of government and military officials to understand the larger picture of the war, specifically the importance of the western theater. The iconic Robert E. Lee seems to have been guilty of this misunderstanding. In the summer of 1863, instead of sending reinforcements to Confederate armies in the West, Lee initiated his own offensive into Pennsylvania. Little effort was made to reinforce General

John C. Pemberton's forces at Vicksburg and, as a result, on July 4, 1863, the fortress fell and the Mississippi River was opened to Federal forces. Only after the Army of Northern Virginia's defeat at Gettysburg and the surrender of Vicksburg did Lee approve the transfer of troops from his army to the West.

By the time the South came to recognize problems with its military strategy, it was too late. Only when the Confederacy's final hours approached did its leaders consider altering their strategic policies and war aims to reconsider the idea of arming and emancipating slaves. In *Confederate Emancipation,* Bruce Levine argues that the proposal might have been more "viable" if enacted earlier in the war; perhaps as early as 1861, after the Confederate victory at Bull Run, when slavery and black freedom were secondary to the North's war aims.

Arguably, the South should have adopted a different military strategy. For the North to win the war, it had to conquer and subjugate the South and its people, an objective finally accomplished by the spring of 1865. On the other hand, the Confederacy's best course of action would have been to mirror the strategies of the colonists during the American Revolutionary War, adopting a defensive strategy with minimal, but well-timed and well-placed, offensives. The colonists focused on keeping a viable army on the field and wearing down Britain's support for the war. The South, however, failed to recognize the advantages of assuming a defensive military strategy. Adopting a more efficient strategy; recognizing the importance of the western theater; refraining from bloody and costly offensives; and making use of all available manpower, including slaves; might have changed the outcome of the Civil War.

Jennifer M. Murray

American Civil War Timeline

1619	English settlers in Virginia purchase 20 Africans as indentured servants from a Dutch ship, leading to the emergence of slavery within 20 years.
1641	Massachusetts Bay Colony legalizes slavery.
1660	Virginia legalizes slavery.
1663	Maryland becomes the first colony to enact slavery for life.
1667	Virginia revokes prior English law allowing freedom for converted slaves.
February 1688	Quakers of Germantown, Pennsylvania, organize the first protest against slavery.
September 1739	Slaves rebel in Stono, South Carolina, after a Spanish decree offers freedom and land in Florida.
1775	The Pennsylvania Abolition Society is organized to protect the rights of blacks who are held unlawfully.
July 1776	Declaration of Independence, which reads, "All men are created equal."
1777	Vermont abolishes slavery.
1780	Pennsylvania abolishes slavery and calls for gradual abolition within the other colonies.
1783	Massachusetts abolishes slavery and grants voting rights to blacks and Native Americans.
1787	Congress passes the Three-Fifths Clause stating that each slave is to be counted as three fifths of a person.
July 1787	Congress passes the Northwest Ordinance, preventing slavery from existing in the new federal territories.
1791	Vermont enters the Union as a free state.

Dred Scott proposes that he has gained his freedom by being transported to a nonslavery state, is submitted to the U.S. Supreme Court. In their now-infamous decision, the Supreme Court declares that Scott is not an American citizen and thus has no right to petition for his freedom.

1858   Minnesota enters the Union as a free state.

1859   Oregon enters the Union as a free state.

October 16–18, 1859   Abolitionist John Brown, hoping to spark a slave uprising and ultimately destroy slavery in the southern states, raids Harpers Ferry, Virginia. Brown fails quickly under Colonel Robert E. Lee's marines and is hanged on December 2. The nation is split in opinion.

November 6, 1860   Republican Abraham Lincoln, whose name is not even on the ballot in the Deep South, is elected the 16th president of the United States.

December 18, 1860   John J. Crittenden submits his six resolutions in the hope of saving the Union.

December 20, 1860   South Carolina becomes the first state to secede from the Union. Ten more states follow in 1861.

January 7, 1861   Fort Marion, Florida, is taken by Confederates.

January 9, 1861   Mississippi secedes.

January 10, 1861   Florida secedes.

January 11, 1861   Alabama secedes.

January 19, 1861   Georgia secedes.

January 26, 1861   Louisiana secedes.

January 29, 1861   Kansas enters the Union as a free state.

February 1, 1861   Texas votes to secede.

February 8, 1861   The Provisional Constitution of the Confederacy is adopted in Montgomery, Alabama. Jefferson Davis is unanimously elected President of the Confederacy the following day.

March 6, 1861   A volunteer army is authorized by the Confederate Congress.

April 7, 1861   General P.G.T. Beauregard orders all intercourse between Fort Sumter and Charleston halted. The following day Washington informs South Carolina that it will resupply the fort by force, if necessary.

April 12, 1861   Confederate batteries at Fort Moultrie open fire on Fort Sumter. Major Robert Anderson surrenders on April 13. The Civil War begins.

April 15, 1861	Lincoln calls for troops to help put down the secessionist movement, but this request is refused by North Carolina, Kentucky, Virginia, and Tennessee. Fort Macon, North Carolina, is also occupied by Confederate troops.
April 17, 1861	Virginia secedes from the Union and Jefferson Davis issues commissions to Confederate privateers.
April 18, 1861	Union soldiers destroy the federal arsenal at Harpers Ferry in order to prevent it from falling into Confederate hands.
April 18, 1861	On the recommendation of General in Chief Winfield Scott, Lincoln offers former Superintendent at West Point, Robert E. Lee, command of the Federal armies. Lee declines.
April 19, 1861	Lincoln orders a U.S. naval blockade of southern ports and calls for the recruitment of 82,000 long-term Union servicemen. This same day, the 6th Massachusetts Volunteers are attacked by a mob while passing through Baltimore, resulting in the deaths of 3 soldiers and 11 civilians.

During the Baltimore Riots, Confederate-sympathizers cut telegraph wires, destroy rail bridges, and smash shop windows.

April 20, 1861	Several bridges on the Northern Pennsylvania Railroad are destroyed by Confederates in Maryland to prevent the passage of troops into Washington. The same day, the Gosport Navy Yard in Norfolk, Virginia is destroyed to prevent it from falling into Confederate hands. The screw steamer *Merrimack* burns to the water line leaving a salvageable hull.
April 20, 1861	The Liberty Arsenal is seized by the Confederates. Robert E. Lee resigns from the U.S. Army.
April 21, 1861	The U.S. Navy partially destroys the Norfolk Navy Yard before evacuating. The Confederates seize the facility that day and begin operating within a few weeks.
April 22, 1861	Confederates seize the U.S. arsenal at Fayetteville, North Carolina.
April 23, 1861	Confederates seize Fort Smith in Arkansas and U.S. officers at San Antonio, Texas. Major

garrisons evacuate and Union forces under Benjamin Butler occupy the forts.

August 30, 1861 Frémont issues an emancipation proclamation, declaring martial law in Missouri. Lincoln modifies it 12 days later.

September 4, 1861 Confederate general Leonidas Polk invades Kentucky and begins constructing fortifications at Hickman, Chalk Cliffs, and Columbus. Polk's violation of Kentucky neutrality proves a key blunder in that it allows Federal forces to enter Kentucky.

September 6, 1861 Grant occupies Paducah and Smithland in Kentucky in order to counter Polk's incursion.

September 18, 1861 Confederate general Albert S. Johnston occupies Bowling Green, Kentucky.

September 20, 1861 Confederate Missouri governor Sterling Price captures Lexington, Missouri, but is soon forced to retreat to Springfield by the approach of Frémont's army.

October 7, 1861 The Confederate ironclad *Virginia*—built atop the charred hull of the screw frigate *Merrimack*—makes its first appearance off Fortress Monroe (Hampton Roads, Virginia).

October 8, 1861 Brigadier General William Tecumseh Sherman assumes command of the Department of the Cumberland.

October 11, 1861 The Confederate steamer *Theodore* escapes from Charleston with the diplomatic commissioners James Mason and John Slidell.

October 21, 1861 Federal forces driving toward Leesburg, Virginia, are confronted at Balls Bluff by a larger Confederate force and are driven back, losing more than half of their numbers. Balls Bluff is the second rout in a row for Federal forces operating in Virginia and thus has important consequences for the morale of the rival armies.

October 29, 1861 Union commodore Samuel Du Pont leads a transport force bearing 13,000 troops to capture Port Royal Sound. Du Pont bombards Fort Beauregard and Fort Walker on November 7, and both forts evacuate by nightfall, leaving them in Union hands until the end of the war.

This success showcases the potential for Federal amphibious operations along the Confederate seacoast.

November 1, 1861

McClellan replaces the old and infirm Winfield Scott as commander in chief of all Union forces.

November 2, 1861

David Hunter supersedes Frémont as commander of the Department of the West.

November 7, 1861

Grant descends the Missouri River with 3,000 men to attack Confederate general Polk's positions 15 miles downstream of Cairo at Belmont, Illinois, eventually being obliged to re-embark his troops and withdraw.

November 15, 1861

Captain Charles Wilkes's USS *San Jacinto* arrives at Fortress Monroe after removing Confederate commissioners Mason and Slidell from the English mail steamer *Trent*. Britain protests, setting off an international incident. The Trent Affair is important because the Confederate government perceives that foreign intervention is one likely pathway for the Confederacy to achieve independence.

December 4, 1861

Henry Halleck issues a series of punitive measures aimed at secessionist supporters in St. Louis.

December 18, 1861

Union general John Pope captures 1,300 Confederates, a number of horses and wagons, and 1,000 firearms at Milford, Missouri.

December 27, 1861

The Federal government resolves its dispute with Great Britain by surrendering Confederate commissioners Mason and Slidell to the British ambassador. The two Confederate diplomats leave Fort Warren, Boston harbor for Britain five days later. While diplomatic, economic, and military irritations between the U.S. and Great Britain will persist, none will be as serious as the Trent Affair.

January 17, 1862

Confederate general Felix Zollicoffer's small army is attacked at Mill Springs, Kentucky, by a Union army of similar size under George Henry Thomas. Zollicoffer's army disintegrates after he blunders into Federal lines and is shot. The Confederates flee, leaving behind 11 field guns, their supply train, and by better than four to one, McClellan displays extreme caution and halts the advance. After two days of careful reconnaissance, McClellan begins siege operations.

April 6, 1862

First day of the Battle of Shiloh. After the Fort Donelson Campaign, Grant's army moves to Pittsburgh Landing on the Tennessee River. Here Grant stops while awaiting reinforcements from Buell. He and his army are overconfident, and consequently ill prepared, when Confederates under General Albert Sidney Johnston launch a surprise attack. To obtain manpower for this attack, Johnston summons men from many places throughout the western Confederacy. It is a calculated risk that fails when the inexperienced Confederates are confused by the area's wooded terrain and their attacks become increasingly uncoordinated as they penetrate deeper into Union lines. In the afternoon of the Battle of Shiloh, Johnston is killed while inappropriately risking his life by leading a charge. His death eliminates

the best chance for the Confederates to drive Grant's army into the Tennessee River. By virtue of tenacious fighting, by the end of the day Grant's army manages to hold a final position along the banks of the river.

April 7, 1862

Overnight, Grant receives major reinforcements when Buell's army arrives. The combined armies, spearheaded by Buell's fresh forces, drive Beauregard, who has replaced the fallen Johnston, from the field. The Union loses about 13,700 and the Confederates about 10,700 at "Bloody Shiloh." The fact that Grant's army was surprised by the Confederate attack and lost so many men leads to popular and political demands that he be cashiered. Lincoln refuses, famously saying that he cannot spare a general who fights so hard.

April 18, 1862

Union commodore David Glasgow Farragut arrives off the mouth of the Mississippi River, with 13,000 soldiers under Butler, and begins shelling Fort Saint Philip and Fort

Jackson. Because the defenders are depleted by the men sent to fight at Shiloh, the Confederates have no answer to overwhelming Union strength. Farragut reaches New Orleans on April 25, compelling the city to surrender three days later.

April 21, 1862 After a short siege, John Pope captures the 7,000-man Confederate garrison at Island No. 10 on the Mississippi River and then joins Halleck and Grant for the advance to Corinth, Mississippi.

May 3, 1862 McClellan's caution provides time for General Joseph Johnston to move to the Peninsula, bringing Confederate strength to 60,000. McClellan's strength rises to 112,000. Johnston resolves to retreat to a better defensive position on the outskirts of Richmond.

May 5, 1862 McClellan resumes his advance, leading to the minor rearguard action at the Battle of Williamsburg.

May 8, 1862 Jackson defeats a small Union force at McDowell, thus clearing his flank for an ambitious but risky advance north down the Shenandoah Valley.

May 9, 1862 Johnston's retreat compels the evacuation of Norfolk. The ironclad *Virginia* is left without a base and is destroyed by its crew.

May 9–12, 1862 Confederate forces evacuate Pensacola after destroying its navy yard.

May 10, 1862 Union forces retake Norfolk, which has been evacuated by the Confederates.

May 15, 1862 The Union fleet steams up the James to within seven miles of Richmond before being repelled by Confederate guns sited on Drewry's Bluff.

May 25, 1862 Jackson interposes his army between converging Union columns and defeats them in detail, culminating in a victory at Winchester, Virginia, that drives Bank's army north across the Potomac River.

May 30, 1862 Beauregard, with Halleck's Union army slowly approaching, evacuates the key railroad hub at Corinth, Mississippi, and retreats to Tupelo.

May 31–June 1, 1862 Battle of Fair Oaks (Seven Pines). McClellan's cautious pursuit brings his army to

August 14, 1862 Confederate General Edmund Kirby Smith departs Knoxville to begin his invasion of Kentucky. He is supposed to cooperate with Bragg's army but poor communication between the two hampers Confederate coordination.

August 17– September 23, 1862 Rampant corruption in the Bureau of Indian Affairs prevents the Dakota Sioux from receiving their treaty-guaranteed food on their reservation; they attack scores of settlements under Chief Little Crow, but are unable to take Fort Ridgley and Fort Abercrombie. They are defeated by Colonel Henry Sibley at the Battle of Wood Lake on September 23. By the end of November, 303 natives are convicted to hang, although Lincoln commutes all but 39 sentences, and the Sioux tribes are expelled from Minnesota.

August 19–24 1862 Pope retires to await McClellan's reinforcements, while Lee probes the Rappahannock defense lines before dispatching Jackson around the Union flank on August 25.

August 27, 1862 Jackson captures the Union supply base at Manassas Junction. He then retreats to an excellent defensive position near the battlefield of First Bull Run. Exhibiting sound strategic judgment, Pope perceives that he can defeat Jackson before the balance of Lee's army can arrive. However, the inability of his cavalry to locate the Confederates and poor coordination among Pope's various commands thwarts the Union effort.

August 28, 1862 Arriving at Manassas Junction and believing he only faces Jackson's corps, Pope sends forces to pursue the Confederates. In the west, Confederate General Braxton Bragg begins his invasion of Kentucky.

August 29–30, 1862 Pope's army attacks Jackson at the battle of Second Bull Run. His piecemeal attacks fail and the arrival of the balance of Lee's army under the capable command of General James Longstreet crushes Union resistance. A near rout ensues, but a gallant rearguard action preserves Pope's army

August 30, 1862 Confederate general Edmund Kirby Smith defeats Union general William Nelson at Richmond, Kentucky, occupying Lexington three days later.

September 1, 1862 Although Pope receives reinforcements and greatly outnumbers the Confederates, his army is demoralized and he retreats toward Washington. Lee pursues, leading to the Battle of Chantilly. Pope subsequently withdraws inside Washington's fortified perimeter. The Second Bull Run Campaign results in a notable Confederate victory during which Lee takes bold chances and outmaneuvers his foes. Union forces fight well but are plagued by divided command and Pope's errors of judgment. The campaign ends with Union forces demoralized and Lee's army ascendant. When Lee assumed army command the Confederate situation looked bleak with overwhelming Federal forces at the gates of Richmond. In three months, Lee has entirely reversed the strategic situation.

September 7, 1862 After defeating Pope, Lee resolves to invade the North. His army crosses the Potomac and marches north, occupying Frederick, Maryland. The Federal army, again under McClellan's command, cautiously pursues Lee.

September 7, 1862 Lee divides his army into two wings with Jackson receiving the assignment of capturing the Federal garrison at Harpers Ferry.

September 11, 1862 McClellan occupies Frederick, Maryland, and one of his soldiers finds a misplaced copy of Lee's orders. Aware that Lee has divided his army, McClellan receives a splendid chance to defeat Lee in detail. However, his innate caution impairs his ability to take advantage of this opportunity.

September 13, 1862 Jackson occupies the heights around Harpers Ferry on the opposite banks of the Potomac and Shenandoah rivers. Two days later the Union garrison of 12,500 men capitulates.

September 14, 1862 McClellan's advance west from Frederick leads to battles at Crampton's Gap and South Mountain.

September 17, 1862 McClellan delivers a ponderous assault retreat after the battle due to lack of supplies. The Union victory at Prairie Grove costs the Confederates 1,300 men and the Union 1,200.

December 12, 1862

The Federal gunboat *Cairo* sinks after striking a Confederate "torpedo" in a Mississippi tributary, thus becoming the first victim of mine warfare.

December 13, 1862

After crossing the Rappahannock River, Burnside's army futilely assaults Lee's position at Fredericksburg. Repeated attacks fail, costing the Union force over 10,000 men while Lee loses about 5,000. The defeat demoralizes the Army of the Potomac.

December 20, 1862

Grant's first plan for an attack against Vicksburg, Mississippi, relies on an advance south along the railroad while a secondary force commanded by his trusted subordinate, William T. Sherman, moves down the Mississippi to attack the city. Confederate cavalrymen commanded by Earl Van Dorn raid Grant's supply depot at Holly Springs, Mississippi, and compel Grant to delay his advance.

December 29, 1862

The second prong of Grant's scheme fails when Confederate general John Pemberton defeats Sherman's army at Chickasaw Bluffs, six miles north of Vicksburg. Sherman is obliged to retreat after losing 2,000 men.

December 30, 1862– January 3, 1863

Rosecrans deploys the Army of the Cumberland along the banks of the Stones River outside Murfreesboro, Tennessee. Bragg's Army of the Tennessee conducts a surprise assault on December 31 that devastates the Union right. By the narrowest margin, the Union center holds. Despite heavy losses, Rosecrans refuses to retire. On January 2, 1863, Bragg attacks the Union left but is defeated. In the sternly contested Battle of Stones River, both sides lose about 12,000 men. Rosecrans, ably supported by General George Thomas, another rising star in the Union command hierarchy, refuses to accept defeat and holds his ground. Bragg decides to retreat, thereby giving the victory to the Union. Coming at a time when Union forces from Virginia to Mississippi had failed, Stones River serves as a powerful tonic for northern morale.

January 10–11, 1863

Two of Grant's subordinates, John McClernand and Sherman, supported by David Dixon Porter's river squadron, invest Arkansas Post and force the 5,000-man garrison to surrender.

January 20–23, 1863

Burnside attempts an envelopment of Lee's flank, but a two-day rainstorm sets in. Roads are reduced to quagmires and the effort, known as Burnside's Mud March, flounders to a demoralizing end.

January 26, 1863

Hooker replaces Burnside as commander of the sick and demoralized Army of the Potomac. He proves a surprisingly able administrator and the army's health and spirit soon improve.

February–April 1863

Around Vicksburg, the winter of 1862–63 features unusually high water, making it very difficult for Grant to advance against the Confederate fortress. During the period Grant tries five projects to outflank the city's heavy guns: a canal

across the peninsula opposite Vicksburg; a more ambitious canal at Duckport to allow transports to arrive on the Mississippi River below the city; the Lake Providence Expedition involving a 400-mile long route through the swamps west of the city; the Yazoo Pass Expedition involving blasting a hole in the levee 325 miles north of Vicksburg; and the Steele's Bayou Expedition. Natural obstacles, high water, and Pemberton's skillful responses thwart all of these efforts. Public outcry against Grant's failures rises.

April 7, 1863

Du Pont leads his ironclads against the Confederates' Charleston batteries, but is badly mauled and forced to retire. Soon afterwards, Du Pont is replaced by Rear Admiral John Dahlgren.

April 15, 1863

Grant embarks on a new campaign against Vicksburg. He intends to bypass the city by marching south along the west bank of the Mississippi River toward New Carthage, where he hopes he will be joined by Porter's fleet.

begins concentrating his scattered forces.

May 12, 1863 With a 44,000-man army, Grant begins his march, encountering an isolated Confederate force at Raymond. The outnumbered Confederates fight a skillful rear guard but fail to slow significantly the Union advance.

May 14, 1863 Grant heads west to engage Confederate reinforcements at Jackson. Here Confederate General Joseph Johnston has begun to assemble forces to help Pemberton in Vicksburg. After a sharp fight, Union troops enter this important rail hub, while Johnston retreats to safety.

May 16, 1863 Pemberton, the garrison commander of Vicksburg, finally decides to challenges Grant's army in the open field. The rival armies clash at Champion Hill. The campaign's decisive battle ensues, a back and forth affair in which Grant's army emerges triumphant. Union casualties are 2,400, while the Confederates lose about 4,000. Most of Pemberton's army retreats toward Vicksburg.

Champion Hill is a crucial Union victory and arguably the decisive battle of the war.

May 17, 1863 Grant pursues the retiring Confederates, encountering a formidable position at the Big Black River. An impetuous assault routs the Confederates and inflicts another 1,700 casualties. Pemberton withdraws inside Vicksburg's fortifications.

May 19, 1863 Hoping to avoid a time consuming siege, Grant orders a general assault against Vicksburg. The defenders occupy an exceptionally strong position and repulse the attack.

May 22, 1863 Underestimating the natural strength of Vicksburg's defenses, Grant orders another general assault. It fails badly with 3,200 casualties. Grant settles in for a prolonged siege at Vicksburg. However, his campaign to isolate Vicksburg from outside assistance has succeeded brilliantly and is widely regarded as his finest maneuver of the war.

May 23, 1863 Union troops under Banks depart Baton Rouge and lay siege to Port Hudson.

June 3, 1863   Unwilling to detach forces to send to the relief of Vicksburg, Lee convinces President Davis that his best opportunity is to launch a new invasion across the Potomac. He strikes north from Virginia with three corps under Longstreet, Richard S. Ewell, and A. P. Hill.

June 9, 1863   A powerful Federal cavalry probe surprises Stuart's cavalry at Brandy Station, Virginia. A sprawling cavalry battle ensues before the Federal cavalry retires. Brandy Station has three important consequences. The probe reveals to Hooker that the Army of Northern Virginia is moving over to the offensive in what will become the Gettysburg Campaign. Stuart is criticized for the surprise at Brandy Station. Humiliated, he resolves to redeem himself as soon as possible. Lastly, the Union cavalry acquits itself well at the battle, giving it confidence for the future.

June 13, 1863   Refused permission to advance against the Confederate capital of Richmond while Lee is marching north, Hooker must instead fall back toward Manassas in the hope of intercepting the Army of Northern Virginia before it can threaten Washington.

June 15, 1863   Ewell captures Winchester, in northern Virginia, routing a 9,000-man division. He crosses the Potomac River into Maryland with the objective of pushing on to Pennsylvania.

June 23, 1863   After six months of inactivity near Murfreesboro, Rosecrans's 60,000-man Army of the Cumberland breaks camp and pushes south. In a skillful campaign, Rosecrans drives Bragg's 45,000 Confederates out of central Tennessee. By sliding east around the rebel flank, Rosecrans compels Bragg to pull back into Chattanooga by July 4.

June 24, 1863   Stuart interprets his orders very loosely and unwisely sets out on a raid around the Army of the Potomac. The raid accomplishes little of value while depriving Lee of his "eyes," namely his cavalry's ability to inform him about Union positions and movements.

Confederates squander another opportunity, again because of the inability of Bragg's subordinates to coordinate their efforts and follow orders. Alerted by two near disasters, Rosecrans begins to concentrate his army behind Chickamauga Creek.

September 18, 1863

Reinforced by elements of Longstreet's Corps from Lee's army, Bragg plans another attack across Chickamauga Creek. During the day, parts of Bragg's army gain a foothold on the Union side of the creek.

September 19, 1863

First day of the Battle of Chickamauga. Bragg's plan calls for the envelopment of Rosecrans's left flank. A confused series of clashes erupts with most units unable to see far because of the wooded terrain. Neither side is able to coordinate its efforts; hence, units fight independently wherever they chance upon their enemy. Although both sides suffer heavy losses, neither gains a significant advantage. During the night, the Union left wing under the command of Thomas erects stout field works.

September 20, 1863

Bragg's plan calls for renewed attacks beginning with his right and passing sequentially to his left. The Confederate attacks fail against Thomas's fortifications. However, Thomas calls for reinforcements. Rosecrans and his subordinates bungle the response, leaving a hole in the line through which surges Longstreet's soldiers. The Confederate attack routs most of Rosecrans's army, but Thomas continues to hold his ground, thereby earning him the moniker "The Rock of Chickamauga." His decisive leadership prevents a Union disaster. The Confederates make a terrible mistake by failing to pursue. This failure allows Rosecrans to retreat to Chattanooga. The Battle of Chickamauga is the bloodiest battle in the west during the entire war, costing the defeated Union force over 16,000 men. However, the Confederates have lost over 18,000 men, a loss they cannot afford.

September 21, 1863

By the night of September 21, Rosecrans is safely ensconced in

Chattanooga. Personally demoralized, he yields the initiative to Bragg, but Bragg can conceive of nothing better than to occupy the high ground overlooking Chattanooga. For the next month, the Confederates try to sever Rosecrans's precarious supply line. Reduced to short rations, Rosecrans's army begins to starve.

September 25, 1863

Recognizing the crisis at Chattanooga, Halleck directs a splendid logistical exercise that moves 12,000 men of the XI and XII corps by rail from Virginia to Tennessee. The former commander of the Army of the Potomac, Joseph Hooker, commands this force. These reinforcements start arriving five days later and help ensure the survival of the Chattanooga garrison.

October 5, 1863

A Confederate submersible slips out of Charleston and badly damages USS *New Ironsides* with a spar torpedo.

October 23, 1863

Grant reaches Chattanooga to assume command of Rosecrans's army. Rosecrans is eventually sent to a

backwater assignment. While awaiting the arrival of the XV Corps under Sherman from his own Army of the Tennessee, Grant makes plans to restore the city's supply line. Meanwhile, Bragg gets rid of tiresome, sometimes disobedient subordinates. The changes of command contribute to the increasing demoralization of Bragg's Army of the Tennessee.

October 26–30, 1863

Grant implements a plan to open a decent line of supply for the malnourished Union troops in Chattanooga. The complex plan is well executed, and on the morning of October 30, a steamer delivers 40,000 rations and tons of forage for the starving horses. The opening of the so-called "Cracker Line" raises the morale of the Army of the Cumberland.

November 17, 1863

Longstreet, with his Army of Northern Virginia force, is detached from Bragg's army. He invests Burnside at Knoxville, eventually instituting a siege.

November 23, 1863

After a month's preparation, Grant's 60,000 Union troops begin to push southeastward out of Chattanooga to break the siege by Bragg's 34,000 Confederates, dug in along the nearby heights. In the center, Thomas's corps moves out onto the open plain and pushes back the rebel picket lines around Orchard Knob, in anticipation of a two-pronged envelopment by other Federal contingents: Hooker, who is to storm Lookout Mountain on the right, and Sherman who is to outflank the Confederates on the left. The next midday, the Union offensive is launched, as Hooker easily carries his objective, although without threatening Bragg's main army. Sherman's corps meanwhile encounters greater resistance among the broken hills at the northeastern tip of Missionary Ridge from the Confederate division of Irish-born general Pat Cleburne, and the Union drive bogs down by nightfall.

November 25, 1863

When fighting resumes on November 25, Grant directs Thomas's corps to pressure Bragg's center with a frontal assault. Against all expectations, 18,000 Union infantrymen surge through the lower rebel trenches at 3:30 p.m.; then, without orders, they scale the 500-foot heights of Missionary Ridge in an irresistible tide led by 32-year-old major general Philip Sheridan. Bragg's army is broken and retreats in disorder, having suffered 8,700 killed, wounded, or captured. Grant's losses are approximately 6,000 men. Sheridan's success makes a favorable impression on Grant. Grant's success at Chattanooga, coming on the heels of his brilliant victory at Vicksburg, convinces Lincoln to offer him the top military command in the entire U.S. Army.

November 26– December 1, 1863

After a long rest following the Battle of Gettysburg, Meade, with 81,000 men, advances across the Rappahannock River. This is familiar terrain to both armies. In Longstreet's absence, Lee has only 48,000 men, yet he uses them masterfully to block Meade's advance at a fortified position behind Mine Run. Meade wisely decides not to attack and the

Mine Run Campaign ends without significant combat.

December 4, 1863

Sherman's corps, after helping defeat Bragg at Chattanooga, raises the Confederate siege of Knoxville. From a Confederate perspective, Longstreet's time in independent command has been a failure.

February 3, 1864

Sherman departs Vicksburg with the XVI and the XVII Army corps, launching a devastating sweep through Confederate-held Mississippi. On February 5, his Union columns pass through Jackson, then level Meridian on February 14–15, before returning into their original cantonments on February 27. The Meridian Campaign foreshadows Sherman's "March to the Sea" later in the war.

February 17, 1864

The submersible *Hunley* slips out of Charleston and sinks the Union steam sloop *Housatonic* by ramming it with a torpedo. The *Hunley* sinks as well, with the loss of its entire crew.

March 8, 1864

Grant is promoted to lieutenant general. He is made commander in chief of all Union armies the following day. Finally, Lincoln has found a general able to devise a strategic plan to win the war and determined to see that plan through.

March 10, 1864

Concerned about a French threat in Mexico, Lincoln wants a military operation to raise the Federal flag somewhere in Texas. Although his generals oppose the idea, Banks is directed to move up the Red River. In cooperation with Porter's formidable fleet of thirteen ironclads and seven gunboats, Banks advances up the Red River.

March 14, 1864

Union general A. J. Smith captures 325 Confederates and 12 guns at Fort DeRussey on the Red River in Louisiana.

March 25, 1864

Forrest leads a raid that levels Paducah, Kentucky.

April 8, 1864

Taylor's Confederates rout Banks's army at the Battle of Sabine Cross Roads, capturing 2,500 prisoners and much equipment.

April 9, 1864

Taylor's pursuit is repulsed with heavy loss at the Battle of Pleasant Hill. In spite of this victory, Banks resolves to retreat. A major contributing factor is the inability of Porter's fleet to advance up the Red River because of low water.

April 12, 1864 Forrest surprises and destroys the Union garrison at Fort Pillow, Tennessee.

May 3–7, 1864 Grant has ordered a coordinated advance by all the major Union armies from Virginia to Tennessee. He personally assumes responsibility for the Army of the Potomac. He reorganizes that army into a simplified structure and appoints Sheridan to command his cavalry. On May 3 the army departs Culpeper, Virginia, and heads southward with 120,000 men, subdivided into five corps, to cross the Rapidan River at Germanna and Ely's fords in search of Lee. The next evening, the Union vanguard camps in the middle of a large forest dubbed "The Wilderness," the same place where it had suffered a bad defeat the previous year at the Battle of Chancellorsville.

Grant's maneuver surprises Lee. With scarcely 70,000 troops and less artillery than the Union host, Lee is characteristically aggressive and opts to attack Grant while the Union army is vulnerable and in motion. Lee conceives that combat in the Wilderness will negate Grant's superior numbers and artillery.

Serious combat begins on May 5. Because of the limited visibility inside the Wilderness, Grant is unable to bring his superior numbers to bear. Fierce, costly fighting takes place, with neither side gaining an advantage. As was the case in the Mine Run Campaign, the tactical dominance of improvised field works becomes apparent.

On May 6, the fighting resumes. First the Federals and then the Confederates gain the advantage. During the battle, both of Grant's flanks are turned. Unlike his predecessors who commanded the Army of the Potomac, Grant ignores the setbacks and maintains the fight. Both sides rest on May 7 and count their losses: Confederates, over

11,000 men; Federals, as high as 18,000. The battle is a draw. However, on the night of May 7–8, Grant makes the key decision to continue his offensive. Grant's willingness to accept losses and keep advancing marks a turning point in the war in Virginia.

May 8, 1864 Union cavalry under Sheridan attempts to seize Spotsylvania Court House in order to get between Lee's army and the Confederate capital of Richmond. By the narrowest, a Confederate force bars Sheridan's path. The scene is set for a ten-day, ferocious campaign that circles around Spotsylvania Court House.

May 9–17, 1864 Frustrated by his inability to defeat the Confederate cavalry, Sheridan receives permission to conduct a massive raid against Richmond. Sheridan's raid will reach Richmond's outskirts. At the Battle of Yellow Tavern on May 11, Sheridan's celebrated opponent J.E.B. Stuart receives a mortal wound. By May 17, Sheridan's command is safely within Union lines well east

of Richmond. From a purely military standpoint, the raid is a mistake, since the cavalry's absence leaves Grant without the ability to scout Lee's position. From a morale viewpoint, the raid finally brings the Union cavalry in the east on par with the Confederates.

May 9–19, 1864 The Battle of Spotsylvania begins when the Army of the Potomac launches the first of a series of assaults against Lee's position. Lee's outnumbered forces utilize well-designed field works to thwart Federal numerical superiority. Grant does not understand the tactical dominance of these works. The result is a series of costly hammer blows as Grant repeatedly orders attacks. By battle's end the Union has lost at least 18,000 men while the defenders, protected by their earthworks, lose between 9,000 and 10,000. Grant again makes the decision to continue to advance in spite of his losses.

May 7–13, 1864 Grant's strategic plan requires Sherman, now in command of the main Union army around

Chattanooga, to coordinate his offensive with the advance of the Army of the Potomac in Virginia. Grant rightly perceives that the Confederates have no answer to a simultaneous Union advance. Accordingly, less than a week after departing Chattanooga with 98,000 Union troops, Sherman encounters Johnston, who has replaced Bragg as commander of the Confederate Army of Tennessee. Johnston's 60,000 men are dug in along Rocky Face Ridge. Rather than storm the formidable Confederate position, two Federal corps pin down the southerners, while Union general McPherson leads the 30,000-man Army of the Tennessee on a wide flanking movement to the right, passing through Snake Creek Gap to threaten Johnston's line of communications. On May 13 Johnston retreats to Resaca.

May 13–16, 1864

Reinforced by Polk's corps from Mississippi, Johnston takes a stand to defend Resaca. Following skirmishing on May 13, Union forces deliver a series of attacks on May 14, none of which achieve much success. On May 15 heavy skirmishing resumes but Johnston becomes aware of Sherman's efforts to turn the Confederate position from the west and south. Johnston decides to retreat and abandons Resaca on May 16. In the battle Johnston sustains some 5,000 casualties, while Sherman suffers 6,000. Resaca is a tactical Confederate victory but a strategic gain for the Union. The features of the Atlanta Campaign are now set: Johnston attempts to lure Sherman into making rash attacks against his fortified position; Sherman continues to press Johnston back toward Atlanta by outflanking the rebels whenever they make a stand.

May 15, 1864

Grant's strategic plan also requires General Franz Sigel to march up the Shenandoah Valley with his 6,500-man army. General John Breckinridge with 5,300 men attacks Sigel near the village of New Market. The Confederate attack memorably features a 247-man battalion of Virginia Military Institute cadets. Breckinridge drives Sigel from the field. Sigel retreats all the way north to Strasburg where, on May 19, he is relieved of command. With the Valley safe for the time being, Breckinridge moves to reinforce Lee.

May 20–June 1, 1864

Grant moves around Lee's right flank at Spotsylvania Court House and marches south toward Richmond. Lee successfully continues to interpose his army between Grant and the Confederate capital. Lee fears that if Grant persists, the Confederate army will end up besieged in Richmond. However, his battered army has lost its offensive punch and so can do little to stop Grant's inexorable advance. By June 1, the opposing armies confront one another at Cold Harbor, some ten miles northeast of Richmond.

May 22, 1864

Banks's Red River Campaign ends. Begun for political purposes, the entire affair proves an unnecessary diversion of Union military resources.

June 3, 1864

At Spotsylvania Court House, Grant enjoys overwhelming numbers with 108,000 men versus Lee's 60,000. However, Grant mistakenly assumes Lee's forces are overextended, and therefore Lee's center must be vulnerable. Consequently Grant orders a direct frontal assault on the Confederate trenches in the hope of achieving a breakthrough. In less then an hour the attackers lose about 7,000 men while inflicting only 1,500 Confederate casualties. The failed assault demoralizes the Army of the Potomac. Grant later acknowledges that the attack was a terrible mistake. Union casualties for the preceding month total 50,000 men, compared to Lee's 32,000; yet Grant is able to replace his losses whereas Confederate resources are almost exhausted.

June 12, 1864

Grant decides to alter his strategy in mid-June, leaving a holding force outside Richmond while slipping the bulk of his army southeastward to approach the Confederate capital through its vital rail hub at Petersburg. The movement begins at nightfall on June 12.

June 14, 1864 In one of the greatest engineering feats in military history, Union engineers build a 2,100 foot long bridge over the James River to allow troops to attack Petersburg. The bridge holds against a strong tidal current and a four-foot tidal change.

June 15, 1864 Grant's shift of focus to Petersburg outwits Lee. Grant's vanguard, under General William Smith, surprises Beauregard's garrison holding Petersburg.

June 16–23 1864 Grant's army conducts a series of assaults against Petersburg's defenses. They are all costly repulses. After a bad defeat on June 22–23 while trying to advance against the Weldon Railroad, Grant resolves to suspend assaults and operate against Lee's communications. Grant's excellent strategy has been foiled because his earlier tactics have made his officers and men unwilling to assault fortifications. Coupled with poor staff work, the Army of the Potomac has fumbled

a fine opportunity to end the war. With both armies exhausted, a long period of static trench warfare begins.

June 27, 1864 For the first time since beginning his campaign Sherman resolves to assault Confederate fieldworks. The ensuing Battle of Kenesaw Mountain reveals to the "western" armies the same tactical dominance of fieldworks that the "eastern" armies have recently learned. The assault fails completely and costs Sherman's army 3,000 casualties. Coupled with failures in the east, this defeat marks the nadir of Federal fortunes in 1864. President Lincoln concludes that he is unlikely to be reelected because the war effort is going so poorly.

On this same day, Lee detaches Jubal Early to threaten Washington, D.C., in order to relieve the pressure on his beleaguered army. The diversionary effort will be recalled as "Early's Washington Raid."

July 5, 1864 Early's army crosses the Potomac and enters Maryland. Authorities in Washington fear for the fate of the capital.

July 9, 1864   Chastened by his defeat at Kenesaw Moutain, Sherman resumes his former approach by again outflanking Johnston. Johnston withdraws to the Chattahoochee River by July 9, only seven miles from Atlanta. On this same day in the east, Early's army defeats a scratch Federal force at the Battle of the Monocacy in Maryland.

July 12, 1864   Early's Confederates encounter the Union fortifications defending Washington. They are held by two divisions of the VI Corps under General Horatio G. Wright, hastily withdrawn from Grant's army around Petersburg, plus a scratch force of rear echelon troops and convalescents. Lacking the strength to conduct an all-out assault, Early can only probe the defenses at Fort Stevens. Inside the fort is President Lincoln. The Confederates suffer 500 casualties before retiring on July 13 toward the Shenandoah Valley. Federal losses are 54 killed and 319 wounded.

July 17, 1864   Sherman again turns Johnston's flanks and Johnston retires inside Atlanta's fortifications. Alarmed at Johnston's seeming unwillingness to hazard a battle to hold the key city, President Davis replaces Johnston with General John Hood. It proves a fateful, and for the Confederates, disastrous, decision.

July 20, 1864   Hood attacks Sherman's army as it crosses Peachtree Creek. The attacking Confederates are repulsed with heavy losses.

July 22, 1864   Hood orders a 15-mile night march to position two corps to attack Sherman's subordinate, McPherson. The "Battle of Atlanta" is another Confederate defeat costing Hood 8,500 casualties. Union losses are 3,700, including McPherson who is killed.

July 28, 1864   Having invested Atlanta from the north and east, Sherman moves to sever Hood's remaining supply line running south from Atlanta. This effort leads to the Battle of Ezra Church, Hood's third defeat in nine days. However, Hood continues to hold Atlanta.

his 60,000 remaining troops to burn Atlanta. The next day he begins "The March to the Sea," an uncontested sweep designed to underscore the South's prostrate condition. Re-provisioned from supply ships, the Federal troops then occupy Savannah by December 21.

November 30, 1864

Following the evacuation of Atlanta, Hood has been trying to cut Sherman's line of supply. When instead Sherman largely ignores this threat, Hood conceives of a last-ditch effort, the "Invasion of Tennessee." On this day Hood, with some 38,000 men, encounters a determined Union rear guard of 32,000 men under the command of General John Schofield. Schofield's defenders man comprehensive field works and repel the determined Confederate attacks before resuming their retreat to Nashville. The gallant, but futile Confederate attacks cost Hood's army over 6,000 men including many of the Army of Tennessee's best known leaders.

December 10, 1864

After cutting a swath of destruction 60 miles wide and 250 miles long, Sherman's army reaches Savannah on December 10, re-establishing contact with Union warships.

December 15–16, 1864

Two weeks after Hood's smaller army, with about 23,000 men, has instituted a loose siege, Thomas, with almost 50,000, emerges from behind his Nashville fortifications to attack Hood. Thomas's tactical plan is a masterpiece. Thomas pins the Confederate right and sends the balance of his force to turn the Confederate left. The outnumbered Southerners cannot man their entire line and are driven two miles back in heavy fighting.

The next morning, Hood stands and fights again, only to see his line once more shattered. This time, the demoralized rebel army retreats in disarray. Thomas's overwhelming victory essentially eliminates one of the two major Confederate armies for the duration of the war.

January 13, 1865

Porter's ironclads bombard the Confederate stronghold of Fort Fisher that guards Wilmington, North

Carolina. Terry's 8,000 soldiers disembark to storm the fort's landward face. The garrison hangs on desperately, so two days later Porter disembarks an additional 400 marines and 1,600 sailors to attack from the opposite direction. They suffer heavy casualties—80 Union killed and 270 wounded—yet nonetheless make it possible for Terry's troops to capture Fort Fisher. The fort's loss closes the South's last major seaport.

February 12, 1865

Sherman's army marches northeastward along the Atlantic seaboard, crossing the South Carolina border. Johnston's army is powerless to stop them as they ravage the countryside and burn Columbia to the ground five days later. The Confederates evacuate Charlotte on February 18.

February 22, 1865

Schofield occupies Wilmington, North Carolina.

February 27, 1865

Sheridan returns to the Shenandoah Valley and embarks upon a brutal, scorched earth campaign to destroy Confederate resources including crops, mills, and livestock.

March 2, 1865

Sheridan runs down Early's Confederates at Waynesboro, Virginia, destroying the last Confederate army in the Shenandoah Valley and capturing 1,600 prisoners and all the Confederate baggage and artillery trains. In the west, Wilson crosses the Tennessee River into northern Alabama to seize the last important Confederate munitions center at Selma.

March 19, 1865

Johnston cobbles together a 21,000-man force to try to block Sherman's advance through North Carolina. At the Battle of Bentonville, the outnumbered Confederates fight a last battle, losing about 1,600 men while inflicting some 2,600 casualties. After the battle, Sherman masses his forces and compels Johnston to retreat.

March 23, 1865

Sherman and Schofield join forces at Goldsboro, North Carolina.

March 25, 1865

Hoping to break the eight-month Union stranglehold on Petersburg, Lee directs a last, desperate attack against the Federal siege lines at Fort Stedman. Although this objective is carried, the Confederate sally

Bibliography

Abel, Annie. *The American Indian in the Civil War, 1862–1865*. Lincoln: University of Nebraska Press, 1992.

Abernethy, Byron R., ed. *Private Elisha Stockwell, Jr. Sees the Civil War*. Norman: University of Oklahoma Press, 1958.

Abrahamson, James L. *The Men of Secession and Civil War, 1859–1861*. Wilmington, DE: SR Books, 2000.

Adams, Charles. *Slavery, Secession, and Civil War: Views from the United Kingdom and Europe, 1856–1865*. Lanham, MD: Scarecrow Press, 2007.

Adams, George W. *Doctors in Blue: The Medical History of the Union Army in the Civil War*. Baton Rouge: Louisiana State University Press, 1996.

Adams, Michael C. *Our Masters the Rebels: Speculations on Union Military Failure in the East, 1861–1865*. Cambridge, MA: Harvard University Press, 1978.

Agassiz, George R., ed. *Meade's Headquarters 1863–1865: Letters of Colonel Theodore Lyman from the Wilderness to Appomattox*. Boston: Massachusetts Historical Society, 1922.

Altsheler, Joseph. *The Tree of Appomattox*. Kila, MT: Kessinger, 2007.

Ambrose, Stephen. *Halleck: Lincoln's Chief of Staff*. Baton Rouge: Louisiana State University Press, 1962.

Ambrosious, Lloyd E. *A Crisis of Republicanism: American Politics during the Civil War Era*. Lincoln: University of Nebraska Press, 1990.

Anderson, Bern. *By Sea and by River: The Naval History of the Civil War*. New York: Knopf, 1962.

Angevine, Robert G. *The Railroad and the State: War, Politics, and Technology in Nineteenth Century America*. Stanford, CA: Stanford University Press, 2004.

Annals of the War. Edison, NJ: The Blue & Grey Press, N.D. [Philadelphia, 1879].

Aptheker, Herbert. *Abolitionism: A Revolutionary Movement*. Boston: Twayne, 1989.

Arnold, James R. *Chickamauga 1863: The River of Death*. London: Osprey Publishing, 1992.

Arnold, James R. *Grant Wins the War: Decision at Vicksburg*. New York: John Wiley & Sons, 1997.

Arnold, James R. *Jeff Davis's Own: Cavalry, Comanches, and the Battle for the Texas Frontier*. New York: John Wiley & Sons, 2000.

Arnold, James R. *The Armies of U.S. Grant*. London: Arms and Armour Press, 1995.

Ash, Stephen V. "A Wall Around Slavery: Safeguarding the Peculiar Institution on the Confederate Periphery, 1861–1865." *Nineteenth Century America: Essays in Honor of Paul H. Bergeron*. Edited by W. Todd Grace and Stephen V. Ash. Knoxville: University of Tennessee Press, 2005.

Bailey, Anne J. *War and Ruin: William T. Sherman and the Savannah Campaign*. Wilmington, DE: SR Books, 2003.

Bakeless, John. *Spies of the Confederacy*. Philadelphia, PA: Lippincott, 1970.

Dalzell, George W. *The Flight from the Flag: The Continuing Effect of the Civil War upon the American Carrying Trade*. Chapel Hill: University of North Carolina Press, 1940.

Daniel, Larry J. *Cannoneers in Gray: The Field Artillery of the Army of Tennessee 1861–1865*. Tuscaloosa: University of Alabama Press, 1984.

Daniel, Larry J. *Days of Glory: The Army of the Cumberland, 1861–1865*. Baton Rouge: Louisiana State University Press, 2004.

Daniel, Larry J. *Shiloh, the Battle That Changed the Civil War*. New York: Simon and Schuster, 1997.

Daniel, Larry J. *Soldiering in the Army of Tennessee: A Portrait of Life in a Confederate Army*. Chapel Hill: University of North Carolina Press, 1991.

Davis, Burke. *To Appomattox: Nine April Days, 1865*. Springfield, NJ: Burford Books, 2002.

Davis, Jefferson. *Papers of Jefferson Davis*. Baton Rouge: Louisiana State University Press, 1971–1985.

Davis, William C. *Duel Between the First Ironclads*. Garden City, NY: Doubleday, 1975.

Davis, William C. *Government of Our Own: The Making of the Confederacy*. New York: The Free Press, 1994.

Davis, William C. "Jefferson Davis and His Generals." In *The Cause Lost: Myths and Realities of the Confederacy*. Lawrence, KS: University Press of Kansas. 1996.

Davis, William C. *Look Away: A History of the Confederate States of America*. New York: The Free Press, 2002.

Dawes, Rufus R. *Service with the Sixth Wisconsin Volunteers*. Madison: State Historical Society of Wisconsin, 1962.

deKay, James T. *Monitor*. New York: Walker and Co., 1997.

Donald, David H. *Why the North Won the Civil War*. New York: Touchstone, 1960, 1996.

Donald, David H. *Lincoln*. New York: Simon and Schuster, 1996.

Donald, David, and J. G. Randall. *The Civil War and Reconstruction*. New York: W. W. Norton, 2001.

Donaldson, Jordon, and Pratt, Edwin J. *Europe and the American Civil War*. New York: Houghton Mifflin, 1931.

Douglas, Henry K. *I Rode with Stonewall*. Chapel Hill: University of North Carolina Press, 1940.

Early, Jubal A. *War Memoirs*. Edited by Frank E. Vandiver. Bloomington, IN: Bobbs-Merrill, 1960.

Eaton, Clement. *Jefferson Davis*. New York: The Free Press, 1977.

Ecelbarger, Gary. *Black Jack Logan: An Extraordinary Life in Peace and War*. Chapel Hill: University of North Carolina Press, 1999.

Eckenrode, Hamilton J., and Bryan Conrad. *James Longstreet: Lee's War Horse*. Chapel Hill: University of North Carolina Press, 1986.

Edgerton, Robert B. *Hidden Heroism: Black Soldiers in America's Wars*. Boulder, CO: Westview Press, 2001.

Eisenhower, John S. D. *Agent of Destiny: The Life and Times of General Winfield Scott*. New York: Free Press, 1997.

Ekelund, Robert B., Jr. and Mark Thornton. *Tariffs, Blockades, and Inflation: The Economics of the Civil War*. Wilmington, DE: SR Books, 2004.

Emert, Phyllis. *Women in the Civil War: Warriors, Patriots, Nurses, and Spies*. Auburndale, MA: History Compass, 1994.

Engle, Steven D. *Don Carlos Buell: The Most Promising of All*. Chapel Hill: University of North Carolina Press, 1999.

Engle, Stephen D. *Struggle for the Heartland: The Campaigns from Fort Henry to Corinth*. Lincoln: University of Nebraska Press, 2001.

Engle, Stephen D. *Yankee Dutchman: The Life of Franz Sigel*. Baton Rouge: Louisiana State University Press, 1999.

Escott, Paul D. *After Secession: Jefferson Davis and the Failure of Confederate Nationalism*. Baton Rouge: Louisiana State University Press, 1978.

Fellman, Michael. *Inside War: The Guerilla Conflict in Missouri during the American Civil War*. New York: Oxford University Press, 1989.

Ferris, Norman B. *The Trent Affair: A Diplomatic Crisis*. Knoxville: University of Tennessee Press, 1977.

Fischer, Leroy H. *The Civil War Era in Indian Territory*. Los Angeles: L. L. Morrison, 1974.

Fishel, Edwin C. *The Secret War for the Union: The Untold Story of Military Intelligence in the Civil War*. New York: Houghton Mifflin Company, 1996.

Fogel, Robert W. *Without Consent or Contract: The Rise and Fall of American Slavery*. New York: Norton, 1989.

Foner, Eric. *Politics and Ideology in the Age of the Civil War*. New York: Oxford University Press, 1981.

Foote, Shelby. *The Civil War: A Narrative.* 3 vols. New York: Random House, 1958–1974.

Fox, William F. *Regimental Losses in the American Civil War*. New York: Brandow, 1898. [Reprinted by Morningside Bookshop, 1974.]

Frank, Joseph A., and George A. Reaves. *"Seeing the Elephant": Raw Recruits at the Battle of Shiloh*. New York: Greenwood Press, 1989.

Franklin, John H. *From Slavery to Freedom: A History of Negro Americans*. 1996.

Frazier, Donald S. *Blood and Treasure: Confederate Empire in the Southwest*. College Station: Texas A & M University Press, 1995.

Freeman, Douglas S. *Lee's Lieutenants: A Study in Command.* 2 vols. New York: Charles Scribner's Sons, 1942–1944.

Furguson, Ernest B. *Chancellorsville, 1863: The Souls of the Brave*. New York: Alfred A. Knopf, 1992.

Gallagher, Gary W., ed. *Antietam: Essays on the 1862 Maryland Campaign*. Chapel Hill: University of North Carolina Press, 1999.

Gallagher, Gary W., ed. *Chancellorsville: The Battle and Its Aftermath*. Chapel Hill: University of North Carolina Press, 1996.

Gallagher, Gary W., ed. *Fighting for the Confederacy: The Personal Recollections of General Edward Porter Alexander*. Chapel Hill: University of North Carolina Press, 1989.

Gallagher, Gary W., ed. *Struggle for the Shenandoah: Essays on the 1864 Valley Campaign*. Kent, OH: Kent State University Press, 1991.

Gallagher, Gary. *The Confederate War*. Boston: Harvard University Press, 1997.

Gallagher, Gary. ed. *The Richmond Campaign of 1862: The Peninsula and the Seven Days*. Chapel Hill: University Of North Carolina Press, 2000.

Gallagher, Gary W., ed. *The Shenandoah Valley Campaign of 1862*. Chapel Hill: University of North Carolina Press, 2003.

Gallagher, Gary W., ed. *The Shenandoah Valley Campaign of 1864*. Chapel Hill: University of North Carolina Press, 2006.

Gallagher, Gary, ed. *The Third Day at Gettysburg and Beyond*. Chapel Hill: University of North Carolina Press, 1994.

Gallagher, Gary W., Stephen D. Engle, Robert K. Krick, and Joseph T. Glatthaar. *The American Civil War: This Mighty Scourge of War*. Oxford, UK: Osprey, 2003.

Gates, Paul. *Agriculture and the Civil War*. New York: Knopf, 1965.

Geary, James W. *We Need Men: The Union Draft in the Civil War*. Dekalb: Northern Illinois University Press, 1991.

Gladstone, William A. *Men of Color: African Americans in the Civil War*. Gettysburg, PA: Thomas Publications, 1996.

Glatthaar, Joseph T. *Forged in Battle: The Civil War Alliance of Black Soldiers and White Officers*. New York: The Free Press, 1990.

Goff, Richard D. *Confederate Supply*. Durham, NC: Duke University Press, 1969.

Goldhurst, Richard. *Many are the Hearts: The Agony and the Triumph of Ulysses S. Grant*. New York: Crowell, 1975.

Goodman, Paul. *Of One Blood: Abolitionists and the Origins of Racial Equality.*

Berkeley: University of California Press, 1998.

Goodwin, Doris K. *Team of Rivals: The Political Genius of Abraham Lincoln*. New York: Simon and Schuster, 2005.

Gordon, John S. *An Empire of Wealth: The Epic History of American Economic Power*. New York: Harper Perennial, 2005.

Grabau, Warren E. *Ninety-eight Days: A Geographer's View of the Vicksburg Campaign*. Knoxville: University of Tennessee Press, 2000.

Grant, Ulysses S. *Personal Memoirs*. New York: De Capo Press, 1982.

Greely, Adolphus W. *The Military-Telegraph Service*. Vol. 4 of *The Photographic History of the Civil War*. Reprint. Secaucus, NJ: The Blue and Grey Press, 1987.

Gresham, Otto. *The Greenbacks or the Money That Won the Civil War and the World War*. Whitefish, MT: Kessinger Publishing, 2008.

Griffith, Paddy. *Battle Tactics of the Civil War*. New Haven, CT: Yale University Press, 1989.

Grimsley, Mark. *The Hard Hand of War: Union Military Policy toward Southern Civilians, 1861–1865*. New York: Cambridge University Press, 1995.

Grimsley, Mark, and Brooks D. Simpson, eds. *The Collapse of the Confederacy*. Lincoln: University of Nebraska Press, 2001.

Guelzo, Allen C. *Lincoln's Emancipation Proclamation: The End of Slavery in America*. New York: Simon & Schuster, 2006.

Hansen, Harry. *The Civil War: A History*. New York: Signet Classics, 2001.

Hardee, William J. *Rifle and Light Infantry Tactics for the Exercise and Manoeuvres of Troops when Acting as Light Infantry or Riflemen*. Philadelphia: Lippincott, 1855.

Harsh, Joseph L. *Taken at the Flood: Robert E. Lee and Confederate Strategy in the Maryland Campaign of 1862*. Kent, OH: Kent State University Press, 1999.

Hauptman, Laurence M. *Between Two Fires: American Indians in the Civil War*. New York: Free Press, 1995.

Hay, John M., and John G. Nicolay. *Abraham Lincoln: A History*. 10 vols. New York: Century, 1890.

Hazlett, James C., Edwin Olmstead, and M. Hume Parks. *Field Artillery Weapons of the Civil War*. Urbana: University of Illinois Press, 2004.

Hearn, Chester G. *Admiral David Glasgow Farragut: The Civil War Years*. Annapolis, MD: Naval Institute Press, 1998.

Hearn, Chester G. *David Dixon Porter: The Civil War Years*. Annapolis, MD: Naval Institute Press, 1996.

Heatwole, John L. *The Burning: Sheridan in the Shenandoah Valley*. Charlottesville, VA: Rockbridge Publishing, 1998.

Hennessy, John. *Return to Bull Run: The Campaign and Battle of Second Manassas*. Norman: University of Oklahoma Press, 1999.

Hess, Earl J. *Banners to the Breeze: The Kentucky Campaign, Corinth, and Stones River*. Lincoln: University of Nebraska Press, 2000.

Hess, Earl J. *In the Trenches at Petersburg: Field Fortifications and Confederate Defeat*. Chapel Hill: University of North Carolina Press, 2009.

Hess, Earl J. *The Union Soldier in Battle: Enduring the Ordeal of Combat*. Lawrence: University Press of Kansas, 1997.

Hill, Jim D. *Sea Dogs of the Sixties: Farragut and Seven Contemporaries*. 1935 Minneapolis: University of Minnesota Press, 1935.

Hoehling, Adolph A. ed. *Vicksburg: Forty-seven Days of Siege*. Englewood Cliffs, NJ: Prentice-Hall, 1969.

Hollandsworth, James G. *The Louisiana Native Guards: The Black Military Experience during the Civil War*. Baton Rouge: Louisiana State University Press, 1995, 2004.

Holt, Michael F. *The Political Crisis of the 1850s*. New York: Norton, 1983.

Holtzer, Harold, and Tim Mulligan, eds. *The Battle of Hampton Roads: New Perspectives on the USS* Monitor *and CSS* Virginia. New York: Fordham University Press, 2006.

Hood, John Bell. *Advance and Retreat: Personal Experiences in the United States and Confederate States Armies*. Bloomington: Indiana University Press, 1959.

Howard, McHenry. *Recollections of a Confederate Soldier, 1861–1866*. Dayton, 1975.

Hughes, Nathaniel C., Jr. *General William J. Hardee: Old Reliable*. Baton Rouge: Louisiana State University Press, 1992.

Humphreys, Andrew A. *The Virginia Campaign of '64 and '65*. New York: Charles Scribner's Sons, 1897.

Hurst, Jack. *Nathan Bedford Forrest: A Biography*. New York: Vintage Books, 1994.

Hutton, Paul A. *Phil Sheridan and his Army*. Lincoln: University of Nebraska Press, 1985.

Jenkins, Brian. *Britain and the War for the Union*. Toronto: McGill-Queen's University Press, 1974.

Johnson, Robert U., and Clarence C. Buel, eds. *Battles and Leaders of the Civil War*. Vol. 1. *From Sumter to Shiloh*. Secaucus, NJ: Castle, 1887.

Johnson, Timothy D. *Winfield Scott: The Quest for Military Glory*. Lawrence: University Press of Kansas, 1999.

Johnston, Joseph E. *Narrative of Military Operations, Directed, During the Late War Between the States*. New York: D. Appleton, 1874.

Johnston, William P. *The Life of Gen. Albert Sidney Johnston, His Services in the Armies of the United States, the Republic of Texas, and the Confederate States*. New York: D. Appleton and Company, 1878.

Joiner, Gary D. *Mr. Lincoln's Brown Water Navy: The Mississippi Squadron*. Lanham, MD: Rowman and Littlefield, 2007.

Joiner, Gary D. *One Damn Blunder from Beginning to End: The Red River Campaign of 1864*. Wilmington, DE: SR Books, 2003.

Jones, Archer. *Civil War Command & Strategy: The Process of Victory and Defeat*. New York: The Free Press, 1992.

Jones, Howard. *Abraham Lincoln and a New Birth of Freedom: The Union and Slavery in the Diplomacy of the Civil War*. Lincoln: University of Nebraska Press, 2002.

Jones, Howard. *Union in Peril. The Crisis over British Intervention in the Civil War*. Chapel Hill: University of North Carolina Press, 1992.

Katcher, Philip. *The American Civil War Source Book*. London: Arms and Armour Press, 1992.

Kenneth, Lee. *Sherman: A Soldier's Life*. New York: HarperCollins, 2001.

Kerby, Robert L. *Kirby Smith's Confederacy: The Trans-Mississippi South, 1863–1865*. New York: Columbia University Press, 1972.

Key, William. *The Battle of Atlanta and the Georgia Campaign*. Atlanta, GA: Peachtree, 1981.

Kolchin, Peter. *American Slavery, 1619–1877*. New York: Hill and Wang, 1993.

Lamers, William M. *The Edge of Glory: A Biography of General William S. Rosecrans, U.S.A.* New York: Harcourt, Brace, 1961.

Larimer, Charles F., ed. *Love and Valor: Intimate Civil War Letters between Jacob and Emeline Ritner*. Western Springs, IL: Sigourney Press, 2000.

Leach, Jack F. *Conscription in the United States: Historical Background*. Rutland, VT: Charles E. Tuttle Publishing Company, 1960.

Levine, Bruce. *Confederate Emancipation: Southern Plans to Free and Arm Slaves During the Civil War*. New York: Oxford University Press, 2006.

Lewis, Charles L. *David Glasgow Farragut*. 1941–1943.

Linderman, Gerald. *Embattled Courage: The Experience of Combat in the American Civil War*. New York: Free Press, 1987.

Linfield, Michael, ed. *Freedom under Fire: U.S. Civil Liberties in Times of War*. Cambridge, MA: South End Press, 1990.

Long, Armistead L. *Memoirs of Robert E. Lee: His Military and Personal History*. New York: Books Sales, 1991.

Longacre, Edward G. *Cavalry of the Heartland: The Mounted Forces of the Army of Tennessee*. Yardley, PA: Westholme, 2009.

Longacre, Edward G. *Lincoln's Cavalrymen: A History of the Mounted Forces of the*

Army of the Potomac. Mechanicsburg, PA: Stackpole Books, 2000.

Longstreet, James. *From Manassas to Appomattox: Memoirs of the Civil War in America*. New York: Da Capo, 1992.

Lonn, Ella. *Desertion during the Civil War*. Gloucester, MA: American Historical Association, 1928 [Reprint 1998 by Bison Books].

Lonn, Ella. Foreigners *in the Union Army and Navy*. Baton Rouge: Louisiana State University Press, 1951.

Lord, Francis A. *They Fought for the Union: A Complete Reference Work on the Federal Fighting Man*. New York: Bonaza Books, 1960.

Loughborough, Mary. *My Cave Life in Vicksburg*. Little Rock: Kellogg Printing Company, 1882.

Luebke, Frederick C., ed. *Ethnic Voters and the Election of Lincoln*. Lincoln: University of Nebraska Press, 1971.

Luraghi, Raimondo. *A History of the Confederate Navy*. Tr. Paolo D. Coletta. Annapolis: Naval Institute Press, 1996.

Luvaas, Jay, ed. *U.S. Army War College Guide to the Battle of Antietam*. Carlisle, PA: South Mountain Press, 1987.

Lyman, Theodore. *With Grant and Meade from the Wilderness to Appomattox*. Lincoln: University of Nebraska Press, 1994.

Lytle, Andrew N. *Bedford Forrest and His Critter Company*. Nashville: J. S. Saunders, 1993.

Mackey, Robert R. *The Uncivil War: Irregular Warfare in the Upper South, 1861–1865*. Norman: University of Oklahoma Press, 2004.

Mahan, Alfred T. *Admiral Farragut: First Admiral of the United States Navy*. New York: D. Appleton & Company, 1879.

Mahin, Dean B. *One War at a Time: The International Dimensions of the American Civil War*. Washington: Brassey's, 1999.

Mahon, Michael G. The *Shenandoah Valley, 1861–1865: The Destruction of the Granary of the Confederacy*. Mechanicsburg, PA: Stackpole Books, 1999.

Marszalek, John F. *Commander of All Lincoln's Armies: A Life of General Henry W. Halleck*. Cambridge, MA: Belknap Press of Harvard University Press, 2004.

Marszalek, John F. *Sherman: A Soldier's Passion for Order*. New York: Free Press, 1993.

Marvel, William. *A Place Called Appomattox*. Chapel Hill: University of North Carolina Press, 1999.

Marvel, William. *Burnside*. Chapel Hill: University of North Carolina Press, 1991.

Maury, Dabney H. *Recollections of a Virginian in the Mexican, Indian, and Civil Wars*. New York: Charles Scribner's Sons, 1894.

McConnell, Roland C. *Negro Troops of Antebellum Louisiana: A History of the Battalion of Free Men of Color*. Baton Rouge: Louisiana State University Press, 1968.

McDonough, James L. *Chattanooga: A Death Grip on the Confederacy*. Knoxville: The University of Tennessee Press, 1984.

McDonough, James L. *Nashville: The Western Confederacy's Final Gamble*. Knoxville: University of Tennessee Press, 2004.

McDonough, James L. *Shiloh: In Hell before Night*. Knoxville: University of Tennessee Press, 1977.

McDonough, James L. *Stones River—Bloody River in Tennessee*. Knoxville: University of Tennessee Press, 1980.

McDonough, James L. *War in Kentucky: From Shiloh to Perryville*. Knoxville: University of Tennessee Press, 1994.

McDonough, James L. and James Pickett Jones. *War So Terrible: Sherman and Atlanta*. New York: W. W. Norton & Company, 1987.

McDonough, James L. and Thomas L. Connelly. *Five Tragic Hours: The Battle of Franklin*. Knoxville: University of Tennessee Press, 1994.

McKinney, Francis F. *Education in Violence*. Detroit, MI: Wayne State University Press, 1961.

McKitrick, Eric L. *Andrew Johnson and Reconstruction*. New York: Oxford University Press, 2002.

McMurry, Richard M. *Atlanta 1864: Last Chance for the Confederacy*. Lincoln: University of Nebraska Press, 2000.

McMurry, Richard M. *John Bell Hood and the War for Southern Independence*. Lincoln: University of Nebraska Press, 1992.

McMurry, Richard M. *Two Great Rebel Armies: An Essay in Confederate Military History*. Chapel Hill: University of North Carolina Press, 1989.

McPherson, James M. *Battle Cry of Freedom: The Civil War Era*. New York: Oxford University Press, 2003.

McPherson, James M. *Crossroads of Freedom: Antietam*. New York: Oxford University Press, 2002.

McPherson, James M. *For Cause and Comrades: Why Men Fought in the Civil War*. New York: Oxford University Press, 1997.

McWhiney, Grady. *Braxton Bragg and Confederate Defeat*. New York: Columbia University Press, 1969.

McWhiney, Grady, and Perry D. Jamieson. *Attack and Die: Civil War Military Tactics and the Southern Heritage*. University: University of Alabama Press, 1982.

Meade, George. *Life and Letters of General George Gordon Meade*. Baltimore: Butternut & Blue, 1996.

Melia, Tamara M. "David Dixon Porter: Fighting Sailor." In *Captains of the Old Steam Navy*. Edited by James C. Bradford, 227–49. Annapolis, MD: Naval Institute Press, 1986.

Meredith, Roy. *Mr. Lincoln's Camera Man: Mathew B. Brady*. New York: Charles Scribner's Sons, 1946.

Miller, Edward A., Jr. *The Black Civil War Soldiers of Illinois: The Story of the Twenty-ninth U.S. Colored Infantry*. Columbia: University of South Carolina Press. 1998.

Miller, Francis T., ed. *The Photographic History of the Civil War*. 10 vols. New York: Castle Books, 1957.

Moore, Albert B., ed. *Conscription and Conflict in the Confederacy*. Columbia, University of South Carolina Press, 1996.

Morris, Roy. *Sheridan: The Life and Wars of General Phil Sheridan*. New York: Crown, 1992.

Murdock, Eugene C. *One Million Men: The Civil War Draft in the North*. Westport, CT: Greenwood Press, 1980.

Murfin, James V. *The Gleam of Bayonets: The Battle of Antietam and Robert E. Lee's Maryland Campaign, September 1862*. Baton Rouge: Louisiana State University Press, 2004.

Musicant, Ivan. *Divided Waters: The Naval History of the Civil War*. New York: HarperCollins, 1995.

Naisawald, Louis V. *Grape and Canister: The Story of the Field Artillery of the Army of the Potomac, 1861–1865*. New York: Oxford University Press, 1960.

Neely, Mark E., Jr. *Confederate Bastille: Jefferson Davis and Civil Liberties*. Milwaukee: Marquette University Press, 1993.

Neely, Mark E., Jr. *The Last Best Hope of Earth: Abraham Lincoln and the Promise of America*. Cambridge, MA: Harvard University Press, 1995.

Nesbitt, Mark. *Saber and Scapegoat: J. E. B. Stuart and the Gettysburg Controversy*. Mechanicsburg, PA: Stackpole Books, 1994.

Nevins, Allan, ed. *A Diary of Battle: The Personal Journals of Colonel Charles S. Wainwright, 1861–1865*. New York: Harcourt, Brace & World, 1962.

Nevins, Allan. *War for the Union, 1861–1865*. New York: Konecky & Konecky, 1971.

Newton, Steven H. *Joseph E. Johnston and the Defense of Richmond*. Lawrence: University Press of Kansas, 1998.

Nichols, David A. *Lincoln and the Indians: Civil War Policy and Politics*. Columbia: University of Missouri Press, 1978.

Niven, John. *Gideon Welles, Lincoln's Secretary of the Navy*. New York: Oxford University Press, 1973.

Noe, Kenneth W. *Perryville: This Grand Havoc of Battle*. Lexington: University Press of Kentucky, 2001.

Oates, Stephen B. *Confederate Cavalry West of the River*. Austin: University of Texas Press, 1961.

O'Connor, Richard. *Hood: Cavalier General*. New York: Prentice-Hall, 1949.

Olmstead, Edwin, Wayne E. Stark, and Spencer Tucker. *The Big Guns: Civil War Siege, Seacoast, and Naval Cannon*.

Simpson, Brooks D. *Ulysses S. Grant: Triumph Over Adversity*. Boston: Houghton, 2000.

Smith, David Paul. *Frontier Defense in the Civil War: Texas Rangers and Rebels*. College Station: Texas A & M University Press, 1992.

Smith, Gene A. *Iron and Heavy Guns; Duel Between the Monitor and Merrimac*. Abilene, TX: McWhiney Foundation Press, 1998.

Smith, Timothy B. *Champion Hill: Decisive Battle for Vicksburg*. New York: Savas Beatie, 2004.

Smith, Timothy B. *The Untold Story of Shiloh: The Battle and the Battlefield*. Knoxville: University of Tennessee Press, 2006.

Soley, James Russell. *The Blockade and the Cruisers*. New York: Charles Scribner's Sons, 1983.

Spencer, John D. *The American Civil War in the Indian Territory*. New York: Osprey, 2006.

Starr, Stephen Z. *The Union Cavalry in the Civil War*. 2 vols. Baton Rouge: Louisiana State University Press, 1985.

Stewart, James B. *Holy Warriors: The Abolitionists and American Slavery*. New York: Hill & Wang, 1996.

Still, William N., Jr. *Iron Afloat: The Story of the Confederate Armorclads*. Columbia: University of South Carolina Press, 1985.

Still, William N., Jr., ed. *The Confederate Navy: The Ships, Men and Organization, 1861–65*. Annapolis: Naval Institute Press, 1997.

Surdam, David G. *Northern Naval Superiority and the Economics of the American Civil War*. Colombia: University of South Carolina Press, 2001.

Sutherland, Daniel E. *Fredericksburg & Chancellorsville: The Dare Mark Campaign*. Lincoln: University of Nebraska Press, 1998.

Sword, Wiley. *The Confederacy's Last Hurrah: Spring Hill, Franklin, and Nashville*. Lawrence: University Press of Kansas, 1993.

Sword, Wiley. *Mountains Touched with Fire: Chattanooga Besieged, 1863*. New York: St. Martin's, 1995.

Sword, Wiley. *Shiloh: Bloody April*. New York: William Morrow and Company, 1974.

Symonds, Craig L. *Joseph E. Johnston: A Civil War Biography*. New York: Norton, 1992.

Tanner, Robert G. *Retreat to Victory?: Confederate Strategy Reconsidered*. The American Crisis Series, ed. Steven E. Woodworth. Wilmington, DE: Scholarly Resources Inc., 2002.

Tanner, Robert G. *Stonewall in the Valley. Thomas J. "Stonewall" Jackson's Shenandoah Valley Campaign, Spring 1862*. Mechanicsburg, PA: Stackpole Books, 2002.

Taylor, Thomas E. *Running the Blockade: A Personal Narrative of Adventures, Risks, and Escapes during the American Civil War*. Annapolis: Naval Institute Press, 1994.

Thomas, Emory A. *Bold Dragoon: The Life of J. E. B. Stuart*. New York: Harper and Row, 1988.

Thomas, Emory M. *The Confederate Nation: 1861–1865*. New York: Harper and Row Publishers, 1979.

Thomas, Emory M. *Robert E. Lee: A Biography*. New York: W. W. Norton & Company, 1995.

Thompson, Jerry D. *Vaqueros in Blue and Gray*. Austin, TX: State House Press, 2000.

Trout, Robert J. *They Followed the Plume: The Story of J. E. B. Stuart and His Staff*. Mechanicsburg, PA: Stackpole Books, 1993.

Tucker, Spencer C. *A Short History of the Civil War at Sea*. Wilmington, DE: Scholarly Resources, 2002.

Tucker, Spencer C. *Andrew Foote: Civil War Admiral on Western Waters*. Annapolis, MD: Naval Institute Press, 2000.

Tucker, Spencer C. *Blue and Gray Navies: The Civil War Afloat*. Annapolis, MD: Naval Institute Press, 2006.

Tucker, Spencer C. *Brigadier General John D. Imboden: Confederate Commander in the*

Shenandoah. Lexington: University Press of Kentucky, 2003.

Tucker, Spencer C. *"Unconditional Surrender": The Capture of Forts Henry and Donelson, February 1862*. Abilene, TX: McWhiney Foundation Press, 2001.

Turner, George E. *Victory Rode the Rails: The Strategic Place of the Railroads in the Civil War*. Indianapolis: Bobbs-Merrill, 1953.

U.S. Military Academy. *The West Point Atlas of American Wars, Volume I, 1689–1900*. New York: Frederick A. Praeger, 1959.

Vandiver, Frank E. *Mighty Stonewall*. New York: McGraw-Hill, 1957.

Vinovskis, Mark A., ed. *Toward a Social History of the American Civil War: Exploratory Essays*. New York: Cambridge University Press, 1990.

Walters, Ronald. *The Antislavery Appeal: American Abolitionism after 1830*. Baltimore: Johns Hopkins University Press, 1978.

Walther, Eric H. *The Shattering of the Union: America in the 1850s*. Wilmington, DE: Scholarly Resources, 2004.

Warner, Ezra J. *Generals in Gray: Lives of the Confederate Commanders*. Baton Rouge: Louisiana State University Press, 2006.

Warner, Ezra J., and W. Buck Yearns. *Biographical Register of the Confederate Congress*. Baton Rouge: Louisiana State University Press, 1975.

Warren, Gordon H. *Fountain of Discontent: The Trent Affair and Freedom of the Seas*. Boston, Northeastern University Press, 1981.

Watkins, Sam R. *"Co. Aytch"*. New York: Macmillan Publishing Company, 1962.

Wayne, Michael. "The Reshaping of Plantation Society Revisited." *Journal of Mississippi History* 54 (1992): 333–48.

Weber, Thomas. *The Northern Railroads in the Civil War, 1861–1865*. Bloomington: Indiana University Press, 1999.

Weigley, Russell F. *A Great Civil War: A Military and Political History, 1861–1865*. Bloomington: Indiana University Press, 2000.

Weitz, Mark A. *A Higher Duty: Desertion among Georgia Troops during the Civil War*. Lincoln: University of Nebraska Press, 2000.

Wert, Jeffry D. *General James Longstreet*. New York: Simon and Schuster, 1993.

Wert, Jeffry D. *From Winchester to Cedar Creek: The Shenandoah Campaign of 1864*. Carlisle, PA: South Mountain, 1987.

Wheeler, Richard. *Lee's Terrible Swift Sword: From Antietam to Chancellorsville: An Eyewitness History*. New York: HarperCollins, 1992.

Wheeler, Richard. *On Fields of Fury. From the Wilderness to the Crater: An Eyewitness History*. New York: Harper Collins Publishers, 1991.

Wheeler, Richard. *Voices of the Civil War: An Eyewitness History of the War Between the States*. New York: Thomas Y. Crowell Company, 1976.

Wiley, Bell I. *The Life of Billy Yank: The Common Soldier of the Union*. Baton Rouge: Louisiana State University Press, 1983.

Wiley, Bell I. *The Life of Johnny Reb: The Common Soldier of the Confederacy*. Baton Rouge: Louisiana State University Press, 1986.

Wiley, Bell I. *The Road to Appomattox*. Baton Rouge: Louisiana State University Press, 1994.

Williams, Kenneth P. *Lincoln Finds a General: A Military Study of the Civil War*. 5 vols. New York: Macmillan, 1949–1959.

Williams, T. Harry. *Lincoln and His Generals*. New York: Alfred A. Knopf, 1952.

Williams, T. Harry. *P.G.T. Beauregard: Napoleon in Gray*. Baton Rouge: Louisiana State University Press, 1954.

Wilson, Harold S. *Confederate Industry: Manufacturers and Quartermasters in the Civil War*. Jackson: University Press of Mississippi, 2002.

Wilson, Mark R. *The Business of Civil War: Military Mobilization and the State, 1861–1865*. Baltimore: Johns Hopkins University Press, 2006.

Winters, Harold A. *Battling the Elements: Weather and Terrain in the Conduct of*

War. Baltimore, MD: Johns Hopkins University Press, 1998.

Wise, Jennings C. *The Long Arm of Lee*. Lynchburg, VA: J.P. Bell and Company, 1915.

Wise, Stephen R. *Lifeline of the Confederacy: Blockade Running During the Civil War*. Columbia: University of South Carolina Press, 1988.

Woodworth, Steven E. *Beneath a Northern Sky: A Brief History of the Gettysburg Campaign*. Lanham, MD: Rowman and Littlefield, 2008.

Woodworth, Steven E., ed. *Civil War Generals in Defeat*. Lawrence: University Press of Kansas, 1999.

Woodworth, Steven E. *Davis and Lee at War*. Lawrence: University Press of Kansas, 1995.

Woodworth, Steven E., ed. *Grant's Lieutenants: From Chattanooga to Appomattox*. Lawrence: University Press of Kansas, 2008.

Woodworth, Steven E. *Jefferson Davis and His Generals: The Failure of Confederate Command in the West*. Lawrence: University Press of Kansas, 1990.

Woodworth, Steven E. *Nothing but Victory: The Army of the Tennessee, 1861–1865*. New York: Alfred A. Knopf, 2005.

Woodworth, Steven E. *Six Armies in Tennessee: The Chickamauga and Chattanooga Campaigns*. Lincoln: University of Nebraska Press, 1998.

Woodworth, Steven E. *While God Is Marching On: The Religious World of Civil War Soldiers*. Lawrence: University Press of Kansas, 2001.

Wooster, Ralph A. *The Secession Conventions of the South*. Princeton, NJ: Princeton University Press, 1962.

Wyeth, John A. *That Devil Forrest*. Baton Rouge: Louisiana State University Press, 1987.

List of Editors and Contributors

Editors

James R. Arnold
Independent Scholar

Roberta Wiener
Independent Scholar

Contributors

James R. Arnold
Independent Scholar

Rolando Avila
Lecturer
Department of History and
Philosophy
The University of Texas—Pan American

Ralph M. Baker
Independent Scholar

Dr. J. Boone Bartholomees Jr.
Professor of Military History
U.S. Army War College

Dr. Jeffrey D. Bass
Assistant Professor of History
Quinnipiac University

Walter F. Bell
Independent Scholar

Dr. Kenneth J. Blume
Professor of History
Albany College of Pharmacy

Ron Briley
Assistant Head of School
Sandia Preparatory School

Bill Cameron
Independent Scholar

Dr. Jack J. Cardoso
Professor of History, Emeritus
State University of New York College at
Buffalo

Keith D. Dickson
Professor of Military Studies
Joint Forces Staff College
National Defense University

Rick Dyson
Information Services Librarian
Missouri Western State University

Dr. Lee W. Eysturlid
Department of History
Illinois Mathematics and Science
Academy

Dr. John C. Fredriksen
Independent Scholar

Dr. Charles D. Grear
Assistant Professor of History
Prairie View A&M University

Dr. Michael R. Hall
Associate Professor of History
Armstrong Atlantic State University

A. W. R. Hawkins III
Texas Tech University

Gerald D. Holland Jr.
American Military University

Dr. Charles F. Howlett
Associate Professor
Molloy College

Dr. Deborah Kidwell
U.S. Army Command and General Staff
College

Dr. Julius Menzoff
Savannah State University

Dr. Wesley Moody
Florida Community College at
Jacksonville

Jennifer M. Murray
Lecturer
Coastal Carolina University

Jason Newman
Independent Scholar

Steven G. O'Brien
Independent Scholar

Leah D. Parker
Texas Christian University

Dr. Paul G. Pierpaoli Jr.
Fellow
Military History, ABC-CLIO, Inc.

Dr. Steven J. Ramold
Assistant Professor
Eastern Michigan University

Charles Rosenberg
Independent Scholar

David Sloan
University of Kentucky

Dr. Spencer C. Tucker
Senior Fellow
Military History, ABC-CLIO, Inc.

Dr. Kathleen Warnes
Independent Scholar

Tim J. Watts
Humanities Librarian
Kansas State University, Hale
Library

Dr. Seth A. Weitz
Assistant Professor
Dalton State College

Roberta Wiener
Independent Scholar

Dr. Anna M. Wittmann
University of Alberta

Dr. Steven E. Woodworth
Professor of History
Department of History
Texas Christian University

About the Editors

James R. Arnold is the author of more than 20 military history books and has contributed to numerous others. His published works include *Jeff Davis's Own: Cavalry, Comanches, and the Battle for the Texas Frontier* and *Napoleon Conquers Austria: The 1809 Campaign for Vienna,* which won the International Napoleonic Society's Literary Award in 1995.

Roberta Wiener is managing editor for the John A. Adams Center for Military History at the Virginia Military Institute. She has written *American West: Living the Frontier Dream* and has coauthored numerous history books for the school library market, including *Robert Mugabe's Zimbabwe.*

Index